LUCHINO VISCONTI

And to Inge

Despite efforts on the part of the author to secure permission for the first four photographs in this book, she has been unable to do so.

ISBN 0-531-09810-9
Library of Congress Catalog Card Number 83-50135

Copyright © by Gaia Servadio, 1982
All rights reserved.
Printed in the United States of America
6 5 4 3 2 1

First published in Great Britain in 1981 by
George Weidenfeld & Nicolson Ltd.
First United States publication in 1983 by Franklin Watts, Inc.,
387 Park Avenue South, New York, NY 10016.

LUCHINO VISCONTI
a biography

GAIA SERVADIO

Franklin Watts
New York 1983

'In my works can be found my whole existence, my whole view of life. . . . There too will be found my *angst* – my anxiety, my fear.'

Gustav Mahler

'He adored Shakespeare, Chekov and Verdi.'

Luchino Visconti of himself

Contents

LIST OF ILLUSTRATIONS		ix
FOREWORD		1
1	Belle Epoque	4
2	Escaping the Cocoon	21
3	The Golden Set	35
4	Flying Free	46
5	New Frontiers	56
6	Changing Roles	77
7	Underground	92
8	Against the Current	116
9	Working with Callas	140
10	The Other Family	153
11	Turning to the Past	174
12	Interior Twilight	193
13	Working to Live	205
14	To Burn Until Death	215
BIBLIOGRAPHY		225
SOURCE NOTES		227
VISCONTI'S WORKS		233
INDEX		251

Illustrations

Between pages 118 and 119

1. Visconti's mother, Carla Erba, in 1897 (*courtesy Luisa Rota*)
2. Don Giuseppe, Donna Carla and Anna in 1910 (*courtesy Luisa Rota*)
3. Luchino aged three with his mother (*courtesy Luisa Rota*)
4. Don Giuseppe, Donna Carla, Guido, Anna, Luigi, Luchino and Edoardo (*courtesy Luisa Rota*)
5. Luchino Visconti in a *tableau vivant* (*photograph Stefano Archetti*)
6. *Tableau vivant* of Tiepolo frescoes (*photograph Stefano Archetti*)
7. Luchino Visconti in Hammamet in 1934 (*photograph Horst*)
8. A scene from *La Terra Trema* (*National Film Archive*)
9. Visconti directing Alida Valli in *Senso* (*National Film Archive*)
10. Farley Granger and Alida Valli in a scene from *Senso* (*National Film Archive*)
11. Visconti at a christening in 1960 (*photograph Pierluigi*)
12. With members of his two families at Sperlonga (*Helene Visconti*)
13. Visconti during the filming of *Rocco and His Brothers* (*National Film Archive*)
14. Visconti with Alain Delon and Annie Girardot (*National Film Archive*)
15. Michelangelo Antonioni with Visconti (*Olympia, Milan*)

Between pages 182 and 183

16. The director at work (*photograph Pierluigi*)
17. Rina Morelli in a scene from *The Leopard* (*National Film Archive*)
18. Discussing a scene in *The Leopard* with Burt Lancaster, Ottavia Piccolo and Anna-Maria Bottini (*National Film Archive*)
19. At his palazzo in Via Salaria, Rome (*Patrick Morin/Camera Press*)
20. Visconti at La Colombaia on Ischia (*Enrico Medioli*)
21. A scene from *The Damned* (*National Film Archive*)
22. Visconti scrutinizing a film set (*National Film Archive*)
23. Helmut Berger (*National Film Archive*)

ILLUSTRATIONS

24 The funeral scene in *The Damned* (*National Film Archive*)
25 Silvana Mangano in *Death in Venice* (*National Film Archive*)
26 Visconti discussing a scene with Dirk Bogarde (*National Film Archive*)
27 Romy Schneider on the set of *Ludwig* with Visconti (*National Film Archive*)
28 Visconti with Enrico Medioli (*Olympia, Milan*)
29 On location for *The Intruder* (*Olympia, Milan*)

Foreword

I have never felt as strongly as some writers on the subject of biographies; some consider such books to be a disreputable craft because in a sense they exploit the dead. On the other hand, works of fiction are also partial exploitations: the novelist uses one or more models for his characters and the source of fiction is frequently a mixture of his own and others' experiences.

I am not, on the whole, a keen reader of biographies, but I have always felt that they are necessarily an interpretation, especially when dealing with a person who has been dead for a long time. Thus, when I was asked to write a biography of Luchino Visconti, a man whom I had known, who had died only a few years earlier, I stopped and thought of my character: no longer a man, but a 'subject' to develop in words. There were many people with whom I could talk, who could bear witness to the stages of a path which started in Milan (a very different environment from what it has now become), went through the glittering Paris of the 1930s, the Italian war of resistance and the years of cultural autocracy in Rome. When my 'subject' became alienated from politics, when he was only marginally interested in contemporary events, I decided not to follow them either. There was also written or tape-recorded material by Visconti himself and interviews given by him, as well as friends, enemies and relatives. I decided therefore that, faced with writing the biography of somebody who was almost a contemporary, I would let the different voices, including that of the protagonist, speak for themselves. Whenever possible, it seemed apt to present history or episodes through people's accounts.

When dealing with somebody who has recently died, his contemporaries are often afraid to recount negative episodes, fearing to offend the memory of the deceased or to appear unkind. The truth is often elusive, or there are several apparent truths, which I have tried to reproduce. Dates are a nightmare: people – as they grow older – forget; others change dates to appear younger. Some people invent, and it takes a long time to discover the lie. Others will reveal only one piece of the story, and the rest will emerge slowly, from other sources, until the jigsaw puzzle is complete.

Sometimes people open up completely, more than one could possibly expect. Others, instead, are afraid: some received me in the company of other friends so that what they did or did not say would go on record. Sometimes I became the recipient of confessions which had nothing to do with the subject. Many people were inarticulate: a house was 'wonderful', a play was 'beautiful'; the art of description is rare, few people are observant and even fewer precise.

On the whole, however, I was fortunate and out of the many conversations I had I was able to retrace the path of my secretive 'subject'. Visconti did not discuss his personal experiences and feelings: he belonged to that generation and class for whom discretion and privacy were part of good breeding. That I should have unearthed certain details of his private life may be judged as disreputable; I did not use all I learned, because some elements were unnecessary, but I recount what seems to me important in explaining the personality of the protagonist.

I do not think that negative information does him a disservice; quite the reverse: Luchino Visconti was a contradictory character, a tormented man. Indeed, the necessity of expressing oneself always springs from traumas and doubts; creativity is seldom a happy process.

Like so many Italians, I am indebted to him. No one of my generation who is in any way linked to the arts escaped the strong impact which Visconti had on the post-war Italian period by bringing to the stage both foreign and Italian contemporary plays.

It is not altogether possible for me to judge what I feel about his character now that I know him better, because my feelings for him developed along with this book, and the 'before' and 'after' merge: maybe what I always suspected came into focus; certainly I respect him more now that I know so much more about his life.

Luchino Visconti projected a sense of authority, even if he merely smiled and shook one's hand; he had that strange regal aura which made one feel grateful for a glance, a smile, a moment of affection. It is difficult for those who did not meet him to imagine the strange hold he had on people – strange and irritating. That is why a large stratum of Italy was against Visconti. I remember being irritated, too, by the many people who would talk about 'Luchino', showing off a closeness which they probably did, in fact, enjoy – and by the elegant teams who followed Visconti's premières. But I was as captivated as most and in fact grew in his shade, in the sense that I saw many of his friends and grasped the type of culture he sowed.

One winter evening in Piazza del Popolo in Rome, when I was with some of his friends who were also mine, he suddenly emerged out of the darkness, a long scarf, a huge dark overcoat, and joined us. His finding us in the darkness, at once, the immediate strength of his presence which precipitated a total change in our conversation and attitude, reminded me immediately of an episode in the *Iliad*, when the humans are suddenly visited by a god in disguise who naturally finds them wherever they are, who joins them and talks to them, but who is not like any of them.

On that occasion he asked me about my work; he had read some of my articles, he praised me and, although I was pleased, I could not believe that he meant it – how could the Olympian god waste time in reading my articles, in detailing them to me, a mere human?

With the Olympian gods he had much in common: capriciousness and generosity, cruelty and humanity. At times he could be the *deus ex machina* who precipitated a situation, for better or for worse.

The last time I saw Visconti he was sitting at a little table, looking extremely pale and thin, and very old. I sat beside him and he told me that he had heard of my house in Scotland, of the flowers, the trees, the landscape. 'You must visit us,' I said. 'When will you be free to come?' He had never been to Scotland and he was not likely to see it ever, he said. 'I am too sick.' He actually used the word *malandato*, which could be translated roughly as 'in bad shape'. 'I am going to die quite soon,' he added, without a trace of sadness. At the time I found it impossible to believe that such strength, such presence, could die; but he was right: he died a few months later.

Readers will find that there is one major fact missing from this account. Where is Visconti buried? There are several versions and theories, but no answer: it is a mystery.

I am profoundly indebted to the many books and publications which I have listed in my bibliography and in notes throughout the narrative. I am also grateful to those who saw me; they are many and their names are in another section of the book. But for this English edition of my book, which varies considerably from the Italian, I would like to thank in particular Maria Denis Guani, who clarified a hazy moment of Visconti's life, and Michelangelo Antonioni. I would also like to thank my patient editor, Alex MacCormick; Maria Ellis, who typed the manuscript and made many helpful suggestions; Martin Paisner, the lawyer who scrutinised the pages which had caused excessive controversy in Italy; and my publisher, Lord Weidenfeld, who first commissioned this book. I thank those photographers and agencies who gave me permission to reproduce their work. A special thanks to the painter Renato Guttuso, who sketched Luchino Visconti in his old age and gave me his permission to reproduce his drawing (with its nice dedication), which was photographed by Stephano Archetti.

Gaia Servadio

1
Belle Epoque

Luchino Visconti's roots, family and culture belonged to Milan, then a centre of the arts, a city where social life was frenetic and *mittel-Europa* in feeling. The Lombard ambivalence towards Austrian and Italian culture produced a musical city. Milan at the turn of the century had that Viennese quality of sombre gaiety, the feeling of providing the last breathing-space left to an upper class which consumed itself in balls and operettas. But behind this Straussian façade, the small, pretty city of Milan was producing what the dying Vienna could not: an industrial élite which was rather prim and puritanical, attached to conventions, and closer in spirit to the neighbouring Swiss than to the Viennese. At the same time Milan also produced dissidence, literature and satire; it looked towards the North, towards Europe, for inspiration, taste and fashions – not towards mainland Italy.

The bourgeoisie which emerged from the austere Longobard-Austrian culture mixed with Italian flair resulted in an entrepreneurial industrial class that was the first of its kind in Italy. This industrial middle class lived in the newer, Napoleonic sector of the city and did not take part in the frenetic social whirl of the Milanese aristocracy. This was more of an accepted fact than a class distinction, since the industrial class had neither the time nor the inclination to dedicate energy to a demanding social life. These families were building their fortunes; only when they had accumulated them did they start moving to palazzos and seeking social recognition and entertainment. Families such as the Pirellis, the Borlettis, the Bonomis, the Bocconis, the Crespis and the Falks started to 'come out' after the First World War.

There was a 'black' aristocracy which was linked to the papacy and the Austrians, and which included such people as the Princes of Belgiojoso and the Counts Borromeo – who even have a saint in the family.[1] But because their links were tenuous – the Vatican is in Rome and the Austrians were no longer the rulers – the black aristocracy was not as rich and important as the 'lay' aristocracy, traditionally pro-French, which included families like the Solas, the Gallarati-Scottis, the Casatis and the Viscontis. The middle class had 'rules of behaviour' which were very strict; the aristocracy, however, could do what it pleased as long as there was no public scandal.

Open house at the Casa Visconti was on Wednesdays, that of the

Gallarati-Scottis on Mondays, the Ricordis on Fridays and Casa Borromeo on Thursdays. 'My mother, like Luchino's, gave large parties. At Palazzo Borromeo, as in all the most important Milanese households, there was open house once a week,' recalls Manolo Borromeo. 'As a child, from my mother's room – the door ajar – I could spy on the adults, and I remember D'Annunzio, at my mother's feet, holding a bunch of violets. There was Arturo Toscanini, who had come round for a glass of champagne before going to La Scala. At five, tea was served; champagne at seven. Then there was dinner at small tables. Afterwards, games like whist in the green salon. There were people who went to La Scala only for the second act of *La Traviata* or the third of *Lohengrin*, not bothering with the rest of the opera. They would call in, then go on to the opera-house, then come back for a round of cards. Rainer Maria Rilke was a friend of my mother's and he used to call in when he was in Milan.'

The two classes dressed differently too. The restrained middle class favoured severe, simple clothes in the so-called 'classic' style. The ladies of the Milanese aristocracy, on the other hand, all looked like the Duchesse de Guermantes. An aristocratic family like the Viscontis gave masked balls and had a private theatre in their house. They were considered eccentric, but the industrial class accepted their originality as a privilege of the aristocracy.

The middle-class families entertained more demurely, each giving a *thé dansant* once a month for the young accompanied by their parents; otherwise the ladies would call on each other at tea-time to leave their cards. Like the aristocracy, they too had fixed days for being 'at home': the first Thursday of the month at the Pirellis, the second Monday at the Crespis; the ladies would call in the evening towards seven or seven-fifteen, but at eight they returned home. The men met at their clubs; their lives were governed by a precise routine. Conversation was limited and there were topics which could not be broached. Sickness was unmentionable, and they were all masters of understatement so, instead of saying that two people were lovers, there was a kind of code: 'those two talk to each other,' they would say. The industrial class was puritanical, unlike the aristocracy.

The house of the Viscontis was one of the most celebrated in Milan. In 1287 Matteo, whose family was so called from their former office of *'vicecomites'* – archiepiscopal judges – was nominated Captain of the People. It is interesting to note that Matteo was a Ghibelline, and the Viscontis always remained Ghibellines, that is to say lay and left-wing. Even Chaucer knew these celebrated names, as the stanza of *The Monk's Tale* headed *De Barnabo de Lumbardia* shows:

> Off Melan grete Barnabo Viscounte,
> God of delit, and scourge of Lumbardye,
> Why sholde I nat thyn infortune acounte,
> Sith in estaat thou cloumbe were so hye?[2]

The dukedom of Modrone of the present-day Viscontis was given to the family by Napoleon. During the Italian campaign General Bonaparte received free forage for his cavalry from the rich, land-owning family of the Viscontis, who were regarded as rebellious and daring for helping the young radical. Lombardy and Milan were Austrian; the Austro-Hungarian Empire stood for reaction, while Napoleon, before he became Emperor, was an innovator, the child of the French Revolution. To side with the young General was 'left wing' – and so were the Viscontis: original, different, unconventional and Ghibelline.

The Visconti di Modrone were numerous and close-knit; in Milan they had two houses, both of which were in Via Cerva. Actually they were not houses, but palaces in the real sense of the word, especially the one in which Luchino's paternal grandfather lived with his sons. On its vast, severe front façade, made more graceful by Baroque convoluted frames around the forty-four large windows and balconies, the palazzo in Via Cerva proudly bore the Viscontis' coat of arms, a viper gulping down a Saracen. The viper had been the coat of arms of the Visconti family which had ruled Milan from the thirteenth century, until the very last Visconti married the *condottiere* Francesco Sforza in 1447.

The origins of this more recent branch of the Viscontis are rather mysterious and it does not matter where they came from but for the fact that, in spite of their tenuous claim, the modern Viscontis firmly made use of that same coat of arms which was Matteo degli Visconti's own, and of those names which distinguished the ducal family (related to all the royal houses in Europe, the English included), such as Barnabo, Uberto, Guido, Eriprando, Luchino, and beautiful names for women, such as Vivide and Violante. They still do.

Luchino's love of music can be traced back through many forebears: his grandfather, Duke Guido, was passionately interested, and a couple of generations earlier Duke Carlo (1770–1836), the first impresario of La Scala, had a liaison with Maria Felice Malibran, the beautiful, quarrelsome Spanish mezzo-soprano, the Callas of the nineteenth century. Following the European trend of those days, the upper-class Milanese seemed to specialize in beautiful social hostesses; the princesses, the countesses, the marchionesses ruled from their salons; in Verdi's time the Countess Maffei and the Countess Eugenia Litta were two of the most celebrated musical women who held distinguished and stimulating salons. When Liszt visited Milan in 1838, Princess Cristina Belgiojioso sent him to Casa Visconti: 'Look for a small piano in the corner of her little salon; open it and play whatever your fingers like. . . .'[3] Milan was European and lay. It felt superior to Rome, intellectually, on every score.

Social status was most remarkable at La Scala. Since 1897 the opera-house had been financed by various families, of whom the Viscontis were first and foremost. This form of private management was always presided over by a

Visconti, at the time by Guido Visconti, Duke of Modrone. Most of the Viscontis were musical. There is a *'saggio di iconografia verdiana'* written by Duke Uberto Visconti in 1913,[4] and Luchino's eccentric uncle, Guidone, was a personal friend of Debussy and Weber.

Until 1815 La Scala was run by a handful of noble families who subsidized the theatre and who owned the *palchi* (boxes). These families, who were known as the *palchettisti*, licensed impresarios to organize operas and ballets. After 1815 the Austrians provided a subsidy, which was carried on by the new government after the birth of the Italian State. But in 1897 the Italian Crown ceded La Scala to the Municipality, which decided to spend its money on more 'important' needs. So, on 6 December 1897, just as the season was due to start, the Milanese were able to read a poster which an anonymous hand had written and placed in front of the main entrance of La Scala: 'Closed because of the death of artistic feeling, of civic responsibility and of common sense.'

The *palchettisti* banded together and set up a council under the presidency of Luchino's grandfather, Duke Guido Visconti, with Boito, the composer and librettist, as Vice-President. Both President and Vice-President decided to hire a professional manager who, jointly with a conductor, would choose the theatre's repertoire: thus the shape for all opera managements was born. Two men were engaged professionally and started organizing the season in 1898. They were Gatti-Casazza, who had some previous experience of management, and the young Arturo Toscanini, who had already distinguished himself and was an experienced conductor. Unfortunately, Toscanini's uncompromising character clashed with the *palchettisti*. However, Duke Visconti was sufficiently enlightened and had the musical judgment to realize that giving way to the young maestro could be advantageous to La Scala.

Toscanini did not really like the Viscontis, especially the generation which followed, because 'they thought that they were the owners of La Scala,' said Toscanini's daughter. He hated the social use of the boxes, the chit-chat and noise during the performances, and the time spent by the nobility in the private drawing-rooms at the back of the *palchi* during the performances. Luchino's paternal grandfather had a remarkable hobby: dressed up as a ballerina, his dark beard tucked inside some lace, he would join the *corps de ballet*; Toscanini didn't find this weakness amusing. He tried to ignore the many extravagant customs of the Milanese and to concentrate on changing La Scala.

Toscanini insisted on several innovations: he installed a new curtain which opened laterally instead of vertically, like the one at Bayreuth; he decided that there should be darkness during the performances (something which the aristocracy hated since one of the main motives for going to La Scala was to be seen), and that ladies in the stalls should not wear large hats. Another of his innovations was the introduction into the repertoire of works by Wagner –

dear to Toscanini's heart, but not to the Milanese. At times there were quarrels, which were often only resolved by Duke Guido's diplomacy: Toscanini and Giulio Ricordi clashed over the score of *Il Trovatore*, which the maestro wanted to perform as originally written by Verdi, and not 'encrusted' by later embellishments.

Duke Guido and Ricordi were to have closer links than those of professional association. Giulio Ricordi (1840–1912) belonged to the third generation of a family which had built up the music publishing house; he was a man of culture who spoke many languages, dressed elegantly and, besides composing music and playing the piano, was a poet and writer. For a composer to be published by Ricordi was an achievement in itself; it also opened the doors of that Milanese society which was so attentive to music – and success. Giulio Ricordi had been Verdi's friend and confidant, and he had backed Giacomo Puccini from the beginning. He had married into the aristocracy: his wife was Giuditta Brivio, daughter of Countess Anna Brivio, a great beauty, a hostess and a powerful woman. Giuditta Ricordi was very musical; she was the closest friend of Fosca Crespi, Puccini's step-daughter. Her only other sister had married Luigi Erba.

Casa Erba was in Via Marsala and was the scene of magnificent balls. The Erbas were one of the few 'industrial' families to have been accepted by the otherwise closed ranks of the Milanese aristocracy. Its enormous fortune was based on pharmaceuticals: an extract of tamarind, which sold particularly well in South America, and a laxative, castor oil, which the whole of Italy had to gulp down once a week 'to cleanse the stomach'.

Luigi Erba, a sweet, withdrawn man of short stature, was a professional musician. He was on the Board of Casa Ricordi and was also a shareholder of the publishing house. His elder brother had no children and so his wealth passed to Luigi's daughters, Carla and Lina Erba. Carla was a beauty, tall and self-confident with languid, velvety eyes. The second girl, Lina, was not so pretty and, like her father, was short. 'But, if I stand on my millions, I become tall,' Lina used to say.

The Erba girls were the richest in Milan. In spite of their 'modest' origins, they were well connected, well read, they knew everybody and were extremely musical – especially Carla – and that was something of paramount importance in Milanese society. When, in 1899, Carla Erba became engaged to the second son of the Duke Visconti di Modrone, it was taken as a matter of course: the rich beauty was to marry an aristocrat of modest means. Their marriage was sumptuous. For their honeymoon Don Giuseppe and his bride went to Paris, where they were often to be seen at the Opéra; during *entr'actes* at the foot of that ornate marble staircase, the pride of the architect Garnier, the elegant Parisians gasped, parted and stopped to stare at the stunning couple.

Carla played the piano like a professional, had met Giuseppe Verdi and knew Toscanini well. She saw Giacomo Puccini often, especially when he came to stay at Lake Como, where the Erbas had a palatial home in neo-Classic-cum-

Art-Nouveau style. Puccini, the protégé of her cousin Ricordi, admired the beautiful, gifted girl. They had first met in the early 1890s when Puccini went to stay at the villa in order to complete the libretto of *Manon* (librettos were always traumatic for Puccini). Later on in life, Puccini would ring up Carla and play his new music for her on the piano. 'But this tune is just like the one in the other opera!' Donna Carla would complain.

Donna Carla set the style in Milan. She dressed in grey and mauve with a halo of chiffon around her head, and she was one of the first ladies to wear real scent. At the beginning of the century perfumes were the prerogative of courtesans and tarts; ladies wore eau-de-cologne or light scents made from flowers or from bergamot. But the climate changed when Diaghilev's Russian Ballet introduced the fashion for exotic tastes, pungent, heavy musk and Eastern shapes, all of which influenced restricted, sophisticated groups.

Donna Carla's husband, Count Giuseppe Visconti di Modrone, was supremely handsome in the fashion of the day – a perfect oval face with dark eyes, shiny jet-black hair slightly *bouclé* over his high forehead and a severe moustache. 'He was an extraordinary human being: Aubrey Beardsley, in black and white. They used to call him Don Zizi,' recollected the Duke of Verdura, who knew both Donna Carla and Don Giuseppe. It was a perfect match. Like his younger brother Guidone, Giuseppe was interested in music and in the theatre. Giuseppe also amazed his compeers by wearing make-up in the evening: powder *and* mascara, when he went to La Scala; but he was an aristocrat and could make his own rules.

When the old Duke Guido died in November 1902, Giuseppe and Carla had been married two years. The Duke had been loved by the Milanese, and had been invaluable to La Scala – he had donated time and a great deal of money to the theatre; he had been eccentric but diplomatic, musical and intuitive. At his death the chairmanship of La Scala went to his four sons, headed by the eldest, Duke Uberto, who was more interested in the social life of La Scala than in the music. When Toscanini asked for a deserved rise in his salary, the brothers told him that he was to receive less than he had asked for, and it was Luchino's father who took him the message. Toscanini turned his back on Don Giuseppe and walked away.

In spite of the fact that Arturo Toscanini was famously sensitive to feminine beauty, he never really took to Donna Carla. He disliked her voice because it was hoarse, and she always talked in Milanese dialect. But she was exceptionally elegant; her dresses were made by Ventura, the foremost tailor of the Italian *belle époque*. Giuseppe and Carla Visconti's private box at La Scala may have been on the first tier because it was the most elegant; but its position – the fourth from the left – was also the most 'musical': from there they could see the orchestra as well as the stage. Their box had a private drawing-room at the back, where the owners could retire for a chat and invite friends during *entr'actes*.

Such drawing-rooms were, in most cases, used far more often than the actual box since the aristocracy had the pick of the ballerinas and ballerinos. It was the custom to call at these drawing-rooms during the performances as well as during the *entr'actes*; at times the fluttering of gowns or redingotes, the sight of spilt glasses of champagne, would signal the caller to withdraw hastily.

The *palchettisti* decorated the boxes, and the small drawing-rooms behind them, as the fancy took them. The Borromeos put mirrors all over theirs, the Viscontis a sombre damask silk from Syria. As for the furniture, any chairs and paintings which were unsuitable at home would generally be fitting for La Scala. 'Do you think this would look nice in the box?' was a sign that the broken-down armchair or the unsteady stool was no longer good enough for the house.

For the premières the boxes of the first tier displayed husbands and wives, jewels and flowers. 'Carla Visconti used to wear yards of mousseline of silk, so much so that in the distance one would perceive a cloud of colour, not her face – even Don Giuseppe was hidden by it. Both of them were so handsome, they were the centre of attention,' Wally Toscanini recalled. Donna Carla also wore fresh flowers in her thick dark hair. Children went to the matinée, not the première; and the men returned alone on the second or third night of the ballet....

At the beginning of Toscanini's directorship, during performances people would chat from box to box until a few minutes before a well-known aria was about to start, and then hundreds of 'Shhhh!' would precede the piece; silence would welcome the tenor's *'Di quella pira'* or the soprano's *'Sempre libera degg'io'* – after the end of which the elegant audience would start talking to each other again. There were certain arias sung by baritones and mezzos which are still called *l'aria del sorbetto*, because it was during these pieces that the public went to 'refresh' itself and consume a water-ice.

La Scala's season started on 7 December, the day of Sant' Ambrogio, Milan's dearly loved patron saint, and continued until Easter. After that the aristocracy would leave for the countryside. They had eighteenth-century villas in the hinterland, in the Brianza. The industrial middle class, instead, built villas near the lakes, since the good land of the Brianza already belonged to the aristocracy.

The Viscontis spent one or two months a year at Grazzano, their castle in the province of Piacenza. The crumbling ruins, built in 1387 by Gian Galeazzo Visconti for the wedding of his daughter Valentina to the Duke of Orléans, had been bought back by the family quite recently. After his marriage to Carla, Giuseppe, who now owned the castle, had enough money to restore Grazzano. With a sense of the theatrical combined with practical flair, he personally supervised the restoration of the property, creating a mock medieval hamlet, a touch of Mediterranean *Meistersinger*, while the few existing walls of the castle were turned into a *belle époque*-style *Trovatore*. The hamlet around the castle was rebuilt as a theatre set, a little square with picturesque corners, and the villagers, who were imported from the countryside, had to wear costumes which Don Giuseppe designed specially for them and for his family. Indeed Donna Carla always wore this Art Nouveau/ Renaissance costume when she was at Grazzano-Visconti. It was the same design for all, except for the hem of the skirts, which was left free for the women to decorate according to their taste and inclinations – musical instruments for the musicians, flowers for the gardener, artisans' tools, etc. The interior of Grazzano-Visconti was likewise theatrical, with frescoes in the style of *Tannhäuser*, and – across the square, in the little church where all the Viscontis regularly went to Mass – the Italian Pre-Raphaelite hand which painted the Holy Family had portrayed the faces of the Visconti family.

In the village, Don Giuseppe started an artisans' school for cast iron and marquetry, which grew into a small industry. Donna Carla did much the same with silks and embroidery. She also developed materials for interior decoration – in Art Nouveau or Neo-Byzantine style – which some ladies used in their private compartments on the Orient Express. The peasant community was turned into an industrious, well-off group of people who have remained strongly attached to the Visconti family to this day. I remember as a child going to visit this astounding community, which, although it was pure theatre, was also constructive; and both villagers and proprietors seemed to enjoy it. 'Don Giuseppe was very like Luchino: he built Grazzano *ex novo* eighty years ago. He liked games, dressing-up, charades, the stage. He was an enthusiast, too,' said Manolo Borromeo.

Although he had no job, since it would have been unthinkable for a Visconti of that generation to be anything else but a gentleman of leisure or a scholarly dilettante, Luchino's father was industrious and inventive. Later he created the GiViEmme (*Gi*useppe *V*isconti di *M*odrone – Emme, in Italian, stands for 'M'), which formed the avant-garde of the industrialization of toiletry products aimed at a middle-class market: *eau-de-cologne*, scents, soaps, talcum powders, which until then had been hand-made products for a small public. He would call his scents after romantic crushes of his: the names themselves are period pieces. There was the *Contessa Azzurra* (the Blue Countess) extract, *eau de toilette* and talcum powder; *Il Giacinto Innamorato* (Hyacinth in Love) complete with de-luxe towelling dressing-gowns made of velvets produced by another branch of the Visconti family. Later, under the Fascist regime, autarchic Italy could not import from France and GiViEmme sprayed the whole country with scents and eau-de-colognes: the later creation, *Tobacco d'Harar*, spelt out the fragrance of the Italian colonial times.

Number forty-four Via Cerva in Milan was an ideal town house for Don Giuseppe's theatrical taste and social appetite. The great inner hall was frescoed and two huge staircases in white marble led to the *piano nobile*, which was adorned by balconies. In almost every conceivable space the masculine building bore the Viscontis' crest, the viper, the *Biscione* as they called it. Great gates in cast iron, marble statues and huge chairs in dark oak left the visitor in no doubt about the power and wealth of the inhabitants of the palazzo. Leaving the hall, the visitor walked through a graceful courtyard, through a vaulted corridor and emerged in an exquisite little garden containing a fountain with marble dolphins and seaweed surrounding a neo-classic white nymph. Around the main courtyard the architect had used columns, arches and terraces to achieve an impression of might combined with voluptuous beauty. The visitor could stand admiringly in that courtyard, but was also tempted to ascend the stairs to the sumptuous *piano nobile*, where there were frescoed halls, vast drawing-rooms, music-rooms and little studies.

In this palazzo at Via Cerva, Donna Carla and Don Giuseppe gave spectacular balls. 'The house was full of flowers and the halls and rooms were fantastic. It was all very theatrical,' Wally Toscanini remembered. 'I met everybody there. There was *diner placé* at small tables on the balcony around that wonderful courtyard, and sometimes there was an orchestra and dancing.'

When Donna Carla and Don Giuseppe went out together in their carriage, people would stop and look at them; some would even come out of the shops. They were extraordinarily young, handsome, gifted and lucky. In Monte Carlo people actually came out of their houses in order to catch a glimpse of them. At the Galleria de Cristofori in Milan, there was a famous photographer called Sommariva, who took portraits of the nobility; in his shop window the velvety features of the First Lady of Milan caught the attention of passers-by. She was like a star, and the Milanese who did not know her by sight would recognize her coach, which bore the Viscontis' crest.

In those days, proper ladies did not walk; instead they had to take the air in their carriages. 'My mother, who didn't have enough money to keep one, rented a coupé every time she went out,' recalled Wally Toscanini. The first lady who ever walked in the city was Countess Edoarda Castelbarco, because she had been ordered to do so by her doctor. She would take walks along the bastions or near the banks of the Naviglio. The Navigli were inland waterways which encircled the city, reflecting the backs of palatial houses, of modest buildings, of flowered gardens. A few boats would sail on these pretty canals; ducks and swans and swallows animated them. The canals were filled in and destroyed during the Fascist regime.

This was the city where Luchino Visconti was born, totally different from what it is now in culture, in mood, in atmosphere and in customs. He was the fourth child of Don Giuseppe and Donna Carla Visconti di

Modrone. When he was born, Mussolini was a twenty-five-year-old Socialist and worked in Milan, not far from Via Cerva.

Of those early days Luchino remembered the well-dressed ladies in feathered hats descending from elegant carriages and going into cafés to drink a *tisane*; he recalled the gardens on the Naviglio and the swallows flying over them before dusk. When night fell, the light of the chandeliers in his house dimmed because they had lit up La Scala, that centre of his and of Milanese life.

The year before Luchino's birth, both his parents had gone to Sicily to help the victims of the Messina earthquake, Donna Carla in a Red Cross uniform, Don Giuseppe with a private ambulance that had been turned into an efficient hospital: it was considered the correct thing to do and the dedicated, handsome Milanese couple were admired and praised for their work. Not everybody knew the couple, but everybody knew of them; they were famous and held that fascination that fortunate people have. Today, popular curiosity is partly quenched by pictures of social stars published in magazines, but then it was the mystery of glimpses caught through the windows of their speeding carriage when the young couple went to the races, or when they were at their box at La Scala, tales whispered, *bons mots* maliciously passed on, all sharpened public curiosity and made the Viscontis into protagonists. They were alert to changes in taste and, as a family, they created fashion spontaneously, just because they had the culture to absorb it and the wealth to apply it. Because of this they were arrogant and well-bred, politely hiding their natural privileges. 'I myself belong to the times of Mann, Proust, Mahler. I was born in 1906 and the world which surrounded me – the artistic, the literary, the musical – was *that* world: it is not by chance that I relate to it.'[5]

Luchino was not born at Via Cerva, but in the house of Anna Erba, his maternal grandmother, in Via Marsala on 2 November at eight in the evening, one hour before the curtain of La Scala rose, and was born under the sign of Scorpio, something to which he always attached great importance; just like his father, Luchino Visconti was superstitious and believed in astrology. Don Giuseppe took part in spiritualist seances which were the fashion then, especially among the aristocracy. 'My father! A nobleman, but certainly neither a frivolous nor a silly man. A cultivated and sensitive person who loved music and the theatre, who helped us all to understand and appreciate the arts,' said Visconti.[6] But it was his mother who totally fascinated him:

> My mother was a *bourgeoise*. An Erba. Her family sold pharmaceutics. They were self-made people; they had started by selling medicine from a cart on the street. My mother loved social life, great balls, glittering parties, but she also loved her children, and she, too, adored music and the theatre. It was she who looked after our daily education. It was she who made me learn the cello. We were not left to ourselves. We were not accustomed to lead an empty and frivolous life, like so many aristocrats.[7]

In his maturity, Luchino was pround of his mother's 'humble' origins, but he was actually distorting history. 'You must never ask the time in our house,' he used to joke, 'because two quarters are missing.' But in fact Anna Erba, his maternal grandmother, had a salon where she entertained the musical and literary world: Ricordi, Leoncavallo, Mascagni, Giacosa, Boito, D'Annunzio and Puccini met one another in her rather sombre, spartan salon.

According to her children and outsiders, Donna Carla was a perfect mother. At night, her hair beautifully dressed and heavily scented, wrapped in silks, she would call on her children and kiss them goodnight. Luchino used to treasure those Proustian moments when his mother, like an apparition, came into his room. Half asleep, he could hear the rustle of her silk and, enveloped by a cloud of her scent, *le Chevalier d'Orsay*, his mother would kneel and kiss his forehead. They had made a pact, Luchino and Donna Carla: before her death, wherever she might be, she would call, and wait for her son to give her a last kiss.

For five years Luchino Visconti studied at home with tutors, as had been the custom in the previous century. Both his parents divided their time between social and family life. His mother was always beside her children, organizing their days, which were planned with an almost military discipline. Before breakfast there was the lesson of harmony and counterpoint. Twice a week Luchino had his cello lesson, and Donna Carla was there early in the morning to wake him up. He often wondered how this extraordinary woman could appear at sunrise, looking fresh and lovely, even when she had been the hostess at a ball which had ended only a few hours earlier.

There were moments in his youth, indeed in his later life, which Luchino Visconti reinterpreted; the unhappy episodes, dramas and humiliations disappeared, coloured by aesthetic, nostalgic visions. It was typical of him that his mother and father's behaviour was never judged by him and only their best side was recounted and remembered. What he did not like of his life he erased, wiped out, dismissed – but secret memories remained and tortured him.

There was a treasured custom: at night Donna Carla would stop for a few minutes – precious minutes which kept her scented presence in Luchino's room – in order to answer a written message which he would leave for her by his bedside. He would try to stay awake in his little room, waiting for the sound of her steps and then, half asleep, he would listen to the pen scratch over a piece of paper – all beloved noises for the child who pretended to be asleep. And then the rustle of her silks would announce that his mother was leaving his room. Luchino's messages to her were, for example, 'Dear Mamma, could you let me go tomorrow to hear la Borelli?' or 'Could I go to *La Gioconda*[8] at the Carcano?' She would generally answer, 'I would let you, dear, if you hadn't walked on the roof' or 'If you hadn't quarrelled with Guido.'[9]

Sometimes when he went to bed early, through his window which opened on to the courtyard of the house, in the light summer evenings he would hear her play the Prelude, Choral and Fugue by César Franck which he was to use in *Vaghe Stelle dell'Orsa* (a film he made in 1965).

When he was seven, Luchino loved to dress his mother for the evening: he would arrange a veil over her hair or a bunch of violets, and choose which jewels she should wear. He would drape mauve, lilac and grey chiffons pinned with a fresh rose and a diamond brooch over her lace.

Carla's sister Lina had also married into the nobility and moved to Via Cerva. Her husband, Count Emanuele Castelbarco, had known the family for many years and was a great friend of both Carla and Giuseppe Visconti. It was almost an arranged marriage, which did not last long.

Carla remained the dominant force in Via Cerva. Her efficiency, energy and beauty were remarkable, and her children admired her authoritarian presence for she required the maximum from them. As Visconti recalled later:

> Mine was such an extraordinary family ... seven children brought up with a wonderful father and a wonderful mother. My mother was involved in everything, but mostly with her children. I remember as if it were now, each of us had an instrument to play and she, in the evenings, came to one's room and pinned up a piece of paper written in her own hand: 6 a.m. cello lesson for Luchino; 6.30 a.m. piano lesson for Luigi. Those were hard days because after the music lessons there was school.[10]

Life was busy. In July the family went to the seaside, in August to Villa Erba at Cernobbio by Lake Como, and in September to Grazzano-Visconti. The Viscontis moved in large units of chauffeur-driven cars across the Apennines or through the Po valley towards the Adriatic Sea. Luchino remembered one such journey, a summer trip, which took place in 1911 when he was five. It was a journey with his family into the mountains, and he vividly recalled the colour of the wild carnations in the meadows and their strong scent, the carriage, the sweat of the horses, and they, the children, taking their turn next to their mother, whose face was protected from the dust by yards of light silk.

Once a year Donna Carla would take her children to Paris to see grandmother Erba, who spent long periods of time at the Hotel Continentale. Like her daughter, Anna Erba had a strong, lively character. When in Milan she led a grand life, entertaining in her house where there was a hydraulic lift which amused her grandchildren. It was a fascinating house for Luchino because next to it and attached to it the Erba pharmaceutical factory was roaring away. Young Luchino would open the door which led to the interior of the factory and had access to the mysterious laboratories. And since the Erba pharmaceuticals had the concession for the Swiss Liebig products, Luchino had the privilege of being able to go through masses of those coloured picture-cards, so popular among children, picking the ones he wanted and filling his pockets with others to give to his friends.

At night when there was a dance, Luchino and the others, Guido, Anna, Luigi and Edoardo, wearing their pyjamas, would creep on to a loggia over the courtyard. 'We would wake up very early in the morning, the music was still playing, we looked at couples dancing.' Luchino's cousin Filippo remembered one such dance after the La Scala première of *Der Rosenkavalier*: for the dinner, Donna Carla had put an enamel rose on every table and each guest was given a silver one; however, the opera had been a terrible fiasco, so the party was somewhat sombre and Donna Carla was annoyed.

In 1912 there were no dances at Via Cerva, because Carla Erba Visconti was in mourning for the death of her uncle, Giulio Ricordi. He had been an important figure in Milan: a man of great charm with a discerning, scholarly mind. Luchino was too young to remember him (he was six when Giulio Ricordi died).

His parents did not have much in common, but they both loved the theatre, they loved acting, and their private theatre in Via Cerva, built by Don Giuseppe, had become one of their main preoccupations: the plays were often performed in Milanese dialect and the prima donna was always Donna Carla. But Luchino's father did not tolerate dialect spoken at home 'for some stupid, strange reason of his own. My mother instead always talked Milanese with her mother and that's how I learned it, through them.'[11] The Milanese dialect and its particular intonation belonged to his mother's side of the family, and Luchino Visconti never altogether lost them.

Luchino's eldest brother Guido, born in 1902, was handsome, with an open oval face, and, because his character was weak, he was Donna Carla's favourite. Then there had been Anna (born in 1903), 'a beautiful woman, a heart of gold', according to Fulco della Verdura. In 1905 Luigi was born and, in the following year, Luchino. After Luchino in 1908 there came Edoardo, handsome, fair and bright.

Life seemed to be perfect and the children were beautiful, but Don Giuseppe was not strictly faithful to his wife. The ladies were greatly attracted to the tall, sophisticated Visconti, but so, too, were a large number of gentlemen. '*A chacun son* hobby,' he used to say. There is a well-known story that when Milan was conquered by Frederick Barbarossa and was about to be razed to the ground, his herald climbed to the highest tower and announced: 'All men and children will be raped, all women will be slain.' Realizing that he had made a slip, he said, 'Pardon, pardon,' at which a voice said: 'Too late, what has been said has been said.' That voice, so the story goes, belonged to a Visconti.

There was a young man whom Don Giuseppe saw for a long while incognito, or so he thought. If this person ever got to know his name, Don Giuseppe romantically declared, he himself would disappear like Lohengrin, on a swan.

Nor was Donna Carla faithful. The upper class in Milan, as in Edwardian Britain, preached strictness, religion and fidelity – they were meant to set an example to the lower classes – but all was known, forgiven and gossiped about, as long as there was no scandal. What is surprising, though, was Donna Carla's rigorous attitude: 'That swine has a lover!' she said once, pointing at a lady with disgust. She would go to Mass every day without fail at 8 a.m., she was engaged in charitable occupations and was considered a saint, although social gossip was rife. But all was well so long as everybody agreed to keep up the appearance of the perfect couple and of the united family. And they all did – for a while.

In later life, when he started talking about it, Luchino Visconti idealized his youth, but what he experienced and never recounted – his parents' irregularities, his own morbid love for his mother, a dramatic separation, scandals and quarrels – went straight into his films. When he was asked why he always put the family at the centre of his stories, Luchino Visconti provided the key to his secrecy:

> Maybe for old reasons of my own, maybe because it is within the family that there still exist those last unique taboos, the moral and social prohibitions, the last impossible loves. In any case the family nucleus seems to me very important. All our way of being, of living, derives from there, from the inheritance we carry with us, from the happiness or unhappiness of our childhood. Each of us is the product of this smallest social cell, before being the product of society. Often an unchangeable product, or capable of modification only with great difficulty. So the family represents a kind of fate, of destiny, impossible to elude. The relationships, the contrasts, the intrigues, the upheavals within the family always interest me passionately.[12]

Family upheavals and family taboos are a strong theme in Luchino Visconti's films, especially in the later ones when he found fewer restrictions within himself and when he allowed himself to express those thoughts and themes which he could not spell out in any other way. Had he had the time to make more films, he might have gone even farther. 'My real dream is to make a film about a great Milanese family, the Visconti di Modrone. A film based in Lombardy from the beginning of the century up till the bombing of Milan. A film which would recount all the stories of my father, of my mother, of my brothers, of all my relatives. One day I shall succeed in doing it; and then, maybe, I shall stop making films about other families.'[13] In fact such a film would have been impossible and his family must have trembled when reading this interview. But he was right: his family's story is a projection of that European culture which drew a last decadent breath during the *belle époque*. The collapse of that social order produced unrest, wars and dictatorships; and those families rose from the ruins dramatically changed – not only financially: their code of behaviour merged with that of the all-embracing middle class. The arrogant freedom, dictatorial inventiveness and panache of such people was gone.

On the other hand, when Luchino Visconti declared that he would have 'stopped making films about other families', he must have been aware that he had been skirting around his own family all the time and that, by illustrating it fully, he might liberate himself as some writers do when they analyse their secrets on paper, as others do when they use analysts as recipients, and yet others when they unburden their minds to father confessors.

His family's world impressed Luchino and it was, in fact, theatre; their parties intertwined with the plays they presented in their private theatre. They staged light comedies, often written and always produced by Don Giuseppe. 'Donna Carla and her brother-in-law, Emanuele Castelbarco, were born actors,' said Wally Toscanini, who saw many such plays and who later married Castelbarco. Milanese society bought tickets in order to see them (performances were given in aid of charity) and delighted in the soirées, which included dinner and witty conversation. These plays were much talked about, especially among those who were not invited and who, out of bourgeois primness or envy, would never have dreamt of taking part in such frivolities. On the other hand, Donna Carla, Don Giuseppe and their friends adored the preparations, the staging and the rehearsals, and they had a professional dedication towards *il Teatrino di Via Cerva*. In May-June 1911 they staged *Per un Bacio (For a Kiss)*, a vaudeville comedy in three acts by Joseph von Icsti; it is interesting to note that the anagram chosen by Giuseppe Visconti to disguise his authorship of this play is Austrian in tone. A fan given to the ladies as a souvenir of the evening bore several images of the play. Over the photographs, beside the date, one can read: *Teatro Casa Giuseppe Visconti di Modrone*.

The sets and the costumes of the plays were accomplished and professional. In the pit, separated from the stage by pretty arrangements of flowers, there were a few instruments to accompany the odd song. In *Gioconda* Don Giuseppe appeared clad in a cloak with a hood, his strong, dark features enhanced by a black wig and thick moustaches. The ladies with him were embellished by veils, flowers, crowns, and the over-stretched gestures of the period: they were meant to be the Muses. On one side of the stage was Gioconda – the model for the *Mona Lisa* – in mock-Renaissance style clothes, and on the other Leonardo da Vinci himself, bearded and curly, a bunch of brushes in his left hand and a vast palette at his feet.

The children were allowed at matinées only, and Luchino Visconti watched his mother, dressed in gold, covered with feathers, veils and flowers, a living Boldini, a magic apparition. She was such a good actress that a professional critic, Renato Simoni, praised her performance in Goldoni's *Gelosie di Lindoro (The Jealousy of Lindoro)* and she was depicted on a full page of *L'Illustrazione Italiana*, the magazine *du bon ton*, in gold lamé and ermine furs. The same gold dress had been worn for the musical comedy *Il Polo si Popola (The Pole Gets Crowded)*, directed, as usual, by her husband Giuseppe. These plays continued to be a centre of activity until the beginning of the war.

Via Cerva provided Luchino Visconti's first experience of a live theatre. The second glittering theatre he knew well was La Scala. The theatre was a sharp and constant theme in Luchino's life. La Scala was more than just a beloved local opera-house: as we have seen, it was part of the history of his family.

By the age of seven, Luchino Visconti was already passionately interested in opera. The dark red velvets of La Scala, those yellow-gold ornate fringes on the heavy curtains, so near to the box where he was sitting – all this formed an image with which he grew up. Visconti loved opera, recognized its passions and believed in them, because he saw opera at its best: from the very start he never saw a ridiculous performance, a hilariously bad staging or a bulging tenor singing atrociously. From early childhood he saw opera conducted by Toscanini, who took opera seriously and was not only the conductor but also the director – at the time direction was hardly considered necessary. No wonder that the conventions of opera were for Luchino as real, natural and modern as those of the straight theatre. He was full of theatrical intuitions and was fascinated by *décor* and costumes, influenced by his mother's flamboyant style. There are several watercolours by Luchino in 1913 which show beautiful women dressed in fox furs, boas and feathered hats; they also show a precocious hand and remarkable observation. He was only seven, but the lines are sure and the colours 'elegant', already consciously so.

The third theatre in Luchino Visconti's early life was the one which he built himself by putting a large sheet across the linen room at home. There, every Sunday, he staged something with his brothers. Later other boys came to join the Visconti brothers and, later still, more intellectual and gifted friends, but Luchino always remained in command. Almost every performance consisted of a Shakespeare play, ad-libbed on the basic plots, which they read over and over again: *Macbeth, Hamlet, Antony and Cleopatra, The Taming of the Shrew*. Much to Luchino's consternation, Luigi often insisted that he wanted to play Hamlet himself, and so Luchino would play the Queen and Rosenkrantz or Guildenstern. His younger brother Edoardo played Polonius and the Ghost.

In 1916 Ida Pace, called 'Nane' by everybody, was born and, two years later, Uberta: the last two girls were forever known as '*le bambine*', the children. Their older brothers adored them, especially Luchino.

So now there were seven children and, in addition to a German governess, Donna Carla engaged a tutor, half-Italian, half-English, called Boselli, to further their education. Luchino, who was then fourteen, later recalled:

> We were trained by a British teacher whom I shall remember as long as I live. He had a mania for training us to mock at danger, to be accustomed to discomfort, and to have prompt reflexes. Perhaps he was a great educator, maybe only a lunatic. When we went out, catching us off our guard, he would suddenly start to run behind a moving tram, like a beech-marten. We had to recognize what was happening even as we recovered from the shock, catch him up and jump on to the footboard. And once on the tram, we

had to put up with the amazed, at times reproachful, stares of the other passengers. Mr Boselli spoiled for us any pleasure in taking a walk because we began to see tramways everywhere or, actually, tramways in ambush, around every corner.[14]

Also, instead of using the stairs, they had to enter their house through the windows by climbing up a rope. This Gordonstoun type of education sounds like a nightmare; no wonder that, for a time in his youth, Luchino Visconti loathed anything to do with Britain.

Meals were a ritual event for the large, elegant clan. The family dinners took place at a long table on which every object was of silver (not polished enough, a chambermaid said later, but that was part of the chic of the Viscontis, to underplay the spectacle), glasses in crystal, shining white Irish linen tablecloths, and for which the servants wore white gloves. Such scenes were often recreated by Luchino Visconti in his films.

There were plenty of jokes at the dinner-table; when the conversation was flowing and everybody was talking, Luigi would sometimes say a rude word, aloud. Only the crudeness of the sound would be caught in the air, and their father would thunder, 'Who said that?' None of them would tell on each other and so they were all punished. Then Luigi would start again on the following night, amid the suffocated giggles of the other children. Or the old butler would be 'degraded', his frogging torn by the naughty boys.

In the summer of 1914, the Visconti family, their maids, wet-nurses, menservants, nannies and tutors went to Rimini on the Adriatic, which was very different in those days. The Tempio Malatestiano was not submerged by tourists and the long beaches were empty, dotted with a few beach-huts and parasols. Few adults swam in the shallow sea, but the children would be allowed to stay in the water for a few minutes; when the skin on their fingertips creased, there was an outcry from mothers and nannies, who would claim that this was the sign that they had been in the water long enough.

During that summer, on the other side of the Adriatic, facing the Rimini coast, a pistol shot at Sarajevo signalled the fall of that Valhalla – the gods fell and with them the world in which they lived. It was not only the beginning of the First World War but also the end of the Austro-Hungarian Empire and the birth of Germany, industrialization, rearmament and unrest; the end of *la belle époque*, that world which Donna Carla and Don Giuseppe symbolized, was near.

2
Escaping the Cocoon

At the outbreak of hostilities Italy was still neutral. Public opinion was divided between the Germanophiles (the majority in 1914) and the pro-Allies. The Church, which had links with the Hapsburg dynasty, was pro-Austrian and the Court pro-German, since it had industrial and banking interests there. Moreover, relations between France and Italy were strained because of France's occupation of Tunisia on which Italy had colonial designs. The lay aristocracy, like the Viscontis, was pro-Allies because of its traditional hostility to the Austrian occupation and because, despite its comprehension of German culture (or perhaps because of it), it felt more closely linked to France. Toscanini was naturally pro-Allies, but Puccini so hated the French that he found himself automatically pro-German (and, later, pro-Fascist).

Donna Carla replaced the German *fräulein* with the French Mademoiselle Hélène, and from Rimini the Viscontis returned hastily to Milan. In May 1915 Italy declared war on the side of the Allies and Austria once again became an enemy country. Part of Palazzo Visconti was requisitioned by the Italian Army and the family moved to one wing. Cousin Marcello Visconti, who later became a Fascist leader, joined the army and wrote letters from the Front. Every night the Visconti children would return home with some Allied soldiers, for it was considered to be part of their patriotic duty to entertain them to dinner. One day in the Piazza del Duomo, Luchino found the mature French poet, Paul Fort, who, after dining at Via Cerva, listened to young Luchino playing the cello.

In the summer of 1916 the family did not return to the Adriatic coast but went instead to Alassio, because the sea air of the Riviera was considered healthy for those who were consumptive and, whether Luchino Visconti knew this at the time or not, his mother was ill. On this occasion their father was not with them. Luchino's sister Ida Pace was born that year, and Don Giuseppe and Donna Carla were on the verge of splitting up. There had been some scandals concerning the family, and satirical magazines like *Il Guerrin Meschino* and *L'Uomo di Pietra* had gone to town. However, in those days, matrimonial crises, especially in that *milieu*, were never followed by a formal parting. By this time Donna Carla and Don Giuseppe each led their separate lives, but still kept up a pretence of family unity. Conventions accepted any kind of freedom from the head of the family, but a woman was not allowed to have lovers, and certainly not openly so. But Donna Carla was a free spirit, modern in her ways and with a very strong personality. She was growing tired of the whirlwind of social life and of the plays, of the comedy, of the demands of a strenuous social life. Don Giuseppe's social appetite, however, seemed unquenchable. He became gentleman-in-waiting to Queen Helen, Victor Emmanuel III's wife, which was an ideal situation, much to his liking. The Viscontis knew the Savoias quite well: the children rode together, and Donna Carla and Don Giuseppe were often invited to Court. The Savoias were not the most intelligent of royal families; they were politically limited, diplomatically unskilled and genetically ugly.

Count Giuseppe was meant to instruct the Queen in taste, literature and manners, for she came from Montenegro, a tiny, mountainous country of sheep and shepherds; the Duchess of Aosta referred to her as '*ma cousine, la bergère*' (my cousin, the shepherdess). Queen Helen was big and dark, much taller than her royal husband, and indeed she had been chosen to introduce healthy new stock into the weak Savoias (certainly there can't have been any political reasons for making an alliance with Montenegro, an operetta-country, now part of Yugoslavia). Queen Helen's mother-in-law, Queen Margherita, had suddenly found herself a widow when her husband, King Umberto, was shot dead by an anarchist at Modena. She thought Queen Helen *grossière* – indeed her gaffes were notorious. Don Giuseppe Visconti was an ideal choice: he was well-bred, poised and literate – and he was a snob. He built a villa for himself in Via Salaria in Rome, next to the Queen's residence, in order to be near her. The King created him Duke of Grazzano and so he finally achieved that title which had eluded him but which he had used, or let others use when referring to him.

The tie between the House of Savoy and the Viscontis was strengthened; and though gossip was rife, the King could reassure himself with the knowledge that, although Don Giuseppe was a *coureur*, he was known also to have special 'hobbies'.

Every so often Don Giuseppe went back to Milan and to Grazzano-Visconti in order to be with his children. In Milan, life continued much as before; as in the rest of Europe, civilians were hardly aware of the hardships at the Front. 'For us boys who were growing up,' said Manolo Borromeo, 'there were small social gatherings, fixed days for tea in the houses of the aristocracy. On Thursdays, it was our turn, the Borromeos; on Friday, the Sforzas; Wednesdays at the Viscontis. During these gatherings Luchino was always the leader – he was younger than all but one of his brothers; in spite of this, we all listened to what he had to say: "Today we play charades!" and "Do this! Do that!" Often at his house we had to listen to a recital by him after tea and cakes. He would start on the cello and we were more or less forced to, you know ... we were boys of nine, ten, we didn't enjoy Brahms. Luchino reproduced this scene in his film *The Damned*, when one of the boys plays the cello behind the curtain.'

During carnival Luchino organized a circus at his house. Indeed, if ever anyone needed something organized, they would ask him. Don Giuseppe must have been delighted by such qualities in his third son – the first three children, Guido, Anna and Luigi, didn't care for the theatre or for organization. 'His father would say to Luchino: "On Monday we give a dinner for forty." Luchino would plan it and dye all the linen tablecloths in pale mauve, put hydrangeas and roses on each table and along the stairs, thus giving the evening a particular flavour. It was a game until the day when he did all this professionally.'

After five years of private tuition, which mostly followed the regular curriculum, Luchino Visconti, aged eleven, started going to school at the Liceo Berchet. A house servant would collect him from school and at about 3.30, after homework, would accompany him to one of the various houses for tea. They played dressed-up charades. Luchino was bossy – 'You will *not* wear that!' – and allotted the garments to somebody else. The governesses and the menservants of the house had to watch the charades and little plays; at times, when they came to collect them, their mothers and nannies also watched. When the gatherings took place at Via Cerva, Luchino would announce: 'Today we won't stage charades; instead I shall play.' At the Borromeos' the games were more boisterous, for there were long corridors in the palazzo in Via Manzoni, shiny with wax, and the boys loved to run and slide along them.

When the weather was good, the chauffeur stayed at home and the boys rushed through the city at full speed on their bicycles jostling hapless pedestrians. Sometimes Luchino's bicycle carried Toscanini's second daughter. Wanda was pretty, serious and sombre – and the young Luchino fell in love with this silent girl. Their first kiss, under a table at Casa Visconti, was disturbed by Fifi, the Visconti boys' beloved smelly poodle. They had numerous pets – dogs, birds and cats. When Wanda became Luchino's girl-friend, everybody smiled, even her stern papa Arturo, who was always thundering about the children making too much noise when they went to play at his house in Via Durini.

Early in the mornings the implacable footsteps of Miss Teresa Mirabello, the piano teacher, tiresomely punctual, would echo along Luchino's corridor with a military sound. Before school, there were two hours of music lesson. In the afternoons after school there were two hours of gymnastics and German lessons. Besides the cello, Luchino studied counterpoint, harmony and gymnastics with Professor Borrelli. In 1920, when he was fourteen years old, he gave a concert at the Conservatory in Milan. The daily newspaper *La Sera* praised 'the young Luchino Visconti di Modrone who showed real promise'.

Always at his mother's side, Luchino went to the concerts of the Quartet Society and both of them would follow the music with their scores. She never missed a single concert, and she would take all her sons, dressed alike, looking striking. On warm spring evenings when she played the piano in the first-floor salon of their home, the rooms where the boys slept would now be filled with the dramatic sounds of *Boris Godunov*, which Toscanini had just conducted at La Scala for the first time.

One day, in the house of some friends, Luchino saw a photograph of Wally Toscanini, Wanda's elder sister, who was one of the striking young beauties of Milan. The Visconti boys themselves had treasured another photograph of Wally, taken from a portrait made of her in the yellow costume which she had worn for a *bal masqué* at Via Cerva. The portrait showed her, slightly mysterious, in full 'Diaghilev' attire – an exotic hat *à la Chinoise* and Eastern pantaloons. In those days all Milan talked about a great scandal: that Wally, aged eighteen, was Emanuele Castelbarco's mistress. Since he was married to Lina Erba, Count Castelbarco was Luchino's uncle; and for such a young girl to have a lover so openly was considered shocking. Under this photograph Luchino wrote: 'Wally when she was not yet a Countess', alluding to her affair with his uncle.

When next Wally met Luchino, who was younger than herself, she said: 'I know what you wrote on a photograph of me. What would you say if I were to write the same under a photograph of your mother?' He blushed and answered: 'That I have been a rascal.' 'Very well,' she said, 'I'll ask your father to slap your face.' She rang up Count Giuseppe, who apologized. 'If I were not limping, I'd come and see you, Signorina Toscanini, but I must beg you to come and see me instead.' He had fallen and broken a leg. 'I am the first to apologize because I am Luchino's father,' he said. Luchino gave Wally a letter which read: 'Gentile Signorina Toscanini, I behaved like an animal and I want to apologize.' Later in life, when Luchino and Wally were great friends, they often joked about this episode.

The aftermath of the First World War brought disturbed economic conditions, which even the golden circle could not fail to notice. Due to the devaluation of the currency, there was serious inflation and the cost of living rose steeply. In the industrial North there were strikes and unrest, and factories were seized by workers. Luchino remembered a summer journey towards Santa Margherita on the Riviera which took three whole days. Their rich-looking caravan of chauffeur-driven cars steered through demonstrations and cities where the workers were on strike. 'It was like the flight from Varennes,' he remarked years later. But it was the first time that the rich felt a *frisson*, a faint suspicion that having money carried a stigma, a pejorative one. The teachings and the images of Marx and Lenin began to appear on walls and the red flag was hoisted near the smoke of the factories. The Russian Revolution, which had shaken the world already undermined by the war, frightened the industrial tycoons, thus helping to produce the conditions which gave birth to Fascism. Germany was responding to defeat with a creative period of dialectics, the period of Fritz Lang, von Sternberg, *Nosferatu* and *Doctor Caligari*. In Italy the new forces of expression – Marinetti's poetry, Balla, Boccioni, the new styles of architecture – led towards populism, towards the titanic strength of the machine, of industry: theirs were totalitarian visions, which flourished as Art Deco, casting aside the attention to detail and convoluted individualism of Art Nouveau.

The old class felt threatened. In 1921 Donna Carla left for Rapallo on the Riviera; her chest was inflamed. Her husband had asked her to go; he had also said that unless all the Erba shares were ceded to him, he would make a scandal about her private life. She gave in. When she returned to Milan, she moved to another house and *le bambine* with Luchino and Edoardo went to live with her, although Don Giuseppe was upset because he was extremely fond of the children: anyway they were to be 'shared', as happens in divorces today. Donna Carla never again set foot in a Visconti house.

Although the children suffered from this separation, it was no great tragedy: they maintained their energetic pace, complicated timetables and whirlwind occupations. There was a nasty scandal when the newspapers published details of the legal case that Lina Erba Castelbarco, with the agreement of Donna Carla, had brought against Giuseppe Visconti. The Erba shares, which belonged to both sisters, had been given to Don Giuseppe without Lina's consent; hence, she argued, they were not his to keep. She won the case, as a result of which the Erbas and the Viscontis were hardly on speaking terms. Donna Carla withdrew from social life; Don Giuseppe did not.

Post-war change pervaded even La Scala, and the system of the *palchettisti* was scrapped. The tiers of private boxes were made available to the general public: La Scala was to become an autonomous institution. A few weeks before the opening of the second 'independent' season in 1922, Mussolini marched on Rome and the King undemocratically asked him to form a government. Almost everybody in Italy was enthusiastic – the march on Rome by the Black Shirts would ensure the end of workers' unrest, of the occupation of factories, of red banners and Marxist slogans – the Fascist regime would exercise discipline in a country which needed it. Few people had doubts; D'Annunzio, the *belle époque* world, the aristocracy, all joined the movement that the middle class had created; the backbone of Fascist 'philosophy' consisted of 'Italianism', the revival of ancient Rome and the supremacy of the Mediterranean basin; it was another expression of the wave of nationalism which had been growing in Europe.

The aristocracy found Fascism distasteful on aesthetic grounds, but necessary: Italy needed a strong hand. Northern Italian industry had nursed Mussolini and had financed the Fascist party, which aimed to put an end to any Marxist whim or longing looks towards Soviet Russia. The events leading to the march on Rome had, however, disgusted Toscanini. In 1919, at a performance of *Falstaff*, a group of Fascists in the theatre had clamoured for the Fascist hymn to be played. Toscanini refused and began the third act of the opera, but the disrupters would not be silent. So he broke his baton and went backstage, furious. A director went to the stage to announce that the hymn would be sung at the end of the performance, the public finally quietened down and Toscanini returned to the pit. At the end the maestro said, 'They are not going to sing a damned thing; the Scala artists are not vaudeville singers.'

Many people were amazed by Toscanini's behaviour, since most Italians believed that Mussolini was the Saviour; many people reproached the maestro, though generally not to his face because his was a 'difficult' character. Toscanini's open anti-Fascism is much praised now, but the Milanese criticized it then.

Mussolini himself paid a visit to La Scala; Toscanini had already met him a couple of times and feared that he couldn't turn his back on him because the autonomous institution of La Scala was permitted to exist only by a federal law. Equally Mussolini and the regime did not want to attack Toscanini – just yet: in Milan the maestro's popularity was probably greater than Mussolini's. But in June 1925 orders arrived from Rome: La Scala should display photographs of the Duce. Toscanini refused to comply. The last of the great events at La Scala before Toscanini's departure for America, before the total stranglehold of the Fascist regime, was the world première of Puccini's last opera, *Turandot*, which the composer had been unable to complete. Luchino Visconti was nineteen and he was there at La Scala with his mother.

Toscanini and Tonio Puccini had commissioned Franco Alfano to finish the opera, but on the legendary night of its première, Toscanini announced to the singers and orchestra that the very first performance would be given without Alfano's ending. And Visconti would later recount this scene – a famous and moving one, when, after the death of Liú, Toscanini, with tears in his eyes, dropped his baton and said to the audience: 'The opera ends here, left incomplete by the death of the maestro.' The La Scala audience reacted with a silence of respect, no one applauded; and then one voice shouted: 'Viva Puccini!', followed by an ovation.

La Scala and Milan fell, like the rest of Italy, into the uninventive, inarticulate grip of the Fascist regime, but Luchino Visconti was not aware of politics at the time and these events did not disturb him. Now a little older, Visconti discovered instead a source of great joy: almost every Sunday after Mass at the cathedral, he went to the Cinema Centrale, often with his father. There he saw his first American films – and later he started going with his friends to other cinemas like the Palace in the Corso.

The summer was shared between father and mother. With his mother, Luchino and his brothers went to Forte dei Marmi, where there were few houses, a deserted beach and no main road. They would leave from Milan and Cernobbio in a large group of cars. 'All of us, with cousins who joined us, girl-friends, menservants – off this column went, with the usual scores of pets. Over the Apennines there was a spot which was our place, near a fountain, so beautiful ... and there the menservants would lay the tablecloths on the grass and we ate a picnic which was carried in those boxes with straw which keeps the food warm. When we arrived at Forte dei Marmi, it was very late at night. He used these images in *The Leopard*,' Luchino's cousin Filippo recalled.

They travelled with all their pets: each of the boys had his own dog, or more than one, and there was the smelly poodle Fifí, who was still the favourite, and various birds. The glory of Grazzano-Visconti had waned – it had become gloomy without Donna Carla, the children were not so happy to go there any longer, but they had to.

Although Donna Carla had opted out of social life, there were still dances in Villa Erba at Cernobbio. A Milanese *grande dame* remembers one evening there. Uberta and Nane were small, dressed in Red Cross uniforms, gazing at the adults. Luchino was a boy of seventeen; he was thin, already tall, with straight dark hair parted at the side, regular features, and was poised and handsome. Old spinsters stood around the walls of the ballroom, commenting and chatting, just like the ball scenes of the film *The Leopard*.

The separation of his parents and their refusal even to talk to each other hurt the adolescent. Luchino Visconti never condemned his parents, because he hadn't been brought up to judge their behaviour and, towards him, they continued to be loving and affectionate. But only their remoteness can justify his sheer idealization of these two human beings, who were beyond judgment and rules and who could do no harm, at least in his later verbal recollections. If one observes his truthful form of recollection – his films – one cannot fail to notice that his family is always the protagonist. All the secrets which he and his brothers kept from others so jealously are revealed, whether in recounting the story of a German industrial family or that of a Sicilian prince, or even when he staged a memorable *La Traviata* at La Scala with Maria Callas. That was his mother's story, or part of it: the consumptive heroine dismissed by society, a victim of conventions. Having idealized her in many of his films, operas and plays, he never quenched his yearning for that figure of perfection – of his idea of perfection – he never came to terms with the fact that she was his own mother: she remained elusive, mysterious and desirable until the very end of her life and of his.

In spite of the rigorous discipline to which he had been subjected – or maybe because of it – at school he was hopeless. He did not study, but he read an enormous amount.

How was it possible for him to study? There were so many distractions and preoccupations. The cinema had become a passion. And he now staged plays himself, no longer with his brothers or with unco-operative aristocratic tea-time friends, but with a more satisfactory group: Ignazio Gardella, who was to become a prominent architect, Vittorio Gnecchi, the son of a musician, Wanda Toscanini and Corrado Corradi, an aristocratic boy – they saw each other almost every day. 'We had met at the Liceo Berchet when we were sixteen. We always had tea together, we laughed a lot and we all had literary or pseudo-literary interests. Luchino had written a one-act play and we were going to stage it. Luchino, of course, was going to be the director,' Corradi later recalled.

There were two girls in the play: one was Luisa Villa and the other Wanda Toscanini. 'We went on rehearsing for over a year – it was really an excuse to meet – sometimes at the house of the Villas, or at the Toscaninis'. Wanda came by herself, but Luisa had a governess who always accompanied her. Or we would meet at Casa Gnecchi, which was in Via Filodrammatici. The actual performance was to be given in Via Cerva, but in the end Luchino's maternal grandmother died and nothing came of it,' said Ignazio Gardella. Of all these years Visconti retained a photographic memory. For example, Gardella recalls an occasion when he and Luchino had both observed a manservant at a Visconti dance who, thinking himself alone, gulped down a glass of champagne. 'That detail was in one of his films, reproduced in exactly the same way.' Casa Visconti still gave some dances and Gardella had been introduced to the household because he had met Anna and Luigi while riding.

At this stage in his life, Luchino was rather wild, witty, exuberant, always in a good mood, but sombre at the same time and affectionate. 'He was profoundly Milanese, not a snob, but with the sense of belonging to the Viscontis, to that very Milanese clan. He was not fond of social life, but took part in it because it was a family custom,' said Corrado Corradi. Luchino and his new friends used to go to La Scala, no longer out of duty but of choice. Gardella recalls that 'Wanda Toscanini's father came to see Luchino and asked us about American jazz, in which he was interested. Once, during a rehearsal, Toscanini got so angry with the orchestra that Luchino and I thought he was going to kill them all.'

This group of adolescents was fairly detached from politics and were neither pro- nor anti-Fascist; they did not discuss politics, they did not notice them. In the evenings they stayed at home, for it was unusual to go out at that age; they studied little. 'And we always bicycled to the Liceo Berchet and Luchino read everything,' said Gardella. But gradually a whole sector of modern and past literature was banned or unavailable, because the regime did not approve of it. For this kind of reason, Luchino began to dislike the petty, genteel, totalitarian regime.

At this time there was no real fracture between the aristocracy, the industrial class and the new Fascist hierarchy, but there was still a separation between the aristocracy and the emerging industrial class. In comparison to the rest of the Milanese aristocracy, which was conventional, the Viscontis were not prejudiced. The conventional members of society condemned them: the plays, the pretty boys, *la dolce vita*. In those years of Fascist gentility, their ways began to shock: their sins were too elegant, their elegance was too sinful. At the same time religion was important to them: there was a private chapel at Via Cerva, one at Grazzano, nuns at Cernobbio (trained by Donna Carla to embroider elegant damasks, white on white), Donna Carla went to Mass every morning, and there was Mass at the cathedral in Milan where Don Giuseppe sang hymns in his beautiful baritone voice. Luchino had inherited a strong sense of religion, of the necessity of pomp and spectacle, but he also had an almost puritanical vision of a pure God in Whom he believed and Who had little to do with the Baroque God surrounded by angels whom he had adored as a member of the Visconti family. His was a severe northern God.

Gardella thought Luchino full of charm: 'They all held a tremendous fascination for me, Wally, Wanda. Luchino didn't have that kind of shyness which so often inhibits adolescents; if anything, he would remain silent and, later, explode with something terrible.' He was rather a bully. He never discussed his private life, because it was something nobody did in his milieu, even at that young age when, generally, adolescents confide in each other. He was fun to be with; he was a leader. He seemed sure of himself, with the rare ability, in an adolescent, of being able to manipulate people, and he seemed to want to prove something – his ability maybe, but more probably he was proving himself.

Luchino did not have much in common with Guido, who was even more good-looking, but rather effeminate – which Luchino was not – and not as bright (Guido was the only one of the four eldest children not to have studied a musical instrument). Guido was his mother's pet but, typically, Guido's allegiance was to Don Giuseppe and, when the Visconti parents split up, he had chosen to stay with his father. Anna was very dark and adored her father. Luigi was also handsome and keen on riding; he was going to follow the family tradition of joining the cavalry. Edoardo looked more like Luchino and was bright. The young Nane and Uberta were adored by, and delighted, everybody in the family.

The boy who had been trained to keep to the rules, whose every hour of the day had been dictated by a timetable and rigid discipline, quite naturally developed into a rebel. He often ran away from home: like a Fabrice del Dongo, he said of himself. Indeed there were similitudes with the protagonist of *The Charterhouse of Parma* – youth, noble birth, beauty, panache, even Lake Como bound the two characters together. But Fabrice had run away from a right-wing pro-Austrian father in order to join Napoleon's army, to fulfil his idealism. Luchino did not hate his father, he merely disliked him. Like Fabrice del Dongo, he loved his mother, but with the excitingly forbidden passion with which the young Stendhalian priest had loved his aunt, la Sanseverina. Fabrice was running away from the Austrians – he was inflamed by politics, Luchino was not: he was searching for a new identity which would free him from his family cocoon.

I was sixteen when I ran away from home the first time. I went to Rome and my father came to find me and then he said: 'Since you are here, stay. But at least, learn something: go and have a look at the ancient monuments.' And he took me, there and then, to San Pietro in Vincoli to see the statue of Moses. My father loved culture, always.... I left huge bills at Baldini & Castoldi,[1] but he never complained. 'Since it's books that you have spent so much on, I don't mind, go ahead.'[2]

After a few days in Rome, he had to go back to Milan and resume his hated studies, but he went on reading voraciously and expanding his taste in literature: once his father told Luchino that he was reading a new book, *Du Coté de chez Swann*, by an unknown writer and it was so beautiful that he read every page over and over again. 'And I,' said Visconti, 'became addicted to Proust, Stendhal and Balzac; I never changed. I never changed politically either. If in politics I ever had any doubts, it was about individuals, not principles.'[3]

In fact, he later changed radically in his political outlook, but he had not as yet thought about politics much. Luchino Visconti was a late developer – the last thing he would have turned towards, in those Milanese days, was *Das Kapital*. Marxism was merely an unpleasant word that conjured an image of illiterate shouting proletarians who killed the aristocracy because they wanted to gain the privileges which Luchino had experienced from the start. Fortunately, however, the Duce and the Black Shirts had put a stop to the 'disorder' that existed only in remote Russia. Germany was in a state of chaos, he heard; nobody in his family or his world was interested in the new, crude, Expressionistic schools which were emerging in Berlin – Grosz, Brecht and Weill were remote from their sense of culture. But Luchino identified with French literature, and Proust in particular; indeed there was a shock of recognition as he compared his own experiences with the narrator's: the social salons, the music – every page could have been a description of his own life as seen by himself. The description of Oriane de Guermantes at the opera the first time the narrator sees her, was for him just as he would have described his mother in her box at La Scala. When he longed for his mother's visit in the night, for her step, her scent and her presence; when he wished to go and see a great actress, la Borrelli, la Duse or la Bernhardt at the theatre and would seek his mother's permission. Marcel's love for Odette's serious daughter was just like Luchino's for Wanda Toscanini; and his parents' relationship with Toscanini was not unlike that of de Guermantes towards Swann.

Sarah Bernhardt appeared in Milan and Luchino went to see her; from Paris the waves of change in fashion and literature spread to Milan. While Josephine Baker's *Revue Nègre* triumphed at the Théâtre des Champs Elysées in that spring of 1925, Diaghilev and Serge Lifar, his new protégé, had been to stay at Villa d'Este near Cernobbio, and called on both Donna Carla and Countess Demidoff, one of the many Russian aristocrats who had fled the revolution. The Russian *belles dames sans merci* were fashionable, they were exotic and typified the mysterious vamp, like a Mata Hari who operated from dark salons decorated with Moroccan pouffes and peacock feathers; they dressed in clothes made by Fortuny (who, after the 'classical' style launched by Isadora Duncan, had abandoned the neo-Byzantine line). In their dark, uterine salons incense burned and a great deal of drugs were taken. Cocaine and opium were the popular, exclusive pastime of the smart set and of the writers. Diaghilev took cocaine, as did Count Ciano, who was an addict (the power that the mafioso Vito Genovese, a killer, acquired during the Fascist regime – he was even received by Mussolini – was due to the fact that he was the supplier of cocaine to Ciano, the Foreign Minister); Cocteau was keen on opium, but took cocaine as well. A sniff and a puff was an accepted part of an evening in the salons of Etienne de Beaumont or Marie-Laure de Noailles. Diaghilev met the nineteen-year-old Luchino at Cernobbio on this occasion – the only time the two ever did; the impresario only had eyes for Lifar (of whom he was very jealous); Luchino was actually thinking of a beautiful girl.

For her Luchino Visconti ran away from home again, and this time it was Guido, his elder brother, who went to collect him. He was punished and sent to a boarding-school with the Calasanziani fathers. But even the monks could not get Luchino to study, so he never passed his final examinations and thus never finished school.

As a last resort, it was decided to send him to work in a family business. Maybe an office would shape him! Not at all; all the secretaries fell for him – and he for them. Besides, he couldn't take desk work seriously.

His father was politely and respectfully told that Luchino's mere presence in the office created 'a state of anarchy', because he was a *coureur* and rather macho in his attitude to women. But women's rationality was limited, he thought; they were the source of disorder and upheavals. Why women should be the source of disorder and upheavals more than men is quite obvious: Luchino's model was his mother, and he would forever identify woman's nature with her passionate character.

Seeing that it was impossible for Luchino to become a disciplined office-boy, the only solution was for him to join the Army, which in any case was part of the family tradition. 'In Africa Guido became Captain of La Folgore; Uncle Luigi and Uncle Edoardo were in the cavalry,' said his niece Meralda. So, in 1926, Luchino went to the famous cavalry school at Pinerolo in

Piedmont, where royalty and the aristocracy sent their children. To the relief of his family he enjoyed it; he was twenty and looked wonderful in his uniform, he was naughty and popular and he discovered that he was an excellent rider. He enjoyed bending an animal to his will, especially an animal as good-looking as a horse. He led a busy social life in Piedmont, for he was invited everywhere and the ladies loved him. On one occasion the Princess of Gerace sent her liveried chauffeur in a Rolls Royce to the barracks to collect Luchino and drive him to the room she had taken at the Hôtel de France in Pinerolo. At their first rendezvous, however, Luchino drank so much champagne as a remedy for his shyness that he vomited all over the Princess.

At Pinerolo, going around with his chums, he had 'caught that disease', which must mean a venereal disease and may have been another component in his gradual sexual rejection of women. At this stage he was sexually interested in women as well as men; later, when he became totally homosexual, he still liked women and needed their admiration, their falling in love with him – but he could not have a sentimental involvement with them. He himself did fall in love, often, very thoroughly and overwhelmingly, but not with women.

He spent the whole of 1927 at Pinerolo, this time as an officer, having emerged from the school a skilled horseman. He joined the Reggimento Savoia Cavalleria, he wore a shiny helmet and thin black moustaches, and he rode wonderful horses. The documents of his enrolment show that he was about six feet tall, had straight brown hair and had been vaccinated against smallpox and typhus.

Once, during manoeuvres, the generals were captured by surprise by a patrol led by the dashing officer Count Visconti. They were not amused at the joke and wanted to punish him, but they mentioned him – unflatteringly – in dispatches instead, because he had powerful, important friends. Apart from his father being so close to the Queen, Luchino had become very friendly with Umberto of Savoia, the Prince of Piedmont and heir to the throne. They used to send each other messages in sealed envelopes, carried by a young *bersagliere*. Rather late in life – he was twenty-two – Luchino began to pay attention to politics. There are some nebulous stories describing Luchino attempting to convince Prince Umberto that Fascism and Mussolini were bad things – but it might be that it was the other way round. Luchino, as he said once, almost became a Fascist. He was impressed by the veneer of discipline and, as happens to military-educated men, he approved of the Army, the conquests and the masculine language.

He was in no doubt about his capacities, but didn't know how to express them. The Army was not enough; he would have liked to write books and plays, but he found this difficult for he was beginning to be gregarious and to fear being alone, confronted with his thoughts on paper. He liked exercising power over others, and they seemed to respond, whether children whom, as a boy, he directed in a play or bullied into listening to his cello, or whether they were soldiers whom he shouted at as an officer of the cavalry. Dressing up in a magnificent uniform pleased him; to ride gave him a sense of freedom, enhanced by the fact that he did it so well; and both men and women admired him.

From Pinerolo he often went to Milan and after a while he decided to move to an apartment of his own in Via San Domenichino, where he lived with a valet and a chauffeur. He would often have lunch at his mother's, where they would have long discussions about people, books and projects. He would also go to Mass at the smart church of San Babila around the corner from Via Cerva. Luigi Barzini, who was younger than Luchino, met him then, in 1927, at his father's house, which was 'the kingdom of Diaghilev': tables covered with objects in jade and gold, brocades, and indirect lighting. He recalls that Luchino was handsome, slightly stiff, and pleased with his name, looks and social standing.

'When we were in Milan we spent two months with each parent,' Uberta remembers. 'When we were with papa and Luchino was at home, he would never go out without coming to our bedrooms to cuddle us and tuck us up. He would whisper: "Do you want a drink of water?" ' The little girls would kick the blankets away in order to make him stay and start the cuddling all over again. He was paternal towards them, almost as though he were repeating the same rite which had given him so much pleasure as a child, when his mother had come to kiss him goodnight. 'He was wonderful, he played with us all the time. In summer we could swim with him for hours; our French governess went mad. At Grazzano-Visconti he would come in dressed up as a ghost and our governess screamed, but we were delighted and couldn't have enough. We were also terrified of our father, who pretended to be strict and shouted at us, but nothing ever happened.' The little girls had a sort of wooden hut in the gardens of Grazzano which Don Giuseppe had built for them; as soon as lunch was over, the little girls would dash there and start cooking all over again: eggs and vegetables, all sorts of things. Luchino and Edoardo came and ate as if it were an inn but 'they never paid the bill, although that was the idea.'

Luchino was never particularly interested in his clothes, but when he needed one shirt he would have a score sent from the shop and try them on at home. Then he would forget to send back those he did not want – a habit he never lost. Pozzi was the first Milanese shop to sell English shirts and cardigans. Don Giuseppe, confronted with huge bills, used to tell Luchino: 'I swear that I saw those Pozzi "Made in England" shirts being made in Rome!' Pozzi went on sending shirts to Luchino Visconti for many years to come.

Count Giuseppe never lost his passion for the theatre, although La Scala was no longer controlled by the Viscontis and Donna Carla was no longer the prima donna of his *teatrino*. He founded and financed the Art Theatre Company of Milan, directed by Gian Capo with quite well-known actors and a new young actress called Andreina Pagnani. This company opened at the Eden Theatre on 28 December 1928 with *The Wise Wife* by Carlo Goldoni. Luchino, who had finished his military service by this time, worked on the *décor* and scenery of various plays, once again absorbed by the professional routine of the theatre. His father was delighted, because he thought that it was a pity for Luchino to waste his talent on military life. The young star of the company, Andreina Pagnani, had just left drama school and Don Giuseppe had a crush on her. Luchino, too, developed a youthful passion for her, although he never told her. The company folded, however, in 1929, only one year after its foundation.

With his new friends Corradi and Gardella, Visconti used to enjoy combing Milan's antique and junk shops. He filled his flat in Via San Domenichino with all kinds of 'amusing' objects: he had a passion for interior decoration. He had a good eye for quality, but also enjoyed what later came to be known as *kitsch* – he loved that in people as well, and was amused by scores of Mesdames Verdurins: *kitsch* people and *kitsch* objects were the same to him.

3
The Golden Set

Luchino Visconti was now twenty-three; he was very rich, he was handsome, he was talented and he wanted to prove himself. Since he had learned only one trade – that of riding, in which he excelled – and horses were preferable to humans (they obeyed without discussion, they were beautiful, they did not sin), overnight he decided to dedicate himself to them totally. His elder brother Luigi was already a skilled horseman and was thinking of setting up a stable. Luchino put this plan into practice.

Riding his own horse Esturgeon in 1929 at the winter races in St Moritz, Visconti surprised everybody by winning, but he was disqualified because he was not officially on the books as a 'gentleman rider'. From then on Luigi rode his brother's horses. Luchino threw himself into training and breeding professionally, and sought the help of a young Tuscan jockey called Ubaldo Pandolfi:

> I was a jockey at the steeplechase with Colonel Forlanini. When Count Visconti met me, he understood that I was a potential trainer and did everything to take me away from my employer, so that I could work with him. When he engaged me, he already owned Esturgeon. He knew little about training and breeding then, but had an enormous appetite for knowledge: we started buying fillies and colts. I trained them and he would watch me while training the young colts and he learned everything by looking: he never asked questions. First I was the trainer of his stable, then later it appeared that it was only him.

Pandolfi would visit Visconti every evening, calling at Via San Domenichino in order to keep his master informed on the progress of the training. Once Luchino had put together his stable he asked for his own colours, white and green. 'He was a gentleman, a bit brusque, a handsome youth; I worked for him for three years.' After that, Pandolfi became trainer for Luchino's brother Luigi. In 1930 Luchino bought two horses from Tesio, who was the top Italian breeder; one was Sanzio, a thoroughbred bay, which he acquired for 1,500 lire, a low sum because the horse was full of faults, but Pandolfi and Visconti corrected them and with him they won the Grand Prix of Milan in 1931. 'We put Sanzio right with patience and work. He was a bit weak in the hind legs and Tesio didn't believe in him. But little by little the horse gained strength. With plenty of exercise, care, massage and medicines we corrected the structure of the horse. Sanzio,' Pandolfi said, 'was a creation of Count Luchino's will.' Patiently, day by day, following a strict programme, Visconti transformed this horse into the thoroughbred which won all his races.

Visconti, his trainer and his horses travelled everywhere, for money was no problem. The Erba shares had been divided among the seven children, and the Visconti side (with the successful toiletry products launched by Don Giuseppe) helped to amass wealth.

When Visconti also won the famous Ostend Grand Prix race in 1932, he gave a grand celebration champagne dinner for everyone in the racing world.

From his flat in Via San Domenichino he moved to one near San Siro, where he kept his horses. 'The Count came to the stables every morning and afternoon, just like a professional, and he took part in the training. He was getting good at it. He had put to stud some mares of very good blood which he had bought in England,' remembered Pandolfi. An event which had particularly stirred the racing fraternity was Visconti's acquisition of a mare which had run third in the Oaks in England. He also bought Lafcadio and Weimar, both of which won several races. Although he learned a great deal from Pandolfi, Luchino was a man who did not need much teaching. He knew about cross-breeding and ancient pedigrees. When he started buying colts, he gave up racing altogether and became a breeder. He did it with passion, judging what each horse needed to do, the way in which it had to be trained. Or he sat at home and worked out on charts which blood should be mixed with which: he had a good memory and patience too. 'He came to the stables with his friends,' Pandolfi recalled. 'I remember Mr Penati and, when he moved on to new stables, Prince Umberto used to come: they were good friends.' Penati was one of Visconti's secret friends, always beside him, until the end of his life. So there was already an all-masculine world of horses, tweeds and whips.

Pandolfi spent two months at Cernobbio, at Casa Erba, working on Luchino's and Luigi's horses – he was there as a servant, but the Viscontis had that aristocratic habit of involving in their family life those who worked for them. Pandolfi, used to see Visconti's mother only occasionally, since she now led a very retired life. Luigi had married Madina Arrivabene, one of the most beautiful girls of the Italian aristocracy; Luchino's younger brother Edoardo was engaged to Niki, Madina's sister. 'Countess Madina used to ride and jump too. At a certain moment in the evening, *la Mamma* would call them all, they would change and dine. One could see that she had authority.' With his father, on the other hand, Visconti seemed rather stiff, Pandolfi recalled. 'But Count Giuseppe was very kind.' At Cernobbio Pandolfi saw the pavilion where Donna Carla kept seven or eight nuns: she was very religious and no longer wore voluptuous mauve veils, but dressed instead in black.

Pandolfi had a room outside Villa Erba at Cernobbio. 'There were many servants and an old retired coachman who lived with them. The Viscontis looked so elegant when they took a walk by the lake, and they already owned a small motorboat and many cars.'

Madina Visconti remembers Luchino in those days sitting for hours on the large yellow sofa at Cernobbio, or crouching on the floor discussing theology with 'our priest', a sort of resident cleric who came for meals and heard Donna Carla's confession. Luchino was rebellious towards the Catholic Church then, but believed in God, though he was no longer a practising Catholic. He often quarrelled with his father, who was religious but also believed in ghosts and spirits, with whom he talked all the time. Donna Carla, by contrast, had withdrawn inside a wall of faith. 'There, at Cernobbio, we sat on enormous yellow brocade settees with wings.... Uberta and Luchino were on the floor, surrounded by their dogs, and Luchino would talk about God, solar rays, physics. The old priest teased him at times,' said Madina Arrivabene. They would gather blackberries and ride and 'there was this extraordinary atmosphere, the priest, the nuns in the pavilion embroidering away....'

He spent some weekends at Grazzano, where his father tried to persuade him to give up breeding horses; he thought that Luchino, whom he suspected of being the brightest of his children, had great talent for the theatre, for *his* theatre. Of all his children, it was Luchino whom Don Giuseppe loved, an almost unrequited love since Luchino adored his mother and condemned his father for the separation and for the scandal of the Erba shares. He was also irritated by his father's more ridiculous characteristics, his over-theatrical mannerisms and his make-believe world which he, Luchino, had absorbed.

'Grazzano amused him,' a close friend of those days recalled, 'it represented his childhood. He also liked the concept of the home, the *décor* and the family. Grazzano had been the Visconti country house and he cared about the Visconti family almost as a matter of course – I would say that he never made any attempt to hide his nobility. He was an aristocrat and demonstrated that throughout his life and art. He was not like a *parvenu* who wanted to belong. He belonged, and it would have been odd for him to pretend otherwise.'

His schoolfriends recognized with amazement the change which had occurred in Luchino: the boy who had been incapable of respecting discipline had become a disciplinarian.

An event had occurred which changed Visconti, something which he never mentioned then and never mentioned later – an episode which had been erased from his life but not from his memory, in fact a watershed in the moulding of his character. Luchino not only liked to race horses, but he had also developed a passion for motor-racing and he had bought a Lancia Spider for himself. From Grazzano-Visconti he would drive to the track at Monza, because he liked anything fast, reckless and dangerous. On the morning of 30

September 1929, Luchino suddenly decided to take his Lancia and asked Macerati, the Viscontis' chauffeur who had been with the family for years, to accompany him to the race. Macerati did not want to go: one of his children was sick, it was foggy and the last-minute request sounded like a typical whim of his spoilt young master. But Luchino shouted and bullied him – he wanted to go there and then, so Macerati got ready as soon as possible. Luchino took the wheel of the open sports car; he was not driving fast because of the fog, but on a sharp bend near Piacenza, a cart full of hay suddenly emerged from the fog. Luchino stood on the brakes: they did not respond, the car started to spin. His chauffeur stood up to see, and a pole sticking out of the cart slashed through his throat. Macerati died a few hours later.

Luchino, who was beginning to enjoy his success, was sought after by men and women, and was gaining a certain degree of self-assurance, was deeply affected by this tragedy: he could not escape his sense of guilt, his anger against himself or his anguish. He did not drive again for twenty years and, when he died, it was discovered that he was still supporting Macerati's children.

Visconti needed to escape, from himself this time, to get away from those self-indulgent whims which had led him to become the instrument of a beloved man's death. He went to stay with his lonely brother Guido in Tripoli, and soon afterwards he departed alone towards the Southern Sahara plateau, the Tassili mountains.

Guido, who in 1924 married a beautiful Florentine, had joined the army and lived in a house in Tripoli which he had bought. Guido's marriage had not survived the honeymoon, and he was sad and lonely. Luchino felt great pity for him and also resented his mother's partiality for his eldest brother.

Luchino must have heard beforehand of the Tassili region, the grand Saharan plateau which, in those days, was almost inaccessible. (It still takes four hours to fly over the vast Sahara, from Algiers to Djanet, the oasis at the foot of the plateau.) Luchino engaged a Touareg guide to lead him on the high desert mountains which only the nomadic Touareg know well, and he also found a porter with a donkey to carry water, the most precious item since, even on the plateau, there are few wells. And off he went, encountering a few wandering Touareg in the spectacular desert of yellow dunes and rocky mountains, living the life of our pre-history, with some goats and camels feeding on the almost non-existent vegetation, small tents fenced in by branches and rags to protect them from the all-invading sand.

The Touareg language is ancient and the writing archaic, still related to hieroglyphics. Led by the two Touareg, with whom he could not communicate except a little in French, Luchino walked through spectacular landscapes: majestic Valhallas crumbling over each other; he would sleep in the open at night, under the deep blue skies starred with billions of twinkling needles. 'Once, but only once, he talked for hours and told me about a youthful journey which he had made following a deep crisis. They were wonderful tales of this journey, alone, in the desert. And he told me this with a certain emotion describing that sky, those nights: he would look at that perfect sky and feel that there was Somebody. He had gone alone apart from the guides, maybe on purpose with nobody of his level with whom to discuss his feelings – and he told me about his meditations. They were not the thoughts of a materialist,' a friend related.

So Luchino Visconti, alone, thought of God, his only salvation after what had happened. Under those skies, in that landscape where he encountered few living things except for flies and scorpions, Visconti spent two months of mystical meditation, of utter solitude – he had a necessary confrontation with his own way of life and with his soul.

Sometimes, when he met a cluster of Touareg, the oldest woman – the Touareg are a matriarchal society – would light a fire with a rare piece of wood, twigs and dry branches scattered in the desert, and welcome him by preparing green tea. The women wore black cloths over their heads, their faces uncovered (unlike the Arab women of the desert), scores of amulets round their necks and colourful clothes. Their features were delicate and, like their men, the Touareg women were handsome. With them Luchino Visconti shared the simple food of the desert, bread, dried dates and water: everything else was a luxury. At night Luchino's guide would prepare the fire, after having searched for and gathered a few twigs scattered by the wind on the desert plateau. During his pilgrimage of guilt he woke at sunrise, when the desert is cold and the light is clear, and drank the coffee made by his guide, who ground a few beans between stones and boiled the water with some lumps of rough sugar in it. At noon, even if it was late autumn, it was too hot to proceed and they would stop to find shade.

The male Touareg looked regal in their huge blue cotton burnouses which hid their faces, a length of which covered their mouths and noses to protect them from sand, sun and flies; Luchino of necessity adopted a burnous, too.

Sometimes he would not encounter a single living presence for days, surrounded as he and his two guides were by jagged mountains in the form of fortresses, giants, monsters and black submarines. He walked through granite gorges and climbed to 4,000 feet to admire the spectacular cave paintings by prehistoric men who had lived in dwellings carved by the wind and sand. These ancient artists had used coloured chalks that still retain their sparkle because of the dryness of the climate. High in the Tassili mountains Visconti pondered on these paintings, witnesses of a culture long since disappeared, taken over by the silent desert; there, too, he gazed at the dark cobalt skies, while he perhaps tried to come to terms with the dilemmas of a young man of twenty-three, longing to express himself; of a man eroded by guilt, a playboy who did not want to be a playboy; of a man who could not fall out of love with his mother, who already felt 'different'. There had been some casual girls in his life, but the most interesting games had been with the boys at the stable, with menservants. And he felt 'different' from his brother Luigi, who had married, from Edoardo, who was to marry, but not so different from Guido or from his father: he felt the weight of a hereditary 'disease', because he was not proud of being 'different'. He would have liked to have children, for he was a conventional man, especially in what concerned the family, which he considered as the only pure nucleus.

At that moment he was also seeking to express himself to God, a mystical God who eluded him but was different from the *chic* Milanese essence of his family's private chapel, or Mass at the cathedral or at San Babila. 'Religion was a thing of his own,' a close friend said:

> I never quite understood it; it was a mysterious side of him. He never talked about it in depth. He certainly was never ironic about it; he had a sense of belief which he passed on to us, a respect for the Faith, believing in something which was not palpable. Faith never appears in his films, but there is no rejection of it either. He never used the character of the priest in a controversial way. Maybe this was because of his education; his sisters and cousins are deeply Catholic, they go to confession, they pray all the time although, historically, his is a lay family.

Visconti's two-month journey, his saga of mysticism and solitude, surrounded by the severe beauty of an alien nature, changed him. He decided to travel more, to go to Paris and to spend less time in Italy. In order to buy horses, Visconti had already travelled to England and France. In Paris he would call on Madina and Niki and their fascinating friends, Serge Lifar, Kurt Weill, Jean Cocteau, Giacometti and Coco Chanel; he had previously met Chanel when she came to lunch at Cernobbio when he was a child. He also saw her and her 'golden' gang at the Lido in Venice – Madina and Niki opened their palazzo and they were all there – Lifar, Misia Sert, the Vicomtesse de Noailles – and they all thought themselves unique, exciting, beautiful and precious. 'During those years I can say that I encountered everybody,' writes Serge Lifar. 'At Venice there were the great popes, like the Viscontis, the Volpi "doges". Between Paris and Rome, society communicated, intertwined continuously. In Paris the people who welcome me were the same ones I met in London, Rome or Venice, all capitals on that axis of a triumphant worldliness.'[1] The more liberated Italians started going to Paris for the ballet, the parties and the people: the *bals masqués, les bals orientals* at the Schiaparellis', at the de Noailles', the lunches at Chanel's, were all becoming legendary.

Luchino Visconti joined the audiences, who were dazzled and educated by Diaghilev's Russian Ballet productions. In the immediate past, the Comtesse de Grehfulle and Robert de Montesquiou had led the applause. Everybody was in love with Nijinsky – Jean Cocteau was totally infatuated by him. Of this same world Stravinsky once declared: 'It is almost impossible to describe the perversity of Diaghilev's entourage.... I remember a rehearsal in Monaco, at which our pianist suddenly began looking very intensely beyond the music stand. I followed his gaze to a Monegasque soldier in a tricorne and then asked what the matter was. He answered: "I long to surrender myself to him!" '[2] So there was this extra factor which attracted Visconti to the Paris set: the sexual freedom. His impulse towards homosexuality, which he considered sinful, was openly condoned by these people. These men and women seemed to switch from homosexuality to heterosexuality with the greatest ease, between a sniff of cocaine and a puff of opium. Cocteau's boy-friend, Jean Marais, was openly his lover just as Lifar had succeeded Nijinsky in Diaghilev's affections. From time to time Luchino Visconti entered this world as the provincial boy, welcomed for his obvious gifts of beauty and wealth, nobility and presence. He knew most of those who went to Venice, including Misia Sert, who was a pace-setter, a remarkable woman who made and discovered talents. Chanel said of her: 'Misia is for Paris what the goddess Kali is for the Hindus: she is the goddess of creation and destruction at the same time.'[3] The composer Satie called her 'the Mother Kill-All', and Cocteau '*la faiseuse d'anges*'. So many people met each other through her: Ravel and Stravinsky were introduced to Diaghilev by her, and through her Stravinsky had a brief affair with Chanel, who felt for Stravinsky a kind of attraction made up of pity for the shyness of the bespectacled man and of admiration for his brain. They would meet at the fashionable and exclusive *Le Boeuf sur le Toit*, the surrealist home of elegance and art, which was nicknamed by Luchino *Le Bluff sur le Toit*.

Another influential figure of the Paris scene was the Vicomtesse de Noailles, who had plenty of blue blood and was said to be a descendant of the Marquis de Sade. ('de Sade! What a beautiful name!' Misia Sert once sighed. 'What wouldn't I give to be called de Sade!') The Vicomtesse de Noailles had a long, severe face, not unlike Virginia Woolf's. Her dark hair was parted in the middle; she was not beautiful but remarkable, and her looks were reminiscent of Velasquez and the Spanish Hapsburgs. Her Paris salon was celebrated for the wits who gathered there – Satie, Picasso, Radiguet – and in her drawing-room were paintings by Goya and portraits of the Vicomtesse by Balthus and Bérard.

The inventive talent of the Russian emigrés was a great, if not the main, contributor to the scene of novelty and a certain degree of democracy, because it was new to mix people from such different backgrounds in drawing-rooms, especially if the drawing-rooms belonged to the de Beaumonts, de Noailles and de Polignacs; and some of the Russian emigrés washed dishes during the day.

Princess Nathalie Paley – at that time Madame Lucien Lelong (her husband was a *couturier* and it was considered a novelty to 'receive' someone in trade) – was the daughter of the Grand Duke Paul Alexandrovitch of Russia, a relative of the Tzar *'de la main gauche'*, as Madina put it. She had beautiful bones, a tiny nose, grey eyes and high cheekbones. Her neck was exceptionally long. Nathalie Lelong was direct and unconventional, surrounded by wits and by handsome people, much photographed, cherished by Cocteau, beloved by Lifar, adored by the Polignacs; and Luchino too fell in love with her. Visconti, who was accustomed to being the object of desire, had found somebody who was even more coveted than himself – and none too interested either. She was the darling of the Paris set, and a close friend of Niki and Madina.

Coco Chanel, the other great goddess of Paris society, who had been desired by most of the Visconti men, took a fancy to the silent Luchino. He was twenty-six – much younger than Chanel – and was certainly aware of her interest. He took to lunching at Chanel's house in Rue Carbon, a great honour since the most glittering, famous and interesting wits dined at her table.

Luchino's German was weak and his English almost non-existent, but his French was fluent and he felt among his own kind with these 'stars', although he was never entirely at ease because he was paralytically shy. He was silent with Chanel, but that was almost a necessity because she was a non-stop talker. Chanel liked the presence of the receptive, handsome youth; the fact that he was an aristocrat and rich also no doubt helped. Luchino loved Nathalie Lelong, who had had an affair with Lifar and several women as well; Chanel had an affair with Luchino, who also loved Niki Arrivabene – they all loved each other and were all beautiful, bisexual and attractive.

So in Paris there were the horses at Longchamps, the parties and Chanel's precious lunches as well. Misia Sert had 'accepted' Luchino, so he could go anywhere. The fact that Visconti was absorbed in breeding horses was, to him, an important factor: at least he was not just another playboy who went to Paris merely for the social scene. He would 'commute' between Paris and Milan, where he still kept his horses but with waning interest. He would spend a week or two in Paris and then take a train back to Milan, for a fortnight or so to see his mother. There were other trips, too, to Venice, to Grazzano-Visconti and to see his brother in Libya: travelling seemed much easier then than it is today and, apart from the fact that money was no problem, there was often no particular reason for being in one place other than, for instance, to see some friends, call on Prince Umberto or watch a race.

In Milan his new stables were ready: it was a lovely building, designed to Luchino's specifications by Piero Tecchia, an architect friend of the family. They were model stables; everybody talked about them: the green-tiled roof, the rooms for the jockeys, trainers and grooms, and the apartment for himself. There he kept about thirty horses, and people in the profession would come and visit the new building of which Visconti was so proud.

Friends came too: Prince Umberto ('the good looks of Prince Umberto seduced all hearts!' wrote Jean Marais) and actors and actresses who came to dine after an evening at the theatre.

Almost every day he would lunch at a restaurant nearby, at Trenno. The head waiter made a point of bowing to him, greeting Visconti and murmuring *'Signor Conte....'* One day Luchino summoned him and asked what the house recommended. 'There is an excellent *consommé nature*, Signor Conte.' 'Consommé is never good,' came the reply – he was already a dictatorial client.

The fact that he often left Milan for Paris, London or, later, Berlin and Munich, signified that Visconti was in possession of a passport, a rare document to possess under a dictatorial regime. Very few Italian citizens had a passport and could go abroad so easily, but his cousin was the Podestà of Milan, the representative of the Fascist party. One wonders what Visconti thought when hearing (certainly not reading, for this kind of news was censored) that the uncompromising anti-Fascist Toscanini had been physically assaulted by rowdies in Bologna and that his passport had been, for a time, withdrawn.

Horses began to bore him, for he had proved that he could master that business, and now that he knew all about it he realized that he must seek fulfilment in another field. In 1934 he sold part of his stables though he was still engaged, with waning enthusiasm, in breeding some colts. He had also quarrelled with the Italian racing association and was to rid himself of all his horses some years later.

The theatre was still close to his heart and with one of his closest friends, Livio dell'Anna, he wrote a comedy in one act: he liked working in a team. And he paid long visits to Paris, where he stayed in Faubourg St Honoré and led a busy social life; but in Milan he needed an occupation to quench his remarkable energy. He embarked on a new enterprise, designing chintzes for sofas and armchairs together with Dell'Anna and Corradi. He drew very well. At the beginning the CVD (Corradi, Visconti, Dell'Anna) was a flop, but then it started doing well – an activity, this, which he totally erased from his later recollections because it did not fit his image of himself.

In Milan he went on combing junk shops, buying Art Nouveau objects, and leading a superficially conventional life. His friends there did not suspect his homosexuality because women were so attracted to him.

Milan began to seem stultifying. Everything exciting seemed to happen in Paris, where he could also see all the films which were forbidden in Fascist Italy, like *The Blue Angel* by Sternberg, and Dali's and Buñuel's experimental films. The Italian cinema strove to depict national life as one of luxury, glory and 'normality'. There were many epic films, mainly set in Imperial Roman times, in which the direct relationship between the glory of yesterday and the glory of Mussolini's Mediterranean empire was stressed and exalted (a few sadistic scenes with Christians being eaten by lions underlined the better, Catholic nature of the present regime and sold the film to a wider public). The modern comedies featured new stars like Vittorio de Sica, the sultry Clara Calamai, the pretty *ingénue* Maria Denis and the actresses Luisa Ferida, Mariella Lotti and Alida Valli. These stars were dressed in approximate versions of eighteenth-century lace or contemporary feathers; they never had lovers on the screen unless they were 'fallen' women; they were ladies in the desert, saved just in time from hordes of black savages by the dashingly handsome Italian officer. Such films were nicknamed the 'white-telephone films'; they never showed the reality of Italian life, poverty, useless wars in Africa or corruption, but were part of the propaganda machine.

Visconti went to see these films, but he was too intelligent to be taken in and his critical sense was too developed to approve of the clumsy dialogue, the approximately accurate *décor* and, more important, the minor role of the director: the stress was on the stars.

Luchino's father did not like Fascism on aesthetic grounds, and he would say so to his son. He loathed the vulgarity of Fascist hymns, the ugliness of the Black Shirts, Mussolini's fatness and the low cultural level of the regime, which was the expression of a new middle class, certainly not an offspring of the aristocracy. He was against Fascism 'because it got on his nerves,' said Uberta. 'When he watched the big parades, he touched wood because he thought the Fascist leaders all dressed in black brought bad luck. He couldn't stand Starace [the prominent Fascist Minister of Propaganda] and, when he saw him, Papà, who was very superstitious, touched wood everywhere. He said to Luchino, "Don't allow yourself to be impressed by people like that!" '

Life at Court suited Don Giuseppe, who had moved to Rome, apart from short spells at Grazzano-Visconti; he enjoyed the 'operatic' side of Court life, the attempt to turn operetta into grand opera. Though the new Duke of Grazzano was not Fascist, many in the family were; when they looked at Europe they saw disorder and inflation in Germany, factories occupied and strikes in France, Spain pushing towards Socialism and they remembered the Red wave in Italy itself. The upper classes and the industrialists felt grateful to Mussolini, even if they did not like the regime.

The Savoias disliked the regime too, mainly on the grounds of rivalry: Mussolini always tried to outdo the royal house, and succeeded with a vulgar flamboyance which disregarded rules of etiquette and was peculiarly suited to the Italians. Under a veneer of mutual respect, there was deep contempt for each other; yet Mussolini was clever enough to make use of the royal house.

The nationalistic tone of the regime limited culture and this was annoying to Luchino; foreign culture was dismissed, ridiculed and often banned. Italian culture itself was provincial enough and, for people like Giuseppe and Luchino Visconti, who doted on Proust, it was too limiting.

It may be that the new regime in Germany, which in 1933 put an end to the vice and disorder of the Weimar Republic, offered a more attractive, serious solution he thought; Hitler, after all, was an Austrian and the Nazis, being German, were more serious and disciplined than the Italians. In his defence, it must be remembered that the Italian press did not at this time criticize the already ugly face of the new dictatorial regime in Germany; Visconti was merely reflecting the attitudes of his contemporaries. So Luchino Visconti decided to visit Germany and study the situation at first hand. Much as he was attracted by Paris, by the disorderly explosion of ideas, by sexual freedom and freedom of expression, his puritan side, his admiration for discipline and for the glorification of the body and youth ideally attracted him to the new Nazi regime.

4
Flying Free

'I have always had a strong interest in German culture, literature and music. After Goethe, I love Thomas Mann. In one way or another, all my films are dipped in Mann, if you look at them. And German music, Mahler, Wagner,' said Visconti.[1] However, there is more to it than that. Visconti was a Lombard and thus a Longobard, a German, which partly accounts for the deep attraction he felt towards German culture and to some Teutonic characteristics.

The end of the Austro-Hungarian Empire had given birth to a particular kind of literature, beloved by Visconti because it moved him deeply. The Austrian literature of the 1920s and 1930s was rooted in the nostalgic memory of the political and cultural humus of an Empire whose passing was recounted, whether with regret by Werfel and Zweig or with ironic detachment by Robert Musil, whether in the epic of Roth or in the satire of Karl Krauss. This literature was a mixture of nostalgia and utopia linked by the vision of the function of an Empire which had already disintegrated. Luchino Visconti always wanted to film Musil's *Young Törless*, perhaps because in this ambiguous story of a German schoolboy can be seen the seed of that sadism which was to germinate into Nazism.

Austria was a cultural mother to Visconti, and what was happening in Berlin in 1933 seemed to be a more dignified version of Fascism, because Nazism was rooted in Teutonic symbolism. He had a fixation about Siegfried, not because of Wagner, who was out of fashion then anyway, but as a mythological hero, the perfect human being, heroic and Aryan. In 1933 and 1934 he often talked about it.

However, one of Visconti's literary 'gods' knew better; as early as 1916, writing to Paul Amman, Thomas Mann analysed the nature of the Germans:

> We are not a nation like others. We are more like Europe in the abstract. In our soul, yes, in the soul of every individual German, the contradictions of Europe are borne out. There is no natural German solidarity and synthesis – only perhaps in music, our homeland, but never, never in the intellect and in politics: which is why it is a mad and un-national undertaking to substitute a literary-political atmosphere in Germany for that of the musical, as the *'civilisation-littérateur'* wishes to do.

We are no nation. National feeling is only spiritually possible with us when we are at rock bottom, when things are going badly ... otherwise it is not possible... [2]

But things in Germany had gone badly: the so-called 'Golden Twenties' had been anything but golden – squalid poverty, inflation and depression; the society of the Weimar Republic which had been born in 1919 stood on shaky foundations. These conditions had given birth to the Expressionist experience, Dada, the *Neue Sachlichkeit*; ideas, 'schools' and trends had erupted everywhere, and political events had been dramatic in Europe.

Visconti's visits to Germany after 1933 were a secret that he never talked about later, because he was ashamed of his early infatuation with the Nazi regime. 'One reason why he liked the Germans was that they are always so single-minded: they believe in what they say, but believe academically. That was the type of thing Luchino was looking for. He was intrigued by the Nazis; also the élite people like Coco Chanel liked the Nazis,' a German friend recalled. His sister Uberta described how Luchino had returned from Germany favourably impressed: 'I remember a ferocious discussion with my father, who couldn't stand them. Luchino had been at a parade, I can't remember where and in which year, probably in 1934: he described the discipline and strength of handsome youths who were carrying something, a huge pole, I think.' Also a school friend remembered that Visconti wrote to him from Berlin asking him to join him. His friend thought that Luchino was interested in Nazism because it was a regime which had given value to the German cultural roots; he was attracted by the idea of strength.

Visconti had also seen and admired Leni Riefenstahl's celebrated propaganda film, *Triumph of the Will*, which she made in 1934 at the Party congress at Nüremberg. He had admired the technical precision, the freedom and strength of the director, the beauty of the photography and also the context. The aeroplane carrying the Führer, the parade in the city, Hitler with his icy glazed look, his little hand responding to the cheering masses – Leni Riefenstahl's film mythically portrayed what had happened, which was realism of a kind, and that reality was beautiful, strong and orderly.

Later, Visconti once, but only once, confided in a friend and described to him some of his visits to Munich, where he would go, driven by his chauffeur, for short stays, admiring Hitler's 'shows', but also longingly watching the blond, sadistic boys in uniform.

When in 1969 Visconti made a film called *The Damned* about the rise of the Nazi regime, he plunged into a world he remembered, which he had seen, and he could not hide the fascination it held for him. 'Let's be clear: I didn't want to make an historical work,' Visconti said of his film about Germany in 1933:

> The rise to power of Adolf Hitler and the political situation in Germany were apparent in this film only as a reflection of and as an influence on the relationships which the characters have towards each other. The historical facts which are described

in this film are really twofold: the fire in the Reichstag, which allowed Chancellor Hitler to erase the constitution, which guaranteed individual and civic liberty, thus getting rid of all parliamentary control and becoming dictator of the Reich; and the Night of the Long Knives, which freed him from a tiresome opposition within the Nazi party and established his alliance with the generals and the upper hierarchy of the army, allowing him to become the supreme head of the armed forces on the death of Hindenburg. But also the slaughter by the Brown Shirts is not recounted in this film with documentary exactitude: it is re-invented, imagined, following my own ideas. The political atmosphere is a main factor in the rush to crime of the Von Essenbachs. It is not by chance that the film starts in 1933: that was a decisive year for Germany. In only twelve months Hitler substituted his own personal dictatorship for the democratic institutions, he destroyed all parties, except for his own, he erased the trades unions, he killed a democratic association, he got rid of the Jews from the professions and from public life, he abolished the freedom of speech and of the press, he suffocated any independence of the Law. In 1933, in the squares of Berlin, books were already being burnt, the Gestapo was institutionalized, already fifty concentration camps were in existence and the opponents of the regime were to die at Dachau, at Buchenwald, at Ravensbrück and at Mauthausen. The Weimar Republic died and the Assassin State was born. The German middle class was finished, while the aristocracy of capital and of industry gave up their power to the new arrivals or tried to share it with Hitler: a new leading class of criminals, of perverted men, was born.[3]

Beautifully recounted by Visconti himself, these events, which were difficult to detect when most of Europe cheered Hitler and even the Prince of Wales didn't hide his enthusiasm towards the new enemy of Bolshevism, were not detected by the young Luchino in the same way as he analysed them later. He did not detect them in France.

By 1933-4, Luchino Visconti was almost a full-time resident in Paris; he used to stay at Le Vouillemont, an hotel which has since disappeared, opposite the British Embassy in Faubourg St Honoré; he knew the city well and loved its restaurants, old corners and little squares. He had discovered a tiny, then unknown shop called Louis Vuitton which made and sold bags and suitcases, signing them with the firm's own initials: L.V., which were not only Louis Vuitton's but also Luchino Visconti's. He would go and order scores of L.V. cases: he was almost their only customer. Visconti launched a fashion because, little by little, friends and admirers were seen everywhere carrying L.V. suitcases, which, at a later date, became a rather snob status symbol.

The arts were still a strong element in Visconti's life; once, when he was in Berlin, he dashed back to Paris in order to see Stravinsky's ballet *The Firebird*. He saw many of the ballets of Christian Bérard, the most famous stage and ballet designer in the 1930s, which stimulated him through their use of colour and their sensuality. Visconti went to see Jean Cocteau's *La Voix Humaine* at the Comédie Française, also designed by Bérard, and indeed he never missed a play by Cocteau.

This production of *The Firebird* was in 1935, the year in which Mussolini attacked Abyssinia, thus isolating Italy even more from free Europe. However, when the 'golden set' and Luchino all moved to Venice, it was as if the city were not even Italian let alone Fascist, apart from some cocktail parties, dances or dinners given by the local Fascist leaders – the powerful Cini, the immensely rich Gaggia or the 'doge' Volpi. The only reason for moving on from one city to the next was to see each other all over again in different environments, in palazzos rather than in *maisons*. Beach-huts had become very fashionable: Chanel's had been nicknamed '*le radeau de la Méduse*', after Géricault's famous painting – Medusa being herself.

Chanel was fascinated by Luchino, but he was holding back. He was flattered by her attention, he liked the world in which she moved and admired her infallible taste and unconventionality; but he found her overwhelming and demanding. Chanel was in love with him, although to say 'in love' is such an approximation when one doesn't know the exact feelings of a woman who was more mature and accomplished than the young Milanese. She was probably enamoured of him, as older women often are of younger men, and she felt she could change him for the better. By then she was the queen, the undisputed authority in Paris, because she was bright, beautiful and energetic. There was, too, a saturnine side to Chanel: 'her sufferings, her pleasure in hurting, her need to punish, her pride, her rigour, her sarcasm, her destructive rage, the single-mindedness of a character which switched from hot to cold, her inventive genius: this *belle dame sans merci* went on to invent pauperism for the millionaire (while eating off gold plates), a ruinous simplicity, the *recherché* of what is not immediately striking: leather on yachts, navy blue and white, the grey shade of her fields of lavender at Roquebrune, her picnics on the River Brenta, the little suppers at La Pausa where people helped themselves. Never was snobbism better directed against itself.'[4]

They went on travelling, purposelessly: these days Luchino was always at her side. He went to stay at La Pausa, Chanel's celebrated villa on the Riviera; this was yet another golden world where the Americans had arrived in precious little groups, their experiences recorded in books like *Tender is the Night*, and where Cole Porter and Somerset Maugham went to meet their own kind. Rory Cameron recalled that 'Chanel's house was between Roquebrune and Cap Martin, and many people converged there. She never gave parties larger than ten or twelve, but then they were all very interesting people, from Poulenc to Lifar.' Her gardens were special; again she was the first to cultivate 'poor' plants like lavender and olive trees, and discard lilies, roses and flowers of that kind. The house was decorated in beige with leather and chamois sofas, pieces of Provençal and Spanish furniture which were then totally out of fashion, and everything was in soft colours like a painting by Zurbaran; she had excellent taste and a total understanding of quality, whether in food, materials or ornaments. Jean Cocteau often stayed with her and once he arrived with a bundle of manuscripts written by Raymond Radiguet, a young friend of his. Chanel told Luchino that these manuscript pages were everywhere in the house and she had had to ask Cocteau to remove them because she feared they might get lost.

Visconti admired Cocteau's work; with his sisters-in-law, Madina and Niki, he would visit the poet in his dark, opium-smelling rooms. Cocteau, however, only had eyes for Jean Marais and anyway Luchino 'belonged' to his friend Chanel.

Torn between the sense of discipline which had been hammered into him during his youth, his inherent sense of guilt, his longing for respectability and puritanism, his almost sinful attachment to his mother (whose devotion to her eldest son always disturbed him) and the sensual atmosphere in Paris, twenty-nine-year-old Luchino made a last attempt at being 'normal'.

In the winter of 1934, while skiing at Kitzbühel, he met Irma Windisch-Graetz, the twenty-one-year-old daughter of Princess Leontine Fürstenberg and Prince Hugo; she was pretty, aristocratic, conventional and German: everything he felt an eligible young woman should be. They met one day at tea, when he was surrounded by Italian friends and she by German and Austrian relatives. It was a classic *coup de foudre* for both the shy, beautiful Princess and the handsome Italian nobleman. They started going out together with other friends, because young women of Irma's background were never alone with one man unless officially engaged. They would dance the polka, and Irma's aristocratic friends judged Luchino a rather difficult character. For one thing he was not keen on sports and had abandoned skiing almost as soon as he had started. He would talk to Princess Irma, whom he called Pupe, about his stables, which were not a financial success, and about literature and ideas. Then one day, when they were taking a walk in the snow, he declared his love to her.

She called him Luchi and found him sensitive, deeply Catholic, a patriot and an ideal companion. Whenever he left Kitzbühel for Paris or Milan, long letters (which were published by an Italian magazine, *Gente*, after Visconti's death)[5] would be sent to her full of news, warm thoughts and longing words. The protected young Austrian princess had no clue to the tempests and passions of her Luchi.

His French entourage, so different from that German aristocratic clan, was busy creating: everybody made films, ballets, paintings, everybody wrote. And he had a whole series of ideas and projects; it was impossible to live in this Paris atmosphere and not get the creative urge.

In February 1935 Irma and Luchino decided to get married. At various times they met in Vienna, in Milan and in Kitzbühel, but it was, apparently, difficult for him to spend any length of time with Irma. In fact, for Luchino

Visconti, who had no ties and no real job, it would have been easy to be near his beloved as often as he wished. Pupe was for him a symbol of purity and normality – and the further away the symbol was, the easier it was to believe in it. He wrote to her about his mother's delighted reactions to their engagement. She was a novelty for Visconti: his love for her was not the tormented brand of passion he felt for his mother, nor the ambiguous relationship he had with Chanel, nor the forbidden liaisons with the boys at the stable, nor the deep attraction he felt for men, which was 'wrong' because religion and society – the society of Milan, but not that of Paris – condemned it.

Princess Irma never met Luchino's parents, but he knew hers. Irma's mother had already given her permission for the marriage, but when Visconti met Irma's father in the spring of 1935, and everybody was talking about the engagement, which was clearly a major social event and the subject of keen interest in international aristocratic drawing-rooms, her father told Luchino that they must wait until he had decided on a profession. Prince Hugo had evidently received discouraging information about his future son-in-law, but he didn't say anything to either his wife or his daughter, no doubt because he wanted to protect them.

Luchino issued an ultimatum: Pupe had to make up her mind and marry him at once. She was distressed; she thought that Luchino's determination to get married immediately was due to a question of pride. But it was not. For Luchino it had become a question of necessity: in Paris he had met a man with whom he had fallen in love and it was nothing like the occasional boy or the capricious homosexual encounters of earlier days. A casual meeting looked like turning into a serious affair. Only 'pure' Pupe could save him. He also felt a deep attraction for his sister-in-law Niki – a sin. Only 'pure' Pupe could save him from incest, complications and guilt.

However, had he married Pupe, matters would doubtless have turned out in the same way as they had done for his brother Guido: a wedding party attended by all those listed in the *Almanach de Gotha*, followed by an immediate separation. This was the only time when he seriously contemplated marriage, and it was an Austrian aristocrat whom he wanted as a wife. The man whom he had met in Paris was, however, a German. His name was Horst, 'a bit of a German face, fantastic features,' as Rory Cameron was later to describe him. 'Luchino was madly in love with him. Many were.'

Horst Horst was a successful and busy photographer. There is a picture of him a few years afterwards, standing next to Gertrude Stein (the latter looking like a fragile old man), with a Marie Laurencin painting in the background. Horst was a young man with a superb profile, sharply defined lips, strong German eyes and straight, cropped, ash-blond hair. His firm jaw and masculine face were typically German; he dominated Visconti: he was the prototype of the kind of man Luchino would always love. 'I met him at Marie-Laure de Noailles' for lunch,' Horst recalled. 'He said that he was going to Rome on the following day. I said: "No, you are not going to Rome, you are having lunch with me tomorrow." Luchino was a man who made one react like that. I never said that to anybody else, I never ordered anybody else about like that.'

Luchino knew nothing about photography, so Horst took him to his studio: 'For the first time he saw what photography was about. Silently he looked: the elegance of it all! Aloof ... wanting to know everything, absorbing everything.' Visconti stayed in Paris merely for the social life: he knew nothing else and he did not like intellectuals. 'For example, Marie-Louise Bousquet had an open salon with a mixture of society people and intellectuals like Gide and the Princess de Polignac, but Luchino never went there, although he had met her. Sitting at a café one night, Marie-Laure de Noailles came by and said hullo. "That old witch," he said: it was not his world, that one. He stayed in the Faubourg St Honoré for some weeks and then went to Milan and Rome and back to Paris again.'

Horst had begun to make his fortune when he succeeded in photographing Chanel:

She had had a row with *Vogue* and no photograph of her was allowed to appear in the magazine. I was sent to her; I photographed her and she said that the photographs were good of the dresses but they looked nothing like her. 'How can I take a good picture of you if I don't *know* you?' I answered. So she asked me to dinner. At that time she had had a row with Iribe, who was her lover, and she was thinking of him when I took my photographs. She adored them. 'How much is it?' she asked me. 'Nothing,' I said, 'to be able to take a photo like that of you was wonderful' – and we became friends.

In spite of the fact that he knew little about actual camera work, Visconti made a short film, as was the fashion among his circle of French friends. It was an experimental film, written, photographed, directed and financed by himself. Visconti had seen experimental films like *Le Chien Andalou*, backed by the wealthy nobility and made by the handsome young Spaniard Salvador Dali, whom he knew, and his friend, also a Surrealist, the Spaniard Buñuel. Luchino Visconti bought himself a movie camera. The story, loosely based on his own life, was that of an adolescent who has love affairs with three different women: an adolescent, a prostitute and an ideal woman, and all three relationships end badly; the boy, who has left the countryside for the city and, in the process, has lost his innocence, commits suicide. The actors were all amateurs, but Visconti's ideal woman was his sister-in-law, Niki. The film was never finished because money, and perhaps inspiration, ran out. 'I remember that he dressed me up in classic Greek garments and made me travel around on Milan's tramways.' Niki, in her flowing dresses, was filmed while passers-by gaped, curious and unaccustomed to the novelty of the cine-camera. Nothing more is known about this film, which went up in flames when the *Palazzo* Visconti in Milan was bombed towards the end of the war. Niki Visconti remembers that, while making it, they all had fun but that her brother-in-law was demanding and, at times, ferocious.

This experimental film, with its slightly perverted overtones, took Visconti a step further away from the conventional life which Pupe offered. And there had been his meeting with Horst, a world apart.

In March, letters from Luchi to Pupe assumed a more detached tone. Pupe could not decide whether to disobey her father's decision that she should wait. Luchino insisted: she had to make up her mind and marry him. But she could not disregard her father's temporary veto. Luchino felt rejected and renounced Irma, marriage and Austrian connections. It was a great disappointment to have been, in a sense, rejected after always having been accepted by everybody. Indeed it was a different Luchino Visconti who emerged from the episode, but Prince Hugo's refusal was not the cause of any fundamental change, though it may have encouraged something that was already there.

When he gave up Pupe, Visconti also gave up his internal struggle. This was not a question just of sexual choice but of his whole way of life; in rejecting the conventional choice of a quiet family life, of children, a conservative aristocratic social life, a nucleus of steady affection, he had chosen the more difficult alternative, that of a nomad of love. Since he was not going to make his mark on life by creating a family, he decided to do so through Art; he determined to do everything well, thoroughly and professionally. But his time was not yet; in art, as in life, Visconti was a slow developer. His existing family therefore remained a constant in his affections.

Niki and Madina had become part of his family and the Viscontis extended their love and interest to all newcomers, only to withdraw it with their disappearance, when it was caused by divorce or death, when the person was no longer able to participate in that clan's outings, picnics or conversations.

With Madina and Niki he was caught up in the life of Paris. 'When we used to go together to Kurt Weill's rehearsals of *The Rise and Fall of the City of Mahagonny*, we also met Brecht. Weill was a friend of mine and of Luchino's,' Madina said. Weill, the artistic Jewish collaborator of the Communist Brecht, had left Germany in 1933 with his wife Lotte Lenya. He must have been the first 'important' truly anti-Nazi person whom Visconti encountered. Madina continued:

Somebody whom I had met at Etienne de Beaumont's had stabbed somebody else because he was courting Nathalie Lelong, but nobody was supposed to know about all this. Those were strange times, it was fashionable to do that kind of thing. And we went to see him in bed, with Luchino, and André Gide was there. And also I remember a great scandal, when Luchino and I went to a first night of a play, *La Fleur du Pois* (*The Sweet Pea*) by Edouard Bourdet, who was not often invited to the de Beaumonts', which was all about homosexuality, and the public shouted so loudly that it had to be stopped halfway, and it was about Etienne de Beaumont, but he didn't take offence – it wasn't the custom to take umbrage then.

At that time Jean Cocteau had just had his play *La Voix Humaine* presented at the Comédie Française; a few years later he was to produce *Les Parents Terribles*, his greatest success. Cocteau was also a journalist; he travelled the world in eighty days for *Paris-Soir*, and produced countless drawings. In July 1937, Jean Marais was once again the lead in Stravinsky's and Cocteau's *Oedipe Roi*, with costumes designed by Cocteau in materials by Chanel, 'some of which were made in metal and so weighty!' Marais recalled. He also produced ballets and films like *La Belle et la Bête*, with sets by Christian Bérard. Luchino saw all these productions, which stuck in his mind. In Fascist Italy it would have been impossible to stage any plays of that kind. Cocteau was constantly ill, partly due to the effect of his smoking opium, and all his friends came to see him in his tiny rooms where he would talk, his long-fingered hands elaborating ideas in the air. Madina and Luchino would visit him in his little flat. The first room, as one opened the main door, was his bedroom, with a large bed in red velvet, in which he lay smoking opium. 'And it was so hot!' Madina said, 'and we would listen to his records, of which he had many. He meditated with his wonderful hands covering his face, and Madame Schiaparelli was there, with her pink hair.'

Luchino and Niki would visit Louise de Vilmorin, who was literate and beautiful, and go to Chanel's small dinner parties, which, according to Madina, 'were so chic, one could die. We also went to the cinema a lot. For us money didn't exist.' True enough: those who had brains, flair, beauty and culture were matched by those who had money but wanted brains, flair and beauty around them. Either one had money, or money came somehow from somewhere. Chanel herself paid Cocteau's debts and for several of his productions, but the Viscontis did not have to worry about money; they had plenty.

When Niki gave birth to her first son at the Grand Hôtel in Rome, Luchino was the first person who came to visit her. 'How was it?' he asked her, to which she replied: 'It was wonderful, superb, but why is it so physical?' He said that the beauty of birth was precisely that: 'Earthy, creative truth. I want to see you feeding your baby,' and then he exclaimed. 'You look like a Madonna feeding the Holy Child!' He found everything aesthetic, Niki commented.

Making private films was the rage in the 1930s; the Vicomte de Noailles made his own experimental ones, besides backing others. *L'Age d'Or* had created a scandal in Paris and led to the Vicomte being barred from the Jockey Club; Fascist youths had wrecked the theatre where the film was shown. It became the main topic of conversation and the subject of disagreement between Right and Left until it was finally banned.

Schiaparelli was the only serious rival to Chanel; she was funny, witty and an innovator – she hated buttons and was the first to use zips. Giacometti, the sculptor, designed jewellery for her boutique.

Madina first met Giacometti at a ball given by the de Beaumonts. 'All the men were in dinner-jackets and, in a corner, I saw this monster dressed in a shocking blue striped suit. He was sitting alone and he wore a red tie. I felt sorry for him, so I went to sit next to him. "I am Giacometti, a sculptor, and I live in Montmartre," he said.' He began by wanting to draw her and then fell in love with her. At the time Feodor of Russia, Nathalie's brother-in-law, was also in love with Madina, and, in order to make him suffer, she would ask him to drive her to Giacometti's dreary studio, 'and Feodor, who was so beautiful one could scream, would wait in the car while I sat for Giacometti.' He lived in Montmartre, had only one blanket and was very shy. It is not hard to imagine this poor man going to Etienne de Beaumont's dances in the evenings, drinking champagne and meeting people like Madina, while in the daytime working in extreme poverty in a dark hole. One can imagine, too, *le beau monde*'s lack of concern for those whose only wealth was their talent. 'I gave him another blanket and a gold watch.' On one of the drawings Giacometti gave Madina he wrote: *'Au pays merveilleux et lumineux que je vois de loin. . . .'*

By this time Visconti was beginning to be completely absorbed by Horst, whom he saw frequently, but he was still trying to hide his new love from his sisters-in-law, from his mentor Chanel and from his friends, although they would have cared little about it. If anything, homosexuality was for them the norm.

5
New Frontiers

'Four years together; it was incomprehensible to me. There was a sparkle, the sort of thing that happens when you are very young and are struck by someone. I never said it to him. I never spelt it out: "You can't leave for Rome, you are having lunch with me tomorrow." It was a mysterious kind of relationship,' remembered Horst. For Visconti, Horst was his first complete love, which he moulded to his need for affection. As Horst said:

> He was definite in his taste. He followed one line. He didn't fall in love often and was not promiscuous and never forgot you. I was the first for whom he had a real attachment. I was faithful to him, because I had no time to be otherwise and I had a lot of work. He understood how important it was to have a job one liked, to have a definite direction in life, where thoughts and feelings were channelled. He was a typical Italian, I've never seen anything like it. He was shy with Coco Chanel, he was also clumsy at times. He never made frivolous remarks; he wouldn't play games. But people wanted him. You could see that there was something there: there was more than anybody thought.

Horst was handsome, rather stocky and articulate. He was sure of himself, of his work, of his choice and was not a *bon viveur*. He was an architect from Hamburg who had left Germany because he did not like Nazism or the atmosphere there. In Paris, before dedicating himself to photography, he had studied architecture with Le Corbusier.

When they met, Luchino Visconti was just a socialite, with no real job or overriding interest in life. He always carried with him two books which he had had specially printed and bound in leather with gold lettering: one was by André Gide and the other was *Death in Venice* by Thomas Mann. He had ordered them in pocket size so that he could take them with him wherever he went.

Luchino and Horst would dine at the Crillon and go to the theatre together; they saw many plays by Jean Giraudoux. *Margot* impressed Luchino. However, to be seen too often with the same man would have unleashed amused gossip, which Luchino feared, for he did not want anybody to suspect that he had a serious emotional attachment to another man. A few months after their first encounter, Horst asked him to stay at Hammamet in Tunisia, where he had a little house. Visconti was seized by panic. What would people say? How would such a visit be interpreted by his elegant friends, the possessive Chanel and his sisters-in-law? Horst, on the other hand, had no such worries: if Luchino wanted to come and stay with him it would be very nice. In which case, he was to appear at Horst's Paris flat early on Thursday morning; from there they would take the train to Marseilles and then the ship to Tunisia. If Horst did not see Luchino on his doorstep, he would proceed alone.

The lean, fragile-looking Luchino and his suitcases did arrive on the Thursday morning, but when Horst and he were on the dockside in Marseilles, by chance they ran into friends from the Paris 'crowd', just the ones Luchino wanted to avoid; he was acutely embarrassed. However, once they were in Tunisia by the sea, sitting in the little garden of Horst's house with jasmine blooming and scenting the night air, he was happy. He felt vaguely superior to Horst and talked a great deal about horses, which did not interest his friend in the least. On the other hand, Visconti did not much care for contemporary art, although Horst and Marie-Laure de Noailles had tried to teach him something about it; Modigliani did not appeal to him, but he loved Old Masters and knew much about ancient art. He would talk of the latter and describe the places he loved to Horst.

At Hammamet they would walk, and Luchino would go to the market to buy Arab clothes, copper vases and carpets. One day, when he and Horst were having lunch listening to the radio, they heard the proud, rhetorical voice of the Italian announcer describe a victory of the Fascist army in Somalia. As the voice revelled in this propaganda, Visconti stood up as a sign of respect – a Fascist *diktat*, to which most Italians had meekly submitted themselves, whenever the radio broadcast war bulletins. He stood, but Horst went on eating. His national pride wounded, Visconti asked Horst to stand. To which Horst replied that he had no intention of doing so, and anyway he was not Italian. Angered, Visconti asked Horst to enquire about departure times of ships and aeroplanes as he wanted to leave Hammamet there and then. Horst did not react at all to this tirade but did as he was asked: he booked a seat on a plane leaving that very evening and called for a taxi. When they reached the airport, Luchino, who could no longer remain silent, complained, 'Why do you let me go?' He wanted Horst to beg him to stay, and the fact that his threat of leaving had not been met with the reaction he had expected tied him to Horst even further. Horst's lack of reaction appealed to him. Visconti and Horst returned to Hammamet and left together a week later, as planned.

The episode of the radio bulletin shows that Luchino was still conventionally Fascist. Edda Ciano, Mussolini's daughter, and her husband, the Foreign Minister, were staying in Paris at this time and were entertained by everybody. To be a Nazi was the fashionable thing; but not for Horst, who had striven to get out of Germany as soon as possible. Horst was a revelation to Visconti, who was astonished by his utter lack of complexity and deviousness. Luchino, on the contrary, was complex and often invented reasons for making himself unhappy or jealous – tricks which Horst dismissed simply as nonsense, being too busy and too sensible to make scenes. Horst thought Luchino had no sense of humour, had the Italian lack of ability to laugh at himself, and lived in a make-believe world, taking his nobility seriously and allowing himself to be impressed by the fact that his father was the Queen's lover.

When they were in Paris, Luchino would often go to Horst's flat or watch him hard at work in his studio. It was not long before friends became aware of their love affair and clearly nobody minded at all: Chanel would ask both of them to lunch. At one of these meals, Visconti met Salvador Dali, but he remained more impressed and influenced by Cocteau and Bérard. Everybody around Visconti seemed to be busy working creatively.

Chanel worked with Dali, Cocteau and Balanchine on ballet and theatre costumes. Horst recalled this atmosphere of creative fever: 'Bérard, Dufy and Tchelitchew designed sets for the plays by Giraudoux; Giacometti made lamps and tables for the interior decorator Jean-Michel Frank; and Louise de Vilmorin made jewellery.' Every conversation he listened to in Paris in those days proved to be a fountain of ideas, Visconti was later to say.

In Paris Luchino went to fewer concerts than he had in Milan, though it was considered smart to go to first nights when Fürtwangler was conducting the Berlin Philharmonic.

Having made his own experimental film and seen every film and play he could, Visconti's true vocation was beginning to take shape, at least in his mind. In January 1935, during one of those short visits to Milan, where he would have lunch with his mother, play with the *bambine*, see his brothers and what were left of his horses and of his Italian friends, he met the Hungarian film director Gabriel Pascal. Pascal liked Luchino, was interested in his ideas, and asked him to work as his assistant on a film which he was going to direct. Luchino was overjoyed: the subject of the film appealed to him, for it was based on *November*, a short story by Flaubert, one of his favourite writers. *November* was to be filmed in London and produced by none other than the famous Alexander Korda. Gabriel Pascal asked Visconti to go to London, talk to Korda and sign a contract as assistant director.

Visconti took the first train to London, a city he usually disliked. Influenced perhaps by Fascist propaganda, he did not like the English either. This time, though, he was excited to be in London and made an appointment with Korda. When he talked to the great producer, however, he realized that Gabriel Pascal's promise had a fragile basis, that the film was still a vague project, not a reality, that Korda was not yet convinced of its worth and that there was no contract to discuss.

Depressed and disappointed, he returned to Paris in order to see his friends. 'Coco Chanel introduced him to Jean Renoir,' said Horst. 'Visconti went to observe Renoir who was filming *La Vie est à nous*, in order to learn.' This was an openly militant film financed by the French Communist Party. Visconti understood quickly: he looked and learned. He first met the French director at lunch with Chanel. The two liked each other, in spite of Luchino's shyness and silence. Renoir was flamboyant enough for two. Chanel explained to her old friend Renoir that her young friend Luchino was longing to work in the cinema and asked for his help. Luchino's life was once again changed: from then onwards, every day he would go and watch Renoir make his film; a year later, in 1936, Visconti officially worked in Renoir's crew, without being paid. It was only many years later that he disclosed the debt he owed to Chanel, a woman who had helped him to find his real path.

'When I was in Paris, I was a kind of imbecile – not a Fascist, but unconsciously affected by Fascism, "coloured" by it; but the people around Renoir were all Communists, card-carrying Communists.'[1] It would be interesting to speculate on the feelings of the spoilt aristocrat as he gradually heard the words 'Marxism' and 'Communism', which until then had sounded to him like terms of abuse, and which, as he came into contact with actual workers – people whom in the past he had seen from a distance, never around the same table – turned into a touchstone of enlightenment.

At the beginning he was looked upon with suspicion. He came from a Fascist country and on top of that he had an aristocratic name and manners: 'Those were the days of the Popular Front. I remember it as clearly as if it were yesterday – the elections, the processions in the Place de la République, the enthusiasm, the vitality of that period, the vigour, the effervescence. . . .'[2]

Visconti's new entourage stimulated him to a fresh political awareness; but political events also called for taking sides. There had been huge scandals concerning the corruption of leading politicians. One particular episode led to a demonstration during the night of 6 February 1936 when thousands of Frenchmen marched to the Place de la Concorde, shouting 'Down with the robbers!' Nervous troops fired at them, killing eighteen demonstrators: it was the most degrading episode of the moribund Third Republic.

During the next few days, crowds invaded the streets singing revolutionary songs; there were speeches, notably by the Socialist leader, Léon Blum, who, in his high-pitched voice, promised a better life and a better deal; and since he was known as a man of probity, the workers believed what he said.

'He [Visconti] arrived at mother's and told us about political demonstrations and meetings of the Popular Front,' Uberta recalled. 'He had gone to one with Chanel, who was covered in fantastic jewels, and they had mixed with huge sweaty men.'

During one demonstration, a crowd of 300,000 Socialist workers led by Blum had merged with the Communists, shouting *'Front unique!'* The Right and the Centre started to paint Blum as the Kerensky of the situation, but intellectuals like Gide, Malraux, Chamson, Schlumberger and Renoir supported the Popular Front. On the other side, the Right expressed its usual point of view: 'It is as a Jew that one has to look at, conceive, understand and defeat Blum.'[3] In the ensuing elections the Popular Front was victorious, and later, in June 1936, Léon Blum was called to the Elysée.

The drama in Europe intensified; the change-over of the leadership from one class to another was delayed – in fact prevented – by wars. Europe had created industrialization and with it a new system of repression. In July came news of the *Pronunciamiento*, the rebellion of Franco, sponsored and helped by the Axis powers enforcing the old order. Under English pressure, Léon Blum decided against intervention in Spain – his biggest mistake. Either Baldwin or Chamberlain (versions differ) said to a French envoy: 'We English hate Fascism. But we hate Bolshevism in the same way. If there is a country where Fascists and Bolsheviks are killing each other, that is a good turn for humanity.'[4]

To the Communist Deputy Antonello Trombadori, who later became a close friend, Visconti would talk about the Popular Front and, because of his political awakening, he began going to see Soviet films by directors such as Eisenstein. This was important because Visconti thus came into contact with another culture which his Italian colleagues could not experience. From being a conventional Right-winger who stood up when listening to Fascist news bulletins, Visconti became attracted by the forces of the Left. Most intellectuals in France were so attracted, because by 1935 Nazism and Fascism had shown their horrible faces, and the Left alone stood against them.

Moreover, Horst's knowledge of and hatred for Nazi Germany had slowly sunk in to Visconti's consciousness. Now that he had forever abandoned conventionality and the pretence of being eligible for a 'good' marriage, he did not need to maintain the respectable veneer of being a Fascist or of being like everybody else. Quite the opposite: he was different now, he had chosen the path of homosexuality, he had a steady homosexual relationship; to Fascist and Nazi eyes he was a pervert. The sophistication of his friends and his culture could not but lead him to reject the gross, ridiculous image of the Fascist regime, especially now that information was beginning to emerge about the harassment of Jews and intellectuals in Germany.

Renoir and the people around him discussed politics all the time: it was impossible to avoid them in the dramatic situation in which the whole of Europe was embroiled, amid the aggression and warmongering coming from the Right, from Germany and Italy.

Sometimes Visconti was invited to dine with the Renoirs and at their house he met Thorez, the leader of the French Communist Party, but he never dared to intervene in the discussions. Renoir had no Party card but was very close to the Communists.

Now, when writing to him, Madina and Niki, who had returned to Italy, had to stop addressing him as 'Count'; he had begged them to do so because his new friends were either Socialists or Communists.

When in 1935 Visconti went to observe the crew filming, he met Henri Cartier-Bresson, who was an assistant director on *People of France* (*La Vie est à nous*): 'Becker was the first assistant director and I was the second; Visconti was sombre and reserved – a calm sort of man. But we were working, you know what it is like to work on a film, one hardly notices other people. He turned up for the first time when we were half-way through the film.' Visconti worked on Renoir's next film, *A Day in the Country*, as third assistant to the director, with Becker and Cartier-Bresson. *A Day in the Country* was taken from a story by Maupassant; it was to be a short film and eventually it lasted only fifty minutes. Renoir and his team, most of whom were unpaid, moved to a location by the River Loing, a few kilometres from Marlotte, where Renoir and his wife Marguerite had a house. 'When writing the script, I visualized beautiful weather,' Renoir wrote. 'I imagined sets cascading with sunlight.'[5] Instead it was a disaster: it rained all the time.

A Day in the Country was a realistic film, which took place on one August day: it is the story of a country excursion by an ironmonger's family; during the outing, the mother and daughter are seduced by two holidaymakers. Sylvia Bataille, with her lovely oval face and eyes of a dove, was Henriette Dufour, the ironmonger's daughter: 'I met Visconti on that film. He was an assistant to the director and was particularly concerned with costumes and hair-styles: he was an incredibly serious worker. He was always there during the filming and was extremely discreet; he didn't mix with others, was neither shy nor loquacious; he paid great attention to everything.' Visconti never talked about his personal life, but this was quite natural, because they only talked about work. He was, ultimately, an outsider; the rest of the Renoir team had been working together, talking together, making politics together for several years. They also had the impression that the man from Milan had no personal life, that he wasn't interested in either boys or girls.

Renoir said to Sylvia Bataille: 'Visconti will look after the costumes for this film.' And this new character turned up from the elegant side of Paris society, the enemies of the Popular Front; but nobody knew about this, although they vaguely suspected it. Before the actual filming started, Renoir had explained to Visconti the type of costumes he wanted for *A Day in the Country*. Visconti had gathered an impressive number of documents on the costumes of the period (1880), which he showed to Jean Renoir and Sylvia Bataille. He had done his research at the Musée des Arts Décoratifs and in books; he was scholarly and cultivated, and he planned the costumes with extreme care. 'We had very little money to spend on costumes, and he had them made in a tiny little tailor's shop, in the Latin Quarter, in an absolutely filthy ground-floor room,' Sylvia Bataille recalled. 'Visconti was always there when we tried the costumes on, arranging the drapes. He would put a pin to create a fold, delicately, unobtrusively. When the fitting was over, off he went.' During the actual filming, he was always on the set. He wanted to learn, but he didn't talk about his desire to master the craft of filming. 'I never imagined that he would become as great as he did, though in fact it was already all there inside him, waiting to come out. Of course he was influenced by Renoir's work.'

Renoir was very friendly with those who worked for him, but when there were people who did not know how to work, he could not stand them. Renoir treated everybody the same – actors, electricians, sound men: if there was no affinity he could not work.

While filming *A Day in the Country* there were a lot of elegant visitors. Luchino was on the set when Chanel came, and with her he was silent, aloof. All the Paris 'crowd' arrived: they were curious about how Renoir was managing to make the film in the way he was, with mostly unsalaried staff. The film was not sponsored by any political group, and it was rare to make a film without substantial backing and without paying salaries; it was solidarity. 'We were all, more or less, on the Left, not all politically engaged, but we knew that we agreed and didn't talk much about it,' said Sylvia Bataille.

Although not communicative, Visconti did not seem lost among the team; he seemed to know what he wanted. Sylvia Bataille observed that it was extraordinary that an Italian could see and understand the deeply French side of the film's story. 'Even the little waistcoat: I don't think that the Italian peasantry wore that garment in 1880. I remember going with him to La Samaritaine, that huge shop where you find everything, in order to look for a girdle with laces which we couldn't find anywhere, and I noticed that he knew La Samaritaine by heart. He was exceptionally precise and observant, and he knew about paintings.'

The odd thing about *A Day in the Country* – a film which was started on 14 July and was supposed to be over in seven weeks – was that it was never finished. By 5 September the team was still on the fourth day of work because of the rain. After eight weeks of enforced inactivity, everybody was in a very bad mood. There were also the usual romantic complications among several members of the crew – notably the break-up of Jean Renoir's marriage to Marguerite, who was also working on the film – but not only that. 'Once, when I went down there to have dinner with Renoir and Sylvia Bataille,' said Pierre Braunberger, the producer, 'they were sarcastic and in a bad temper. I was disgusted. I said: "Jean, you are my best friend and because this film was meant to be a collaboration between three people – you, Sylvia and me – if you feel like this, we'd better call a halt." Next day they stopped shooting.' A fortnight later Braunberger regretted having wasted a great deal of money simply because of his pride, and he tried to finish the film with what material he had. He asked Jacques Prévert to write a new script, which was refused by Renoir, who then accepted another version.

Sylvia Bataille recalls that shooting stopped, with the film unfinished, because the principal actor had fallen and injured himself, and there was no more money. The hotel would not let them leave until their bill was paid and she had to go to Paris, leaving her small daughter to stand bail for her. 'The film eventually made a lot of money. It is still shown but we never got a penny.'

He wasn't paid either, but for Luchino *A Day in the Country* became an all-important point of reference; by watching Renoir, he learned: he silently studied everything – actors, camera movements, lighting. One day Renoir, who liked having Visconti around, gave him a typed translation of James Cain's *The Postman Always Rings Twice*: Duvivier had given it to Renoir because he thought that Renoir could do something with it. Renoir gave it to Luchino because he thought that Luchino might use it, one day.

Luchino had finally found his vocation, the channel for his artistic fulfilment, and he was aware of it: his life would be in the cinema, and he would assert himself by making good films – like Renoir's. Many of those who knew him at this time, his family included, said: 'One would never have guessed that he would have become Visconti!' – and this was precisely his motivation: to show that he could assert himself on his own ground, working, ferociously and professionally. Moreover, his sudden shift to the Left was not insincere, as many accused him of being, then and later; for an intelligent man in the 1930s it appeared impossible to do otherwise once he became aware of what Fascism and Nazism were like. It was also a way to differentiate himself from his family; it was to throw away the past, the Milanese aristocracy, Pupe's family and their rejection of him.

Once the filming was over, Visconti returned to Italy. Duke Giuseppe, who had seen his son's sketches for the costumes for *A Day in the Country*, was critical of them, his sister Ida remembers. He would go and see his mother, who was fascinated by his stories about Renoir and Chanel, and the latter would ring up 'and [she] talked and talked; at times Luchino put the telephone to one side as she went on talking.'

Milan was no longer just the city where he grew up, the city of his parents' separation and of painful recollections: it became a city which offered him a job. A Milanese theatre company engaged him to design the décor and costumes, and to be the assistant to Renato Simoni, the director. For the first time Luchino Visconti's name appeared in the credits. The first night of *Carità Mondana (Social Charity)* by Giannino Antona Traversi – a poor play – took place in Como. Andreina Pagnani, the same actress who had been helped by Don Giuseppe years before, was the star. One month later, in

November 1936, for the same company, Visconti designed *Sweet Aloes* by Jay Mallory, the pseudonym of actress Joyce Carey.

Having left behind the elegant crowd in an almost revolutionary change of scene, Visconti sought out the company of his old friends from Milan, and with Corrado Corradi went on a tour of the eastern Mediterranean, first to the Aeolian Islands and then on to Greece aboard a Greek fishing-boat. 'He was not a passionate sea-lover, but our voyage was a discovery of the classical world. It was a wonderful time, a very hot July, and we slept on deck.' They would fall asleep looking at beautiful clear skies. He had a taste for nature; maybe he enjoyed a composition of different elements more than a single item. They would climb for hours up to the top of Mount Etna on Sicily; they would swim. Then, in August, they sailed on to the Greek Islands, and Visconti kept an account of his journey in a diary, written in a rather florid and convoluted style.

On Delos he could almost believe it was true that the twins Artemis and Apollo had been delivered there by Leto; he was particularly sensitive to that kind of atmosphere.

As a companion for this long sea journey, Visconti had chosen one of his closest and oldest friends, a man who belonged neither to the glitter of the Paris élite, nor, certainly, to the Left; a man with whom he could not talk about film-making. Corradi was an easy friend who represented the normality of his schooldays in Milan, who knew his family and remembered his youth.

Then, almost immediately after his return from Greece, Visconti went to New York for the first time; later he returned to the United States for long stretches. This visit, motivated by a man towards whom Visconti was attracted, coincided with a temporary break in his affair with Horst. The two had been drifting apart, Horst totally taken up by his work, Visconti by his new group of Left-wing friends. It is possible that his journey to Greece with his old friend Corradi was due to the interruption of what had been an all-important and monagamous love affair.

On this first trip to New York Visconti discovered that he did not like the city or even the country. He did not like Anglo-Saxons anyway. 'Anything English he was weary of, just to be contradictory, and, like Chanel, he hardly spoke the language,' said Horst. It was not a happy experience for Visconti because he had gone to New York to see a man 'spoilt, depraved and extremely rich. I don't know why he did it. I wasn't jealous, but I told Luchino that he wouldn't have been happy with him,' Horst recalled. This is one of the most confused and secretive episodes in Visconti's life. On one of the few occasions he referred to it, he censored his reason for going to the USA and said that he visited New York and Hollywood to talk about a film on Chanel's life, a project of which nothing is known. In Hollywood he called on Douglas Fairbanks and Mary Pickford, whom he had met when they stayed at Villa d'Este near Cernobbio. 'He never wanted to work in the USA, he went there incognito,' stated Manolo Borromeo, who had visited Hollywood a few months earlier.

While he was in New York Visconti went to see several plays and made mental notes on the different styles. He felt depressed, lonely, deceived. 'He came back from the USA all yellow with jaundice: he did not like Hollywood,' Uberta said. He had hated the whole experience.

Back in Italy he worked on the scenery and costumes of a rather indifferent play called *The Journey* by Henry Bernstein, which was staged in March 1938, once again starring Andreina Pagnani, of whom he was again vaguely enamoured; he would follow her everywhere, but she was hardly aware of his interest in her.

Horst came to see him when he was in Italy. Once Visconti booked him a room at the Grand Hotel in Rome, not next to his own but to another boy's, whose room was between his and Horst's. 'He did that kind of thing in order to make himself jealous, to torment himself,' said Horst. On the following morning, although nothing had happened, he made a terrible scene and Horst took the first train back to Paris; but he found Visconti in the next compartment.

The European world to which Visconti so closely belonged was moving towards war. To a friend in Paris, Toto Guptman, Visconti said that had Italy attacked France, he would never have taken up arms against that beloved country. By now it was all clear: Hitler's drive to war, Mussolini's totalitarian regime, the limitations of cruelty, of tyranny. Chamberlain's behaviour at Munich could not but confirm Visconti's contempt for an Empire which had let itself be cheated by two monsters. Horst fled Paris and sailed in the *Normandie* on her last voyage to New York. His departure marked the very end of their long love story.

In January 1939 Visconti's mother, who was in the mountains at Cortina, called him. She was about to die, she said, and was keeping her promise, remembering their old pact, that she would wait for him. When he joined her he was just in time to hear his name whispered by her. She was fifty-nine.

Part of his world collapsed: the person for whom he had sublimated his feelings since childhood, to whom he would tell all (or almost all), a mother he had never grown out of, beautiful and elegant, strong-minded and exacting, had died. She, who had been the harbour of his gloom, the wit who would advise him, who redeemed his losses with her mere presence, had gone: he was now alone. She had died before her son could show her that he was the one who had absorbed what she had planted: of all her children, he was the closest to her – not Guido, whom she had loved the most, as mothers do love their weakest child, and who lived virtually in exile far away in Tripoli. Not Luigi, who had married Madina Arrivabene and was totally devoted to horses. Nor Edoardo, who was not interested in artistic things, nor Anna, who was on 'her father's side' and lived with him. Not even the two *bambine*, who had grown up close to this fascinating woman when she had renounced her social life to dedicate herself to the family: Ida Pace, called Nane, was full of charm and warmth, while Uberta was like her in looks. But none of her children, except perhaps Edoardo, who had married Niki, had the sense of freedom, the flair for life that Donna Carla emanated; certainly not Luchino, who was persecuted by a Northern type of guilt. 'His mother's death was a trauma for him,' said Corradi. 'He had a religious crisis, in fact more than a crisis, a marked return to the Faith. She herself had been very religious and he had inherited her profound belief.' From Cortina her body was taken to Milan, and all her children, Guido included, gathered for her funeral.

Luchino Visconti was in a state of despair. He had just moved house once again and now lived in a flat in Corso Porta Nuova: he shut himself in his rooms and preferred not to see anybody, except Corradi, who would call sometimes and find his friend prostrated by grief. Luchino refused to be best man at Corradi's wedding, which took place two months after Donna Carla's death, though he was at least present in the church at his friend's wedding. He was happy to think that Corradi would settle down to a quiet family life.

Only an absorbing job could have distracted Visconti from his despair, and it came in the form of a telegram: 'I leave for Rome to film *La Tosca*, come, Jean Renoir.'[6] The film was to be partly backed by Italy in an ephemeral attempt to show that the Fascist regime was culturally open.

The choice of Renoir, maker of *La Grande Illusion* (1937), an anti-war film, and a lieutenant of the French Army, was part of a political operation to show Italy's independence from Nazi Germany, with which there were tensions, notably after Hitler's invasion of Austria. Mussolini himself had asked the French Government to 'send' Renoir to Italy to teach at the Experimental Film Centre, the school for the cinema industry, and to direct a film of *La Tosca*.

On 1 September 1939 Hitler had invaded Poland and on the third the United Kingdom and France had declared war on Germany, but Italy had remained neutral. There was another political twist in the planning of *La Tosca*: France was keen to detach Italy from Germany and to assure her neutrality, and so Jean Renoir was sent to Rome as soon as the Italian regime's request arrived.

To arrange things neatly, Renoir engaged Carl Koch, a German, to work on the script and later on the filming. Koch was anything but a Nazi, quite the opposite: he had been a close friend of Bertolt Brecht and Kurt Weill. He was 'a spirit of the universe, a bit like the philosophers of the eighteenth century', wrote Renoir. 'Koch was a fat German who loved his comfort, a *gourmand*, even a *gourmet*, sophisticated to his fingertips, indifferent to politics but capable of coming to blows over a symphony or a good painting.'[7]

In Rome, Koch installed himself in a nice house, to which he invited what anti-Fascist intellect there was available, including young intellectuals interested in films, most of whom had jobs connected with a magazine called *Cinema*, edited by Mussolini's son Vittorio, who had some vague interest in that field. By one of those anomalies which are typical of any tyranny, *Cinema* was allowed more freedom than any other publication. This was partly due to the fact that the editor did not bother reading the articles and that the Party dared not criticize or censor a magazine edited by Vittorio Mussolini. These men, mostly in their early twenties, were the brothers Massimo, Gianni and Dario Puccini, Mario Alicata, Giorgio and Giovanni Amendola, Giuseppe de Santis and Pietro Ingrao, and most of them were already in the clandestine Communist Party. They sought out Koch's company, not only because the man was close to Renoir, who was a symbol of free expression, but also because he was an intelligent anti-Nazi; his wife, Lotte Reiniger, was also well known for having invented a new technique using animated silhouettes on film: in 1926 she had made the first full-length cartoon film in the history of the cinema.

La Tosca, based on Sardou and Puccini, was not an easy script to write, but it was an appealing idea to make a film in Fascist Italy which dealt with injustice and tyranny; a couple of sympathetic lovers defeated by a bigot, a bloodthirsty dictator whom any attentive audience would easily equate with Mussolini. The way in which Renoir conceived this historical film was similar to what Visconti did later in his masterpiece *Senso*. The story, from the very beginning (Angelotti's escape) to Tosca's suicide, was to take place in twenty-four hours, moving fast, in a 'detective film technique', as Renoir said. The camera was to follow the hero and heroine all the time: 'We shall see these people in anxious flight, we shall be able to penetrate Rome's streets and show many aspects of that city, together with them. We shall get to know the countryside and ancient Rome: we shall penetrate inside Castel Sant'Angelo, the Farnese Palace, the famous church where the first part of the story takes place.' The streets would be crowded with bourgeois, peasants, soldiers and merchants wearing the costumes of 1800. 'My ambition is to give the impression that the cinema was already in existence in Directoire times and that Rome should appear as if in a documentary filmed then.'[8] The idea of making a documentary using detective film techniques was not going to be too rigorously carried through; Renoir believed that the public was lazy – people bought a ticket in order to be entertained – and so he would use simplifications. For example, one was that of 'establishing a frontier between the two sets of characters', and, since the fashion of the upper classes in Italy then was similar to that of the Directoire in Paris, Renoir was going to use 'correct' 1800 costumes for the hero, Cavaradossi, and his friends, while the Right-wing Queen of Naples, Scarpia and the court at Palazzo Farnese would wear costumes reminiscent of Louis XVI's times. Obscurantism versus

Enlightenment explained visually in the design of the costumes: this was an idea which appealed to Visconti.

Visconti worked on the script with Koch and Renoir and loved the challenge; *La Tosca* was going to be made by his master and he had a primary role in its preparation and filming. He took Renoir around Rome looking for the ideal locations; they went to Tivoli and combed ancient Rome – Renoir loved the city and enjoyed seeing it with Visconti; the two became real friends. Renoir was delighted with his young colleague, who could detail historical events and lead him around 'that wondrous city'; Visconti himself took in the full beauty of Rome, its tender blue skies, its crisp wind, the gardens laced with Corinthian capitals, the Romanesque churches. He also realized that he had to make the city his base if he wanted to work in the cinema, because, despite the Fascist directors and their cinema, there were groups of young people who liked him at once, seeing in him both a friend of Renoir and a man who had seen plays and films and read books of which they had been deprived.

In Rome Visconti took a flat in Via Kirchner, in the Parioli district and plunged into work. The Italians he began to see and the company he kept were totally different from the ones he had frequented in his earlier Italian days. 'I met him with Renoir when he was working on *Tosca*,' said Giuseppe de Santis, who was to become a film director himself. 'Gianni Puccini and I had heard a lot about this young aristocrat who wanted to work in the cinema on his own account, and Luchino immediately understood us young men, a group of anti-Fascists based around *Cinema*. I made friends with him at once; those of us who were opposed to the regime didn't talk very openly, but he followed what we wrote and we wrote a bit in cypher, but a cypher which was intelligible to whomever had the means to interpret it.' De Santis, Puccini and Ingrao had been friends since childhood, and they trusted each other enough to speak their minds – a dangerous thing to do at a time when people were sent to prison or banished for thinking differently, and everybody denounced each other.

Gianni Puccini was at the Experimental Film Centre, and de Santis was a writer who knew other writers and painters who would not accept official Fascist recognition, the great leveller of culture. Pietro Ingrao had started working for the clandestine Communist Party in 1935, and he was well initiated in political work by the time he met Visconti. 'That was a world of intellectuals, Roman students detached from and tired of Fascism, of the political disintegration,' Ingrao explained. 'There were those who had immediately moved to the Left, others who had a Liberal-Socialist dilemma.' There was a continuous debate among those in the literary and cinema world who were in the Liberal, Socialist, or Communist camps (one cannot talk about parties, except for the Communist Party, which already had a clandestine structure); they would debate the best way to achieve liberty and democracy: it was a stimulating and forbidden dialogue. They would discuss the need to achieve some form of realism in the context of a national cinema which was insipid and conformist. The literary idol then was the great late nineteenth-century writer, Giovanni Verga, because of the realist nature of his social analysis. The magazine *Cinema* was important because it relaunched a kind of literature which contained social themes; also, there was the political and conspiratorial link. Since Verga, a Sicilian, was a recognized master, it was possible to find and read his books, and, instead of describing wondrous armies winning wars, he wrote about men who became bandits out of despair, about the Mafia, which Fascism claimed to have erased, about adultery and poverty, injustice and hunger; in short, he wrote about Italian social realities, he was a realist. 'The link with Visconti,' Ingrao said, 'had first of all an impact on the level of cultural and artistic interests. Not only had he a relationship with Renoir, who had chosen a different path from the commercial established one, he also clearly wanted to get involved in directing films, trying to build around himself a group of collaborators. That was the entourage of young people with which he sought a contact. When he came back to Italy he established contact with those young men who were linked to a literary background.'

However, as the filming of *La Tosca* started, Italy declared war on the Allies. A few days after the beginning of filming, Jean Renoir had to leave: 'My parting with my colleagues was despairing. Leaving Luchino Visconti I was full of regret for all the things which we could have done together, but hadn't. I owe to him my understanding of that sensitive Italian world; he had helped me in several films, like *A Day in the Country*. In spite of the feeling of deep friendship which linked us, I was never to see him again. Such is life.'[9]

Koch, who had a German passport, stayed on in Italy and took over the direction of *La Tosca*. Michel Simon, who played Scarpia, had a Swiss passport and could stay as well. Visconti became first assistant to Koch and together they tried to carry on Renoir's work.

But Koch was no director; he had been chosen by Renoir as an assistant because he was German and a friend. 'He was a bureaucrat,' de Santis said, 'but *La Tosca* would have been a bad film even if Renoir had directed it.' Jean Renoir himself never saw it, but heard that it was no good. Visconti only referred to it once, saying that it was a bad film; all copies have been lost.

La Tosca over, Luchino was determined to make his own film. His new friends used to meet at his flat in Via Kirchner, which became a centre of exchange and work. 'Luchino's flat was beautiful, all decorated; we lower-middle-class boys from the provinces were not accustomed to décor,' de Santis commented. They began to work together, de Santis and Visconti. With Koch, Visconti worked on subjects for films; one was *Don Juan* or *Dance in the Village*. But with de Santis he found more common ground: both of them had read and loved *Le Grand Meaulnes* by Alain Fournier, and this common recognition was an important link; both of them had also read Verga's books. 'We tried to work on a treatment of Fournier's book for the screen, but we had difficulties because his widow was neither enthusiastic about the cinema nor was she keen to sell the copyright to some unknown people who were also Italians, enemies. So we started working on Verga,' recalled de Santis. Visconti also approached Ingrao and Alicata, asking them to work for him in his search for a subject which would give him the opportunity to make the realist film he began to visualize.

Alicata was a southern Italian, articulate and an intellectual, a man with great energy and love of life. Those who knew him – he died in 1966 – whether friend or foe, were won over by his intelligence. Ingrao was, and is, a more withdrawn person, careful and reasoned, a man of intellectual honesty and physical courage. The mere fact that Visconti recognized at once these men's gifts is a tribute to his judgment. At Via Kirchner, Visconti had a Polish manservant who tended to be a snob and always addressed Alicata, de Santis and Puccini as 'baron' or 'count'. These Communist intellectuals, who came from the provinces and did not have a penny, had a hard time convincing the Pole that they were simply 'Mister', not even 'Esquire': he was, however, determined to use some kind of title – like 'doctor' – even for these men who, late in the evenings, would leave the flat in Via Kirchner exhausted and walk for an hour or so before returning to their modest houses.

With Alicata and Ingrao, Visconti worked on *Jeli the Shepherd*, a short story of jealousy and betrayals: Jeli, who sees his woman Mara dance with a rich man, kills his rival. There were other stories by Verga that both Ingrao and Alicata discussed with Visconti and on which they prepared treatments for potential scripts. They also plunged into Melville's *Billy Budd* and *La Dame aux Camélias* by Dumas, a typical theme in Visconti's work: he was interested in a certain type of realism and enjoyed evoking an era. The Ministry for Popular Culture, to which the treatment of *Billy Budd* was sent, reacted with a negative note.

Visconti had plenty of ideas and talked about a number of possibilities, many of which came from American literature of the 1930s because, strangely enough, these works were passed by the Fascist censors since they depicted America as a decadent society in crisis. Thus all of Steinbeck's books, James Cain and even Hemingway (who was published in an anthology of American modern literature) were allowed in Fascist Italy. 'Visconti was also keen on the Russian novelists, whose work he knew well, and on the realist literature of the nineteenth century; we also talked about Proust,' said Ingrao. This was the point of their encounters; Ingrao and Alicata, who were both in their early twenties, about ten years younger than Visconti, wanted to revive the social realist literature as a means of attacking Fascism. Verga had tried to relaunch Realism against Decadence in order to return to a literature which held the key to the description of society. Visconti had similar interests and looked for social ideology, his own great motif: the sunset of a certain world, the dusk of the society in which he had grown up. It was clear that the texts which this group of men discussed contained a social element: the clash of classes, the taste of an era, the reconstruction of an environment, were all themes which appealed to him.

Aside from the stimulus and the possibility of earning something, the work which Visconti gave Ingrao and Alicata was useful for conspiratorial purposes: it offered them an official reason for meeting (frequent encounters had to be justified to the police; the OVRA, the Fascist secret police, kept an eye on those who met too often). Ingrao and Alicata could thus see each other every day to discuss politics and to prepare subversive leaflets, which they regarded as their prime task. In 1939, furthermore, various Communist leaders – such as Natoli, Lombardo-Radice and Amendola – had been arrested. Ingrao, Alicata and Bufalini became the leaders of the clandestine Roman Communist Party.

De Santis and Gianni Puccini were also engaged in Party work, but were very secretive – they had to be – and not a word was whispered to Luchino Visconti, their employer. Visconti, being a private and silent man, would ask no questions; he was interested in one goal, that of finding the ideal subject for his film and to be allowed to make a good film which would astonish people. The idea that his young friends were active in clandestine political work must have crossed his mind – being no fool, he must have guessed – and it must have thrilled him: he was by now totally committed to the anti-Fascist cause, and he enjoyed the taste of the forbidden and risky. Ingrao said that once he and Alicata had a treatment of a story which 'we had to give to Visconti at the end of September and we had spent all the time in clandestine activity; so that on the last three nights we worked non-stop in order to finish our work and meet our deadline.'

Though they kept their activities secret, they did talk to Visconti about politics, and about Fascism. But there were limits. 'We had an incomplete idea of him then. He was a very intelligent man, a man of culture, who had some bizarre sides; after all, he was always an aristocrat.' They were suspicious of his social life and did not understand his aims. Here was an aristocrat who valued intellect and wanted to create a circle of anti-Fascists working for him – why? Visconti's fever to create, his determination to find 'his' film – witnessed by the quantity of scripts, subjects and treatments he commissioned at the time – seemed amazing and anomalous. Everyone was suspicious in those days. The boys from the provinces knew that Visconti had perceived their potential and they had seen his; besides being sympathetic and well-read, he was rich and was an excellent cover: an aristocrat, the son of a duke, a friend of the Savoias! He was one of the last people who would be suspected of anti-Fascist activity.

They asked him to write for the magazine *Cinema* (many of Visconti's articles were actually written by the group together) and his name reassured the editor. Michelangelo Antonioni was one of those bright young men who could no longer bear the intolerance of Fascist official culture. He had already heard a great deal about Visconti, but had never met him. He belonged to the same circle and knew Alicata, Gianni Puccini and Giuseppe de Santis. He had arrived in Rome from Ferrara and joined the editorial group of *Cinema*. Antonioni and Gianni Puccini together wrote an article for *Cinema* in which they said that film-making was the new art which should exploit and include all others.

Antonioni first met him at 'Via Veneto, at one of those cafés on the upper part of the street; it was called the Golden Gate. I think Luchino had just lost his father because he was dressed in black, all in black; I was impressed by his utter self-assurance and by his way of looking at the passers-by as if they were his. It was his way, this austere authority, a graceful one, because he was a well-bred man; his family background was apparent in him. He was also generous with his friendship. On that occasion he was with Alicata and either Giuseppe de Santis or Gianni Puccini.' Antonioni joined the group who worked on the treatment of possible stories for Visconti and noticed that when there were decisions to be taken, Visconti used absolute determination; he never saw him having any doubts, or at least he was never aware of it. But if he liked an idea, he pondered, he absorbed it and made it his own. Among these younger men, necessarily his inferiors, Visconti was coming into his own. They were stimulating; his search for a story for a film was stimulating; the limitation of censorship was stimulating too.

In June Visconti published a controversial article in *Cinema* called 'Corpses', in which he expressed his desire to see the Italian cinema take a new, more interesting direction. He was working on several film treatments and scripts including *Adrienne Meusurat* by Henry Green, *Herr und Hund* and *Unordnung und frühes-Leid* by Thomas Mann, *Ethan Frome* by Edith Wharton, and he also bought an option on the film rights for three of Giovanni Verga's works: *Jeli the Shepherd*, *The Lover of Gramigna* and *I Malavoglia*, two short stories and a major novel.

'With Puccini, de Santis, Alicata and Ingrao, we started working on film projects which might interest us,' Visconti wrote:

> Our first project was a treatment for the screen of a short story by Verga, *L'Amante di Gramigna*. . . . We took the script to the Minister of Popular Culture, Pavolini, who kept it for a long time. Once Gianni Puccini was called by the Minister – I can't remember for what reason – and on his table he saw the script of our film marked with a blue pencil: 'Enough of these bandits!' When he came back from the meeting, Puccini told me, 'Look, that film will never go through.' It did not. A theme of that kind was taboo.[10]

The cast had even been selected for *The Lover of Gramigna*; Luisa Ferida, a star of pre-war Italian cinema, who was later executed for collaborating with the Germans, was to play la Peppa. But even after Puccini's visit to the Ministry, Visconti would not give up: he took courage and went to see

Pavolini himself. He remembered having to wait for half an hour while the Minister was trying on a suit (a white one for the summer); after the tailor left, Visconti talked to Pavolini, but though the Minister seemed to be convinced, the offending script was never released.

At about this time, Visconti saw not only the anti-Fascist group around *Cinema* whom he employed, but he had also made a number of new friends in the cinema world and in the arts. He knew most of the stars of the time: Maria Denis, who had the looks of a young Ingrid Bergman with a stunning, pure face, was a friend. 'Our encounter was beautiful. He was a man full of charm, intelligence, culture. A woman could be very attracted by a man like Visconti. And I was fascinated by him.' She described their friendship as a close, stimulating relationship, as 'an *amitiée amoureuse*' which had intellectual overtones and did not involve their physical lives, 'on a plane of mutual attraction, a friendship completed by mutual interests.'

She used to spend a lot of time with him – she was a famous actress involved in the cinema, a world which attracted Luchino – and with his family, Uberta and her husband Renzo Avanzo. In spite of being an actress, she was a serious girl, who could not go out without her father's (an officer of the *carabinieri*) permission, a highly moral girl. And that could not but attract Visconti.

Jean Marais, who went to stay with Visconti while he was preparing *Ossessione*, recalled that at his house he had met 'Anna Magnani, Massimo Serato and Vivi Gioi. Maria Denis was often there; she seemed to have a great influence on him. She was beautiful. Clara Calamai was also in love with him: he had a physique which fascinated women.'

From occupied Paris, Jean Marais joined Visconti at the latter's invitation. 'He hadn't changed since Paris. When I first met him, he was thirty; I saw him again when he was thirty-seven. Later, when he was more successful, he grew more secure – mind you, he always gave that impression, even when he was not.'

Among Visconti's new friends was the Sicilian painter Renato Guttuso, whom he had met at Arduini's, a bookshop in Piazza di Spagna, which had become a meeting place for young intellectuals. Guttuso and Visconti had talked about Verga, also a Sicilian, and the painter, who like almost everybody else (apart from Visconti) had no money, found himself working for Luchino. It was Visconti's way of linking people to himself, being generous to them, helping them, but also establishing their inferiority.

Luchino and the Puccini brothers went by train to visit the latter's father, who lived in southern Italy. The countryside was beautiful, but old father Puccini was the main point of interest: he had met Verga and they had become friends. He gave Visconti a tatty old postcard of the village of Acitrezza, which was the location of Verga's masterpiece, *I Malavoglia*. On his return to Rome (it was 1941), Luchino kept it by his bedside, looked at the wild, rough landscape and decided to leave once again and go to Sicily to visit the place which had inspired his new literary hero. He left alone on a long uncomfortable train journey to Catania, and from there he went to Acitrezza, a tiny, poor, beautiful village of fishermen. Visconti was amazed by Acitrezza, by Sicily, by its bleak beauty and its ferocious poverty. He felt he had had a revelation: he, a man of the North, had no notion of the South with its social injustice and its dark beauty. On his return to Rome, he asked Guttuso to make a series of drawings of Sicilian fishermen, keeping *I Malavoglia* in his mind.

Apart from making these new friends, Visconti now plunged into homosexuality as a serious choice. He may have had a strong feeling for Maria Denis, a momentary attraction to Clara Calamai, but women were too demanding for him. Although not persecuted as in Nazi Germany, homosexuality in Fascist Italy was condemned and derided; Italian males were supposed to be strong and virile, and officially immune from this perversity. This may possibly have appealed to Visconti all the more: the clandestine nature of his sexual life, the possible danger, the 'anti-Fascist' connotations were all an added attraction to something which was already part of his life. Besides, after his mother's death, he had sublimated his feelings for the woman who had cost him so much suffering, but who had given him so much pleasure and interest, who had been the model for any involvement; her death made the idea of repeating a similar involvement with another woman impossible. Also the idea of creating a family cannot have appealed to somebody who had witnessed the life of a family like his, tormented and turbulent.

Visconti had fallen in love with an actor called Massimo Girotti. With his green eyes, virile jaw and strong body, Girotti had the masculinity which appealed to Visconti. People who saw them at the time have described how Visconti slowly circumvented him; for Girotti was not a homosexual, and that was part of his appeal.

One day Girotti sent Visconti a very offensive letter, insulting him and his family: he wrote that they were all debauched and depraved. Visconti was mortally offended. He called two friends, the lawyer Livio dell'Anna and the painter Renato Guttuso, and told them that they were both to be his seconds for a duel. They naturally tried to dissuade him, but since they were unable to do so and since they had no idea of how to behave in such circumstances, they bought a copy of the *Manual of Chivalry* in order to find out the rules of the game. They then went to the Roman hotel where Girotti lived, but all they found were a few of the actor's friends, who tried to show them some love-letters from Visconti to Girotti. Abiding by the rules of chivalry – in all senses – the two men said that they were not interested and kept silent. And waited. When Girotti finally arrived, they stood up and told him: 'You have been challenged to a duel; you must appoint two seconds.' Guttuso and dell'Anna explained what the rules were, but then persuaded Girotti to write a letter of apology to Visconti, saying that when he had written the insulting letter he had not been in possession of his faculties. The apology was delivered to Visconti at once, and that night they all dined together – Visconti, Girotti, Guttuso and dell'Anna – at Ranieri's, Rome's best restaurant, as Luchino's guests, of course. The two seconds, as was the rule, received beautiful presents: Visconti sent them each a wallet in crocodile skin, an extravagant rarity in those years of war.

The way Visconti lived was beginning to stimulate curiosity and malicious gossip in Rome. His was a flamboyant life-style and his behaviour was eccentric – not so much in his way of dressing or talking, but in his cosmopolitan love of grand parties, excellent cooks and perfectly trained servants, his liking for a social life which did not conform to the middle-class ways of Fascist Italy and his taste in literature and the figurative arts. But his social life was often linked to work; he mainly saw people in the cinema world.

Because *The Lover of Gramigna* was clearly not going to get a certificate from the censor, Visconti remembered the novel which Renoir had given to him, *The Postman Always Rings Twice*, of which he had a French translation. Visconti and his team decided to work on a script based on James Cain's story, changing the characters and the environment. It was to become a totally Italian story, told in realistic terms, of the poor strata of Italians, shot in a dull, unheroic environment. The script of *The Postman Always Rings Twice*, which had already served as the source for a French film in 1939[11] and was to be filmed by Tay Garnett in Hollywood in 1946, was passed by the Fascist censors. Visconti attributed getting permission to shoot the film to the fact that the story was based on an American novel: but he also had friends in the Ministry of Arts, such as Attilio Riccio and Eithel Monaco. It was indeed a revolutionary script, it was just what the intellectuals around *Cinema* had worked and hoped for, a film which described everyday life rather than luxurious environments or heroic battles. The film told the story of obsessive passions in the truck-drivers' world of the Po valley, and the course of the action was embedded in a hostile, sad landscape. The landscapes for *Ossessione* were of paramount importance for a realistic film which told the story of a destructive sexual passion – a subject about which Visconti felt strongly. Travelling northwards and searching everywhere, he had found an ideal setting in the flat landscape around Ferrara: he was now alone, in command of his ideas, his film and his crew, with ultimate responsibility for his first film. He had to succeed, he had to amaze the public and he had to assert himself. This was to be his most important battle. In the context of what was called the 'white telephone' era of Italian cinema, Visconti's realism amounted to a revelation.

In December 1941, while Visconti was in Ancona, still searching out the locations for *Ossessione* with de Santis and Dario Puccini, the news came that his father had died at Grazzano-Visconti. De Santis and Puccini offered to go with him.

They all left together on a difficult car journey towards the North; wartime in Italy was apparent only in the scarcity of food and petrol. When they arrived at Grazzano, they found that all the brothers had arrived except Guido. Luchino was distraught. The funeral was eccentric and grand, and particularly odd for two provincial young men like Puccini and de Santis: medieval costumes worn by villagers, and music; Don Giuseppe must surely have had a hand in arranging such a theatrical event. The new Duke of Grazzano, Guido, remained in Tripoli and refused his inheritance. The castle at Grazzano went to Anna, Giuseppe's favourite daughter, who kept it as it was; the beautiful villa in Via Salaria in Rome went to Luchino.

When he returned to Rome, once again in mourning, Visconti left Via Kirchner and moved into his father's former villa, a sumptuous, airy house. He was very thin and dressed entirely in black with black sunglasses. He had found his ideal actors for *Ossessione*. For the lead role of Giovanna he had tried to engage Maria Denis, since he liked to work with those he loved, but she had to be discarded, for her face was too pure for a 'vulgar' role. So he rather courageously put Anna Magnani under contract. She was a young actress who had only been used for comedies and this was to be her first dramatic role.

6
Changing Roles

In June 1941 Visconti started filming, but almost immediately his heroine had to be re-cast. Anna Magnani was pregnant. She did not want to confess this to Visconti because she judged intuitively that this film, directed by an inexperienced newcomer, would have been important for her career. She was also very taken by the handsome, stern aristocrat and feared his reaction, so she tried to conceal her pregnancy and joined the film crew at Ferrara. She felt unwell, however, and confessed the cause to Visconti, who did not create the predicted scene, but she had to give up the role of Giovanna. Clara Calamai, the star of the day, was persuaded to take the part, which was totally out of her usual range. So Visconti had to be content with a second choice; but it was a characteristic of him to turn an actress who had been imposed on him by circumstance into the best possible solution, adding an almost indispensable quality to the film. Calamai's polished face provided an added reason for Giovanna's desire to break away from the poverty of her surroundings and her ugly husband; she achieved a wickedness and a passive sensuality where Magnani might have produced an overdose of anger. 'We chose her also because she would give us a veneer of respectability in the eyes of the Fascist authorities,' Giuseppe de Santis added. She was a star of many 'official' films, but it was amazing that both actresses – Magnani and Calamai – had been so keen to work for the inexperienced Visconti. 'I was so impressed by him,' Clara Calamai said. 'He was so young. *Mamma mia*, he was so nasty – a medieval lord with a whip in his hand – especially in those early days.' When he first saw her, she had a raucous voice because she had a cold, and not her usual melodious, child-like tone. 'The voice is perfect,' he said. He started to dishevel her tight perm. They were in Ferrara in a squalid hotel; the make-up man, who was called de Rossi, had the task of making Calamai's face look working-class; Visconti wanted a hairstyle which looked natural. He decided on a make-up which she thought looked horrible. While Visconti began explaining the character to her, Clara ordered a chilled lemonade. This was exactly the kind of thing which provoked the eruption of the volcano. Unexpectedly, violently, his temper exploded: 'Listen when I talk to you, you stupid fool.' It is amazing that someone directing his first film, dealing with a star, should assert himself at once in this way. 'He was a fabulous director, he would bend us to his will; I felt what he wanted from me even if I had my back turned to him. Girotti was not up to it, but Visconti would get angry with me, not with him,' Clara Calamai recalled. 'I fell madly in love with him, not only because he treated me so badly but also because women like to be dominated: he enjoyed making people fall for him.'

Visconti tried to educate Girotti by making him read books. 'One could see Girotti change: Luchino had the power to change men. Little by little Girotti was subdued, his eyes dilated, he became a succubus. Luchino enjoyed teasing him; he made me kiss him at length in one scene and then he would hate me for it.' When Girotti had to slap her on the face, Visconti insisted that it should be violent. 'I cannot hit her harder, otherwise I'll kill her,' Girotti said. She received three of these blows: Luchino enjoyed watching it. There was a scene in which Girotti had to break a glass inadvertently – he could not do it and had to repeat it many times. Visconti lost his temper. On the table there was a vast quantity of glasses: he picked them up one by one and threw them on the floor, just by Calamai's feet. The pieces of glass were flying around her face. Nobody spoke. The destruction of the glasses took place in deadly silence. 'I had turned into a stone. On the other hand, I didn't even dream of protesting – by then I was madly in love with Luchino.'[1]

The theme of *Ossessione* was freedom and, at that particular moment, freedom meant antagonism to the regime; 'These themes were contained throughout the dialogue,' said Massimo Girotti, 'and Visconti had technical difficulties in making me express them. In fact I suffered like hell! He was frank with me, I knew him fairly well and we talked....'[2]

The film was only loosely based on Cain's melodramatic novel: the characters took on Italian connotations and names, and the locations were those of a forgotten provincial town. A man called Gino arrives by chance at a country inn and has to stay on as a labourer, because Giovanna, the innkeeper's wife, claims that he has not paid his bill. Actually he has, but she wants to keep him because she is gripped by desire for him, and he for her. They leave together but, after a brief while on the road, she turns back because she cannot face poverty and discomfort. Some time later, the innkeeper and his wife encounter Gino by chance, and the husband insists that he should come back and live with them. During the journey, Giovanna persuades her lover to murder her husband in a staged accident. When she collects her husband's insurance, Gino suspects her of having used him; they now mistrust each other and he despises her greed, her need for comfort. He spends an afternoon with a woman who, in spite of being a prostitute, is purer than his mistress. When they drive away to escape arrest, their car skids off the road and Giovanna dies.

'The term "neo-realism" was born with *Ossessione*. From Ferrara, I sent the first shots of the film to my editor, Mario Serandrei. After a few days, he wrote to me saying how much he liked the scenes and he added: "I don't know how to define this kind of cinema other than as 'neo-realistic'." '[3]

That Visconti directed *Ossessione* with a firm hand amazed those who worked with him, like de Santis, who had studied at the Film Centre, and who knew much more about the technicalities of the camera and lighting. Luchino had almost no training or experience, but from the very first he knew where to place the camera and the actors. He consulted his crew on the delivery of lines, on the script, but never on the technical level. Visconti was a dictator on the set of *Ossessione*, but an extremely hard-working one. If filming started at 5 a.m., he would actually make a point of being there before any of the technicians. He knew the script by heart and had an obsession about realism: if the table had to be set, the spaghetti on it had to be properly cooked and the bottle was actually full of wine.

'His sense was intuitive and atavistic, a sense also possessed by Renoir – it is natural, if there were no Masters, there would be no Culture,' said de Santis, his assistant. He had no doubt about how to direct actors – *Ossessione* was a story where the psychology of the characters was subtle, it had to be interpreted. He was also the producer: the film was entirely financed by Visconti. As he finished each roll of film, he would send the negative to Rome for processing and, later, he was told that every scene was immediately subjected to a form of pre-censorship.'

From time to time filming stopped, when money ran out. At the same time, Italy was losing the war. 'While we filmed *Ossessione*, Luchino was worried about his brother Guido, who was fighting in Africa,' de Santis remembered. On 28 October 1942, a car came up the road which links Ferrara to Polesella; the crew, filming the final dramatic sequence, saw an administrator and Visconti's cousin emerge from the car with grave faces. The cousin took his relative by the arm and walked away from the set, along the road, until they were so far away that they were two specks in the distance. The crew learned that Visconti was to leave that same evening to join his family: his brother Guido had been killed in Africa. Giuseppe de Santis was to proceed with the filming.

There are stories about Guido Visconti, the Captain of La Folgore, who at El Alamein ran towards the enemy carrying a flag and shouting 'A Visconti does not bow to the Windsors!' These words may well be apocryphal; on the other hand, it is likely that Guido sought to die in a way that was tantamount to committing suicide. He left money to be distributed to paupers: 500 lire to each family, quite a substantial amount in those days. 'He was a weakling with the profile of Malatesta,' said a relative. 'I remember Guido, Luchino and their mother dining together, the boys in dinner-jackets; Guido sparkled with beauty.'

His house in Libya was left to Luchino, but it was in a shambles. All Guido's possessions were sent home. 'We still have his suitcases. We opened one and some of his ties fell out. What memories that brought back! I gave the order to lock it up at once,' one of his sisters said. Guido's suitcases were never opened again, and this detachment from things which had belonged to a dead member of the family was typical of the Viscontis, Luchino included.

Guido's death was a sad waste: this handsome man had never lived his life fully, he had been forgotten by everyone since that was what he wanted, his death was pointless, fighting for an evil regime, with no glory. Once again the Visconti family gathered at Grazzano-Visconti: they were fewer this time. Guido's body arrived from Africa; the funeral ceremony took place in the private chapel of the castle; it was a simple, wartime funeral, quite different from the flamboyant, exotic one which had accompanied Guido's father to his tomb.

Luchino returned in haste to Ferrara, for he wanted to complete his film and money was running out; Italy was beginning to realize that she was at war, and there were virtually no cars, no petrol and few trains. Moreover, the filming of *Ossessione* had already taken seven months. In spite of the war, life seemed to go on, though news was scarce and distorted unless one listened to the BBC, which most Italians did, although it was forbidden. Mario Chiari, Visconti's new friend, was an intelligent architect, who had returned from the Russian front with tales of defeat, of the useless loss of lives and of Italian soldiers sent to be massacred with no equipment – all this had not previously been known. The Italians had not been told about the collapse on the Russian front or of the sufferings of both invaders and invaded. Chiari recounted how Russian villagers helped the retreating Italian soldiers, who had neither clothes nor food. If they had to spend the night out of doors it was the end, and they knew it. Often the Italians would fraternize with the Russian villagers and together they would fight against the Germans – their allies – who were trying to occupy the village.

'I was a friend of the three Puccini brothers,' said Mario Chiari, 'and Gianni Puccini told me "Visconti would like to meet you." I came back from military service; *Ossessione* was about to be shown.' Visconti had not been called to arms because of a special law: if a family already had two sons at the Front – which was the case with the Viscontis – the others were not conscripted. One can only speculate what Visconti would have done had he been called to fight for a cause which he now despised.

Jean Marais had been staying at Via Salaria in Rome. 'His film took a long time to make but, before I went back to Paris, I saw the first rough cut – or one of the first – and I marvelled because to help pass the time in Rome I had seen a lot of Italian films, and all of a sudden *Ossessione* struck a totally different note from everything else that was being made, and I felt so proud – as one is proud of one's friends doing well – and I said to myself: this is a great film director.' Even with Marais, Visconti was secretive, almost ashamed to give away any details of his life. 'He never talked to me about the fact that he had been Renoir's assistant – I should have put the question to him: why don't you ever tell me? Nor did I know about the short experimental film he had made.' Visconti was already forming a different type of friendship, with people he could talk to and discuss things with; those who were a source of relaxation, with whom he could play games like riddles, were different and there was no need to talk to them – and Jean Marais belonged to this second category.

Naturally the film caused surprise, even alarm, but it also won recognition. Even Fascist intellectual circles admired the film intensely. The group around *Cinema* advised Luchino to organize a showing for intellectuals like Longanesi, Guttuso and Moravia. Although the latter's name did not appear in the credits of *Ossessione*, because he was a Jew and a well-known opponent of the regime, he had revised the script, rewritten some dialogue and introduced a few new ideas.

In a programme note for *Ossessione*, Visconti wrote: 'My first concern is to tell stories of men living through events, not events for their own sake. Of all the tasks concerning me as a director, the one that excites me most is working with actors, finding human material out of which to create new men....' Indeed Visconti was interested in moulding his actors, in creating unexpected characters out of film stars known for different characterizations (for example, in *Ossessione* Clara Calamai, the elegant vamp of the time, played the sluttish innkeeper's wife, and Massimo Girotti, who had been known solely for his beauty, became a kind of tormented Jean Gabin).

The film was given its first showing on 16 May at the Arcobaleno cinema in Rome, where '... a new Italy, never seen in official documentaries, appeared before the eyes of the audience,' a critic wrote.[4] Enthusiastic applause during and at the end of the film welcomed this showing. Leaning against the wall at the back of the hall, half-asphyxiated by the heat and by his feelings, Visconti saw Vittorio Mussolini, the editor of *Cinema*, who angrily shouted: 'This is not Italy!' and went out slamming the door. Visconti was congratulated and shook scores of hands. There had been shouts, screams and insults, but also enthusiastic applause.

The film was given a showing in Ferrara, where it was immediately seized by the magistrate; at Salsomaggiore, after the first night, the archbishop came to bless the room; in other cities it was banned.... But Mussolini had it screened at Villa Torlonia and he personally decided to pass it: Visconti never understood why. After that, *Ossessione* was shown in some cities.

But the *bien-pensant* opinion, the commercial distributors and, mainly, the Church were opposed to *Ossessione*, which showed human weakness as a natural factor and recounted squalid episodes concerning unheroic characters. There was even a homosexual in the script, the Spaniard, who was depicted as a sympathetic character. The theme of male companionship as a better alternative to passion was offensive. The fact that a whore was a purer figure than Giovanna was also at odds with contemporary ideas – and even Gino, unconventional and passive, was an anti-hero. His cap, his clumsy way of walking, belonged to the French cinema, and so did those smoky rooms, the ugly outskirts of a city, village fairs and adultery. The community in which the protagonists lived was mean and gossipy, with the exception of Gino, who was a tramp. The homosexual was the symbol of liberty; and it is not by chance that the character was depicted as a Spaniard, a nationality which reminded everyone of a civil war which, at the time, had become a political myth. *Ossessione* was not only the meeting-point of French cinema and of the American New Deal combined with independence from Fascist themes, it also contained a condemnation of the cultural mentality on which the regime was based.

In October 1942, Visconti wrote an article for *Cinema*, which, despite events in the country, managed to continue publication; shortage of paper, printing ink and men, personalities on the verge of collapse, a war being lost: all this is only evident in the fact that the issue covered two months instead of one. As usual the article contained the key to an understanding of dissent, in words which are difficult to grasp now when one is not living under a dictatorial regime which bans nonconformist thoughts; the same lines – half sentences, messages in cypher – are detectable in Soviet intellectual circles, those few lines which the censors overlook, and so they get printed in a text which the public understands at once. For example, in this article by Visconti, published in moribund Fascist Italy, he wrote: 'Cinema attracted me because it brings together and co-ordinates the desires and needs of many people, striving for a better world. Clearly this need for co-ordination greatly heightens the director's human responsibility. However, as long as he is not corrupted by a decadent vision of the world, this very responsibility will drive him towards the right direction.'

Decadence was the cultural expression of D'Annunzio and of the Fascist regime – it was fake; realism was the expression of freedom and reality – it was a political choice. Yet Visconti had been groomed in decadence, to which he returned in later life, when it became an aesthetic rather than a political choice; in any case, his decadence was cosmopolitan, lacking the nationalistic connotations of Fascist make-believe. He adopted realism when decadence was the accepted line and he moved to decadence when realism was.

Back in December 1942, a few months before finishing *Ossessione*, Mario Alicata had been arrested for his political activity. By this stage Visconti knew that most of his group had been active in the struggle against Fascism. Whether he knew that Alicata was the editor of the clandestine Communist daily, *L'Unità*, is doubtful.

Towards the end of that year, Ingrao, who was on his way to Rome from his village in the South, telephoned one of his political colleagues from the station. He was told – in code – that Alicata had been arrested. He understood at once that their little group was in danger and he entered a clandestine world. 'We had already agreed with Alicata that, if one of us was arrested, the others would join the comrades in Milan.' Ingrao knew that he should not return to his own house and so, from the station, he went to the villa which he knew was beyond suspicion, that of his aristocratic friend Luchino Visconti. That night there was a party, with Anna Magnani, Maria Denis, Jean Marais and other people from the cinema world; Ingrao was not much in the mood for chatting, for he was worried (he does not enjoy parties anyway): 'I didn't tell him that I was leaving; he certainly knew about Alicata's arrest – nothing was said openly, but he certainly knew by then what we were up to. We asked few questions, that was the rule: never ask. But I knew that I could go and stay at his house that night.'

After Ingrao's escape, Visconti grew closer to Alicata and went to see him in prison, taking books and paper and giving him work to do. Alicata started working on a treatment of *I Malavoglia*, Verga's masterpiece, which was to be filmed by Visconti years later under the title *La Terra Trema*.

On 18 January 1943, from the prison of Regina Coeli, Alicata wrote to his wife that he was worried about the overdone elements of *Ossessione*. By stating this view Alicata was striking a sensitive chord: the over-explained, the over-stressed was always a fault in Visconti's work, and some of his films missed being masterpieces precisely because of this lack of subtlety. In his almost Teutonic determination that the public should not miss anything, the abundance of explanation often became overwhelming and occasionally even offensive: art rests on the suggestion, on the theme which is fully understood by the craftsman, but is understated and can be interpreted and absorbed in different ways and on different levels.

In a later letter to his wife dated 12 November 1943, Alicata discussed his commission for the treatment of Verga's novel *I Malavoglia*, which Visconti had asked him to do while in prison – a way of giving employment and financial help to his friend.

Mario Alicata was released in April, but he was kept under surveillance; he could not be active, and such was the case for many others: fewer people and houses could be used for clandestine activities. Giorgio Amendola returned from exile to lead the Communist Party. 'As soon as Alicata was out of prison,' he wrote, 'he talked to me about Visconti and he told me that he would meet him in order to ask him to join the Party.'

The Roman base of the clandestine organization had become No. 2 Via Ruffini, a house belonging to the Lombardo-Radice family. Lucio and Laura (who later married Ingrao) were both engaged in clandestine work. The illegal Communist Party which Amendola now led in Rome had a united policy which was backed by the workers in the North, who actively undermined the regime by organized strikes. The Communist Party was the only anti-Fascist organization on a national scale; outsiders were impressed and members were proud of being in it.

In July it was the turn of Gianni Puccini to be arrested and the group felt it was under siege, though Visconti provided a safe and unsuspected harbour. By this stage, Visconti knew all about the Party's activities and he was entrusted with maintaining contact between members of the group. He had become an active opponent of the regime.

Visconti's friend Renato Guttuso received a telephone call in code: 'I was to collect Commander Gallo at the station.' Gallo was the cover name of Luigi Longo, the Commander of the anti-Franco Garibaldi Brigade in Spain. 'He was famous, a legend.' Naturally stations bustled with spies and surveillance, and indeed Gallo was returning in order to lead the armed resistance in Italy. 'I had been told to look for a man wearing a cap and carrying a newspaper under his arm; I didn't know what he looked like.' There were no password sentences, because it was too dangerous. 'When we saw him, he asked. "Are you waiting to collect somebody?" After that I took him to Luchino's.' Once again, it was the safest house and the most trustworthy owner, who asked no questions; the anti-Fascists had been trained to secrecy and Visconti had been educated to it.

Visconti decided it would be a good idea to join his brothers briefly at Cernobbio. He had not seen his family for a while, and he also needed to collect some money: the pharmaceutical industry was one of the few which in wartime was booming. One night, from Villa Erba, Luchino and his brothers could see flames redden the sky: Milan received the most violent bombardment of its history. The brothers decided to go at once to the city, for they feared that Via Cerva might have been destroyed; when they succeeded in reaching Milan, they found their *palazzo* and the surrounding area still burning. They called the fire brigade, which barely existed, but, unable to find any assistance, they hastily looked for a water tender and, working throughout the night, succeeded in saving part of their old home.

When Visconti arrived back in Rome, there was a sudden but not unexpected development: on 25 July 1943, Mussolini was summoned by the King for a private audience and, on his way out, he was arrested and dispatched to a secret place in the southern Apennines. The head of the Armed Forces, General Badoglio, was appointed Prime Minister in his place. Suddenly the air was bubbling with elation, in spite of the fact that everyone knew that the first moment of freedom after twenty years of tyranny was going to be brief. There were fifteen German divisions already in Italy, of which six were armoured, against ten Italian divisons which were hardly in a fit state to fight. The Italians had few reserves of petrol or automatic weapons, and only light tanks, while the German panzers swept the field. It was taken for granted that the Allies would land north of Rome, cutting the country in two; in the event, Rome remained occupied by the Germans for ten more months. In his book *Letters from Milan* Amendola wrote that he knew that there was little time left for liberating the political prisoners who were still in gaol. Those who came out of prison or returned from banishment also needed help. 'So, we formed a committee for welcoming political prisoners, a committee in which all parties were represented. The presidency of this committee was unanimously given to Prince Doria, who had been banished because of his stern anti-Fascist behaviour and who, after the Liberation, became the first mayor of Rome.' Visconti, too, belonged to this committee.

Many Italian soldiers returned eagerly to rejoin their families or to prepare to fight the Germans. 'We were all militants,' Guttuso said. 'Those in need went to Luchino's house.' Seven Sardinians who had left the anti-Franco Front arrived in Rome and were housed by Visconti in his garage. 'The Spanish Civil War was a catalyst for our political choice, for all of us, and Luchino was with us. When one needed money, housing or clothes, Luchino was always the first to give.' From the German-occupied North came Scoccimarro, one of the clandestine leaders of the Communist Party, in order to co-ordinate action, and he found a hiding place in Visconti's house, where he stayed for a week. 'I went to see him a couple of times,' said Amendola, 'and we dined together with Visconti, who introduced himself as a comrade.'

Apart from Prince Doria, Visconti and Guttuso, the Committee for Assistance to Those Persecuted by Fascism included Umberto Morra, later the principal of the Italian Institute of Culture in London, Laura Lombardo-Radice, who became a prominent Communist MP, Marco Cesarini-Sforza and Mario Alicata. One of the committee's most important tasks was to obtain the release of Left-wing political prisoners whom the authorities were unwilling to free, especially if they were Communists. Time was short, it had to be done as quickly as possible, before the Germans reached Rome. The Italian Government was seeking an armistice with the Allies; this was no secret, but everyone knew that when it was officially announced Germany's revenge would be swift. The Communists were putting pressure on Badoglio to negotiate an armistice as soon as possible – and the Allies concentrated their bombing on Italy to hasten the decision.

Umberto Morra recalled an expedition to Regina Coeli, Rome's prison; the little group had gone to collect Prince Doria at his palace – for once they had used a coach and horses, though usually they walked everywhere, cars having almost totally disappeared. An old woman appeared in the entrance hall of the palace and Visconti, who had kept his good manners even in those times, recognized the old princess, bowed to her and offered her his seat in the coach. The group went to see the prison warden in order to obtain the liberation of the Communist and other political prisoners before the Nazis arrived. Alicata pushed Luchino ahead: 'Let the Duke lead the way as he looks so distinguished!' Since the warden refused to recognize the committee as an official body, Visconti signed a paper taking personal responsibility for the release of the prisoners, thus also associating his name with an anti-Fascist organization.

The atmosphere was electric; many clandestine activists returned to Italy. The German *putsch* was expected from one moment to the next. The sole issue of *The Italian Worker*, a magazine edited by Mario Alicata, appeared on the streets as the Germans were entering Rome by Porta San Paolo. It was distributed while people fought in the streets. But when the Germans finally arrived in Rome as enemy occupiers, the committee was dispersed.

On 8 September, Badoglio had announced the armistice between Italy and the Allies, and overnight the German Army turned into an occupying force. The Allies had decided to form a second front in Italy, as a diversionary tactic to keep the maximum number of German soldiers on Italian territory. At 6 p.m. on the day of the armistice, Italians had heard on the radio that the Allies had landed at Salerno. Amendola had gone to the Ministry of Industry and found it deserted – there wasn't even a porter – but when he opened the door of the Minister's office it was not empty: 'They have left me alone, they deserted me, they fled!' the Minister told Amendola. The King and General Badoglio had run away with the whole royal family and the Supreme Command; they had not notified anybody, nor had they left any orders – and the Germans meanwhile were heading south towards Rome. The news spread rapidly, there was panic everywhere and the Italian Army was divided and demoralized. It was now the turn of the clandestine army, of the partisan groups, which many people – but not as many as is claimed today – hastened to join; all anti-Fascist parties joined forces in a Committee of National Liberation to deal with the confused, dangerous times and to face what was going to become a fierce civil war, waged alongside an international conflict.

Luchino Visconti was still at Via Salaria, with the Sardinians in the garage, but now he was exposed and could no longer hide behind his aristocratic name. Some friends came to collect the Sardinians, as there was a ship to take them home, but there was room only for six. Paolo Mocci, who was the commanding officer, said that it was his duty to send the others to safety; he would stay behind and wait for another chance.

Suddenly, Rome was occupied, German cars and trucks were all over the city: deportations, requisitions, thefts and mass arrests followed. Rome was looted, once again, by the Germans. Luchino Visconti began to consider going southwards, across the lines. Mario Chiari, who had moved to Via Salaria and knew what the Germans were capable of from his Russian experience, was adamant, saying that he could no longer live under a Nazi-Fascist regime and that he had to leave, even if he risked his life.

The Germans needed the capital, now an open city, as a base for reinforcements to send on to their southern front. Rome was no longer under the control of an intolerable but disorganized dictatorship: the city was under the drastic rule of the SS and OVRA, the Fascist secret police. Special interrogation centres were set up; from the one in Via Tasso, which was the SS centre, few came out alive.

A former bed-and-breakfast guest-house on the corner of Via Principe Amadeo, La Pensione Oltremare, which was later to be the subject of a film by Visconti, became the interrogation centre of the Italian 'Special Squad', under the command of Pietro Koch, a tall Slav. However, the Pensione Oltremare was too small, too central, and the inhabitants of Via Principe Amadeo soon understood the purpose for which the *pensione* was used, because they could hear the screams of those who were beaten up and tortured there. So in the spring of 1944, the Special Squad moved to the Pensione Jaccarino, which was on the corner of Via Sardegna and Via Romagna. This location was more suitable to Pietro Koch's purposes because the house stood isolated, in a fairly large garden.

A few days after 8 September, Mario Chiari and Luchino left together for Tagliacozzo, in the Abruzzi, where Massimo Girotti had gone. The journey took a couple of days though it was only about seventy miles. Luchino's sister Uberta had stayed behind in Rome with her small child, so he returned to Rome to collect her. Uberta Visconti had married a lively man called Renzino d'Avanzo, the son of a forceful baroness, who had been one of Italy's motor-racing aces. Their son, Carlo Libero, was two then; Luchino was very fond of his nephew and had asked his sister to call him Libero, which means 'free'.

While he was away, Maria Denis ran his house in Via Salaria; she was put in charge of the dogs, of the sizeable staff, was left money for their wages, and she made sure that everything was running smoothly. The woman who was doing all this was not a sweet old maid or a loving unmarried relation, she was one of the greatest movie stars of her day, a fact which underlines the fascination that Visconti, by now a man of thirty-seven, held for so many. 'I offered to take charge of his house and, in fact, he gave me all his family jewels, which I took to my house and hid until after the war, when I returned them to him.' She used to go to Via Salaria very often; one of the servants was the 'gardener', Paolo Mocci (the Sardinian officer of the Garibaldi Partisan Brigade). But she did not know this.

For a while Visconti and the others stayed at Tagliacozzo. One day, when German tanks arrived in the village's main square, Mario Chiari observed an old peasant woman wearing regional costume who, as if talking to herself, exclaimed: 'I wonder where next they are going to make the poor people cry!' Visconti said, 'Moravia would give his right leg to be able to write a sentence like that.'

Tagliacozzo being full of Germans, Uberta bought a house in a nearby hamlet called Verrecchie, where there were some peasants farming. A few weeks later, in the woods, they found some American and English prisoners of war who had escaped from trains, and they started to help them. Chiari and Visconti were in double danger: they had to avoid any encounter with the Germans and the Fascists because they would have been treated as deserters, and they were also assisting the enemy – an offence punishable by death. They decided therefore to leave Verrecchie and head towards the Allies, taking the POWs with them.

Captain Richard Edmunton-Low of the King's Grenadier Guards was an aristocratic type. Visconti dressed all the other POWs like Italian peasants, but the Captain was so tall that he could not find any clothes to fit him until he came across the military uniform of a former Fascist. Thus, dressed in this unlikely outfit, the British officer walked through the Italian countryside. Main roads and large villages or towns were the most dangerous places, because they were used by the Germans. It was safer to go through the mountains. To head for the mountains became a euphemism for saying that one was fleeing the Germans, because in the valleys there were roads and thus Germans. They had decided to cross the front line, bringing themselves and the prisoners of war back to safety.

In order to go south through the lines, the group of men had to cross the main road to Sora, which was used by reinforcements on their way to Cassino and was therefore a dangerous and busy spot. 'We had decided to cross it at dawn.' While they waited, their money and food ran out, so they were dependent on peasants and shepherds for their sustenance. 'We slept in hay in the rain. We had nothing, we were in danger of being denounced – and it was cold.' Before attempting the crossing of the main road, Mario Chiari and Visconti had found a haystack in which the POWs could sleep, but there was no room for them. 'I am terribly tired,' Luchino told Chiari. 'What wouldn't I give for a hot bath and one night in a real bed!' Alone, Chiari went down to Piscistrello, a small village. It was under curfew and there was nobody in the streets. He knocked at the house of the priest and the door was opened by a frightened-looking sacristan, whom Chiari asked to wake the priest. He was an old, sympathetic priest, typical of the countryside, and Mario Chiari waited for him to get dressed before telling him: 'I travel with a famous person who is very tired. Before getting back on the road, he would like to have a bath and to sleep in a bed. But I absolutely can't tell you who he is and neither you nor the sacristan must see him.' There then took place an amusing scene, typical in a way of the disorderly and dangerous moments of wartime: the priest locked himself in one of his rooms, the sacristan boiled some water and Luchino had a bath, shared a whole chicken with Chiari, and then went to sleep in the priest's bed.

Whenever they emerged from the woods, the men were in danger of being seen. Once again, trying to cross the road to Sora, this assorted group of Americans, British and Italians, led by Captain Low, climbed down towards the road, where they suddenly spotted a group of German soldiers.

One of the soldiers was turning and would surely have seen them had it not been for a peasant who came by with his cart full of hay, screening them while they ran for cover. They were beginning to feel it would be impossible to cross the road. Later on, hiding every now and then in deserted huts, they reached the valley and Chiari went ahead to explore the lie of the land – one man alone was less obvious than a group, most of whom could not even speak Italian. Once, travelling like this, they found a lonely woman in a small house, who was eating a soup made of dry bread and maize without salt. 'I have nothing,' she said to Visconti, but she gave him some of her soup. The men were always hungry.

Some of the Americans fell ill, so they stopped for a while in Settefrati, where a doctor gave them hospitality and assistance. Visconti was enjoying a challenge, the danger and also the realization that he could endure a life of deprivation. Perhaps his old Anglo-Italian tutor had been of some use after all.

They left Settefrati, which was becoming dangerous, and moved to a house in the open countryside; but suddenly the owners of this new refuge arrived to take possession of their house. 'I remember a magnificent scene,' said Mario Chiari. 'They arrived by cart, which seemed to contain the entire household: the grandfather sat in an armchair, which was carried like a sedan-chair, the old paralysed grandmother sat among the silver, the milk bottles, the nappies for the babies. . . .'

So, off they went to live in a grotto on the mountainside, where it was cold and they felt gloomy because it was Christmas time. 'Luchino and I were in another grotto, near the one where the Allied soldiers slept, with a shepherd called Stefano. Luchino had neuritis in his arm, which made him suffer tremendously. The snow fell. The Allies had landed at Anzio, missing the chance to make a sweep. Our Americans were ill and we decided that if by a certain date the Allies had not arrived, we would have to turn back and take the sick POWs to Rome.'

It was the Americans who felt most acutely the distance from their families; they were more vulnerable than the English. On Christmas night they wanted to go to Mass, but the area was full of Germans. Mass was at 8.30 in the evening and the priest, who had been forewarned made them come down from the church tower so that they could take part in the Mass from behind the curtain of the organ-loft. On the other side, in the church itself, there were thirty or forty German soldiers singing Christmas hymns. The whole village knew that the prisoners were hiding behind the curtain listening to Mass, but nobody gave them away.

While Visconti was on the run, Via Salaria continued to be used by various people as a haven. One day a tall, handsome man rang the bell. The man turned out to be none other than Pietro Koch, who was in charge of the

Pensione Jaccarino, whose name had already become infamous. Koch's men had surrounded Visconti's house and were looking for Paolo Mocci, who, they believed, was hiding there. They failed to find him, but in the gardens they found several bombs. From then onwards anybody who had anything to do with Via Salaria was under suspicion and so was Maria Denis.

Visconti meanwhile was still in the mountains and knew nothing of all this. Uberta returned to Rome, where there was hardly any food but where, at least, she was safe from bombing. However, as the Allies advanced, as the bombing increased and more ground was lost, the vindictiveness of the Germans became harsher. The Resistance, especially in the North, was well armed and well organized. In Rome operations were organized by the GAPs – armed partisan groups – to sabotage reinforcements, blow up railway lines, shoot spies and Fascist bosses and kill Germans. But for each German killed, it was decreed that ten Italians would be shot. Clandestine leaflets and newspapers were still printed and distributed; militants were imprisoned, tortured and shot or sent to extermination camps.

By now the group in the Abruzzi was on its way back to Rome. In one village, posters were stuck all over the walls stating that any peasant who owned a pig had to give it to the Nazis on the following day. 'Some boys came to see us and told us about this, asking us to come down and help,' Mario Chiari recalled. 'It became like St Bartholomew's night. A pig is a treasure, especially when there is no food.' So, all through the night, every single pig was slain and pieces of meat were hidden everywhere: in the church, in the bed of a woman who was having a baby, under the roof. In the morning, when the SS came, there wasn't a single pig in the whole area.

In January 1944 they were all caught while resting in a wood. It was undramatic and unexpected: suddenly they found themselves surrounded by SS, who searched them (they carried no arms) and made them walk ahead of them with their hands up. Luckily, they were seen to be of some immediate use because an SS General was due to arrive the following day in a village nearby and the prisoners were ordered to sweep the streets. 'But almost at once, Allied planes began to bomb the village. You should have seen the Germans, who always prided themselves on their courage! They fled and hid in cellars, anywhere they could. In a second there was not a single German in sight. We all, very calmly, crossed the village with the brooms in our hands and, since they were brand-new, we presented them to an old woman in the street who was looking amazed at this odd scene.'

In February 1944 the men, hungry and exhausted, most of them sick, were back in Rome – the last part of the journey having been covered in a German lorry ('Luckily the Germans were stupid, too!'); Visconti and

Chiari found a way of getting the sick Americans to hospital. No one denounced them because there was no question of who was the enemy.

'I decided that, as soon as the American soldiers were well again, I would set off once more with them and with Luchino,' said Chiari. But Visconti, who now used the cover name of Alfredo Guidi, was undecided because a new idea gripped him: not of running away, but of taking an active part in the fight against the Nazis.

7
Underground

At the very stage in his life when he had finally found the channel for expressing his energetic self, and had achieved a measure of success in it; when he had found a way of life that gave him the inner security that had eluded him before; when he had achieved the freedom to express his strong sentimentality and the passions of his private nature; when he had become aware of his ability to captivate men and women, intellectuals and comrades; at this moment, Luchino Visconti was ready to give it all up. This time it was not in order to turn the page on another chapter of his life, but by putting his life at serious risk.

Having decided to be militant, he asked the Catholic-Communists whether he could join their ranks (the Catholic-Communists were an anti-Fascist group which included many intellectuals with Marxist leanings; it was later dissolved on the orders of Pope Pius XII). A friend told him that he was too well known and that he would be more useful in his role of helping and providing shelter, but his old group, most of whom were either in prison or in hiding, welcomed his decision. 'In those days Luchino hid hand-grenades, small arms and dynamite,' said Laura Lombardo-Radice. 'He also walked round Rome distributing leaflets and the clandestine Communist paper, and seeking new places to print illegal literature.' Visconti was even more secretive than usual about this eventful page in his life story. That he joined an actively militant group in the armed struggle has been doubted, but Giuseppe de Santis is adamant and he lived through this period with Visconti: 'During the resistance we had exact orders from the Party, Trombadori, Puccini and I. Luchino felt that he was being excluded from militant activity and he asked to join the GAP, the armed partisan group. He was a man of great courage and he would have done it with great vigour. He was a man of absolute seriousness; he was welcomed into the group and he was given a weapon. This is a fact, it happened.'

The actions of the GAPs were directed by the Communists; from them the Allies asked for information, for sabotage and for diverse kinds of offensive action against the enemy. Besides engineering landslides, placing mines to blow up transport, cutting the telephone and electricity wires, the GAPs also carried out death sentences on those among them who had become spies for Pietro Koch or for the Germans.

Visconti decided not to go back to live in Via Salaria, which was still guarded by Maria Denis. After his return to Rome, the Gestapo arrived at Luchino's house when he was making one of his rare visits home, but he escaped just in time by throwing himself over a wall into the garden. In the house at the time were six or seven people under suspicion and the raid was probably the result of information provided by a spy. More specifically, Mario Chiari remembers that on that evening, at the beginning of March 1944, Rinaldi Ricci, Guttuso, Luchino and himself were in the house; there were also stacks of *L'Unità*, the clandestine Communist Party paper, ready to be distributed, and some dynamite:

> It was ten o'clock in the evening and the city was under curfew, when suddenly the door bell rang. In came three SS men with an Italian interpreter. He said that there were people living in Via Salaria and that it was obligatory to register the names of those who stayed in a house, but that there was no official record of them. But I said that this was a private house, and I took them upstairs. Also with us was a very young boy, a Communist called Roberto Venditti, who courageously said, 'Would you like some brandy?' and poured them four glasses. They asked about the gardener and, while we were playing for time, Paolo Mocci – God knows why –came in and they took him away. Perhaps Mocci feared they would burn the house down if he did not give himself up. From that day on we never went back to Via Salaria; Luchino went to live at his sister's.

Mario Chiari still thought about going back to the mountains and was waiting for a lorry which would also take the now-recovered American and British POWs. But on 23 March, 'Luchino, Gianni Puccini and I heard an explosion without understanding what it was; we saw the Germans run.'

With a surprise attack the GAPs had killed thirty-two German soldiers in Via Rasella, a road in the centre of Rome which runs down the hill from Via Quattro Fontane. Kappler, who was in command of the SS in Rome, immediately rounded up 335 people from the ranks of the political prisoners at Regina Coeli, the Pensione Jaccarino and in Via Tasso (the Roman Gestapo centre) as well as priests and young boys from the streets. Among them were Paolo Mocci, who had just been arrested at Visconti's house, and Montezemolo, the Piedmontese officer who had taught Luchino cavalry tactics at Pinerolo. German lorries took these people to a spot near the Via Appia called the Ardeatine, the site of some abandoned quarries. The prisoners walked to their death in the small, dark tunnels of the ancient quarry, where they were shot by the SS. Some died at once; others bled to death in the darkness of the dusty tunnels. After this, the Germans blew up the quarry, blocking the entrance in an attempt to cover up their crime. The Allies were approaching and by now the Germans knew that victory was escaping them and that they might have to account for their crimes. A boy, who had followed the lorry into which his father had been pushed, a few days later took a group of civilians to the quarries and they dug until they reached the heap of bodies. Luchino Visconti went to identify Paolo Mocci's corpse, which he only recognized from the pullover he had been wearing, for by then the bodies had decomposed.

After the explosion in Via Rasella, the SS and the Special Squad under Pietro Koch and his aide Bernasconi intensified their brutalities. The ferocity with which the Germans tortured those arrested and the atrocious deaths of those who refused to talk, made the activists who were still free realize what methods were used to extract information. Throughout March more partisans were shot, but also more sabotage operations were carried out: the partisans fought against their own fear of reprisals by hitting back.

Mario Chiari returned to Via Salaria a few days after the explosion in Via Rasella:

> I was in the house alone when Bernasconi came in; he had surrounded the house with sixty men. He said that he had caught a man called Fabiani, whom Luchino had employed some time earlier. They wanted to kill me there and then, but (and this was typical of the SS, some of whom had arrived with the Fascists) they said that that would have spoiled Luchino's green carpet and that my blood could have been evidence against them. They said: 'Where is Luchino?' I answered at once that he had left for Milan on the previous Wednesday. I don't know how it came into my head, I just said the first thing which came naturally. Maria Cerrutti, the housemaid, came in and they asked her: 'Where is Visconti?' and she said: 'He left for Milan last Wednesday.' She had read my thoughts, I don't know how.

Mario Chiari went to his room and, seeing that his money and gold chain had disappeared, he complained that they had been stolen. 'The SS searched all the Fascists and, while this was going on, the telephone rang, and I answered – it was Luchino. I simply said: "I don't know where he is," and put the telephone down. Luchino understood at once.' The SS wanted to take Chiari away for interrogation at Via Tasso, which meant being tortured and then shot, but his life was saved by a short Italian policeman who insisted that he was in charge, not the SS. 'No,' he said, 'I shall take him to San Vitale prison.' While he was in prison, they beat him up and made him watch others being tortured, as a way of intimidating him. After he had been in prison for a week, a lawyer joined Chiari in his cell: 'They even put me in jail!' he complained, to which Chiari replied, 'But look, today all honest people are in jail!' One day, looking down from the window of his cell, Chiari saw Gianni Puccini walking up and down the small courtyard, arm-in-arm with a guard.

Maria Denis and Visconti met secretly in churches, changing church every time, 'for the pleasure of seeing each other: at the same time I would give him news of his friends and house. I never asked any questions. It was too delicate a moment.' Around the end of March, Maria Denis was arrested and taken to the police station in Via Genova. There she found Mario Chiari, also under arrest. 'I spent all day with the Commissar, but he was a good man, he understood that I was merely looking after Luchino's house – at that time women did not mix with politics.' She was allowed to go home.

But at the central police station Maria Denis had learned that Via Salaria was under suspicion, that bombs had been found in the garden and that a boy from the GAP squad, who had found shelter at Luchino's villa, had been arrested there. 'I began to be worried because my situation was becoming dangerous. They might have thought that since I looked after Luchino's house I was involved in their political activities.'

A few days after her arrest and dismissal by the central police, Maria Denis had an appointment with Luchino at one of the 'the usual churches', but he did not come and she was worried. She rang up friends of Visconti and learned that Luchino had been arrested. It was 15 April 1944, the day Visconti was supposed to take part in his first GAP action. 'He was to kill somebody. I think he was arrested because of a spy among us.' By then every member of the group had been caught.

Visconti recalled the episode years later: 'I was arrested in an apartment in Rome: one of those flats from which one left for clandestine operations. I was caught with a gun in my pocket. I was taken to the Pensione Jaccarino, their base, and thrown into a cell.'[1]

When he was arrested he was also carrying false documents in the name of Alfredo Guidi, but he was wearing one of his shirts with the initials L.V. 'I am Luchino Visconti,' he said at once. Again he recalled:

> They took me to the Pensione Jaccarino and for twelve days they kept me locked in a toilet without giving me any food in order to weaken me and make me talk. They didn't succeed, so they put me in a cell with the others. I was not tortured, only beaten up: all of a sudden, they would come into the cell, twice, three times a day, and they beat us up. During the nights we gave support and help to those who, after interrogation, had been hung from the ceiling by their arms, people who were almost dead, with all their bones dislocated, covered with blood and crippled by torture. I saw the most atrocious things of my life there.'[2]

Franco Ferri, a young Communist who had met Visconti in the GAP, was also taken to the Pensione Jaccarino. He encountered Visconti, who was being moved to the coal-cellar for interrogation. As their paths crossed, they pretended not to know each other. Ferri realized at once where he was being taken, because the group had a detailed plan of the house and one of its members had even succeeded in escaping from the infamous *pensione*.

On the night of Luchino's arrest, Maria Denis was in a terrible state; she cried, she could not sleep. Towards midnight she took a strong sleeping-pill and, at last, she went to sleep. But an hour later she was woken up by two men who were standing beside her bed, with machine-guns in their hands. Her father was furious: these men were behaving as if the law did not exist. 'You have no right to come into a house like this!' But they ordered her to get dressed, they put her into a car, then blindfolded her and drove to a place which she had never seen before, which was the Pensione Jaccarino.

She was taken into a room where a tall man with a thin moustache sat behind a desk. Maria Denis did not know it then, but the man was Pietro Koch.

That night, Maria Denis was interrogated for five or six hours; the tall, handsome man would ask her questions and underline part of what he wrote down in red; then he would leave the room, as if to compare her story with somebody else's. 'The whole atmosphere was meant to intimidate me,' she recounted years later. She, on the other hand, was a brave woman; she had that kind of 'metabolism' for which fear came 'after', and Pietro Koch was impressed by her behaviour. 'I've had important people here, kneeling and crying; instead you just sit there calmly.'

But when he started asking questions about Luchino Visconti, Maria's eyes filled with tears. 'I see that you feel very strongly about this man.' 'Yes, he is an exceptional person,' she answered.

At one point Maria Denis asked, 'What are you going to do with me?' 'I'm going to keep you here, at my disposal,' he said. 'Look, I'm the daughter of an officer of the *carabinieri*: if you exercise power of this kind, you must either jail me, if you have evidence against me, or you must let me go.' 'I want Visconti to be confronted by you.'

Maria Denis was pleased: she liked the idea of seeing Luchino. With her eyes she could have told him a lot of things, including the fact that she was not going to abandon him to his fate.

Then she was blindfolded once again and taken home, but this time Pietro Koch accompanied her in the car. 'Remember,' he said to her, 'you cannot leave.' The fact was that he had fallen in love with the famous actress who was also a stern and courageous woman. He had been deeply impressed by her.

On the following day Maria Denis got in touch with Luchino's family and told them about her encounter and her second arrest. They begged her to keep in touch with Pietro Koch. Baroness d'Avanzo said, 'You are the only person now who can give us news of Luchino! When Koch rings you up, ask him to lunch, try to get to know him and see what we can do to save Luchino's life.' She agreed for Luchino's sake.

They lunched at the Restaurant Belvedere. He told her about his life; though his parents were German, he said he hated Germans. Despite this, the Italians had behaved atrociously, Koch thought; they had declared war, and now that they saw the tide turning they were changing sides. He found it unforgivable that an ally should turn against the Germans in this manner. Maria turned the conversation to Visconti, telling Koch about the artistic value and qualities of her friend, and then she asked him how she could help him. 'I see that you are very fond of that man and see things differently from me,' Koch replied.

After the lunch, Maria reported back to the Visconti family. Uberta had left Rome, but some days later her mother-in-law, the Baroness d'Avanzo, said she had found another way to help Luchino, this time through Pietro Koch's second-in-command, Bernasconi.

Maria Denis saw Pietro Koch again and had lunch with him once or twice. Meanwhile he would ring her up and send her flowers to show that he was very taken with her. And one day he showed how much he loved her: 'I've sent Visconti under a false name to San Gregorio, where he will be safe.' Pietro Koch had 'hidden' Visconti from the Germans by putting him incognito into a kind of open prison which had been a foundling hospital. In fact the Germans started looking for Luchino, and two days later Maria Denis received an ominous telephone call from the SS at Via Tasso: 'Signorina,' the voice said, 'we need to talk to you. Shall we come for you or will you come here?' 'No, no, I shall come to see you,' she said, fearing her father was too ill to bear a visit from the SS as well and, indeed, he died soon afterwards.

Pietro Koch called her too. She told him that the SS wanted to see her in Via Tasso and he insisted that he should accompany her. He was worried: it was he who had hidden Visconti from the Germans.

She was interrogated for four hours. 'I had to say why I was looking after Visconti's house and whether I was in the know about his political activities. Nothing came out which could have damaged me or Visconti.' Or Pietro Koch, who was waiting for her downstairs at the grim house of torture, and greeted her with great relief. 'One never knows what the Germans will do!' he said.

Three days went by and Pietro Koch, who clearly could not keep away from Maria Denis, rang her up: 'Today we're going to see Visconti,' he told her. He came and collected her, and on the way to the San Gregorio he stopped at the Pensione Jaccarino. 'Please, wait for me a moment.' And he left her in a room alone for half an hour.

On that very day Ferri, who had hopes of being released, was taken to Koch's empty room, where he waited for him for several hours. Through the curtains, on the other side of the office, he saw Maria Denis, also waiting. Although he had never met her, he immediately recognized the famous actress; knowing that she had been close to Visconti, he assumed that she must be the spy who had betrayed them all to the Fascist secret police.

The Pensione Jaccarino was feared for the squalid, inhuman conditions in which the prisoners were kept and for the beatings they received, but people were rarely killed there. The 'hole' was the lavatory in which Visconti was kept during his first days; it was a smelly latrine used by the staff at the Pensione Jaccarino and it was ninety centimetres wide by one metre in length. Prisoners would be left in this tiny place for days – the air was foul. At one time, Fortunato Pintor, whose nephew had been killed by the Fascists, shared this filthy latrine with Visconti and a great friendship was born. After interrogation, the prisoners would be sent to the coal-cellar, under a sloping roof, which was very cold at night and crawling with insects and human beings. The coal-cellar housed most of the prisoners. It was a horrible place; at its highest point the roof measured 1.75 metres; it had a tiny opening at the height of the pavement, was without light, and it stank from the excrement of the prisoners.

One morning, all the prisoners were taken up to the terrace, where they were told they would be shot because of their political activities. Visconti too was taken up to the terrace, but it was a charade, merely part of the scheme to demoralize the prisoners. When they were all lined up, facing the black barrels of the guns, helpless, waiting to be shot, they were told to go back to their cell.

When Visconti arrived at San Gregorio, his face was swollen and his body heavily bruised. It was 27 April 1944 – he had been at the Jaccarino for twelve days. In the normal course of events he would have been sent to the Regina Coeli prison, which was better than the Jaccarino because of the food and because people were allowed to get some fresh air once a day, but the danger there was that political prisoners could be rounded up at any moment by the Germans and taken away to be shot, especially before the arrival of the Allies, which was clearly imminent.

Visconti's life had been saved by Pietro Koch. Since Visconti was out of danger, Koch had no other excuse to see Maria, so in order to see her again he suggested going to see Visconti together at the San Gregorio. 'Beforehand we went by Via Salaria to collect things which Luchino wanted, such as clothes, whisky, ink and paper. Luchino was very moved and sent me a beautiful letter,' Maria recalled.

It was at this point that Maria realized that she had to look after herself. 'Many had told me that there was gossip, that I had been seen with Pietro Koch in an open car – gossip was rife. I had never thought that it could have been interpreted in any other way. I was frightened.'

The Allies never came, but things could not go on in the same way forever and there was Maria Denis courted by a torturer who, for her love, had hidden a man from the SS and had saved his life. But what did he want from her? Or, rather, how long was he going to wait? When Visconti was in the safety of San Gregorio, Uberta came back to Rome. Maria Denis went to see her expecting her help. 'I was convinced that they would say go and hide where we have been hiding, but they only said, "What can we do, Maria?" I found myself alone with all my problems and I was worried, extremely worried, with a great deal of bitterness in my heart.'

Pietro Koch was a man of twenty-six or twenty-seven. He knew that he was doomed. He used to say that he knew that he would be shot, that they had lost the war, that there was no point in worrying – he would just carry on in his sadistic, fatalistic way.

Because Maria Denis was a famous actress, he respected her – still. But her reputation was ruined. Her father insisted that she should leave as soon as possible. So, she sought help from a great friend of hers called Mario Guglia, who was hiding at the Golf Club of Acquasanta, near Rome. She packed her suitcase and went there, hiding and waiting for the Allies. But Pietro Koch was looking for her everywhere. He sent Bernasconi, his second-in-command, to Via Salaria, where Uberta pleaded with him for Luchino's liberation from San Gregorio. Bernasconi found out that Maria Denis was at the smart Acquasanta Golf Club.

Koch and his squad encircled the club and found Maria Denis, but with her, too, were others also in hiding; a fight broke out and Mario Guglia and all the men were beaten up and taken to the Pensione Jaccarino.

Maria Denis was put under pressure: she was an Italian star, she was told, she had to leave Rome, which was about to be taken by the Allies, and follow them to the North, to the real Fascist Italy. Koch was leaving and he wanted her with him.

But the young woman, with great ability and force of persuasion, told Koch that she was apolitical; she wanted to stay where her family was, with her father who was ill. 'I've been an actress, now I am a normal person. I don't want to go through changes unless you want to tie me up and take me away by force – something I think you won't do.' With her strength of character she persuaded Koch. He insisted, however, that he would keep those who had been arrested with her at Acquasanta. Again she pointed out that he had only gone to the club to look for her, because he wanted contact with her. 'And you know that I want to hide at the Acquasanta because my father wanted me to get away from you. I feel responsible for these people. Either you let them all go or I stay with them.' Koch freed them all.

On 3 June, when the Allies were almost at the gates of Rome, Visconti was released from the San Gregorio prison.

Maria Denis kept to her house, claiming she was ill, but one day she received a telephone call from Koch. 'I would so like to say goodbye to you.' 'I'll meet you at the church of St Therese,' she said, 'so that I shall be able to thank you.' Because he respected her, he had saved Visconti's life and had behaved decently towards her.

When they met in the church, which was very near her house, she found the courage to tell him that he was crazy, that he should have changed his way of life, that he was harming too many people. 'All is over, I know. I shall be caught and I shall be condemned. I cannot change. I wish you all the best for your life.'

He went out of the church and Maria Denis never saw Koch again.

On the fourth, the Anglo-American forces entered Rome while, from the northern part of the city, the Germans were leaving. There was no popular insurrection against the Germans to aid the Allies' entry into the city, in spite of the hopes and the endeavours of the GAPs and of the partisans: a few people had been brave, but most were cowards and Fascists.

'On the morning of 4 June,' said Mario Chiari, 'I was in a cell with an old trade-unionist; he was called Cantini, a good Socialist who had spent most of his life in jail or in banishment; we could hear the sound of bombing. "Have a look, and see what is happening," Cantini told me. From the window I saw a scene which was worthy of Eisenstein: I saw the Fascist guards tearing the Fascist badges from their jackets, replacing them with metal stars – those of the regular army – a precise gesture, but so full of significance, indeed worthy of Eisenstein's visual genius.' The warden of the prison, who was later killed in an atrocious way, assembled the inmates and told them they could leave, but he advised them to wait for a while because the Germans were taking away and killing any men they found in the streets.

On that very day Pietro Koch fled too, following the Germans north towards Florence. A man from his squad went to see Maria Denis. 'I had a letter from Koch to you, a letter of ten pages, but I was afraid and I have thrown it away.' The German Army was withdrawing, crowding the streets, black, covered with blood; with them was a famous funeral carriage containing paintings and stolen valuables. They looted and killed. The only bridge which was passable in Rome, Ponte Sisto, was thick with German tanks, while on the banks of the river the Roman urchins were see-sawing, sunning themselves, swimming and passively watching yet another invader retreat.

After his release, Visconti returned to his house, where he had a bath (absolute bliss!) and slept once again in his own comfortable bed. As the Germans fled from Rome, he went out to look round the city, almost delirious with happiness. A new life and a new Italy would rise from all the suffering, horror and dirt. On the evening of the fourth, Luchino Visconti and Mario Chiari met in Via Veneto; they had not seen each other since their imprisonment. They talked for a while and then went to Piazza Venezia, where the first Allied jeeps had arrived: the moon was shining, they were happy; they discussed their adventures. Late that night they went to Rosati's, where there was a good barman who mixed them two stiff drinks – a rare treat in those days. Outside in the streets American lorries with loudspeakers drove round Rome announcing the landings in Normandy.

Many friends had died, many had suffered; for those who had lost relations and friends or been maimed, life would never be the same again. The last few years had been terrible, but life had to go on and for Luchino Visconti it would unfold in a new way: the war and his work in the Resistance had matured him and sharpened his sensitivity. He began once again to fill Via Salaria with parties, with friends who were interesting, old friends as well as some new ones acquired during recent months. One of his new friends was Ferri, the young Communist whom Visconti had encountered at the Pensione Jaccarino and who, unseen, had observed Maria Denis waiting in Koch's office. He still believed that it was she who had betrayed the group to the Fascists, for many actresses had indeed been collaborationists. One evening in June 1944, Ferri, who was a young student, found himself at Via Salaria, in a glittering company. Even in those days, when Rome was starving, there was food and wine and menservants at the house in Via Salaria. Ferri said something, which he cannot remember, against Maria Denis. Visconti, who knew that he owed her his life, did not defend her reputation then or later.

She returned to Luchino's house and he was as sweet and affectionate towards her as he had always been, but he never referred to what had happened. 'I had the impression that he didn't want to talk about it,' said Maria Denis. And anyway, as a reaction to the war, Via Salaria was always filled with people; it had become difficult to talk, to exchange ideas as they had before the war. Now there were always many visitors coming and going, things had changed.

One day, when Maria was at Via Salaria, a friend of Luchino's asked him how he had managed to get out from the infamous Pensione Jaccarino. He answered, 'Uberta saved me.' Maria Denis left the house, disgusted and humiliated. She never went back.

This episode affected her deeply. 'It was as if I had seen a man going under a lorry; I had helped him and I had been told that I had pushed him instead. I was deserted by everybody, confronted with gossip.'

She had loved him, she had looked after his house without having been told that Villa Salaria was under suspicion, she had sought the company of a very dangerous man in order to save Visconti. She had loved him and he had loved her, in his way: his behaviour was unpardonable.

There may have been a complicating factor in Visconti's behaviour in this matter. By dismissing Maria from his life, Visconti got rid of womanhood once and for all. Only much later in life was he to be attracted by another woman – Maria Callas – and that was another kind of link based on artistic admiration.

Visconti never referred to Maria Denis again, not even to close friends. It was a marked trait of his character that he had the ability to erase from his memory anything that was unpleasant and to accept into it only those events that enriched his store of experience or – as we have seen – to elaborate them to make his participation in them suit his vision of himself.

With Maria Denis he dismissed, too, phases of his wartime experience: the phase when he had been a Fascist and even a Nazi sympathizer, and his phase of inactivity and non-participation. In 1942 and early 1943 he had become an anti-Fascist to the extent of making his film *Ossessione*. Only in the last months of the war had he actively helped by sheltering people and hiding arms, and by aiding the English and American POWs. Later, but only for a brief period, had he played an active role – but he had been arrested on the very first day of real action. In his later recollection, Visconti's war experience became one of continuous militancy from beginning to end. There is no doubt, however, that he lived those last few months with courage, generosity and honesty. Visconti emerged from the war and prison a new man: stronger, more secure in himself and with newly-found self-esteem. Few intellectuals of his generation behaved as he did; indeed most of the film directors who, with him, produced the post-war neo-realist school of films had been silent or even friends of the Germans.

Visconti rarely spoke of this period of his life. (Jean Marais, when asked what he knew about Visconti's imprisonment, was amazed: 'He never mentioned that to me!' he exclaimed.) Nor did Visconti mix his Communist friends with his cinema friends – he liked both groups in different ways. He also felt a sense of gratitude towards the Communist Party, which had opened his eyes and had welcomed him without asking questions, trusting him. Among its ranks he had met the most interesting people of his adult life and indeed he had chosen well – Alicata, Ingrao, Laura Lombardo-Radice, de Santis, the Puccini family. He had joined forces with the Communist Party because of its militancy against Fascism and Nazism, but there was also a certain amount of Marxism there. Certainly, when he felt attracted to the Communist Party, he had read nothing by Marx, whose works were banned. His later understanding of Fascism and Nazism as being the result of warfare by the industrial class against the emerging working class was Marxist. It was not capricious of him to join the Communist Party, it was not merely an act of rebellion against his old ties; his was a gesture motivated by the belief that the existing class structure was dangerous and unjust. With the mind of an aristocrat – but even more that of an intellectual – he hated the middle classes, their comforts and motivations, their customs, their ignorance and their way of life, and he certainly felt more at home with a peasant or a fisherman than with the bejewelled wife of a lawyer or with a banker. He felt at home with the Communists he knew and now with the others who, after the Liberation, were emerging from a clandestine way of life. 'Luchino always considered himself a Communist,' Laura Lombardo-Radice said. 'He was not the kind of Communist who would go to the Federation or cell meetings, and he didn't bother about carrying a card. He gave money, he helped, he kept in close touch. Luchino lived during this time – the Resistance, his imprisonment, his hiding of arms – in a sporting, lordly way; these are very fine pages from his life.'

For aiding the POWs Visconti received a certificate from the American General McNarney and from the Supreme Commander of the Allied Forces in the Mediterranean, Field-Marshal Alexander.

After the Liberation of Rome, Visconti's house in Milan and most of his family were cut off in the non-liberated area of Italy, which put up a formidable resistance to the Germans and thus experienced a longer and harsher occupation. Mussolini was set up by the Nazis in a northern republic, *la Republica di Salò*. All industries, including that of the cinema, were moved to the North. Those who did not go, like Visconti, were considered traitors.

Visconti's younger brother, Edoardo, became a Partisan. Cut off from the Erba business in the North, Luchino was without money, but life was nevertheless exhilarating: there were so many things to do, there was a whole country to rebuild and he, Luchino Visconti, was going to contribute to the creation of new, clean, democratic institutions.

Most of his childhood friends, and Milanese society in general, could never understand Visconti's new enthusiasm for the Left and what they saw as his 'betrayal'. He was attacked either as being a *poseur* or as a traitor to his class. His way of life and homosexuality never created any scandal, but his joining the Communist ranks provoked resentment. Communism was still a dirty word in those circles, it was the number one enemy; the Italian Communist Party had not yet become 'fashionable' among the intellectuals. Corrado Corradi, his old friend, who belonged to the élite of Milan, said: 'Luchino had been arrested together with militants of the Left. My impression is that he was exploited politically, and his beliefs were more theoretical than practical. But they made a banner out of him. Our ideas were entirely different – these political changes happened during the war, he was opposed to the war.'

Manolo Borromeo, his friend from the days of polite, aristocratic tea parties, was harsher and accused Visconti of being a Communist with servants in white gloves. 'If you really believe in Communism, you should give everything you have to the poor, not live like this,' Borromeo used to tell him. 'He accused me of having been a Fascist, just because I had done what everybody else had.'

The Milan of Visconti's childhood was gone – La Scala had been damaged, Toscanini was abroad, the Navigli had been covered up, his parents had died and his palazzo in Via Cerva had been bombed. His old friends thought and behaved differently from him and, although he saw them from time to time, his links with Milan were severed.

Rome was beautiful, the climate was sweet, the air crisp, the hills flowering with acanthus, the ancient monuments overgrown with wild flowers, the sunsets orange and pink, and there he had a lovely house, surrounded by scented gardens. It was not an industrial city – Rome then had a working population of half a million and was a small, compact capital; the orgy of cement, indiscriminate building and mass immigration from the countryside was to start a decade later. It was also the only Italian city which had not been bombed during the war. From the spring of 1944 to 1948 was a wonderful phase for Visconti and everyone was full of hope. That the Italian governing class would turn out to be dishonest and corrupt, as if the Resistance had never existed, was unthinkable.

Visconti felt he had a mission to educate and spread the culture of which Italy had been deprived for twenty years. It was not populism – he never directed his voice to the masses – it was a compulsive mission. In June and July 1944, together with Rinaldo Ricci, Franco Ferri and Mario Chiari, he worked on a project for a film: *Pensione Oltremare*[3] was a story of a partisan very close to his own experience at the Pensione Jaccarino. In *Pensione Oltremare* Visconti wrote a scene in which a German soldier caresses a naked woman with his hand gloved in black leather, and his collaborators, who did not know that Luchino was homosexual, disagreed with this scene, which seemed to them gratuitous. 'Why a black glove?' Ferri would ask. 'It's more carnal,' Visconti would answer.

At this point in the project, Ferri and Ricci left Rome to join the Resistance Army in the North, where the war was still in progress. Visconti, instead, joined the commission for purging the cinema world of those who had collaborated with the Germans. The committee which was set up in July 1944 consisted of writers and film people. It was never very harsh, but Luchino's joining it underlines his desire to recreate a new Italy with better, more honest institutions.

There were several films Visconti wished to make. He went to see the scriptwriter Cesare Zavattini, because he wanted him to work with Alicata on a short story by Maupassant called *Les Tomales* – which Zavattini judged an 'odd' idea. Then Visconti worked with Michelangelo Antonioni on a couple of film treatments. Antonioni was a shy, handsome young man, who was extremely professional and hard-working. 'I worked on two films with him, films which were never made. One was about a little orchestra of women playing at the Front for the soldiers: it would have been the first neo-realist film. We wrote a treatment.' Vasco Pratolini, a well-known Italian writer, and Gianni Puccini also worked with Visconti. In the morning these young men would go to Via Salaria and work all day in a room in a small tower. The mere fact of being in such a beautiful, luxurious villa seemed to them amazing, but they found Luchino Visconti was even more astonishing: he was strong-willed and dictatorial, but could also be friendly and generous. A fire was lit in the room at the top of the tower and the young men would work all day at a large table in the centre of the room. Antonioni recollected that: 'In the morning we used to sit around a large table with sharpened pencils, as though we were in an office, and Luchino, rather like a schoolmaster, used to ask for new ideas on the next scene. Pratolini was there as well. I had an advantage over the others – in that I slept little, I suffered a bit from insomnia, so that when I arrived at Via Salaria I was wide awake. "Ragazzi," Luchino used to say, "what did you come up with last night?" Since I had the time to develop some ideas the others would be angry with me. A crackling fire burned in the chimney. One day he read the only copy of the script. "*Ragazzi*, all we've done so far is a *stronzata*," and, to our horror and astonishment, he threw the manuscript into the fire. He didn't like it; we had to start writing all over again. Maybe he was right. He also liked to make a scene, because he had a strong sense of drama; the stronger the gesture, the better the scene.'

In Visconti's recollections, this script failed because of the blindness of the producers, not because he burned the work of three brilliant Italians; he may have been right, but there is sadism in the act. He could get away with it, however, because he was the man who had filmed *Ossessione* and had been in the Resistance, because he was autocratic and because he was already something of a myth.

The second and last project on which Antonioni worked with Visconti was *The Trial of Maria Tarnowska*, a true story which he had longed to do all his life. Luchino was short of money, because his income from the family business in Milan was blocked by the war; he let his house in Via Salaria and went to live in two small flats, one for himself and one for his menservants, at the Hotel San Giorgio, a grim building near the Central Station. However, Visconti had enough money to pay Antonioni and the other young writers; they would go to the Hotel San Giorgio each winter morning and write all day. Their meals were served in the room where they worked and, when Luchino had to go out, he would lock them in. When spring came the script for *Maria Tarnowska* was further developed on the beach. These outings became grand expeditions. 'We used to work on the film on the beach of Fregene, which was empty and beautiful. We took a huge basket which Luchino's maid prepared and La Gina, an excellent restaurant, filled it up with food and wine. Without knowing it, we recreated the atmosphere of Maria Tarnowska's world, with Luchino's friends who were extremely elegant and spoke French,' says Antonioni. 'We shared the writing between us. There was one scene in which Maria Tarnowska is in her bed at the Hôtel des Bains and the waiter serves her breakfast. Luchino wanted me to write this. I said, "No, Luchino, if there is somebody who knows what is on that tray it is you, not me. You are the only one who knows what a Baltic countess would have ordered." And for this little scene of a waiter bringing her breakfast, he wrote twelve pages. It was a beautiful script: the story of a murder seen from three points of view. Maria Tarnowska was a tall, fascinating woman who lived in Venice and was married unhappily; her lover was called something like Pitoeff and she had a suitor called Perrier. Perrier was the one who was persuaded to kill her husband. She was tried and sentenced to eleven years. When she was taken to the Tribunal, in a gondola, escorted by the *carabinieri*, everybody came to see this beauty. They had to change her police escort every day because the policemen fell in love with her. One day, my mother-in-law, who was a tall, beautiful Venetian, went to the trial and she was taken for Maria Tarnowska and almost locked behind bars.'

Once again Visconti had sensed talent in Antonioni, an unknown, shy man from Ferrara. Incidentally, all the people mentioned above who were locked in the room at the Hotel San Giorgio later went on to produce fine books or films. Visconti liked to 'invent' people, to discover them and immediately give them impossible tasks.

'For *Maria Tarnowska* we went to the Lido in Venice, to the Hotel des Bains, which he wanted to change completely. It would have been a wonderful film: it was a murder story set in a *mittel*-European background, a world he knew well, into which he was born,' says Antonioni: 'The film was to be produced by Alfredo Guarino, who was the husband of the star Isa Miranda, who was to play the title role. One day Luchino decided that he could not do the film with Isa: 'Now Alfredo is coming, and I'll tell him.' We begged him to change his mind; we were also worried about our work. But Luchino just told him: Alfredo became as white as a sheet and we put him on a wonderful sofa in Via Salaria and left him there, in pain.'

While preparing films, Visconti was also planning to go back to his first love, the theatre; he persuaded an impresario to mount a production of *Les Parents Terribles* by Jean Cocteau. He rehearsed for sixteen days with a cast who thought he was mad.

Andreina Pagnani, who by now was a famous actress, was once again his leading lady; there were fierce arguments when he ordered her to wear no make-up, to look ugly and dishevelled, and say her lines from a bed. Mario Chiari designed the scenery, but Visconti, as became his custom, took the credit for this as well.

The actor Gino Cervi, who was a member of the company, urged his colleagues to be brave: he was sure that the 'ordeal' would last for only one or two nights because the play was sure to close. He was wrong: *Les Parents Terribles* was an enormous success and the audience climbed on to the stage to touch, kiss and shake hands with the cast. The play ran for a month and made more than enough money to pay off the deficit of the previous season. The impresario was so delighted that he offered Visconti a bonus of 3,000 lire. The actors were astonished. The extreme realism of the direction and of the scenery was the novelty which took them by surprise: it was a memorable theatrical début for Visconti. Not only was *Les Parents Terribles* a rather difficult play, but Visconti had caused chaos in the way he cast his actors. For example, Andreina Pagnani was accustomed to playing juvenile parts, but she was cast in the role of the mother. On the afternoon of the première (because there was no electricity in Rome, the performances took place in daytime) the myth of Luchino Visconti was born. Public recognition of his talent had not come about before because few people had seen or heard of *Ossessione* and many of the critics had dismissed him as a rich Milanese who made movies in order to have a good time; but when he left the Eliseo Theatre, knowing that he had been recognized as a professional, he was a happy man.

Visconti's realism had arrived on the stage: *Les Parents Terribles* opened on 30 January 1945. The critics were appalled by the audacity of the text and even more so by that of the director, but agreed in placing both on a high level. At the same time, Giorgio Strehler, also a new young director, began producing plays in Milan, starting with Camus's *Caligula*. Visconti and Strehler built the Italian theatre, and Visconti acknowledged that fact. Theirs was a 'cleaning up' operation, which needed discipline. Visconti abolished the prompter and forbade improvisation (stars would improvise new lines when they'd forgotten the right ones); he insisted that the usually tardy public should arrive at the theatre by the advertised time for curtain-up. Visconti was doing for the theatre what Toscanini had done for opera fifty years earlier.

'*Les Parents Terribles* was wonderful,' Antonioni remembers: 'a theatre style which was very modern, but which went to the core of truth. When he took a play he was able to penetrate it deeply, better than a film script. In the cinema there is the fundamental factor that a film is illustration, photography; and Luchino was a very great illustrator and at times he could not avoid illustrating the story he was going to tell. While on the stage, everything had to be invented, and he needed to "live" a text, he worked more on the text for the stage. He had the theatre in his body, he had the sense of the theatre he created. With actors he would recite their parts and he was excellent. He acted very innocently, in life; he didn't do it out of exhibitionism; but he acted a bit.'

Luchino lent money to those of his friends who had none and never expected it back, as Antonioni knew from personal experience. He also recalled that 'We spent a lot of time together; I went to the theatre while he was rehearsing, every night; we met at his house, or at the Cinema Club. Those who were part of his group, like me, felt that he was the central figure. To be with Luchino was incredibly amusing. The relationship he had with his friends was never monotonous. He always needed to create some slight upheavals in order to enrich, to feed a friendship. He had many homosexual friends, but he expressed his homosexuality in a virile way, almost as an outsider. He never extolled or made his homosexuality public.'

After the success of *Les Parents Terribles*, Visconti chose Pagnani and Pierfederici (who had played Michel, the son) for his second play, *The Chandelier* by Alfred de Musset. However, Pagnani and Visconti quarrelled 'over a piece of nonsense' said the latter, and he left the company a few days before the first night, demanding that all 'his' actors follow him. Pierfederici and Girotti did leave with him, but the others stayed. At the last moment, Pagnani gave the leading part to Giorgio de Lullo, an unknown actor in the company whom nobody, least of all Visconti, had noticed. Later on Visconti claimed that he had advised Pagnani to cast de Lullo, but this is untrue: Pagnani and Visconti, having quarrelled ferociously, were not on speaking terms. It was also difficult for Visconti to come to terms with the fact that the ultimate boss of the company was not himself, but Andreina Pagnani. Back in the days when she had acted in the company financed by his father and, later, when he had worked on the scenery for her in Como and Milan, Visconti had been enamoured of her. Casting her as the mother in *Les Parents Terribles* and thus reducing his former idol physically to the ruinous wreck of a spoilt bourgeoise with her hair visibly dyed and her fact without attraction, gave him an intimate pleasure.

When *The Chandelier* opened, everybody talked about the 'revelation', by which they did not mean the play, but the new leading man, Giorgio de Lullo. Visconti, who was in Milan, was longing to see de Lullo; when he finally met the young actor, who was dashingly good-looking, reserved and sensitive, their great love was born.

The second play Visconti directed was *The Fifth Column* by Ernest Hemingway. It was translated by Suso Cecchi d'Amico.[4]

The action of *The Fifth Column* is set during the Spanish Civil War and expresses views that were unacceptable to the Italian public at this time. The play was a flop and was taken off after only seven days. An old gentleman in the audience, when he heard the notes of the *Internationale*, shivered and turned pale, looking around fearfully; another lady was waiting to see a fifth column appear on the stage. After the flamboyancy of *Les Parents Terribles*, Visconti directed *The Fifth Column* in a slightly 'dry' manner and the production was austere. Visconti had also chosen a beautiful leading lady who had been a variety artiste but, sadly, could not act. Because of his urge to 'create' actors, Visconti sometimes used people of secondary talent who could not live up to his demands.

In May 1945 he signed up with Lux Films to shoot *The Grapes of Wrath*; he worked on the screenplay with Giuseppe de Santis, Mario Alicata and Antonio Pietrangeli, but the film was never made. He was, meanwhile, also working on other plays, reading and writing too. In fact, at this time, he was producing an enormous amount.

The manuscript of a novel – started but never finished – betrays his mystical philosophy of the moment. He had often longed to express himself in writing, but his prose is florid and convoluted. He wrote diaries which, however, never betray his actions, only his thoughts and impressions. He started novels and plays and he always had a principal role in the writing of his own scripts. In the sketch of the novel which was to be called *The Experiment* the figure of the woman is characteristically that of a fragile and stupid being, a person who agrees to be locked up, whose only merit is beauty. Locking up was also a 'hobby' of Visconti's, both metaphorically and materially.

While Visconti was writing, reading, preparing scripts for the stage and screen, taking part in the anti-Fascist commission and quarrelling, he also contributed to a documentary sponsored by the Psychological Warfare

Board's Film Division, under the general direction of Mario Serandrei, the man who had hailed the first sequences of *Ossessione* as they arrived in Rome from Ferrara. The film was called *Days of Glory*. And for this film, on 4 July 1945, in Rome, he filmed the trial of Pietro Caruso, former Head of the Fascist Police of Occupied Rome, of his aid Roberto Ochetto and of Pietro Koch, head of the Pensione Jaccarino. The trial lasted one day. Visconti was called as a witness for the defence, but instead he stood up and accused Koch: he said that Koch and his squad were animals, a horrible, cruel bunch. Indeed he had seen the most atrocious scenes of his life take place at the Pensione Jaccarino. Pietro Koch then said that he did not ask for anything; Koch's lawyer told Visconti to stop.

What did Visconti feel when, with an unsteady camera in the darkness of Rome's Palace of Justice, he filmed the face of Pietro Koch?[5] On film one sees the impassive features of the former terror of Rome, standing, surrounded by the judge, the barristers and a huge crowd. Koch and Caruso were sentenced to be shot on the following day. Ochetto was given a life sentence. Visconti's camera zoomed into a close-up.

Before the trial Visconti and his camera had registered a horrifying sequence of scenes. Carretta, the governor of Regina Coeli (who had advised prisoners not to leave at once because of the danger from the retreating Germans) was recognized by the crowd as he entered the Palace of Justice, escorted by the *carabinieri*. The mob shouted and surged towards him. Visconti was pushed about and his camera jostled as he tried to frame the gates of the Palace of Justice, surrounded by a crazed mob. Carretta, separated from the *carabinieri*, could be seen being beaten by hundreds of fists. The unsteady images showed violence and then a body falling into the River Tiber: Carretta was thrown from the bridge of the Palace of Justice. It was a wild, inhuman scene. He fell into the Tiber but miraculously was still alive; he got up and, since he was in a shallow part, walked along the river bed, but boats appeared from everywhere and started to pursue him. When they caught up with him, the oarsmen rained blows on his head until Carretta was under water and every time he tried to emerge they struck him again, until finally he was dead.

The murder of Carretta is a strong, painful image, but forms only part of this long documentary which recounted the German occupation of Rome and showed the Fosse Ardeatine and the partisans in operation.

On the day after the death of Carretta and the trial, Visconti and his camera crew were at Forte Bravetta: we see a truck arrive and stop on an empty esplanade. Out of it emerge some *carabinieri* and then Pietro Caruso; the light is harsh with few shadows, it is 2 p.m.; the guns crack and Caruso falls. After this, Pietro Koch emerges from the truck, tall, smartly dressed, with his straight hair shining. Once again Visconti's camera shows the masculine structure of the Fort and pans to a lonely chair where Koch is to be tied up.

Koch kneels in front of a priest, who gives him the Absolution *in articulo mortis*, he crosses himself and kisses the rosary. He then sits on the chair and is bound but refuses to be blindfolded. The guns crack again. Koch's body jumps, and then falls with the chair; the time is 2.18 p.m. 'Facing Koch's execution,' Mario Chiari explained, 'Luchino just felt that he was present at an act of justice. Before everything else, Luchino was a philosopher.'

A new group of people had gathered round Visconti – a new passion did not necessarily exclude old faces, and some of Visconti's old flames were still about. 'Luchino was then thirty-eight or thirty-nine and he liked to surround himself with younger people,' said Patroni Griffi, a playwright who had arrived from Naples with some bright people like Francesco Rosi. 'I was about twenty-two then, and we all dined at his house. He didn't much like the company of intellectuals, of his contemporaries, of society. We went to his house and found that he had prepared fantastic dinners, beautifully laid tables, as if he were expecting the King – and yet it was only us, young boys he was entertaining. . . .' These young men, who had grown up during the war, had never before seen anything like it: the professionalism of the cuisine, the elegance of the house, the variety and quality of the drinks, menservants in white gloves, beautifully trained, a crackling fire and games, like charades and quizzes, after dinner.

Visconti went on working. His third play was another work by Cocteau, *La Machine à Ecrire*. For this he used a different company, that of Laura Adani, his future sister-in-law.[6] A promising young actor called Vittorio Gassman played two roles, that of Pascal and of Massimo. It is a story of anonymous letters which upset the seemingly peaceful life of a provincial town. While *La Machine à Ecrire* was playing – it was coolly received – Visconti was rehearsing *Antigone* by Jean Anouilh with Rina Morelli and Paolo Stoppa (who were to be his two most faithful actors) and Giorgio de Lullo. With *Antigone*, which is a short play, Visconti also staged *Huis Clos* by Jean-Paul Sartre. Both authors belonged to the post-war Existentialist school of philosophy. *Antigone* was staged very simply: the actors sat on opposite benches in contemporary dress as if they were taking part in a rehearsal. Rina Morelli as Antigone (the Partisan) on one bench faced Créon (Pétain) on the other. *Huis Clos* was more disturbing and aggressive; in Rome it was icily received and a large part of the audience walked out, but in Milan it was a triumph.

Such companies, then as now, used to tour Italy, playing the provinces as well: what was shocking for the capital was even more so in the Italian provinces. On the other hand, the provinces were starved of culture; with these tours Visconti rallied talent from all over Italy, the young wanted to know him, to be part of his 'court', and everybody wanted to be able to refer to him as 'Luchino'. He provided a form of shock therapy. Being a homosexual, he was a liberating influence to those who were like him, and a loathsome symbol to well-to-do families: Visconti became the target of atrocious jokes. Though he was reviled, people felt compelled to attend his opening nights, even if only to denigrate them. He loathed the vulgar jokes about him, but was able to bear the blows and never retaliated even when cruel jibes appeared in the Right-wing press. Because of the realism of the texts he chose and the way he staged them, Visconti became known in Italy as 'the director of the soiled beds'.

On 30 October the première of his production of *Adam* by Marcel Achard, starring Laura Adani and Vittorio Gassman, caused a sensation because the play dealt with homosexuality. The critics labelled Visconti 'the *enfant terrible* of the Italian theatre', but he was no child: he was a man of thirty-nine who knew what he was doing, and he wanted to confront the public, he wanted to stimulate and educate – and he wanted to prove himself. 'When *Adam* was performed in Milan, I was flabbergasted,' said Pier Luigi Pizzi, who was to become a famous designer and producer. 'I was passionately keen on the theatre and some friends and I became enthusiastic admirers of Visconti. During that performance chairs flew in the air: Visconti was never loved by the public.' The play certainly encountered problems: in Milan the police were called in, in Como it was banned on the opening night, and in the end a veto by the Patriarch of Venice after a full-house première there ended its existence.

The plays were staged quickly, one after the other, as though Visconti were in a hurry to fill the gap caused by so many years of cultural inactivity and of Italian texts only. As he rehearsed one play, he would plan another, think of ideal actors and discuss new possibilities. All the plays that he staged in this period (the end of 1944, 1945 and 1946) were seen by the Italian public for the first time.

Visconti next directed an American text, *Tobacco Road*, from the novel by Erskine Caldwell, which opened in Milan in December 1945. It is a play about hunger and sex, nymphomaniacs, children and incest. Giorgio Strehler, who two years later was to found Il Piccolo Teatro in Milan, wrote on the only occasion he discussed Visconti in print and the last time he worked as a theatre critic: 'Visconti's direction, so accurate in the technique of acting, has shifted the accent from the religious motivation in the text to the political, which, in the play, is incidental. Luchino Visconti is Communist, while Caldwell, before being socially polemical, is a writer who believes in the religious mania of his characters.'[7]

Once again this play caused havoc: at one point the public started screaming and Laura Adani had to beg the audience to let them continue the performance. At the end of the play, admirers clambered on to the stage to shake hands with the cast, while other members of the audience booed and screamed '*Basta!*'

Throughout that year, protests, shouts and booing accompanied Visconti the length and breadth of Italy. Later he was to look back with nostalgia on the days when the public reacted and came to blows in the theatre. His public and pupils continued to turn up for first nights, fights and scenes of triumph.

If he did not like an actor, Luchino could make his life very hard; he would ridicule some and treat others like jesters, but if he were pleased he could be considerate. He would lend money to those who had none and then be 'offended' when the person tried to return it. He would also 'invent' work in order to finance painters, writers, scriptwriters or actors. With some he had an understanding; others he shaped by insults, such as Mastroianni, who said, 'Visconti put me in the theatre and taught me most of what I know, not only how to act, but what to choose, a certain taste. I feel rather privileged because, thanks to him, I entered the theatre through a golden door.'[8]

Beaumarchais's play *The Marriage of Figaro*, which opened at the Quirino Theatre on 19 January 1946, was Visconti's first 'spectacular', almost operatic treatment of a play. It involved a great deal of money, numerous actors, music (not by Mozart but by Renzo Rossellini) and ballets. The cast, except for Vittorio de Sica (Figaro), was almost the same as that with which he was to form his own company in November of the same year.

The choice of Beaumarchais was deliberate: the play carried a message which had caused it to be forbidden for over twenty years. Anything that Visconti staged at this time was part of a massive attack on the old; his aim was to rouse the public and prepare them to create another kind of Italy. The choice of these plays today may not sound very adventurous and some of the scripts were admittedly not even good, but the attitude of that member of the public who, hearing the notes of the *Internationale*, looked around and shivered, is indicative. The situation can be compared with what would happen in the Soviet Union if it were to become a democracy: Soviet audiences would be confronted with 'forbidden' themes, with political freedom, with the staging of plays which had never been seen before because of censorship, breaking the tradition of acting, filling theatres with a new, different public instead of with smart *apparatchiks*.

In *Figaro*, actors spoke and danced in a palace which was divided into rooms and a staircase with the lighting picking out the space needed for one scene, and the rest left in darkness. The orchestra was on the terrace, and de Sica would walk among the stalls reciting his monologue, which thus became a dialogue with the public.

After the Liberation Visconti had met Antonello Trombadori, who became his confidant. Trombadori was the son of a painter; when he was very young, he had been in the clandestine Communist Party. He was an articulate and easy-going man; he was well connected with the intelligentsia of Rome. 'I had been arrested in 1941,' said Trombadori, 'but I knew about Luchino. I knew that he was a man of the Left, who declared himself to be a Communist, who had been in France. Information on intellectuals concentrated on the political environment they moved in – Visconti was an anti-Fascist, thus he was a Brother.' After the Liberation, Trombadori, a populist (the opposite of Visconti), was put in charge of the Communist Party's cultural affairs; he started an association of men connected with the cinema and this was how they came to meet. 'He was about to stage Sartre's *Morts sans sépulture*, but I said to him "You can't do that, just after the war; you are putting Nazis and Partisans on the same level – it is too schematic. Later on it could be done. Life is, alas, more complicated, but at this moment of struggle it would appear as an anti-Communist play.' Visconti had submitted the text to Trombadori because he had wanted to consult him and, through him, the Party. Of this drama, Sartre had said, 'My characters ask themselves a question which has tormented men of our generation all over the world: how would I resist under torture?' and it is clear that Visconti, who had had these thoughts at the Pensione Jaccarino, was fascinated by such a theme. 'And I wanted to show in particular,' Sartre went on, 'that kind of intimacy which arises between the torturer and the victim. The first needs to humiliate the second, to lower him to a cowardice similar to his own.'

The decision not to stage this play, which was actually ready, 'was not a directive of the Communist Party,' said Trombadori. 'It was due to a continuous discussion between Visconti and me, but through me he saw the Party and wanted to be at peace with it. It was important to him: his was a moral choice, nearly religious, easy to explain in an aristocrat, almost a kind of self-punishment, a limitation he imposed on himself, that of arriving at a point where discipline becomes a blind act, within a reasoned choice. His was not a fanatical choice; on the contrary, Luchino was a man of reason. He arrived at it by reasoning, then reason became a feeling.'

Trombadori was a friend of Palmiro Togliatti, who in 1944 had arrived in Naples from Moscow, rallying the Communist forces behind a policy of non-revolution. Not only had he a directive from Moscow (at Yalta, Italy had been alloted to the Western Front), but he also wanted to avoid a civil war, which, in Italy, could have become like the Spanish Civil War: Togliatti agreed with the government's decision when it ordered the partisans to give up their weapons. He became Minister of the Interior and, since he had heard of Visconti and liked the theatre, he asked Trombadori to introduce him. Theirs was a formal relationship based on deep mutual respect: Visconti treasured the fact that Togliatti came to his opening nights, sitting in the front row, and that during the second entr'acte he would visit him backstage – he would not go at the end, when Luchino's dressing-room was crowded with friends and admirers; Togliatti's visits and his reasoned comments were discreet, and Luchino would not let anybody else enter his room when the head of the Communist Party was with him. Togliatti was a man of considerable intellectual power and charm as well as being scholarly and intuitive. Visconti was both impressed by him and flattered by his friendship. More than liking him, he adored him: Togliatti became a kind of father-figure, distant yet concerned about what Visconti did, a person to whom Visconti wanted to prove himself.

In May 1946, before the first general election, Visconti published an article in *L'Unità*, the Communist Party paper, which shocked his former world and his relations. It was entitled *The reason why I shall vote Communist*: 'There is still a fear of "Communism", fear of making an enormous mistake, of the totalitarian state, of the control over the liberty of expression, the stifling of initiatives and all other nonsense. It seems to me that these are childish fears.' Italy, he wrote, could not but become Socialist and, since the monarchy had been inept, he was going to struggle for what the Communist Party wanted: a parliamentary republic. It was impossible, he stated, to doubt the will of the Communist Party to be part of the democratic institutions of the country: it was that very Party which had fought for liberty against Fascist dictatorship. Religion was going to be respected, he said, and that was an important point for him. Visconti did not believe in art as a form of propaganda; on the contrary, art had to express and clarify the feelings of man living among men. 'He was very keen on the Communist Party, he shared its views, he always voted for them. He would always defend the Party – not with noisy imbecility, but on a high level,' says Giorgio Ferrara, the film director, who wrote a book on Visconti. 'He suffered for these contradictions, an aristocrat with money leading a certain kind of life; more than just being attacked, he was ridiculed.'

In June 1946 Visconti worked at the polling station for the national referendum on whether Italy should remain a monarchy or become a republic. The referendum went, marginally, in favour of the republic, and into exile went the monarch of a few weeks, King Umberto, Visconti's former friend in the days of the Pinerolo stables.

At last Visconti was to make another film, this time based on *I Malavoglia*. Trombadori arranged that the Communist Party would put up the sum of six million lire, on the assumption that the film would be a documentary about southern Italy, and this enabled Visconti to start filming; but at some point Visconti confessed to Trombadori that *La Terra Trema* – this was to be the title of the film – was not going to be a documentary and that the Communist Party could not become a film producer.

While working on this film, Visconti announced the formation of his theatre company, a kind of Italian National Theatre. In a letter of intent he stated that his repertoire was going to be selected only on artistic criteria, staging classics, but also contemporary plays. The company included actors like Rina Morelli, Paolo Stoppa, Giorgio de Lullo and Massimo Girotti.

Visconti had also dug out some *monstres sacrées* like Tatiana Pavlova, Memo Benassi and Mariella Lotti. When he went to see the latter, Maria Denis was there by chance. Before he arrived Mariella Lotti, who was a beautiful star of the pre-war cinema, asked her friend Maria whether she minded meeting Visconti. 'No,' she said, 'I suffered a lot, but I would like to see him.' When he arrived, Luchino was sweet and charming to her, as if they had been seeing each other all the time, as if nothing had happened. But Maria looked him straight in the eye and said, 'I'd like to play the truth game with you.' He said nothing and then left.

While he was rehearsing *The Glass Menagerie*, Patroni Griffi talked to him about a friend of his who was determined to work in the cinema and had written a thesis on Verga's *I Malavoglia*: 'Luchino felt a certain diffidence about the recommendation, but he agreed to meet Francesco Rosi and, when he saw him, Luchino said he wanted to have him photographed and use his image in the play he was staging. He needed the photo to depict a POW, and that is the way Rosi made his first appearance on stage.'

In Florence, where he had gone at the invitation of a group of enthusiastic boys who had staged *Les Parents Terribles*, he met the bright, handsome, young Franco Zeffirelli, who immediately made a strong impression on him. A spirited Tuscan, Zeffirelli played the part of Dmitri in *Crime and Punishment* alongside Girotti and de Lullo. He did not, however, appear in the cast of *The Glass Menagerie*, which opened a month later on 13 December 1946. Then Visconti surprised Zeffirelli and Rosi by asking them to be his assistants on the film he was preparing based on *I Malavoglia*.

Franco Zeffirelli did not act in the following productions, *Life with Father* and Anouilh's *Eurydice*; he wanted to work on the production side of the business; he was a good designer and was to take the place which had, until then, been Mario Chiari's. 'When he set out to make the film' Patroni Griffi commented, 'Luchino called on Zeffirelli and Rosi and asked them to work on a most demanding task, that of making a film without a script.'

8
Against the Current

'*La Terra Trema* is one of the best films I've ever seen,' says Antonioni. 'There is no shade of illustration; in it Luchino felt his theme and his characters as if they had come out not from a story which he had to treat for the screen, but from the very earth, from Verga, from Sicily, from that culture which, strangely, he felt very deeply.'

The landscape of Acitrezza, near Catania in eastern Sicily, was wonderful and tragic; the story was the eternal one of the bully subjugating the weak, which was not only the theme of *I Malavoglia*, but was also true of that environment: Visconti redeemed the sense of defeat in Verga with hope for a different and better future, but one which was distant as well. *La Terra Trema*, which deals with the life of fishermen, was to be the first part of a threefold documentary; but it was the only one produced (it still bears the subtitle of *Episodio del Mare*). The films about the sulphur-miners and the peasants were never made. Visconti was not concerned with, he did not even think about, the commercial possibilities of the film: he wanted it to correspond to his plan. As he said:

There was no pre-established script; I would leave it to them. For example, I would take two brothers and tell them: 'Look, this is the situation. You have lost your boat, you are paupers, you have nothing to eat, you don't know what to do any more. You want to escape, but you are too young, and he wants you to stay. Tell him what it is that drives you away from here.' The dialogue started like this, I gave a hint, they brought ideas, images, colour. Then I would ask them to repeat the text, sometimes for three, four hours, as one does with actors. But I never changed the words. When Brancati, who is an excellent Sicilian writer, heard these dialogues, he exclaimed 'They are the most beautiful in the world! No one could have ever written anything like it.'[1]

In Sicily the days and nights of intense work and exhaustion began: working sixteen hours a day, many scenes were filmed at dawn and the crew, after finishing work, had to return to their modest hotel at Catania, one hour away from Acitrezza. One of Francesco Rosi's tasks was to note details for continuity. It was an almost impossible task, and yet all-important since there was no script, just a guiding story, a thread; improvisation built up realism, realism had to be reproduced. Visconti had come to the conclusion that neo-realism was losing credibility:

Thus at a certain point the need arose to return to fundamentals, to truth, and to do so without any tricks, without a pre-established shooting script, without real actors, just following reality and truth. And *La Terra Trema* was also a difficult enterprise, with high and low moments, crises and halts, but one which we succeeded in bringing to a conclusion. I remember that at the time my professional conscience told me 'You must do it, you must finish this film without making any concessions. On the contrary, you must demonstrate that this is the right way and that other approaches are wrong now. . . .'[2]

The images were beautiful: black-shawled women against overcast skies, impassive, wrinkled expressions, close-ups of weather-beaten faces. The strong sounds of the sea seemed to efface all others, suffocating the soft voices of the fishermen, the calls, the rushing footsteps: sound was stronger than vision, and more evocative.

Convinced that the moment of revolution was near, in *La Terra Trema* Visconti showed the conditions suffered by the exploited Sicilian proletariat. The plot followed the basic outlines of *I Malavoglia*; it concerned the struggle of a family – the Valastros – which subsisted on a hostile sea, the source of its livelihood. Verga's pessimistic and fatalistic view of the family ruled by necessity alone was changed in the film. In both book and film the fishermen are defeated, but while in Verga the enemy is the sea, in the film the enemy is the exploitation by other men. The fishermen depend on the wholesaler who owns their boats. The Valastro family attempts to escape from this exploitation by mortgaging their house and setting up an independent business; but one night they are caught in a storm and their boat and their livelihood are destroyed. In Visconti's version, Verga becomes Marx when 'Ntoni Valastro's consciousness is awakened and, disgusted by the miserable prices offered for the night's catch, he leads a revolt among the fishermen. The wholesalers call for the police and 'Ntoni is arrested. At the end of the film 'Ntoni talks to a little girl and it is to her that he articulates the message of the film, the need for collective action.

Zeffirelli was working on this film for the first time as assistant director, and even the camera man, Aldo, who was to become one of the greatest in the profession, was new to the job. Visconti had asked Aldo to work with him because he admired his work; besides, after the war there were few technicians available, especially if one did not want to use those who had worked for the Fascist film industry. 'Luchino was a man who always gave one a sense of responsibility. He was a Maestro in the literal sense of the term – a man who taught, educated, helped you to know yourself,' said Rosi.

Money was beginning to run out. From Acitrezza Visconti rang Mario Chiari, who was working on an epic film called *Fabiola*, asking him to go and see his accountant in Milan for some more money. 'Count Visconti is going to ruin himself!' the good old Milanese solicitor would whine from the other side of a desk, opening his arms and handing over the money.

Sicily was very poor then, though perhaps not as sad as it is today, when concrete, over-crowding, consumer pressure and the Mafia have proliferated. What was clearly visible then was the extreme poverty. Living in Sicily was a painful experience for Visconti, because of the poverty and because it was the stronghold of the Mafia, which had rallied around the ruling party, thus providing votes and parliamentary seats. Corruption, *omertà*, intimidation and injustice were the rules. Added to which, Visconti carried with him the banner of a party which was to many people anathema. The anti-Communist campaign during the general election that had followed the referendum on the monarchy had been fierce: it was said that every vote for the Communist Party was a vote for the Iron Curtain's annexation of Italy, and priests in their Sunday sermons suggested that it was a mortal sin to vote Communist. It required courage to be an open supporter of the Communist Party at such a time. Those six months were an important experience for Luchino. It was also a bitter time for men who, like him, were committed to the Left: Visconti felt a sense of powerless humiliation when the Communist and Socialist parties were 'expelled' from government, and Togliatti agreed to resign his ministerial post. It virtually amounted to a *coup* – excluding from government the architects of the Resistance movement. Such events could easily have led to revolts and unrest, because many people felt that the Left was the only group which had fought Fascism, hence the only nucleus which could build a non-Fascist state. Some Communists felt that the Party should have reacted and, although this has never been officially confirmed, there is documentary evidence which indicates that the Communist Party could still have counted on armed units, the remnants of those GAPs which had 'disobeyed' by not giving up their arms after the Liberation. Togliatti, however, resisted any such temptation.

In April 1948 the Popular Front, a coalition of Communists and Socialists, was defeated; two months later the leader of the Communist Party, Palmiro Togliatti, was shot and severely wounded. For a time it looked as if civil war might explode in Italy; the Communists mounted a military occupation of several cities including Genoa, Porto Marghera and Abbadia S. Salvatore. It was a spontaneous and angry move, but the Party recalled its men to order: Togliatti feared the ghost of civil war and the distant prospect of foreign intervention. He knew Stalin well.

From Sicily Visconti followed the political developments; he would ring up his friend Antonello Trombadori in Rome – in those days it took hours to put through a call from Sicily to Rome – but he was totally absorbed in making his film, which he intended should be a political and ethical statement. In *La Terra Trema* he did not wish to copy life, but he did want to produce it anew, using the authenticity of the environment.

1 The richest and most beautiful girl in Milan: Carla Erba, 1897

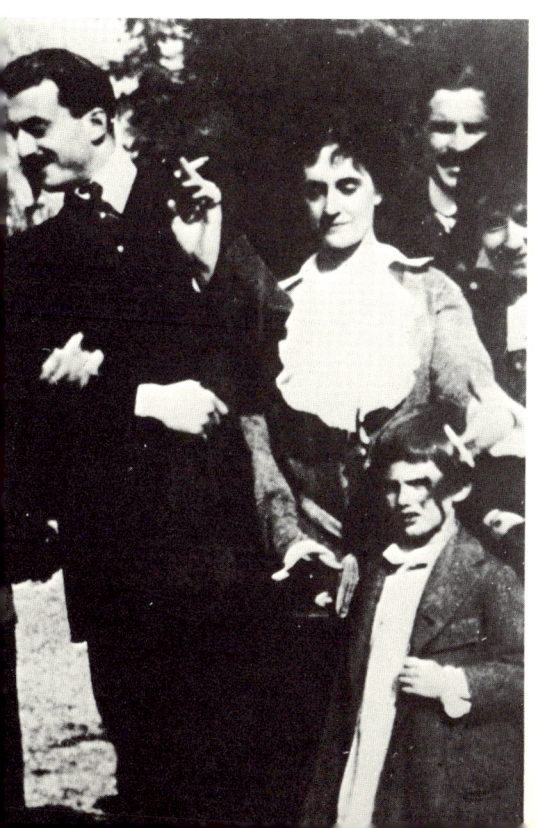

2 An unhappy marriage: Don Giuseppe with his ailing wife on his left and their daughter Anna at Grazzano-Visconti, 1910

3 Luchino aged three with his mother at Grazzano

4 The family before the separation: (*right to left*) Luchino's parents, Guido, Anna, Luigi, Luchino and Edoardo, 1914

6 *Tableaux vivants* at the royal palace: Luchino as a page (*right*) to
the aristocracy; (*below*) recreating Tiepolo's frescoes of *chinoiserie*
at Villa Valmarana, 1929

7 Luchino Visconti in Hammamet, 1934, taken by Horst

8 A scene from *La Terra Trema* (1948) – this was considered a daring image at the time

9 Visconti directing Alida Valli at La Fenice in 1953 for the opening sequence of *Senso*

10 Farley Grainger and Alida Valli in *Senso*. This scene was filmed at Lonedo, Palladio's very first building

11 Visconti acting as a godfather to the first son of Lucia Bose Dominguin (*right*)

2 Members of his two families together [in] 1963 at Sperlongha: (*below, left to right*) Visconti, his youngest sister, Uberta, [a] friend, his brother Edoardo, Princess [C]ercolani and (kneeling) his nephew [C]arlo d'Avanzo; (*above, left to right*) [F]ernando Scarfiotti, Enrico Medioli and [F]ranco Mannino, who soon after married [U]berta

Checking a camera angle during the [fil]ming of *Rocco and His Brothers* [in] Milan

14 With Alain Delon and Annie Girardot on location for *Rocco*

15 Michelangelo Antonioni (*left*) worked frequently with Visconti

Visconti's behaviour towards his crew was most demanding: at times his angry scenes humiliated and wounded; he could not tolerate imprecision, which his Lombard personality regarded as deliberate obstruction. He was kind to his crew in some ways, but he could also be extremely cruel. Visconti would emerge from his tantrums only when he realized that he had been wrong and wanted to be forgiven – without saying so. 'During *La Terra Trema* he treated Zeffirelli and me like animals,' recalled Rosi.

In the end he produced a film which was three hours long and in which the main characters were real fishermen who spoke an incomprehensible dialect. No one wanted to have anything to do with it; the distributors wanted to cut it. Visconti put Rosi in charge of the film. 'After editing it with him, Visconti turned me into a Neapolitan bulldog, guarding the film, because they wanted to cut it. They would come unexpectedly into the cutting room but I was there, next to it.' Visconti also insisted that Rosi should be in charge when *La Terra Trema* was shown at the Venice Film Festival. The two of them had gradually become friends through their work, which was Visconti's mainspring and motivation. 'It was trying to work with him. It was like being under a constant examination, you had to prove yourself continuously,' said Rosi.

La Terra Trema was not a success at the festival and was attacked by most of the press, and even more so by politicians, who accused Visconti of damaging the name of Italy abroad by exposing poverty and misery. Visconti remembered it vividly: 'I can't tell you what happened when the film was shown! I stood at the back of the hall and I could see these beautiful ladies in furs who, half-way through the film, got up without any sign of shame or embarrassment.... "What a thing!" they said. "How disgusting!".... And then, off they went. But I never lost courage, never.'[3] When the film was shown abroad, though, it was hailed as a masterpiece. At that year's Venice Film Festival, Laurence Olivier's *Hamlet* won the first prize.

Making *La Terra Trema* had taken almost a year; in August Visconti was in correspondence about another project: staging *Orlando Furioso* at the Prato Verde della Meridiana, in the gardens of Boboli, for the Maggio Musicale of 1949. Visconti's idea was to stage Ariosto's *Orlando Furioso* by dividing the scenes so that they would be played in different parts of the garden, but this project eventually fell through. He then thought of staging *Lorenzaccio* at Palazzo Pitti and, typically, he conceived the action in a really grand manner: he would assemble the public in a courtyard, which would have to be built on the level of the first floor, and stage the action inside the rooms of the palazzo. In this way, the public would have been in the middle, and the actors would have done their plotting in the very rooms where plots had been made and unmade for centuries. But the location was judged impossible.

Visconti then began working on a grandiose production of *As You Like It* with his own new company in Rome. He conceived it as a 'fantasy, a dream, a fairy-tale'. To visualize this concept he called on Salvador Dali, whom he had met through Coco Chanel; 'she suggested that I should work on that play,' said Dali, recalling those days. A great draughtsman, exploiter of dream visions and Freudian symbols, Dali had defected from Surrealism; he had become religious, painted holy themes and sympathized with the Franco regime. He liked Visconti, but criticized him politically: 'High society was crazy about him. He ate off gold plates, he was a Communist who only liked luxury.' During 1948 in Rome he, his wife Gala and Zeffirelli saw each other constantly. Dali would comb the Roman specialist shops with Zeffirelli looking for ornaments, silks and *bon-bons*, because Dali insisted that the actors on stage should eat real cakes. Visconti used to discuss Dali's personality with him, much to the painter's pleasure. Dali also worked on the lighting of his scenery and costumes. His sets were partly inspired by Bomarzo, that extraordinary garden of carved monsters in the Roman countryside, which at the time he wanted to buy. On the stage there were elephants with obelisks like Bernini's sculpture and a Palladian temple which exploded into four parts; it was a dream of fantasy and unreality. *As You Like It* got a mixed reception: it was certainly beautiful and different, but using Dali was criticized by the Left, who maintained that he was too close to Franco for comfort. So much so that a prominent Communist wrote an attack on the production for *Rinascita*, the weekly edited and founded by Togliatti, who did not publish it. Instead the head of the Party asked Visconti to write an article explaining his own interpretation of *As You Like It*. In *Rinascita* Visconti wrote:

> It is said that by staging Shakespeare's *As You Like It* I have abandoned neo-Realism. This impression arose from the style of the décor and of the acting, and because of my choice of Salvador Dali. I ask to be forgiven by those who like this imprecise terminology. Neo-realism was a point of departure; it is now beginning to become a label which somebody has stuck on us like a tattoo. And instead of meaning a method of identifying a certain moment, it becomes a limit, even a law. Do we already need limitations?[4]

With the help of Togliatti, Visconti won this vital battle. Had he been 'abandoned' by the Communist Party, Visconti would have felt an orphan once again, and more so.

He continued to produce a prodigious amount of work: he planned a film based on *Chronicles of Poor Lovers*, a novel by Vasco Pratolini, a Communist writer; the scenario was written by Zeffirelli, Sergio Amidei, Pratolini himself, Antonio Pietrangeli and Visconti. The film was to be financed by Raoul Lévy and Edoardo Visconti, Luchino's younger brother. The cast consisted of Gérard Philipe, Marguerite Moreno, Massimo Girotti and a newcomer, the ravishingly beautiful Lucia Bosé who, after she had won the title of 'Miss Italy', had become a close friend of Luchino's. She had fine features, elegant allure, she was witty and she had the colouring and the looks of a Visconti. But *Chronicles of Poor Lovers* fell through: it would have cost too much and the producers had to back out. (The film was made ten years later by Carlo Lizzani, with a different script and a different cast.)

Following its success on Broadway, Luchino decided to stage Tennessee Williams's *A Streetcar Named Desire* (and, perhaps influenced by Williams, he himself grew a black moustache, which did not suit him). The play opened at the Teatro Eliseo in Rome on 21 January 1949; it was designed by Zeffirelli, and in the cast were Marcello Mastroianni, Vittorio Gassman, Rina Morelli and Franco Interlenghi. It was not a great success and some critics accused Visconti of imitating Kazan's realism, but Franco Zeffirelli's costumes and scenery were much admired.

Visconti admired Franco, who was an orphan (his mother had died when he was a child and his father, having married again, had never acknowledged him); he was talented, alert. For Visconti, Franco was a kind of adored son whom he had adopted and formed, and who, like all bright children, was rebellious and anxious to escape. Zeffirelli, for his part, wanted to find his own way. As a young boy he had formed a theatre company in Florence, where he had been the director, the designer and one of the leading actors.

Zeffirelli, like Visconti, loved opera. In spite of his travels, his plays and his generally busy life, Visconti had not deserted melodrama: he would go to the opera whenever there was something he wanted to see. In Rome, in the autumn of 1948, he heard a fat, young soprano sing at the Opera House; she was Greek, married to an Italian, and her voice was extraordinary, with a unique middle range. What struck Visconti even more than her musical gifts was her sense of the stage. Her name was Maria Meneghini Callas, as she was known then; and Visconti started sending her bunches of roses with admiring little notes – but never went to see her backstage, never met her.

Knowing that Visconti had a profound knowledge of music, the impresario Siciliani wrote in January 1949 asking him to produce Verdi's *Otello*: it was the first time that he had been officially asked to stage an opera. However, Visconti turned it down because he was too absorbed in his theatre company. Despite this, he still pursued Maria Callas from a distance and, with his friends, went to every performance of hers in Rome. She asked to meet the famous director who sent her bouquets and at last, in February 1949, they met. He went backstage to her dressing-room and she was immediately attracted to this handsome, self-assured director who knew so much about music. She asked him to work with her and the famous man boldly answered, 'Come back to me with this request when you are sixty pounds lighter.' The odd thing was that she did: her determination to work with him and to please him made her do it.

In February 1949 Siciliani wrote again to Visconti from Florence. The Maggio Musicale was still trying to secure him as a director; many alternatives – *La Mandragola* as well as *Il Lorenzaccio* – had been turned down.

Caro Visconti,
I refer to our conversation in Rome last week, which I prefer not to consider as definitive. I therefore suggest something else for the next Maggio – as I've told you many times, your presence would be particularly welcomed, by the Committee as well as by myself. What do you think about Shakespeare's *Troilus and Cressida*? Need I emphasize how well this play would adapt to the natural environment of the Boboli gardens? And wouldn't this be the typical and traditional play – in the best sense – of the best Maggios? I know that you are very familiar with this magnificent text and I think I know too that you have considered staging it....

Zeffirelli started work on the play at once. He was given some 'grand' directives by Visconti, who, in the meantime, had to fulfil an obligation to the actor Vittorio Gassman; and while everybody else was busy preparing *Troilus*, Visconti staged *Oreste*. It was a baroque, extravagant, operatic spectacle; *Oreste*, by Vittorio Alfieri, was a text which Visconti did not like, but the staging of it had been a condition of Gassman joining the company. Those who saw *Oreste* still remember it as a grandiose extravaganza: Visconti had ripped out the stalls and used this space for the actors instead. As Alfieri was an eighteenth-century writer (the French Revolution was round the corner, the monarchy was sinking), Visconti staged the play in Versailles under water. On the stage behind a gauze screen there was an orchestra playing Beethoven symphonies which successfully drowned out most of Alfieri's pompous lines. But it was a *capriccio* – and an expensive one, too. Gassman was furious: he attacked Visconti and later left the company in order to work under his own direction.

Even more flamboyant, grandiose and, many people said, extravagant was his production of *Troilus*. The initial designs had envisaged the two camps with a real harbour full of water and ships for the Greek fleet and, on the other side, the walls and city of Troy. Naturally the people in charge at the Maggio thought the probable costs excessive. Imagine digging a harbour in the Boboli Gardens, which lie behind the Palazzo Pitti in Florence! So they sighed with relief when they saw the second project, which concentrated the action within Troy itself; the city was enclosed by walls and the 'Greek action' was to take place outside, two hundred yards from the city walls.

In the end Zeffirelli's design was one of the most beautiful ever to be seen on stage – if the gardens of Boboli can be called a stage. It depicted Troy as a Persian miniature, with a shifting perspective which enabled the public to see the action around roads, houses, palaces and walls because the scenery was not painted – it was built: Troy was recreated in detail. There was Hecuba's house; and during rehearsals arrows indicated 'Priam's garden', 'Cassandra's room': it was like a folly. Piero Tosi, a friend of Zeffirelli's, brought some drawings for *Troilus* for Visconti to see. But Visconti, after looking at them, told him to wait, saying he had plenty of time to develop; instead he employed him as a scene-shifter. Tosi, who hoped to design for Visconti, was naturally hurt.

The sets for *Troilus* were so huge that Flora Carabella, who was engaged to Mastroianni, could not find him for a whole day. 'If he's a Trojan,' someone said, 'you'll find him inside the city!' Actually he was a Greek – outside the walls. Patroni Griffi recalls that, when he went to see his friends rehearsing, the first thing he encountered was a flying bottle thrown by the angry director, who had forty days to rehearse this epic piece of theatrical *panache*, which was to be performed for only eight days. The actors were exhausted by Visconti's demands. All the Italian theatre was there: besides the names already mentioned, there were Paolo Stoppa, Franco Interlenghi, Renzo Ricci, Massimo Girotti, Sergio Tofano, Memo Benassi, Rina Morelli and Elsa de Giorgi (a writer, famous for her beauty, who played Helen). Provençal troubadours sang to the accompaniment of flutes and lutes. Cressida's long procession passed through the Boboli gardens, with horses and a fantastic retinue. There was no doubt whom Visconti favoured: he was on Troy's side – and Troy was depicted as a weak Europe, while the Greeks were conceived (though not too obviously so) as polished, 'new' Americans who came to invade and erase the old customs. Foreign tourists who saw *Troilus and Cressida* (the first performance was on 21 June 1949) were amazed and shocked: how could poverty-stricken Italy stage this kind of production just after the war? And was this the same man who directed *La Terra Trema*? It was unbelievable. The production amazed everybody. Critics, the general public, friends and foes alike could not help but admire the grand concepts of Visconti's interpretation: it was a triumph.

Visconti was moving towards luxurious staging simply because poverty seemed to evoke the need for flamboyance. Unconsciously he was also asserting the role of the director – a concept which hardly existed in the Italian theatre – in a violent way. Actors liked to work for him, despite the fact that he was overbearing. At times he imposed his personality as director by despotic and exacting demands. But although he had a sadistic attitude towards actors, he also adored them, especially the famous old ones, whom he would rescue from oblivion (as he had done with Tatiana Pavlova, or Ruggero Ruggeri, whom the company nicknamed 'the corpse'). Visconti also adored reminiscing about Eleonora Duse or Sarah Bernhardt.

In the same year, Visconti rented a white tower called La Colombaia on the island of Ischia in the Bay of Naples. He was not particularly keen on swimming, but he liked the blue sea and the lush, scented vegetation of such islands. Ischia was to become his favourite refuge, while he hardly ever went to the house in Tripoli which Guido had left to him.

After spending a month on Ischia, in August Luchino went to see Horst, who had rented a small house in Austria. They had written to each other, after all these years, and decided they wanted to meet again. Visconti had misgivings about going to Austria because the Italians were disliked due to the fact that Italy had robbed Austria of the Tyrol. Horst thought that all this was nonsense; the villa was in the mountains, isolated – too simple, he feared, for Luchino. Horst had a friend living with him, the first Englishman Luchino ever liked. In addition, he enjoyed the beauty of the scenery and the fresh air.

Despite such distractions, Visconti did not enjoy holidays; he preferred working on a script with friends, planning a new play and talking about work. After a week in Austria, he therefore returned to Via Salaria.

Corrado Corradi, the old school friend from Milan with whom he used to comb the antique shops when he was staging a play, went to stay with him. It was a friendship which never died, and whenever Corradi went to Rome he would stay at Via Salaria, in spite of the few interests they now shared. Corradi was a nobleman who ran his own estate; he had a wife and children, and was not interested in politics or show business. He and Visconti led independent lives and met only for meals.

At night, Luchino seldom went out, so instead people came to see him; he disliked being a guest, but enjoyed being the host. At the pinnacle of his career, he still found time to choose the menu and type of champagne, and to worry about the china on the table. He had taken to drinking very strong filtered coffee from which emanated an almost intoxicating smell, and to be asked to prepare this special coffee for Luchino was regarded as a sign of high favour. Corradi would observe the ritual of the coffee being prepared in one of the many drawing-rooms at Via Salaria, or on the terrace, in the garden, under the portico, in the library – in any one of the many rooms which looked like Visconti's film sets, drooling mastiffs on the floor, mantelpieces crammed with beautiful objects. Sometimes they went up to the first floor, which was less opulent than the ground floor but fresher and cosier, and Visconti would drink his immensely strong coffee on the verandah which was full of doves and flowers – he had green fingers and a non-Italian love of plants. Or Visconti might take his coffee in his bedroom, which was crammed with icons (they had not yet become fashionable), bronze sculptures, paintings and photographs of friends.

His taste in dogs would change; at one time he had a passion for basset-hounds, at another for Alsatians, which he liked to breed. He would give puppies to his relatives and friends – another sign of favour. At this stage in his life (the end of 1949) it was the turn of ferocious mastiffs, and old friends like Corradi observed that he was more sure of himself now, and more irascible and demanding; he knew he had become 'the myth', that every production of his was regarded as a major event. Because he had asserted himself, he began to be more outspoken; he would speak quickly, with authority and humour; never asking, but commanding with a mixture of privileged impatience and liberal concern. He was hungry to create; he wanted to achieve.

In 1950, though, many of his projects fell through. He worked on a scenario of Merimée's *La Carrozza del Santissimo Sacramento* (*The Coach of the Blessed Sacrament*), which he wrote with Zeffirelli, Antonio Pietrangeli and Suso Cecchi d'Amico, the first time he used this future regular collaborator for a film script.

There was another project on the life of Petipo, the nineteenth-century Neapolitan actor, in which he wanted to use Totó, a supremely gifted and popular Neapolitan actor whom no 'quality' director would touch. (Visconti always showed courage in his projects.) There was also a story about a dancing competition, and one about a Milanese family from the industrial aristocracy (his own). Again he became part of a cultural association, called Partisans for Peace. Giuliano Pajetta of the Communist Party remembered a meeting at his house: 'This association was a cultural thing, linked to the Party.' Because *La Terra Trema*, which was being shown, hailed and loathed around Italy, was a highly political film, Visconti became a target and a symbol. In that very August, for example, *La Terra Trema* was prevented from being shown at Prague for the World Peace Prize because the producers thought that, had it gone to Prague, the film might have been harmed commercially.

Visconti also instituted a literary prize for the best first book and, in the same mood of constructiveness, he joined a group of people who created 'Antiparnaso', an association for the 'modernization' of opera. The lyric theatre had been neglected during Fascist times: the young considered it dead. When the 'Antiparnaso' decided to sponsor a production of *Il Turco in Italia*, an amazingly modern opera by Rossini, Visconti entrusted Zeffirelli with the design and asked Maria Callas to sing the leading role. Later on that year the director of the Rome Opera House tried to tempt Visconti into directing *Zaza* by Leoncavallo, which was to star Callas and Tito Gobbi; but Visconti turned it down. He was not interested in Leoncavallo's music and was now aiming at a great occasion to make his opera début.

Although Visconti was liked by impresarios, he was persecuted by officialdom. Having been one of the first intellectuals to rally to the Communist Party, his plays and films were considered controversial, they had to be eradicated. A lesser man might have gone to work abroad, but Visconti's Teutonic determination to achieve his aim created difficulties for magistrates, police, bishops and deputies, for the stern Milanese was actually stimulated by such persecution: 'If *Carlton-Browne of the F.O.* had been made in Italy,' he said a decade later, 'the Boulting Brothers would have spent a total of a hundred years in jail.'[5]

In February 1951 Visconti staged *Death of a Salesman*, the first play by Arthur Miller to be performed in Italy; many critics again said that Visconti had copied Kazan's 'raw realism' – a comparison he disliked. To Milan he brought a slightly changed version of his production of *A Streetcar Named Desire*, and to the Venice Theatre Festival, *Il Seduttore* by Diego Fabbri.

In Rome he met one of his great idols, Thomas Mann, at the home of Alba De Cespedes, a writer who worked for Mondadori, Mann's Italian publishers. Luchino Visconti had started working on a short story by Mann called *Mario and the Wizard* (*Mario und der Zauberer*), which was to be a kind of opera-ballet to be performed at La Scala. The music was to be written by Visconti's new brother-in-law, Franco Mannino, a conductor, composer and pianist, whom Uberta Visconti had married after the annulment of her marriage to Renzo d'Avanzo. Visconti was writing the libretto. Mann had already published *Doctor Faustus*, which international criticism had labelled as an expressionist work; Visconti thought that it was about expressionism, but was not itself expressionist. Mann looked like a bureaucrat; he could have been the general manager of a corporation or a civil servant from a ministry. He was attentive and kind, and Luchino was shy with him. Mann spoke good Italian (his daughter had married an Italian) and the two men settled down to discuss *Mario and the Wizard*. Before arriving at any conclusion, Mann asked many questions. When Luchino told him how he had treated the subject of *Mario and the Wizard*, there was a sudden embarrassment because Thomas Mann kept silent. But then, slowly, the man whose writing Visconti worshipped started to comment that he had arrived at the same solution himself and said, 'I had feared that you might have misunderstood my short story, because it is not expressionist.'[6]

It was at this same meeting that Thomas Mann told Visconti about an occasion when he saw an aged 'queen' on his way to Venice, his sweaty hair dripping dye over his forehead, an image which Visconti was to associate with Mahler, probably misunderstanding Mann, who talked in a very low voice. But certainly, on that occasion, Thomas Mann was giving Visconti a visual hint, an image, closely related to the mood in which he approached the Lido and the writing of *Death in Venice*. In 1911 the Manns had gone to the Grand Hôtel des Bains on the Venice Lido; it was the last time they went there before the war. They had arrived in the third week of May by boat from Brioni, whence they had fled because the Archduchess of Austria was staying at the same hotel as they were. She had the tiresome habit of coming down to dine two minutes after all the guests had sat down so that everybody had to rise for her. The same happened when she left the dining-room a few minutes before everybody else did. This typical royal whim of enjoying the visible exercise of power irritated the always irritable writer and was the reason why Thomas Mann went to Venice and saw Tadzio, his mother, and the beautiful family of children all neatly, elegantly and identically dressed. Had Thomas

Mann gone back the next year, it might have been Luchino and the beautiful Donna Carla with her children who would have captured Mann's imagination; and this is partly what interested Visconti in Mann's short story, *Death in Venice*.

Thomas Mann had met Mahler the previous summer, in 1910, and was in no doubt about the musician's genius, as he told his wife Katia: he had had the impression of having met a genius 'devouringly intense', as he later called Mahler.

Thomas Mann and Visconti were to meet and talk twice more. Visconti felt deeply the privilege of having talked to Mann, having listened to his voice, having confronted that intellectual, laboured genius. The outcome of the encounter was that the writer ceded the rights of all his short stories to be set to music by Mannino. The contract for *Mario and the Wizard* was signed on 27 August 1951. As well as writing the libretto Visconti was to direct the ballet for what was to be a 'choreographical action' – a phrase they coined to describe a mixture of ballet, opera and theatre.

The themes of Thomas Mann's novellas were of course symbolic (one of the strong threads that must have appealed to Visconti was disease and abnormality as a source of spiritual life). *Mario und der Zauberer* (1930) is a clear parable of the Italian Fascist dictatorship, and was denounced by the Nazis in 1933. The conjurer-wizard, Cipolla, a clear allusion to Mussolini, deprives his spectator-victims of their wills and makes them perform all sorts of nonsense, thus revenging himself for his deformity. A young manservant, Mario, is one of his victims who, when in a trance, is compelled to kiss Cipolla while, on the opposite side of the stage, other victims dance. But Cipolla has pushed his victims too far and Mario, awakening from his trance, kills the wizard.

The choreographer Visconti used for this ballet was Leonide Massine, who had worked with Diaghilev. Massine, a handsome White Russian, lived with his wife in a beautiful *Directoire* tower outside Naples and was a romantic character whom Visconti brought back from oblivion. Jean Babilée danced the part of Mario when it was performed, much later, at La Scala in 1956; Thomas Mann's daughter, Elizabeth Mann Borgese, congratulated both Visconti and Mannino; but *Mario e il Mago*, which won the Diaghilev Prize, was never performed again. 'The character of the wizard,' said Mannino, 'was acted, because it was a composite work, neither opera nor ballet. Luchino used to play that part fantastically [in rehearsal]! I would have liked him to do it: he was a born actor!'

Visconti and Mannino worked closely together; Mannino had to go to his house at Via Salaria: '... Even if he expected nobody for dinner, his chef from the Abruzzi was ordered to prepare dinner for fourteen every night "otherwise he gets out of practice", Visconti used to say.' Mannino spent long months too at La Colombaia on Ischia, where Visconti surrounded himself with friends and what was immediately labelled 'his court': Walter Chiari and Rina Morelli, Paolo Stoppa, Suso Cecchi d'Amico, and Franco Zeffirelli, also Gnam Penati and Massimo Girotti. There they lived, mixing work with sunbathing, while Visconti planned his garden, which was to become spectacular. 'I had hired a piano, which was in the living-room, where we also had meals,' Mannino recalled. 'In the evenings we would play the games Luchino loved, like charades. In the daytime I composed and played, and the chef, who besides being a good cook loved music, would "compose" menus calling his dishes *L'Appassionata*, *Il Notturno*, etc.' In the evening Visconti, as was his custom, would discuss the menus which his chef proposed for the following day and he would also study. He found the time to do everything and was always perfectly briefed.

'Before buying his house on Ischia,' says Antonioni, 'he used to rent a castle on the harbour and I used to go and stay there often, and Clara Calamai was often there: it was very beautiful. There one spent evenings which – how could one say? – were different because Luchino created a different atmosphere. He was a man full of irony; he would say, ironically, "Let's go out and watch the moon." But we went out and watched the moon and enjoyed the wonderful scenery. He loved games like a child. Some of the games at the castle were naughty. We played murder in the dark, the light went off and the "detective" stayed away for a long time: in the darkness everything would happen; I was delighted, there were wonderful women there.'

La Colombaia (the Dovecote) was on a wooded hill looking over the blue sea of Ischia, an Arab white tower and white terraces, with gardens extending through the wood which ran down to the beach: Visconti had planted a sea of blue hydrangeas which filtered through the green of the wooded path; little guest-houses were scattered around the wood, their paths joined in a white alley which led to the sea. When he later succeeded in buying the tower (at the time he rented it), he furnished it all in Art Nouveau, Liberty prints, Jugendstil *objets d'art* and paintings, sculpture and furniture – years before the revival of those styles. It was an impeccable collection and, although theatrical, the house was comfortable; the terraces over the sea were shaded by stupendous parasols, and ancient Neapolitan tiles glittered in the sun. Drinks were sipped there, while meals were served in the living room. The chef enjoyed a joke invented by Visconti, that of reproducing the most precious vases by Gallé or Lalique in fine caramel. When they were brought to the table, the frightened guest would see the host smash the one served on his plate with the point of a knife and, invited to do likewise, would hesitate – thus provoking hoots of laughter. By combing small markets for Art Nouveau pieces, Visconti once again launched a fashion, copied first of all by his 'set' and then by others: the strength of Visconti's personality is demonstrated by his rediscovery of a trend, a painter or a style which was immediately copied, from the Louis Vuitton suitcases to the Lalique vases. Like all men of culture and taste, he was ahead of fashions because he anticipated them and, unwittingly, 'launched' whatever he touched.

At La Colombaia the furniture was Charles x, sculptures were by George Minne and vases by Hugo Leven, Lalique, Gallé and Joseph Hoffman. Visconti's bedroom was adorned by several Klimt watercolours, and there were voluptuous angels by Polowny of the Wiener Werkstätte. He was beginning to appreciate Mahler, who then in Italy and elsewhere was a forgotten composer, and he liked listening to Wagner and Verdi. At La Colombaia, as in every house of Visconti's, music was frequently played. But, surrounded by friends on Ischia, he would also sometimes sit on the terrace in silence. Suso Cecchi d'Amico remembers how important silence was for Visconti – often a silence to be shared.

Alberto Fassini, the young son of the owners of La Colombaia, saw Visconti on a beach where the Fiocchi family, relations of the Erbas, had a house: 'I was about eleven then. Uberta was there with her little son and I think Luchino was in a boat. I shouted "Signor Visconti! Can you give me a lift?" I wanted to meet him so much. We talked about Callas, whom I also already admired, and about music. Callas brought us together.' He joined the army of Visconti's worshippers. Visconti was a wizard, and he liked those who loved him. He chose to have a restful social life shared with close friends, to whom he offered the best food and drinks, and the most beautiful décor. Outsiders felt excluded and envious, but every now and then new people would join this adoring but witty and articulate court. There were the boys from the provinces, awakened by Visconti's plays, enchanted by his intellectual breadth. A newcomer to his circle was Elsa Morante, then married to Alberto Moravia; she was intelligent and handsome, and fell in love with Visconti, who loved her too, but she followed the pattern of those women who, because they were too intelligent, 'led to upheavals'. They would spend long hours together talking: she was stimulating company, but a rather close, mysterious character. She was a challenge to Visconti and he could not but be flattered by her total attention. He adored that, and almost demanded it from people around him, provoking friends and colleagues, women and men to fall in love with him – which was easy enough: it was a hecatomb.

At this time Visconti felt bitter towards the Italian cinema world, towards Cinecittà, which was conventional, fearful and which turned down many of his projects. He despised Cinecittà for its ignorance and its corrupt power; there was never money to produce his films. He had given up *Chronicles of Poor Lovers* and *The Coach of the Blessed Sacrament*. He found the finance, however, to make a 'social' documentary, which was produced by Marco Ferreri and written by Vasco Pratolini. It deals with a terrible sexual crime which had just taken place in a derelict area of Rome (the rape and murder of a little girl, a morbid theme such as always appealed to Visconti), but it was banned by the Italian censor and was only shown in France in 1953, under the title *Notes sur un fait divers*.

Visconti also worked on another project, *Il Marchese del Grillo*, a film which should have been produced by Salvo d'Angelo, but that fell through, and as a last resort d'Angelo offered him a script by Zavattini. 'The story of *Bellissima* is that of a woman or, better, of a crisis: a mother who has not fulfilled her small middle-class aspirations and tries to achieve them through her daughter. But then she becomes convinced that, if she wants to better herself, it is not in this way that she will find her improvement. At the end of the film she returns home, pure as she had left it, but with the knowledge of having loved her daughter badly and, moreover, bitter about things which she has had to do in order to reach that world which she thought wonderful but which, ultimately, was deplorable.'[7]

Anna Magnani was at that time the great protagonist of neo-realism; she had had to drop out of Visconti's *Ossessione* because of her pregnancy, but she had starred in Rossellini's *Rome Open City*; she had the physical and intellectual qualities of the woman of the people. Predictably she fell madly in love with him in a passionate, frustrated shower of emotions, which Visconti managed, at times, to control, but they also quarrelled continuously and at times ferociously. Together they changed the original dialogue, which Magnani would *ad lib* (Visconti was the only Italian director then who refused to dub voices and remake sound-tracks in the studio).

For the costumes and designs, Visconti engaged Piero Tosi, the blue-eyed boy whom he had treated badly when he brought him some sketches of *Troilus* to see. Piero Tosi was to become Visconti's best designer and his most tormented collaborator, who worked for him until the very last film. 'My encounter with Visconti was not based on esteem,' Tosi remembers. 'I was very young then, and I didn't know how to work. It was a fatiguing business, because he hardly spoke to me throughout the film. Those were the last days of neo-realism. There were no costumes, really, and no tailors; I used to improvise the stuff. Up to *Senso* he was very hard, medieval in tone: age softens everything. His relationship with me developed out of a real esteem for our work, but it was not easy. Not that he needed to be convinced – things always needed to mature with him, until they became his own ideas.'

Bellissima was the least 'Visconti' and the most 'Italian' of all his films: Zavattini's influence on the script was strong and it was not one of Visconti's favourite films. It is a film full of humour and irony, and Anna Magnani, the *monstre sacrée* of those days, created a wonderful character: the most lovable, kindest portrait Visconti ever made of a woman. There is a deep knowledge of human nature in *Bellissima*. It is the story of Cinecittà, the gross, callous cinema world versus the simplicity of little people. A radio announcer gives details of a competition: a film director is looking for the most beautiful girl in Rome to star in a film (it was at the time when films like *Song of Bernadette* and *Lassie*, with underdeveloped teenagers, were very successful). Anna Magnani played the role of a working-class mother; we see all the others at the film studio in Cinecittà, and there is hostility in Visconti's images of other middle-class mothers, but not for Magnani. The mother's simplicity and her ambition channelled through the child, Maria, are exploited by all, but in the end the child is triumphant and even the mother gives up the idea of *'la più bella bambina di Roma'* (which Maria certainly is not) being the star of the film, even if Maria through pushing and pulling is actually selected for the part.

The beauty of the film rests on the observation of the attitudes of a certain Roman middle stratum; but the delightful, cruel and true details of Roman life mean that *Bellissima* loses some of its context when seen outside Rome – even in Milan some of the observations were alien and lost.

Bellissima was another kind of experiment, another exercise in Visconti's search. He had approached the reality he was seeking by making Anna Magnani re-invent her own character. In order to do this, he forced her to be present at all the filming, even in scenes in which she was not acting. Anna Magnani, however, was only too pleased to be near him all the time, to get up at 5 a.m. every day and go exhausted to bed at midnight: she was in love with him and made no secret of it.

No moment of *Bellissima* is gratuitous. Even the strange opening sequence, over a funny passage from Donizetti's *L'Elisir d'Amore*, was not casual: the miraculous 'liquid' sold by a rogue to the simpletons is like the cinema world. The true protagonist of *Bellissima*, which almost erases the strong presence of Anna Magnani, is Rome, the target of Visconti's satire – a city seen with contempt but understanding, with disgust but not with rejection: an ornamental Eastern crowd, noisy and depraved, inept, vulgar, unproductive.

Visconti may have liked the film so little because *Bellissima* was the fruit of a strong collaboration with Zavattini and Magnani – and he did not like either sharing ideas or acknowledging that he had done so. When he saw it again on television years later, he was ill and close to death, and Magnani had died. They had been friends, they had quarrelled and, at times, did not speak to each other for months. Once she 'cut' Visconti for years because, when he was a member of the Venice Film Festival jury, Visconti had personally vetoed Magnani's award for *Suor Letizia*, a film in which she starred, directed by Camerini, and which he thought a poor film; Anna Magnani could not understand how a close friend could refuse to favour her. He was a northerner, she a southerner.

In 1952 Visconti worked on his greatest theatre productions: Goldoni's *La Locandiera* and Chekov's *The Three Sisters*. He became recognized, respected and admired, whereas hitherto the general public had mainly associated his name with scandal. Therefore he mellowed a little: he was less nasty, though not less demanding. But things which he had liked doing in the past (such as keeping a company of actors waiting around through the night until he found the perfect object, like the whistle in *Eurydice*), he would not do now that he was surrounded by awe and respect. *La Locandiera* (*The Innkeeper*) was a rarely-staged play and Visconti's aim was to erase the mannerisms which usually encrusted productions of eighteenth-century works (Mozart had suffered from the same fate). *La Locandiera* was pale, dry and unusual. Visconti had thought of the characters as objects, like opaque bottles. Tirelli, who later worked with him, recollects seeing it: 'Goldoni? Like this? It looked like Longhi, like a realistic play ... it was a revelation.'

Because the visual effect was to be so important and because Visconti was a man who wanted the best, and as he could not engage Longhi or Chardin to design the scenery for *La Locandiera*, he asked Morandi. But the venerable old painter refused: he hardly ever left his house in Bologna, where he lived with his sisters, two skinny old maids who were totally dedicated to the recluse. So Visconti asked Tosi to work on *La Locandiera*. 'Visconti wanted to give the play a precise pictorial formula, a mixture of Morandi and Longhi, though he never told me this, because he didn't express himself in words,' said Tosi.

Piero Tosi, who had studied at the Academy of Florence with the painter, Ottone Rosai, was terrified of Visconti and was a cultivated young man with a touching sensitivity. In spite of the fact that Tosi was paralysed by shyness, Visconti understood the boy's potential; besides, Tosi was able to stand up to him whenever he thought that Visconti was wrong. 'In the first scene the walls of the inn were all pale yellow, the door was large, he wanted the sky to be blue – all the rest was beige. I didn't agree with that.'

So the shy young Tosi went to Bologna to meet Morandi, who was even more shy. Tosi was received by Morandi's old sisters at the front door of their simple house which was full of nineteenth-century furniture. Morandi, a man of great modesty, told him that never in his life had he been to the theatre, he had not even seen a backdrop. Tosi had brought with him his sketches for *La Locandiera* and showed them to Morandi. Against Luchino's will, Tosi wanted to remove the windows and to have the sky in the same colour as the ground. Morandi agreed with Tosi and said '*Finestra, no!*' ('a window, no!'). Tosi asked him to write this on the sketch itself. Morandi added, 'The sky is always in the same colour as the ground.' Visconti accepted Morandi's corrections and from then on he trusted Tosi.

La Locandiera was born out of intense collaboration and preparation, but also out of confusion. Tosi said: 'The stage, in Luchino's mind was to be "space". There were immense quarrels in our working relationship; after thirty years of working together he still called me "*tu*" and I called him "*lei*", although it was the snob thing to do to *tutoyer* Luchino; but some people finished up by becoming his jesters. Those were always fatal relationships.'

Visconti's second great achievement was his production of Chekov's *The Three Sisters* with sets designed by Zeffirelli and the costumes by Marcel Escoffier. As Visconti himself put it:

> In my theatre career there are two elements of equal importance. The first is Chekov's plays, which I staged relatively late out of deference. Chekov is the author whom I consider the greatest, on the same level as Shakespeare and Verdi. Speaking of Verdi, I touch upon the other element. There is something I want to say first: Stendhal wanted the following engraved on his tombstone: 'He adored Cimarosa, Mozart and Shakespeare.' On the same lines, I would like the inscription: 'He adored Shakespeare, Chekov and Verdi.' Verdi and Italian opera were my first love. My work almost always betrays a touch of the operatic, whether in my films or in my plays. I've been accused of that, but actually I take it as a compliment. So, on the one hand, Chekov (*The Three Sisters, Uncle Vanya, Tobacco Damages Your Health*), on the other, Verdi (*Traviata, Macbeth*).[8]

Chekov's deep nostalgia for the past and the aristocratic world which was doomed to crumble was similar to Visconti's; and in *The Three Sisters* Visconti started to stage his autobiography, something which from then onwards he was going to do more and more explicitly.

Visconti sent Escoffier a detailed sketch for the costumes throughout the play, specifying the shades and the moods; he also sent him a photograph of his mother wearing an afternoon coat at Grazzano-Visconti, which was used in that production. In fact Visconti brought the time of the play forward, so that it would coincide with the fashion he remembered, when his mother was already moving in that same kind of society.

New friends arrived. One such was Enrico Medioli, a young man from Parma, defiantly dressed in red cashmere, who became Visconti's close friend and collaborator, and was near to him during his illness, until the end. Medioli was one of those middle-class young men, too intelligent to be content with provincial life and culture, who had been staggered by Visconti's productions and personality. The shock of recognition had been the stimulus; he, like others, needed to develop his talent in a new environment. From Parma there was also Maurizio Chiari, a witty decorator with a wonderful eye; and Alberto Arbasino, a young writer who was publishing articles about the Sitwells and Old Vic productions, and who came from near Pavia; his writing displayed wit and culture, the novelty of an 'invented' language, plunging from opera to literature, from pre-pop to 'in' jokes. There was Filippo Sanjust, a sombre, intelligent man, who spoke numerous languages and dialects, lacing his conversation with quotations. These were all people who started 'growing' around Visconti, and because of him, in the post-war Italian cosmopolitan cultural world which could not have come about without him.

In the summer of 1952 Visconti went to stay with Suso Cecchi and her husband Fedele d'Amico, who had rented a house at Santa Marinella, at the seaside near Rome. He had just filmed an episode of *Siamo Donne* (*We Are Women*); it was fashionable (that is, profitable for the producers) to turn out films in episodes with four or five well-known directors and stars. This was a rather poor film in which the stars played themselves (Alida Valli for Franciolini; Ingrid Bergman for Rossellini; Isa Miranda for Zampa; and Anna Magnani for Visconti). But during that summer Visconti and Suso tried to work on different projects. One was a film called *Marcia Nunziale* (*The Wedding March*), which was a true story. It was inspired by a woman who had committed suicide and it was a negative judgement on the institution of marriage. From her tragedy and the collapse of her marriage, there followed the stories of the lawyers, their interests and their marriages, and the film was meant to be a cry of need, a demand for divorce, but because of the power of the Church and the Christian Democrats, the producers refused to finance such a project. They suggested something 'safer', like a historical film, a film with 'production value' in colour. The producers, Lux Films, knew that Visconti continued to be a particular target for attacks: in the following year, for example, Visconti could not stage *Il Trovatore* for the Maggio Musicale Fiorentino simply because he was a well-known Communist.

So Visconti turned his attention to a short story by Camillo Boito called *Senso*. Apart from Chekov's monologue, *Tobacco Damages Your Health*, and Euripides' *Medea*, both staged in Milan (Mario Chiari did the costumes for both), 1953 was almost entirely taken up with working on *Senso*. This was to be an amazing achievement, a superb film and a breakthrough: it was the first time that history had been treated seriously in a film, instead of merely as an excuse for telling a story: in *Senso* the fashion and the events of the time were respected, the portrait of the society was rigidly accurate, the story of the film was not an excuse for the historical background, and history became the protagonist.

Visconti, like most creators, worked best when strongly inspired by love; all his films were made as the result of a strong involvement on his part, and he referred to this quite often. *Senso*, the passionate story of an aristocratic woman who demeans herself for love, was made in his own image; he was Livia Serpieri, who almost revelled in debasing herself with an enemy soldier, a typical Austrian, younger than herself.

The Italian Risorgimento, the aspiration for freedom and the belief in a political change which in fact did not come about, reflected modern history, something which Visconti was living then, the turn of events after the liberation of Italy from the Fascist regime, the gradual take-over by the Christian Democrats, who had the same faces and *mores* as the old Fascist bosses. The development of the script of *Senso* went through various stages, changing continually, elaborating, even after filming had started. The opening sequence, which has remained a famous *tour de force*, shows the

Venice Opera House during a performance of *Il Trovatore*. After the credits, the caption: 'Venice, Spring 1866. The last months of the Austrian occupation of the Veneto. The Italian Government has signed a treaty of alliance with Prussia, the war of liberation is imminent.' On the stage, a tenor, dressed in thirteenth-century medieval style, sings *Di quella Pira l'orrendo fuoco* and the camera pans over the opera-house to reveal the Austrian officers filling the dress circle and, in the boxes, the Venetian aristocracy. As the tenor finishes his famous aria, in which he urges his men to attack, and as the chorus sings *All'armi, all'armi*! (To arms! To arms!), some patriots are seen passing leaflets from hand to hand; the act of the opera ends, a girl shouts 'Foreigners out of Venice!' and a shower of patriotic rosettes in the Italian national colours covers the muted applause of the Austrian soldiers, dressed in beautiful white uniforms, and the enthusiastic clapping of the Italians: in Technicolor the drama has started in a profusion of magnificent details. The good-looking and spiteful Austrian officer, Lieutenant Franz Mahler (Farley Granger), makes an offensive remark about the Italians and the Marquis Roberto Ussoni (Massimo Girotti) challenges him to a duel. From a box, Countess Livia Serpieri (Alida Valli) has seen what has happened; Ussoni, her cousin, is an underground leader of the patriotic movement. She, a woman of the aristocracy, faithfully married to an older, conventional man, decides to go and see Franz Mahler and persuades the cynical officer to abandon the duel: drama is for the stage, she reminds him nervously. The operatic drama on-stage, instead, develops in real life, and intentionally Visconti twinned the two, pointing out that opera is purer and more economical in its description of passions than other forms of theatre. Instead of fighting the duel, Franz denounces Ussoni; Livia sees him again, while Usssoni is sent into exile; the Austrian officer follows her, through the night, from *piazzetta* to *calle*, his white cloak a ghostly apparition in a picturesquely blue, unforgettable Venice. They fall in love and spend time together in a boarding-house; then Franz leaves. Livia waits for his return and one day a messenger comes and gives her an address: Livia rushes out, thinking to find Franz, and her husband, Count Serpieri, secretly follows her; when she is about to confess to her husband, the door of the secret *rendez-vous* opens and Ussoni is there to tell Livia that he has clandestinely returned to Venice in order to collect money for the partisan cause. Livia is so tormented by the knowledge that she would have preferred to find Franz and that she has forgotten about her cousin and the partisans, that she confesses to her husband; but the latter chooses to disbelieve her, thinking that Livia wants to protect her cousin. Anyway, the weak Count Serpieri, who previously sided with the Austrians and had 'repudiated' Ussoni, now wants to make friends with him: the political tide has changed, turning against Austria. The Serpieris leave for their country villa (Lonedo, Palladio's first design for a country house) and Franz breaks in. She hides him, makes love to him, adores his sleeping features: but he wants the money to bribe a doctor to declare him unfit for military service. His reasoning is not totally despicable: battles are fierce and bloody, and if he loves her he must be near her; he could desert, but if he were to be caught, he would be shot. With a medical certificate he could be in Verona, near his regiment, and live for her. Livia gives him the money collected for the partisans: by now she has totally debased herself, she has lost her faith in the cause and she has betrayed Ussoni's trust. The deep effect of this scene is underlined by the music (Bruckner's Seventh Symphony), as she wanders along corridors, desperate, in a black shawl. In spite of the fact that Franz has told her not to join him in Verona, Livia goes and finds him drunk, a wreck, in the company of a young prostitute, and he insults her, wounding her deeply. She takes her final debasing revenge: she goes to the Austrian command to denounce him as a deserter. The Austrian general, who understands her motivation, urges her to reconsider her decision: denunciation is the worst infamy. Franz faces the firing squad and Livia crawls through the streets, surrounded by squalid and drunken soldiers. Livia is morally dead, Franz has been shot. At the end of the film Austria is celebrating the victory of Custoza, but it is a crumbling empire and as the Austrian empire declines, Italy is taken over by the bourgeois state. Livia's husband, an opportunist whom she has never loved, moves from the Austrian side to that of the Risorgimento; the survival of Serpieri and the disappearance of the idealist, the pure Ussoni, are a strong message in the film, and the political parallel between nineteenth-century and post-1943 Italy is clear: the nation which emerged from the war of liberation was not, after all, different from what it had been before. The new élite is the same as the old: the film shows implicitly the lack of ability of the Italians to change their ruling class.

An important sequence in *Senso* was censored by the Ministry of Defence: Ussoni arrives with the partisan forces but is informed by the regular army, by officialdom, that his services are not required. The partisans were Left-wing, an embarrassment to the new Italian monarchy. The final victory should not and could not be shared with the Left; it was the army's job either to lose or to win.

Visconti was therefore desecrating the myth of the Risorgimento; *Senso* struck at Italian nationalism. Visconti described his aims thus: 'To begin with I had thought of *Senso* as a historical film, I even wanted it to be called *Custoza* after the battle, but there was a cry of indignation: the production company, the minister, censorship ... at the beginning they didn't even tolerate the title *Senso*; during the shooting of the film the title was *Summer Tempest* [*Uragano d'estate*]. My intention was to trace a picture of Italian history, in the course of which would be portrayed the personal story of Countess Serpieri; but even that, after all, was the representation of a certain class. Even the ending was different: filmed at night time, in a street in Trastevere.'

The first version did not end with the death of Franz: one saw Livia walk past drunken soldiers and the final sequence showed a young Austrian, totally drunk, who sang a song of victory and, while crying, he shouted 'Long live Austria.' But the producers thought it 'dangerous'. Visconti, of course, did not agree: 'For me it was much more beautiful. One left Franz to his own affairs, we gave up Franz's story! It didn't matter whether he died or not! There was no point in seeing him executed. So we were left with her, who ran to denounce him. She passed among prostitutes and became a sort of tart herself. Then she fled, shouting 'Franz! Franz!', and we panned on to the young soldier, symbol of those who paid for victories and really cried, cried, shouting 'Long live Austria!' I had to cut a great deal and the negative was burnt . . . the real ending of *Senso* was that young soldier, a small Austrian farmer who had no responsibility and who cried because he was drunk. Or rather, he sang because he was drunk and cried because he was a man, he cried 'Long live Austria!' on the day of a victory which was empty, because soon Austria will be destroyed, as Franz said in his room. This was *Senso*. . . .'[9]

Colour was used as a means of expression, the shades were suggestive, sometimes invented, as in the Venice sequence where Livia's glowing awakening to sensuality made the use of colour an intrinsic part of the story.

Franz was not a clear-cut 'baddy', but the son of a dying empire, who recited Heine; Livia had the haughty arrogance of her birth. Alida Valli, who had never been a remarkable actress, although a very popular one in Italy, emerged as an unforgettable Countess Serpieri. Visconti's first idea had been to cast Ingrid Bergman and Marlon Brando. But Rossellini would not allow Bergman to make the film, about which she was very sad, she told Visconti. Lux Film Productions did not want Marlon Brando and insisted on Granger.

Visconti had asked Marlon Brando to come for a film test and he was enthusiastic about the young actor's professionalism; Brando's cynical features made him the perfect Austrian soldier of the decaying empire. Brando had read a rather bad translation of the script, which was later given to Tennessee Williams to render into English. Anyway, the producers declared that Brando was finished as an actor and that the up-and-coming star to launch was Farley Granger.

Once again Piero Tosi was summoned: Visconti wanted him at all costs. Tosi did not want to work with Visconti because he was terrified of him; Visconti sent Tosi terrible letters and even got the Minister for the Arts to intervene. When Tosi finally accepted, he went to Rome only to discover that Luchino had disappeared for three months in order to study and find the locations. Then Tosi spent two months with him on Ischia; Visconti would lock him up in the tower so that he would have to work all day. A number of people were staying at La Colombaia; they went to the sea and sometimes Tosi went too, but he was shy; he was a boy from the provinces, and he refused to go to the beach, to be naked in such beautiful company, which played games and seemed so at ease. Luchino worked, too, and made others work: from them he took what he liked. He demanded that Tosi should restrict and reduce until a design became as pure as possible, a pictorial abstraction. Visconti unlocked Tosi from the tower: 'Is the work ready?' he would ask and pick up the drawings which he liked. He wanted everything to be exact and was attentive to detail. And what he decided became law, it was not a subject for discussion.

Visconti was now the great director surrounded by the respect which follows a Maestro, and after *Senso* he reached the peak of his fame. When he entered a studio, a theatre, any place, the electricians and other workers fell silent. He projected a sense of discipline; but he could also be sensitive to the mood of actors. During the shooting of *Senso* there was a moment of great tension when Alida Valli was acting a scene with a peasant who could not remember his lines and, on the twenty-third take, the peasant, who was playing a coachman, once again got the lines wrong. 'I cannot go on any longer!' Alida Valli said, exhausted. Visconti turned to the crew: 'Madame Valli is tired, we'll break now, tomorrow we start again. It's her face which will be appearing on the screen, and if this is what she wants to do....' But he reminded her that she had responsibilities towards the film, too. For Alida Valli, *Senso* was a tremendous effort but it was the most important film of her career.

The making of *Senso* was full of 'disasters' – indeed Tosi remembers the first few days of work. They were filming at the Fenice Theatre in Venice very early in the morning. In the nineteenth-century theatre only men and prostitutes occupied the stalls, and when Luchino arrived he saw the men wearing black top hats. He screamed at Tosi and Escoffier, 'Ignoramuses! Imbeciles!' because in those days they wore grey (not black) top hats at the opera. 'If you had read Stendhal or Balzac with more attention,' he said to them, 'you would have known.'

One hot, sunny day, while filming a sequence of *Senso* with the peasants working in the fields, a peasant offered Tosi and some of the men a glass of sweet wine and so they lay drinking in the hay in the granary. Aldo, the cameraman, told Luchino, who was looking for them, where they were and what they were doing. They were four or five minutes late for filming, something which Visconti could not tolerate. Faced with the sight of the young men, relaxed and a bit groggy from the wine and heat, a rather sensual scene, Visconti started shouting: they were all to go home and stay away for two or three days. But Tosi was forgiven – an unusual sign of favour.

While Verdi gave *Senso* its musical backbone, Visconti also used the Teutonic architectonics of Bruckner to accompany some scenes of the film. He had asked for advice from Fedele d'Amico, a musicologist, and when Visconti said that he wanted to put Bruckner in *Senso*, d'Amico told him that it was folly. 'In fact it was perfect,' d'Amico said later. 'I hate Bruckner, I don't understand how people who go to the cinema could take pleasure in listening to him; nevertheless, it worked.'

When *Senso* was shown at the Venice Film Festival officialdom decided to boycott it. It created havoc; the authorities said that it defamed the Italian armed forces. The film critic of *Osservatore Romano*, the daily paper of the Vatican, was a member of the jury that year and maintains that the Christian Democrat Minister for the Arts told him to go to the Festival with a large sum of money and make sure that *Giulietta e Romeo*, a mediocre film by Castellani, won the first prize; on no account was the prize to be given to *Senso* because both film and director were Communist. When the critic in question, Piero Regnoli, answered that he had to see the films before making any promises, the Ministry sent somebody else to intervene with 'the members of the jury who, without my knowledge, were almost all bribed'. *Senso* did not get the prize;[10] *Giulietta e Romeo* did. Curiously enough, Marlon Brando, who acted in *On The Waterfront*, was also a loser at the same Festival: the jury opted for Jean Gabin. In the United Kingdom, *Senso* was screened as a dubbed travesty called *The Wanton Countess*, and in America it was never shown because it was thought the public would not stomach a hero who made his mistress give him money.

The enthusiasm of the inventive post-war years was over; Luchino began to perceive the strength of Italian '*Transformismo*', that everything should change so that everything should remain the same; Visconti photographed and captured this concept with contained anger, and because what he portrayed was true, his films were disturbing. Visconti probably did not realize how perversely prophetic he had been, but it is all too clear today how right he was in his analysis.

9
Working with Callas

Opera was not a new channel in Visconti's life: it had been the coherent stream running through his films, plays and education. Many times his projects for operas had been frustrated, either because he had been busy, had not been sufficiently interested in a specific opera or because of political reasons. But the fact remains that impresarios continued to approach Visconti, and that Visconti went on looking for the right opportunity, because he wanted to stage opera in 'his' way, in a way which was to change the role of the opera director. Opera until then was not considered 'cultural', its conventions being so far removed from reality as to alienate the educated public; that an opera should even have an 'important' director was an innovation in itself.

On the other hand, Visconti wanted to work in opera because he wished to change its concept: beneath the conventions of the libretto, he believed, opera was not only 'cultural' but alive. His concept was mainly due to the fact that he had grown up at La Scala, where he had seen opera conducted by Toscanini, a man who believed in the cultural and topical elements of this art form. Visconti was responsible for putting opera back on the cultural circuit and for giving it social prestige. He knew that the sweeping passions of opera were easily understood by the public, which is why it was so popular, and with his highly professional background he wanted to stage opera as rigorously as he did films and plays. Intellectuals did not go to the opera then; opera, like the *corrida* in Spain, was regarded as a self-indulgent pastime of the lower classes.

Faced with the problem of staging opera, Visconti decided to take it at its face value: he was going to reproduce opera as it was written. The key to the sets, to the changes of mood and tempo, and to the level of acting would be dictated by the music. He was essentially a man who always acted out of conviction and did not fear the ridiculous, which he seldom perceived, and in any case did not see in opera. Neither did he believe in justifying opera: if we understand and enjoy the conventions of the stage, we go to the theatre; otherwise we stay at home.

In 1951, Visconti had backed a new production of *Il Turco in Italia*. He had already become an addict of Maria Callas's particular tone of voice – a vast range, with husky, odd middle tones, not in the pure *bel canto* tradition, but intent, vibrant and expressive. La Scala was rather cold towards Maria Meneghini Callas, because Antonio Ghiringhelli, its general administrator, supported another more conventional-sounding soprano, Renata Tebaldi; between the latter and Callas there was already a rivalry, mostly created by the press and by fans. According to Visconti, 'in actual fact they went about their work and paid no attention to each other.'[1] On the other hand, Maria Callas had not made it easy by being quoted in the press as saying: 'If the time comes when my dear friend Renata Tabaldi sings Norma or Lucia on one night, then Violetta, La Gioconda, or Medea the next – then and only then shall we be rivals. Otherwise it is like comparing champagne with cognac. No, with Coca-Cola.'[2]

Certainly Visconti preferred champagne and he already had his eye on Callas – and she on him.

'For all of us discovering Callas was important,' said Alberto Fassini, who was to become an opera director himself. 'Luchino used to go and see her in Rome, he listened to her rehearsing, he sent huge bunches of roses to her hotel. They had become friends, but there was no talk about working together then.'

In January 1952 Ghiringhelli had written to Visconti about the possibility, suggested by Visconti, of staging *Don Carlos*, an opera which was out of the repertoire at the time. Ghiringhelli also asked Visconti whether he would stage *Debora e Jaele* by Ildebrando Pizzetti, a contemporary composer who did not interest him. This proposal was not accepted, but in September he tried again, suggesting Pizzetti's new opera *Cagliostro*, which was to open the season together with *l'Incoronazione di Poppea*. Visconti answered with a long telegram (the telephone hardly worked, it took hours to get through from Milan to Rome and vice versa) saying he was not interested in a contemporary work, he was looking for a nineteenth-century opera.

His name as a director had already appeared in La Scala's programme for the 1953-4 season, not with an opera but for the *Azione Coreografica* (Choreographic Action) of *Mario e il Mago*, for which, as we have seen, he had also written the libretto. But *Mario e il Mago* had to wait because the public at La Scala had booed the appearance of a car on their sacred stage in another opera, *La Gita in Campagna*, by Peregallo; the authorities, fearing that the various bicycles necessary for *Mario e il Mago* would provoke the public's further fury, cancelled the performance.

Also in September the San Carlo Opera House in Naples asked Visconti to direct Verdi's *Otello*, but he turned it down because he could only have rehearsed with the company for nine days (the opera was then poorly directed by Rossellini). In July 1953, Antonio Ghiringhelli suggested *Rigoletto*. However, Visconti was working on *Senso* and could not spare the time. In 1954 he asked Visconti again: would he like to direct Spontini's *Agnese di Hohenstaufen*? Once again Visconti was unable to do so. Never the less, he was shortly to make his opera début with another work by Spontini, about which he said:

> *La Vestale* is a difficult opera to stage because it needs great style. This Maria gave it. For me she was a wonderful instrument, which could be played as I wished and which responded in an inspired way. How different from contending with a singer from the old school! As the High Priestess, Ebe Stignani was hopeless with her two stock gestures, worse than a washerwoman on stage. Unbearable! She was the antithesis of Maria, who absorbed and grew from day to day. How, I don't know. By some uncanny theatrical instinct, if put on the right course, she always exceeded your hopes. How beautiful she and Corelli [the tenor] looked during the love duet in the temple, the sacred flame flickering from the altar; they looked like pure physical beauty, figures from neo-classicism, reborn.[3]

There was much that they shared: both Callas and Visconti were extremely professional and sought perfection, both had a sense of their own value and a passion for their work; they had stature and they were tyrants in their own way. They were both strangely insecure, needing the reassurance of each other's fame, and in spite of their overwhelming success neither was happy. Both were also secretive. Their partnership created a musical feast, the rebirth of opera as a cultural spectacle, as drama, as beauty.

They worked closely together: Callas wanted Visconti near, always. She had fallen in love with him and become yet another of his victims; but he, this time, had fallen for her too.

Adriana Asti, a tiny, delightful actress, describes those days: 'At Via Salaria there was Franco Zeffirelli and la Callas, who sang and played at the piano: she was in love with Luchino and he with her; he was always rather in love with the people who fell for him. He was a great conqueror and he wanted people to love him and he, in his way, reciprocated, also vexing them at the same time; he was extremely jealous of these people: he was terrified if they had other friends.'

They would go to the sea at Ostia, near Rome, Maria and Luchino and the 'court'. Maria would undo her hair which fell, black and long, around her waist and reminded Luchino of his mother's. He caressed her hair and admired her trim body: by then Maria only ate lettuce leaves. She looked like a vestal and moved like one.

La Vestale was written in 1807, at the height of the Napoleonic era. It tells the story of a vestal virgin who betrays her gods and sacrifices her virginity for love. The scenery and costumes, which Visconti asked Piero Zuffi to do (he had to redesign them twenty times), were neo-classical in style; the perspective suggested vast airy spaces.

There are several notes of Visconti's on the movement of the chorus; a spectacular funeral procession with priestesses carrying garlands was one unforgettable image. Movements had been taken from Canova's sculptures, from the paintings of Ingres and David; visually the inspiration came from a grand, neo-classical style which corresponded to the music. When the curtain rose, Callas was seen veiled, leaning against a pillar of the proscenium which had been incorporated into the scenery. Visconti and Callas had worked endlessly at her 'gestures': 'We selected them from the French tragediennes, some from Greek drama, for this was the kind of actress she could be – classical. Today some famous singers try to imitate what Maria did, but they only make fools of themselves.'[4]

At a certain moment [Visconti said] Maria began to fall in love with me. It was a stupid thing, all in her mind. But like so many Greeks, she had a possessive streak, and there were many terrible jealous scenes. She hated Corelli, because he was handsome. It made her nervous – she was wary of beautiful people. She was always watching to see that I didn't give him more attention than I gave her. And she disliked the baritone, Enzo Sordello – who knows why? – and did not want to do a scene with him in the last act. 'Look, Maria' I told her, 'we can't change the baritone or the opera just to please you!' But I could forgive her anything because she did all I asked so scrupulously, so precisely and so beautifully. What I demanded she gave me, never adding anything of her own. Sometimes during a rehearsal I would say, 'Come on, Maria, do a little by yourself, do something you like,' but then she'd ask, 'What should I do? How am I to place this hand? I don't know where to put it.' The simple fact was that, because of her crazy infatuation, she wanted me to command her every step.[5]

Visconti, La Scala and Callas formed a trio which had all the magic ingredients: the excitement of quality, novelty and that elegant glamour which Visconti carried with him. People queued for days and booked in advance – something unusual then. Although the public realized that these performances were exceptionally good, the critics were hostile: Visconti and Callas were massacred, insulted and regarded with suspicion; the predominant attitude was that Visconti was a dilettante, a lord from the Renaissance who enjoyed himself playing the opera director, in direct contradiction of his political affiliations.

Others took Visconti more seriously: Toscanini went to a rehearsal of *La Vestale*, which was to open the 1954–5 Scala season in December. Victor de Sabata, who was then the artistic director of La Scala, Antonino Votto, the conductor of that production, and Maria Callas went to greet him. To be back in Milan gave Visconti a strange pleasure, the feeling of recapturing the scent of the fog, of reliving dramatic and happy moments of his childhood, of seeing his brothers and Toscanini, of working at La Scala, that bastion of Milanese life which had been part of the Viscontis' way of life also. Camilla Cederna, who interviewed him at the time (she knew him well already), described him physically:

A pale man with black eyes and a sad expression goes in and out of La Scala these afternoons, while rehearsing the ballet of *La Vestale* in rigid neo-classical style. He is still a young man, in black and white, without shades, and talks with passionate violence. The critics from the extreme Right detest him, reproaching him for having bartered the helmet of the Savoy Cavalry for a working man's cap – while on the Left, they reproach him for having kept too elegant a touch in directing his plays, the hand of a lord; while those who love the theatre praise him and so do the young, who consider him a Maestro of direction. One can already speak about 'his' school; his well-known pupils are Franco Zeffirelli, Mario Chiari, Franco Rosi, Rinaldo Ricci and Francesco Maselli; among the designers, Marcel Escoffier and Piero Tosi.[6]

On the first night of *La Vestale*, Toscanini sat in Ghiringhelli's box and at the end, responding to frenetic applause, Maria Callas walked over to his box and handed him one of the bouquets sent by her admirers. The critics were lukewarm, but the public and, above all, musicologists applauded the production of the opera. After the performance Toscanini and his daughter Wally, Carlo Maria Giulini and Visconti went to a restaurant to celebrate. Visconti recalled events thus:

> Later il Maestro called me. He said: 'I very much like what you are doing but you must understand that my eyesight is poor. I find this Callas woman very good. She has a beautiful voice and is an interesting artist, but her diction is unintelligible.... Opera is theatre and the words are more important than the music.' I was stupefied – surely Toscanini did not mean this – and I explained that Maria Callas was a Greek-American and didn't speak perfect Italian. But Toscanini stuck to his point. 'No! No! You *must* hear every word, otherwise it's a concert.' You see, Toscanini was a man of the theatre. He came from a century when people attended opera as we do movies and plays. Can you imagine anyone today watching a film not understanding a word but being fully satisfied?[7]

After the war, Toscanini had returned to Milan from the States and at La Scala he had conducted concerts, but no opera, because at his age he found it too fatiguing. He was eighty-seven by then, but still energetic and full of ideas. Luchino Visconti, the friend of his daughter Wanda when they were children, the boy whom the Maestro had seen at Via Durini so often, whom he had shouted at when he was too noisy, who would stage plays with Wanda as the leading actress, was the perfect director to stage the *Falstaff* which he wanted to conduct.

Visconti went to see Toscanini at his house. 'At the time, the small opera house, La Piccola Scala, was under construction. The plan was for il Maestro to inaugurate it with *Falstaff*, which he wanted me to stage. I often went to his house to discuss this, and one day he expressed the wish to watch one of my rehearsals.'[8]

Toscanini liked the straightforward way in which Visconti approached opera – that was his own concept too: to take a valid masterpiece and analyse it, enhancing the context. He had sent Visconti a copy of his recording of *Falstaff* (1950) with a dedication: he hoped that their work would be fruitful. To Visconti, Toscanini explained his ideas with lucidity: he wanted 'the real *Falstaff* in which the characters would act the comedy even more than sing it.' When attending rehearsals of *La Vestale*, the Maestro would discuss Spontini and make observations about the performance, but he would always go back to 'their' *Falstaff*. 'Who would ever have thought,' Toscanini used to say, 'that I was going to work with the boy whom I used to scold for riding his bicycle too fast with his books and Wanda on the handlebars?'⁹

Falstaff was announced for the 1954-5 La Scala season; but La Piccola Scala was not ready and Toscanini insisted on staging Verdi's most mature opera there and not at La Scala, because he wanted to conduct *Falstaff* in more intimate surroundings, as he had done in Busseto in 1913 and 1926. 'Why don't you young people try to think up something different and suggest it to me?' Toscanini would say to the grandson of the president of the board who had first engaged him in 1898. 'I can only imagine the old scenes – the usual tavern, the usual garden. Suggest something fresh, something nice.' After one performance at La Scala, they dined together and Toscanini smiled at Visconti and drank to 'our *Falstaff*'.¹⁰

But a few days later, when Toscanini started discussing the casting of Falstaff with Ghiringhelli, he became so happy and worked himself into such a state that he had a mild heart attack. Wally Toscanini told Visconti that their *Falstaff* could not be translated into reality: her father was in no state to conduct it.

Later Visconti described how Toscanini had listened to his own recording of *Falstaff*, beating time as conductors do, already working at it – but he had forgotten a few bars. He fell into a deep melancholy. Toscanini then said, 'I am going to die far from everybody, in some wood, in America. Nobody must see me!'¹¹ He was ashamed of his old age, of his mind which no longer worked well, and yet he had not lost his lucidity. After a concert at which they had heard Beethoven's Seventh Symphony conducted by a German, Visconti related that Toscanini said to him, 'Those trumpets! Really! Why are they so loud? I came back home and played my Seventh on the record player, in order to check if my trumpets also came in so loudly. No, they came in right, not so strong.'¹²

La Piccola Scala opened in December 1955 with *Il Matrimonio Segreto*, conducted by Sanzogno and directed by Strehler; thirteen months later Toscanini was dead.

With Toscanini living in seclusion in an American forest in order to hide his old age, La Scala lost that halo of continuity, that touch of magic, though it remained the most beautiful opera-house in the world, with its maze of corridors, the ushers in stylish livery, the large dressing-rooms, the stairs and the glittering theatre. Nowhere holds the same spell for an opera lover. Even for a man of Visconti's success, to be working at La Scala and to have been picked by Toscanini must have felt like an extraordinary privilege. 'But my goal is Verdi,' said Visconti at the time.¹³

Before staging *La Traviata*, his 'point of arrival', Visconti directed Callas in *La Sonnambula* by Bellini, which opened on 5 March 1955. It was a triumph of *bel canto*. 'Callas was never that capricious myth created by the press,' said

Piero Tosi, who recalled the impression that she created during the famous sleep-walking scene in the second act:

> Her steps were like those of a ballerina and when she stood still she took a dancer's fifth position. Of course Luchino had coached her in these details, but it was *how* she did them. Though the critics hated it, for me the second Act was the most beautiful of all – the Count's room at the inn, the neo-Gothic beams – the kind of wood that at night gives off the colour of pale violet. The Act and the mood were almost metaphysical. Half the stage was illuminated by the moon, the other half dappled with shadows and light; Callas entered from the rear, a sylphide tripping on a moonbeam. She crossed the stage on a diagonal of light, singing her dream of her fiancé, pretending to ascend the church steps for her wedding. She was enchanting. When the Count touched her shoulder, she fell to the floor, but very softly. Later, she had to lie on a sofa and her pose was exactly period Louis-Philippe – pure 1830. When the villagers arrived with lanterns, the moon faded and the spell was broken. One of the things critics complained about was that I had dressed the villagers like ladies and gentlemen – the women in shades of pink, grey, pearl, and the men in black with white gloves. But Luchino and I had intended to evoke a lost, divine, melancholy era. Critics never understand.[14]

For this opera, too – the story of a young maiden who is believed to be unfaithful to the local landowner because she sleep-walks at night – there exist Visconti's detailed notes on the movements of the chorus and several actions 'to invent'.

He must have been stimulated to stage *La Sonnambula* by Maria Callas and because the conductor was Leonard Bernstein. When, a decade later, he was asked by Sir David Webster, then the General Administrator of Covent Garden, to restage it there, he turned down the offer and handed over the London *Sonnambula* to Enrico Medioli and Filippo Sanjust.

Maria Callas was now transformed, not only physically but also intellectually: she dressed soberly and beautifully, her commanding profile was framed by jewels and her long black hair, which so pleased Visconti, was entwined in an elegant simple style. He gave her a great deal of advice about clothes and what to read. 'Poor Gian Battista', her husband, was almost nowhere to be seen.

In a filmed interview for French television, made at that time, Maria Callas, sitting on Visconti's left, was almost always in profile gazing at Visconti. Hers was the expression of the woman in love, proud of her man who is doing the talking, dominated and wanting to be dominated; she was not the aggressive woman in total command which had previously been her attitude, as Visconti recalled:

> To start with, Maria's infatuation had not abated and she seemed more possessive than ever. She couldn't bear me paying attention to anyone else, especially to Leonard Bernstein, our conductor, who was so amusing, such a wonderful friend. We were together a lot, and Maria spied on us even when we went outside the theatre to have a

coffee or take a little walk. Once Lennie and I went to visit her at her hotel because she had a painful carbuncle on her neck. When the moment came to leave, we said: 'Ciao, Maria! Get well!' and headed for the door. 'You stay here!' she commanded me, 'I don't want you to go off again with Lennie!' My God! in those days she could sometimes be an absolute fool.[15]

During that period at Casa Ricordi he met Gian Carlo Menotti, who was already famous and had come from the States for a performance of an opera of his at La Scala. They became good friends.

When, in *La Sonnambula*, Callas – kneeling next to the tomb – sang '*Ah, non credea*', she begged Visconti to be in the wings, close to her, in order to tell her if the tone of her voice had been pure and her phrasing good. And he had to lead her to the wings and prod her to go on. Each time he did so she would ask him to walk nearer the open stage. His presence made her feel happier and more secure, and she had even demanded that his scented handkerchief should be placed on a divan where she had to lie for her love scene. When Callas (Amina) awoke for her jubilant reunion with her fiancé, Visconti lit up the auditorium of La Scala, including the gigantic chandelier on the ceiling; the lights rose with the *cabaletta* of the aria. Visconti thus transformed Amina's grand finale into the coronation of Maria Callas as the great soprano of La Scala, its queen, its *prima donna assoluta*. It was both her triumph and Visconti's: everybody wanted to see the production and musicians travelled from all over the world to witness this gem.

It was, however, *La Traviata* by Giuseppe Verdi which Visconti had longed to stage. If *La Sonnambula* was an ideal vehicle to show off Maria Callas, *La Traviata*, which he staged in May 1955, was to show off his own approach to Verdi. When it was first performed *La Traviata* had created a scandal because it dealt with a contemporary subject – and its heroine was a prostitute. Visconti advanced the action of this opera to a date which was nearer to Visconti himself and to his family, because Violetta's tragedy, Marie Duplessis's or Marguerite Gautier's saga – that of paying for having loved, of becoming the victim of convention – was his mother's too. Indeed Maria Callas looked a bit like Donna Carla Visconti: tall, elegant and passionate, with long black hair; Visconti reinterpreted *La Traviata* with his mother in mind.

La Traviata is one of the most popular operas in the world, but it is also a complex work. In it the heroine, the only sympathetic person on the stage, is a prostitute; all the others around her reflect middle- and upper-class hypocrisy and act solely out of selfish motives. It is as modern now as when it first opened: how would a contemporary father from the upper-middle class react on learning that his only son has left everything for a prostitute who keeps him and that his daughter cannot marry because of the scandal?

Maria Callas delivered the realistic interpretation which Visconti had asked of her, the opposite of the stylized *Sonnambula* or *La Vestale*. When Violetta heard Alfredo's voice in Act One, she ran downstage to the window. It was nerve-racking to see Callas running towards the pit: she was so short-sighted and naturally did not wear glasses for performances.

The concept of this Violetta was close to Visconti's understanding of love: in the famous aria '*Ah, fors'è lui*', Violetta realizes that if she falls in love, she will lose her lucidity and her capacity to enjoy life: here is a woman who lives egoistically, taking from others, in danger of seeing her role reversed.

During rehearsals di Stefano often arrived late; he did not like Visconti's concept of *La Traviata* because it concentrated on Violetta. So there they were on the stage, she and Visconti, acting out the love scenes between Violetta and Alfredo.

'Luchino was very much in love with her,' Alberto Fassini said, 'and she was jealous of the oddest people. "I can't see you, but I smell you," she would say. They often saw each other, they rang each other up. He used to tell me "Your Maria rang," he knew how much I admired her.'

La Traviata was not hailed as a critical success, but the word went round that it was not to be missed. Claudio Abbado, who was then a student of twenty-two, went to La Scala to see this *Traviata* and to listen to a conductor he admired; he was amazed by the whole performance. A man of few words, Abbado remembered how exciting and perfect in its dramatic entirety *La Traviata* had been: 'It was magic and realistic at the same time. The character of Violetta had been rendered to the full.' In later years, Visconti talked to Abbado about working together, an opportunity that sadly never came about.

There were often incredible rows. Visconti felt that he had to be in command and not even La Scala intimidated him. When rehearsals took place, he did not want anybody on the stage apart from those who had to be there. If his orders were disobeyed or ignored, his voice would become more and more thunderous and he would scream, furious, like Jupiter in a rage. Once Visconti shouted at some people, 'I don't want anybody on the stage!' But the master of the chorus crawled from one side of the stage to the other. Visconti immediately jumped up like a hawk. 'This is a shit theatre! *Basta*! Have you finished walking up and down the theatre? I'll kick you in the arse!' At another time, he was with a friend and wanted to go backstage to see Callas, but an usher would not let him through. He got angry and uttered the futile words, 'You don't know who I am!' To which the usher answered, 'Yes, I do, and in the end we are the same, you and I, we'll both die!' Visconti, 'No! You will! I shall not!' He often laughed at the recollection of this exchange and it became a standing joke; he had been caught out – by himself – in a childish outburst.

On the other hand, he could also be extremely patient, working with Callas on the smallest detail until it was perfect. A week before going back to Rome, he went to see Maria in her dressing-room at La Scala; he wanted to thank her and to say goodbye. They had worked together magnificently.

During the intermission of Act Three of *La Traviata*, they exchanged sweet farewells and then he left her to change from her ball costume into the nightdress of Act Three, and he joined some friends having dinner at the Biffi Scala, the famous restaurant which is attached to the opera theatre. But a few minutes later, Luchino and his friends were startled by Maria's appearance in her ball gown, covered by a cloak. 'Go away!' he shouted, 'What are you doing here?' She embraced him with tears in her eyes. 'I had to see you once more and say goodbye again!' How terrible, Visconti thought, had she already changed into her Act Three costume and entered that smart restaurant in a nightgown! Visconti was prudish about those he loved, especially women, his women. He disapproved of *décolletée*, if they had lovers, or if they did not behave impeccably, in a rather Victorian fashion. He was even shocked if he saw his young nieces in a night-club.

His visit to Rome was in order to stage Arthur Miller's *The Crucible* and *Uncle Vanya*, another beautiful interpretation of Chekov. He was returning to the theatre and to his actors, a company he loved. But nothing was quite the same, because following a terrible scene between Visconti and Zeffirelli, Franco was ostracized by almost everybody: Visconti was all-powerful in the theatre.

The actress Lilla Brignone was looking for a director for *Lulù* by Bertolazzi, which she wanted to act with her own company. Neither Strehler not Visconti could do it, so she asked Zeffirelli. He was enthusiastically accepted and set to work, but when Visconti heard of this he let Lilla Brignone know that if she employed Franco Zeffirelli, she would never see him again. Lilla Brignone could not afford to spite the great man of the theatre and, without telling Franco the truth, she 'withdrew' her offer, but told the real reason to a third party. Naturally, in a matter of days the truth got back to Zeffirelli: 'A designer yes, a director never,' Visconti had pronounced.

Matters reached a climax when, in the middle of the night, opposite the Piccolo Teatro in Milan in the snow, the two had a very heated discussion and parted hating each other.

Zeffirelli had good grounds for his hostility. Visconti felt angered and humiliated at having been found out in a weakness – particularly strange in a man who liked to 'make' people and see those who had worked with him launched on a successful career. The truth was that Visconti did not want Zeffirelli to launch out on his own and be independent of him.

Over-night Zeffirelli's name became unmentionable. Bice Brichetto, who adored Visconti, suddenly realized that he would not speak to her. What had she done? Visconti had heard that she had talked to Zeffirelli. 'But how was I to know? Until yesterday you were the best of friends – at least warn me!' she told him.

In 1955 Visconti met Adriana Asti, who was acting in Lilla Brignone's company. She was pretty and very alert. 'Naturally I had fallen a bit in love with him, like everybody else. He came to see me rehearsing a play by Goldoni – *The Fan* – and, when he was in my dressing-room, he told me to discard a big wig I was supposed to wear: he gave me a little secret direction, ignoring the official director of the play. We became friends.'

She was Milanese, like him, and they would talk together in dialect. In November 1955 she played in *The Crucible*: 'It was a very difficult play and he was very nasty,' Adriana remembered; 'there were legends about his immense nastiness, and the way in which he frightened people. He was a bit cruel, he thought that actors should be dominated, but he could make stones act. He himself was a divine actor, he would play all the parts, and when he read a new script to us one thought, "My God! I'll never make it!" He was very gifted. He would reduce actors to the most infinite admiration for him – those who were more independent, who refused to yield to his conditions, would be thrown out. One actor once said: "I would do this differently." He was kicked out.'

Visconti even found the time to work on a kind of vaudeville, called *Festival*, in Milan: such shows were in fashion when, after so many years of poverty, there was a desire for luxury, leisure, feathers and sequins – but Visconti's conception of vaudeville was so expensive that *Festival* was cut down and only retained a few of Visconti's ideas – and his signature as a consultant.

He went back to Milan in April 1956 to stage *Mario e il Mago*, that 'choreographic action' for which he had written the libretto and which had been withdrawn from La Scala's season in 1954. Thomas Mann had died the previous year (1955) and maybe Visconti had lost faith in the work, but nevertheless it won the Diaghilev Prize. He started working on *Così fan Tutte* for the Salzburg Festival following an offer from Herbert von Karajan; Lila de Nobili had been engaged; but it fell through. It is a pity that Visconti did not stage this sublime opera at this time when he was at the peak of his inventiveness, authority and understanding. *Così fan Tutte* was (and is) rendered as a piquant comedy in that eighteenth-century mannered style of powdered dolls in pink and blue parlours, while in fact it is a sombre, realistic opera. But Visconti was never a great Mozartian although, with *La Locandiera*, he had touched the same chords.

In June 1956 *La Locandiera* was chosen for the Festival of Nations in Paris, and Visconti set to work again on that successful production; he returned to Paris in June, back to the city which had formed him, back to his restaurants, his favourite shops and to Coco Chanel.

Suso Cecchi d'Amico, who was with him on this and other journeys to Paris, enjoyed going around with him looking for a restaurant which no longer existed, or finding a little corner shop. One afternoon, Visconti asked her if she had brought a suitable dress for the opening night; Suso Cecchi d'Amico, who is a rather stern woman, said she had brought a smart short black dress. 'Impossible!' he cried, and since this conversation was in the Faubourg St Honoré and they were near Cardin's, Visconti decided to go in and have a look: a suitable dress could certainly be found and, since Cardin was a friend of his, the house would be able to make the alterations very quickly. 'I was in despair. I couldn't afford such a dress, but Luchino could not understand it because he had no idea of money. Nor could I let him buy it for me. I was hoping not to find a dress which suited me.' Instead, alas, Visconti practically dismantled the shop, and a suitable dress was found. Feeling ashamed and intimidated she turned it down, saying that she did not want it after all. And for the first night of *La Locandiera* Suso wore her short dress. *La Locandiera* was a great success in Paris: it was Visconti's first play to be seen abroad and the French public was to become his most faithful.

While in Paris Visconti saw Horst again: they always remained friends, but there were things which irritated Horst. Visconti enquired after Horst's mother. 'I answered: "She is in East Germany." He said: "She must be happy then, it's wonderful to live in a Communist country." I replied: "Last week she went to a village to get some coal because she couldn't find any and her mini-wagon collapsed. My mother spent all night in the cold wagon in the rain rather than abandon the coal." There was no answer.' Visconti believed then, in a strangely Teutonic way, that Communist societies had achieved true Communism and that any reports to the contrary were merely propaganda. So convinced was he of this that, when he learned of the Hungarian Revolution, he was profoundly upset and in November 1956 he signed a collective letter addressed to the Soviet Writers' Union deploring the invasion of Hungary. Many famous people had not wanted to sign or, even worse, had evaded the issue: they were not at home, they did not answer the telephone, they did not want to commit themselves. Fedele d'Amico recalled that 'when we asked for his signature, he knew immediately that he should sign the letter.' It was important that the signatories should belong or be close to the Communist Party, not outside it.

Visconti directed two more operas with Maria Callas in 1957, both at La Scala. *Anna Bolena* by Donizetti was their first joint success, recognized by both public and critics, but although Visconti took Donizetti seriously, he did not feel for the score in the same way as he did for some other operas. In *Iphigenia in Tauris* by Gluck, Visconti dismissed the Greek classic style and, instead, reflected the baroque music by using Tiepolo's frescoes at Palazzo Labia in Venice as his main source of inspiration. Maria Callas, in white satin, tiara and pearls, was an apparition out of one of the *trompe l'oeil* paintings on the palazzo's staircases. Both productions were successful, but they were more mannered and less inspired. Anyway the great statement of opera as theatre, which embraced the direction, the setting, hard work and conviction, had already been made. Maria Callas had been crowned: she had shown herself to be not only a superb singer but also a splendid actress.

Their special partnership came to an end when, in 1959, Callas met Onassis and, although the affair enhanced Callas's social fame and position, it damaged her singing career. Visconti was furious: 'the vulgarity of the creature, those eyes like a dog!'; the 'tortoise' he nicknamed Onassis; 'and with poor Meneghini around, poor Battista!' as if he himself had behaved any better! Visconti never talked about his affair with Callas, because he hated to publicize his private life. In a way, he was more likely to let others know about his relationships with men than with women, and he had been very fond of Maria Callas. Not only did he admire her, but he felt he had made her into a real star. Later, when she had lost her voice and started appearing in recitals with di Stefano, Visconti commented sarcastically that 'those two should go around with a begging bowl'. He was saddened by her appearances on the stage once her voice had gone, because he felt 'his' Maria was humiliating herself.

Later Callas talked negatively about Visconti. Since every opera critic always said that she had been 'created' by him, she tried to demolish Luchino Visconti's reputation as a director by ridiculing him. On the same occasion she said that Mozart's music was poor; on both counts she was wrong.

10
The Other Family

Visconti had become the centre around which the young, the intellectuals and the beautiful gravitated, a point of reference for the theatre as well as the cinema and the opera world; at the same time, those who did not belong to his world felt excluded. He had become a sort of demi-god, an enigmatic Sphinx, important, universally known, like a star; and, like a star, maligned, envied and admired. His position of total privilege irritated many; he was derided for his political stand, for his homosexuality, for his love of luxury and for being privileged; some of the comments, printed nicknames and gossip stung him and, though he pretended not to notice, vulgarity humiliated him.

The fact is that the people who were excluded, or felt they were, resented him; after such success, a general irritation, always aroused in Italy by those considered too fortunate, began to spread. He felt it and although he pretended not to be affected by hostility, he was, because he was still vulnerable.

The end of the 1950s was an incredibly busy period of his life – theatre, opera, friends, admirers, enemies. A great deal of work, and each film corresponded to a passion; a love affair renewed him, but he was captivated only by those who treated him badly, by those who, after resisting, yielded and then would torment him. The energy that Visconti consumed by being in love was frankly amazing. If the object of his passion did not humiliate him, Visconti would humiliate his partner; there were some terrifying scenes in which Visconti would reduce the momentary object of his love to tears, showering him with insults: it was Visconti's vengeance on the boy for not having been debased by him. His was a violent, passionate nature and, in his constant need to be loved and humiliated, it was also a very insecure nature. He was the product of a disorderly family, of lack of real affection in his childhood and, however often he exalted his family in interviews and recollections, he felt towards it the masochistic attraction of the rejected, the only relationship which ultimately satisfied him. Any fulfilled love failed from the start.

He would never talk about his homosexuality, even with his most intimate friends. Antonello Trombadori once made a joke, which he regretted at once. He was reading a newspaper and saw that a homosexual who had played a small part in a film by Visconti had been murdered. 'Luchino,' he said, 'I don't want to think that one day I'll open a newspaper and find your name like this.' To which Visconti replied that there were different kinds of homosexuals, that he would never have 'gone with a tart', that he needed to build up a relationship and that he needed to fall in love. Later on in his life, an episode took place which underlined his attitude. He was dining with friends in New York when one of them asked Visconti to take him to a 'gay' bar. Visconti exploded with anger: 'A gay bar?' he thundered, his voice carrying all his contempt. 'When I was young, homosexuality was a forbidden fruit, something special, a fruit to be gathered with care, not what it is today – hundreds of homosexuals showing off, dancing together in a gay bar. What do you want to go there for?'

He loved to go to the movies. 'We would go to the cinema almost every night, at 10.30,' said Peppino Patroni Griffi, the playwright. Once, when they both went to see *Doctor Zhivago*, which Visconti liked very much, as they were leaving the cinema, Visconti whispered to Griffi: 'Let's go upstairs and see it all over again, hiding, otherwise they'll lynch me.' He knew he was not 'supposed' to like the film intellectually. He still read a great deal and from France he would receive all the new publications. In those days most objects were not as costly as they are now and not many people had his culture, taste and money: Visconti bought a series of drawings by Odilon Redon in Vienna and he 'discovered' Chini, a turn-of-the-century Italian painter who had designed sets for Puccini. Patroni Griffi recalled, 'His houses were full of paintings. What didn't he spend on gardening! He was not a modern man. He always portrayed an era, a special time of history, a special family, with that key character who was his mother. The mother in *The Damned*, the mad mother in *Sandra*, the mother in *Bellissima* – all portrayed the mythical and mysterious character of his own mother. He spoke about her little, but as if talking of a goddess. I never heard him talk about his father, but he loved all those episodes of the "good" Milan, connected with La Scala.'

What outsiders called with contempt and envy his 'court' (his friends, admirers, former lovers, actors and actresses) had become his family. He really loved the company of his friends, especially when this was not demanding, requiring no real discussion or deep thought, but laughter and games. He transferred his strong paternal sense to these young people; his concern was to make something out of them, to make them work. 'After Luchino's death, for example,' said Suso Cecchi d'Amico, 'a magazine purchased Luchino's letters to Helmut Berger. Everybody worried about the scandal, but they were the letters of an angry father: you can't do this, you can't spend so much, you mustn't behave like that. . . . He had difficult children.'

He enjoyed his family; he would go and stay at Sperlonga with a niece of his, and there 'Uncle Luchino' delighted in playing games with the children. Once again, as he once had with his sisters when they were children, he would dress up in elaborate ways. He used to be '*zia Amalia*' (Aunt Amalia), as his sister revealed:

> He would force everybody to work and sew and prepare his costume. He wore a delicate veil over his face and nylon stockings and lipstick and high heels and a skirt. He needed a week to prepare such costumes, imitating the boring old ladies who came to tea; he also wore a large hat with lace and gloves without fingers. Aunt Amalia had really existed; she was an aunt of Luchino's, but she had been dead forty years. Then he would become a witch and would switch off all the lights and the children would run away, desperate . . . [his sister revealed].

Although he expected relaxation from his friends with laughter, jokes and games, Visconti was also demanding. His younger friends had to be cultured and this was tested repeatedly by what were called 'Society' games, which always had something to do with history, literature or music. It was no good hoping to keep Visconti's company if one had not read and 'digested' Proust, Mann, American literature, Balzac and Stendhal, if one did not know Verdi and Wagner by heart, and if one did not have a wide knowledge of history. Although Visconti was not very articulate, rather the opposite – he spoke well, but preferred to listen – a new kind of language developed around him, including new words and expressions, the art of comparison between different trends, building imaginary bridges between cultures. This affected the writing and manner of speech of many of his friends.

Though he was accused of being a 'decorator', he was far from it: though Visconti considered décor essential in the recreation of an historical moment, as indeed *Senso* had demonstrated, it was a means, not an end, and he exercised it with no restraint, but with exactitude. The research into the fashion of a particular class in a particular period resulted in a perfect historical transposition.

Christmas was a double rite for Visconti's true family and for his 'other' family. During the weeks preceding Christmas Visconti would be seen in Via Condotti buying presents for everyone. Every gift was thought out, for the child, for the grown-up, for the star, the singer, his menservants, his relatives. They were unique presents and he would spend time and money to find the right one for the individual person. 'He would start months in advance. He bought and bought. He had a voracious appetite for buying,' his niece said.

By now he was earning a lot of money; he was rich anyway because of his shares in the Erba pharmaceutical business, but he spent money so freely that he was often in debt. For Christmas he spent alarming amounts. At midnight on Christmas Eve he went to Mass with his family – a grand Mass in some beautiful church. The family – especially the brothers – always tried to gather for festivities. 'The odd thing was that when the Vatican replaced Latin with Italian he welcomed it. He said that it was so helpful, that now he understood every single word of the liturgy,' his sister said. And yet it went against his character to approve of the erasing of the ancient tongue, of the universality and nobility of Latin. Religion was important to him, though he rarely discussed it because he felt it was too intimate to dilute in words.

On Christmas morning the tree and the lunch were at his sister's house and he would arrive with a suitcase full of marvellous parcels for his relations, and each year he would choose a different theme for his packaging and tree: one year it would be silver and white, another gold and green, yet another black and pink, and he would spend hours choosing the wrapping-paper, ribbons and baubles, writing on each little card an apt dedication.

From mid-afternoon on Christmas Day through to the small hours, Via Salaria was open house: nobody was invited but friends were expected to call in (Visconti was most offended if he noticed that somebody had not come); friends brought greetings and collected their presents, which were to be found under the huge Christmas tree in a gigantic, glittering heap.

Everybody brought his or her present, which Visconti would unwrap impatiently with the curiosity of a child and the greed for novelty, typical of the rich. 'It was a nightmare; as early as November we would begin discussing what to give him,' Adriana Asti recalled. 'It wasn't easy. He loved presents which people had taken trouble over.' Those who called on him on Christmas Day were friends, his 'other' family, because he had found the affection and the devotion he needed in this entourage.

I first met him in the summer of 1956, while I was on holiday at Castiglioncello, where I had met the children of Fedele and Suso Cecchi d'Amico. I was an adolescent, but had already seen some of Visconti's theatre productions in Parma, and I was familiar with his films because I had worked in a cine club.

The d'Amico children talked about 'Luchino' as a mythical presence, so that when one day he arrived at the villa he was already a hero, carrying with him the disturbing presence of fame. The other people at Castiglioncello also belonged to the cinema world: some – like Mastroianni – were already stars; but none had, not even remotely, the same effect on me as that exercised by Visconti's hawkish profile and erect head of black hair seen in the distance. Visconti liked life at the d'Amicos', the spartan but cared-for dining table, the hours of work in the shade of the pine trees. When he was there, we adolescents were asked to keep quiet, to go and chat somewhere else, and we would leave the house, which was lovely and old-fashioned, and would hear his Milanese voice and catch a glimpse of his dark bushy eyebrows. Shaking hands with him felt like being presented to royalty and his smile was similarly interpreted as a sign of benign benevolence which could change the fortune of one's life: he had an air of authority.

When he was at Villa Bologna with Suso, they were working and he rarely swam with us, perhaps just a dip before lunch, and Visconti would rarely join in – he cared little for swimming – but I remember him on the beach, in a blue bathing-suit, relaxing and joking with us in the water.

In the summer of 1956 Suso and Luchino worked on the scenario of *White Nights* (*Le Notti Bianche*, inspired by Dostoievsky's book, written in 1848 one year before his imprisonment).

After *Senso* Visconti acquired the reputation of spending too much money; he did not have any work in the cinema and Marcello Mastroianni was longing to play a good part in a quality film. Suso Cecchi d'Amico therefore suggested making a 'small' film produced by a co-operative; each of them would pay a share: Visconti, herself, Mastroianni and a young producer called Cristaldi. 'They were all at Castiglioncello. Luchino was my guest. Marcello arrived and we started looking for a modest subject for a small film. We used to go to Leghorn, where part of the city is made out of canals, and it occurred to me that it would be the perfect setting for a short story by Dostoievsky, with only two characters. My father suggested *White Nights*.' The story and theme of *White Nights* was freely adapted from Dostoievsky's sad account of his own solitude. A man meets Natalia, a lonely girl – the man has no friends – he is a stranger in the city: St Petersburg for Dostoievsky, Leghorn for Visconti. For months the girl has been waiting for her lover to return; at the end of the film he does, and the man is even more lonely than before. Mastroianni was the lonely man, and Jean Marais the lover who comes back to Natalia.

So they began work. 'We started in an expensive way because he signed up Maria Schell; she was fashionable then and she didn't want to be a member of a co-operative,' said Suso.[1] Then they went to Rome, and Visconti said, 'This story is something special, in a theatrical sense: the décor should be all fake.' The sets were built at Cinecittà, and the partners of the co-operative trembled; Luchino was, as usual, overspending. 'We had rebuilt a city! And there was this character who hardly appears: I went to Paris with Luchino and we met Jean Marais. Luchino told me, "Look, I've never made anything with him, but he could play the part." ' Suso rang Mastroianni and they were both alarmed, because Marais had been engaged, and he wanted to be paid. There was no money, and no distributor wanted to advance any financial guarantees.

Visconti decided that the fog in *White Nights* was to look fake as well, and thus the studios were filled with white gauze. 'According to him,' Suso commented, 'he was being economical, but he was so impractical. Today they make wallpapers which imitate perfectly any material, including damask; but he didn't even want to see them. He looked through a book of patterns and instinctively chose what cost twelve times as much as the rest!'[2]

White Nights had a great influence on the new French school of directors, but it was hardly noticed in Italy.

It is a charming, elegant film in black and white, deliberately artificial. As usual, the music in *White Nights* was carefully thought out. The musical theme which stresses Natalia's love is an arrangement of the love-potion theme from *Tristan and Isolde*. When Natalia is taken to the opera to see *The Barber of Seville*, the aria we hear is Figaro's *'Donne, donne eterni dei, chi v'arriva a indovinar. . . .'* (Women, eternal gods, who can possibly guess what you are thinking?) – another clue, just as the message *Il Trovatore* had been all-important in the opening scenes of *Senso* and *L'elisir d'amore* in *Bellissima*. Another thing to stress about this unexpected film of Visconti's is that it was made soon after the Twentieth Congress of the Soviet Communist Party, whose revelations left Visconti disorientated. Indeed *White Nights* is a totally apolitical film. It is a cameo, full of clever observation. The settings of Leghorn have been reproduced with intentionally flat effects, the lighting is diffused as in the Venice sequences in *Senso*, when Livia runs through a gloomy, empty, blue Venice.

Talking about *White Nights*, Jean Marais burst into laughter:

> It was typical of Luchino! We knew each other well. Each time he came to Paris I saw him, we dined together. . . . He said that he was looking for an actor for *Les Nuits Blanches*. 'This is a character who appears not throughout the film but just at the beginning and at the end, but one has to think about him as if he has been there all the time.' This is what he said to me. I told him that maybe I could help him and asked him to mention a star who had the 'physique' and the personality for that character. To this he answered, 'You,' to which I said immediately, 'Then why don't you ask me to play it?' 'Because it is a tiny role.' 'But I would play anything for you, even if I appeared only for a second,' I said. And that is how I came to play that character. It was a strange film, done entirely in the studio. I had been warned by everybody that when he worked Luchino was terrible, but I didn't find him so: he was correct, calm and precise in his directions.

Some critics hailed *White Nights* as neo-romantic; others wrote that Visconti had abandoned neo-realism to take a dangerous 'poetic' path: it was not a success. The public deserted the gloomy story in black and white, and the members of the co-operative lost a great deal of money, but *White Nights* launched Mastroianni as a major actor.

Jean Marais was a friend with whom Visconti shared many memories and experiences. Once when they were in Rome, Visconti, Marais and Massimo Girotti went to see Mistinguette. They went for a laugh because Visconti liked anything camp, but, as Marais recalled, 'It was awful, she was very old. She wore a terrible royal blue dress and a royal blue hat with feathers, many of which were broken, and the dress was uncomfortably tight on the rolls of fat on her body. She sang some of her famous songs, lifting her skirt, but from one side one could see her knees swathed in bandages. Oh, it was so sad! And then she descended among the public singing *"Je cherche un millionaire"* – I'm looking for a millionaire – and when she came to sit on Girotti's knees he was terrified and shouted "Ahh!" Mistinguette must have been eighty-two by then.'

In 1957, besides the two operas at La Scala, Visconti staged two plays, August Strindberg's *Fröken Julie* (*Miss Julie*) and Carlo Goldoni's *L'impresario delle Smirne* (*The Impresario from Smyrna*).

On 24 September for the West Berlin Festival he staged the ballet-play *Maratona di Danza* (*Dance Marathon*), with music by Hans Werner Henze. 'I was at the Festival and we spent some time together,' said Fedele d'Amico, 'and I followed the rehearsals of this strange work, which was rather badly constructed. It was a fake pantomime, a purely mimic spectacle in which, from time to time, there were some spoken lines; and this fact broke up its design. It was rather long, drawn out and boring.'

Visconti had met Henze, the German composer, in 1955 at the Milan house of Fosca Crespi, Puccini's heiress. At the time Visconti was financing the dancer Jean Babilée and his company, and at the beginning of 1956 he asked Hans Werner Henze to write the music for a ballet-drama. Visconti had written the libretto himself: the story of a dance marathon which takes place in the squalid suburbs which were growing around Rome. 'The libretto of *Dance Marathon* was very beautiful,' Henze said, 'it was an object of realistic art, like the American realistic art of today. Kienholz's work was not dissimilar.' Typically Visconti never mentioned that the idea for the work came from the American book *They Shoot Horses, Don't They?*, which was enjoying a great success at the time and was later turned into a film. He transposed the story from California to the Roman suburbs where, in those days, such awful competitions took place. 'The idea also came from Renzo Vespignani's paintings, which depicted lurid satellite cities around Rome; in fact his sets were splendid: a sheet of glass covered the ceiling, reflecting the dancing couples.'

While working, Henze would play to Visconti on the piano what he had composed; Visconti would then demand changes, 'always on the lines of realism, which was very difficult for me because I was involved in serial dodecaphonic music then, which was the main preoccupation of contemporary composers at the time. I even had to compose a pop song, which in the performance was played on a record. He was dictatorial, but in a very persuasive way. It was difficult to say no to Luchino. He explained what he wanted in a few words and left a lot to one's imagination. Like all the people who worked for him, I became a pupil, yearning to learn, because he evidently had something my generation had lost, that type of culture received from a strong middle class, a patrimony of ideas, as well as those of taste.'

They became very close, and Visconti would sometimes write to Henze every day. Henze's personality was an unusual challenge to him; his intellectual level was higher than that of the people with whom Visconti usually liked to be involved. 'I consider myself a bit of a product of his; he was able then to be interested in the work of so many young people, he was a man who could communicate. His non-conformism, his undaunted drive fascinated me.' And Henze liked Visconti's pride, something aristocratic and at the same time peasant-like. 'In his private affairs he was simple, human.'

When they went to Berlin together, the city was not yet scarred by the Wall and they used to go to the theatre almost every night. Visconti was a little disappointed by Brecht, but wrote a fan letter to Fritz Kortner, the expressionist actor, who had fled Germany in 1933 and who was then directing *Hamlet*. At the time Visconti was very anti-German; Henze was under the mistaken impression that he had been tortured by the Gestapo and that a weakness in his left ear came from blows he had received during his imprisonment. Clearly, Visconti was to redevelop his devotion to German culture and to give in again to his Teutonic streak.

Henze liked *Dance Marathon*, although his music played a secondary role, merely an appendage to the libretto, to the ballet. 'He was like a magician when working, the way he moved people, organized the effects of colours, of groups. At the same time one could observe in his work the touch of the dilettante, the mistake of the amateur which betrayed the great effort of his work and reminded one that he was only human.' Henze thought that this element, this 'chic', a kind of English aristocratic attitude towards work, was present in all his productions.

One month later Visconti was asked to stage Kleist's *The Prince of Hombourg*, but he thought the play should be turned into an opera (Visconti would write the libretto) and he asked Henze to compose the music. 'For me as a German, a drama of that importance where all the sounds were already there! It seemed impossible!' But to say no to Visconti, even on these grounds, was unacceptable: he retaliated, threatening to break their friendship. He would write postcards, '*Le Prince de Hombourg pour notre amitié.*' He was furious.

After that, Visconti never asked Henze to work for him again, though he would work with inferior musical talents. The fact was that Visconti did not like a relationship of equality, either in love or in work. He was no longer interested in listening to the opinions of others, and he began to surround himself with inferiors to whom he could dictate. By making this choice, he was cutting himself off and losing the stimulating friendship of many talented people.

At this time Visconti worked on another opera, Bellini's *Il Pirata*, which never saw the light of day. He also started studying a French version of Eugene O'Neill's *Long Day's Journey Into Night* for the French actress Edwige Feuillère. And he had yet another idea which fascinated him, but which came to nothing: a documentary in Tibet.

It was in early 1958 that popular recognition for *Ossessione* came at last, because Visconti succeeded in putting his old film together from a series of fragments which he had found at the Cinetecà Nazionale – the negative had been destroyed during the war. He also staged Arthur Miller's *A View from the Bridge*, using Sicilian dialect, something which, initially, disturbed Miller. The American playwright was then considered the major realistic voice in contemporary theatre; Visconti wrote an article in the form of an open letter to Miller, explaining that only two of the characters were going to use Sicilian dialect and that this was an important point for the Italian public 'in order to show the difference between newly-arrived immigrants and Italians who have been long enough in America to adapt themselves to local ways'.[3] He also wrote that he himself had used the same dialect for his *La Terra Trema* and that some of the most important contemporary books in Italian literature had been written in dialect – one of which was Pier Paolo Pasolini's *Ragazzi di Vita*.

Visconti never liked Pasolini much. He may have admired his scholarship, but he resented his open homosexuality, the display of vulgar words and, later, Pasolini's crude films. They were actually at different poles: Visconti was as constructive as Pasolini was destructive.

While Visconti was in Paris working on *L'Impresario delle Smirne*, Edwige Feuillère's agent took him to Alain Delon's dressing-room; they had never met before, in fact Visconti had never set eyes on Delon, but the script was ready for *Rocco and his Brothers*, his next film. It is said that Visconti saw Delon and exclaimed '*C'est lui!*' and didn't even bother to talk to the young man.

Visconti was staying with his valet at the Berkeley Hotel in Avenue Matignon. Nearby, in Avenue Gabrielle, there was a house which he wanted to buy; it looked slightly Italianate, with large windows overlooking the Champs Elysées, and it even had a Proustian connection – the first meeting between Marcel and Albertine had taken place near there. It is odd that Visconti, who loved Paris so, never bought a house or a flat in the city. On this occasion, and after many years' silence, he rang up Sylvie Bataille, who was married to the psychoanalyst Jacques Lacan. 'We had an appointment at the Berkeley and I didn't recognize him because I saw this strong man; when I had first met him he was a thin, small youth.' For a short time, this very secretive man went to see Lacan as a patient: was it merely curiosity about analysis or was it due to a real need to know himself?

From Paris, where he had seen many of his friends and shopped in a number of his old haunts, he went straight on to London. For the first time he was going to work on an opera outside Italy. Sir David Webster, General Administrator of Covent Garden Opera House, had asked him to direct an opera and Visconti had gone back to his old idea of doing *Don Carlos* – which, to be correct, should be *Don Carlo* when sung in the Italian version.[4] Curiously enough, this was one of Verdi's masterpieces which in the 1950s was still out of the repertoire. Because of its Schiller roots, it was performed almost exclusively in Germany, in a dark Spanish Inquisition context: the public at large and opera-houses had dismissed it as an impossible piece. *Don Carlos*, like many of Verdi's operas, had a troublesome life: literally at the last minute Verdi, who had written it for the Paris Opéra with a French libretto, had to cut almost an hour off the playing time. The opera had further suffered by repeated cuts. There was a first act set at Fontainebleau; it was about the joy of Elisabetta di Valois at the news that she would marry the handsome Spanish prince, followed by the meeting between the two exalted royal fiancés, ending with the bitter realization that the old King Philip II, Don Carlos's father, had opted to marry the French princess himself. Visconti and Giulini the conductor decided to reinstate the first Fontainebleau act (even if not in its entirety) and to cut a scene from the fourth act (when the King of Spain is protected by the Grand Inquisitor from a popular insurrection).

'*Don Carlos* was a watershed,' said Sir John Tooley, who worked then as Webster's assistant. 'It provided a great stimulus to Covent Garden. It was an eye-opener.' Scenery and costumes were historically accurate for the period and distinguished the two courts. Princess Elisabetta appeared first in an olive-green dress, wearing a bejewelled hat, straight from *l'école de Fontainebleau*. At the end of the first act, the palace in the distance shone with lights for the festivities: a Queen for France! while a couple of cuddling peasants disappeared in the forest (they have disappeared from the production as well, alas. Visconti's original concept has lost many of its details). San Giusto was like a Flemish painting, a grey nave dominating an alienated black prince, always dark and solitary, like Hamlet, as in the music which Verdi composed for that character. His friend Rodrigo's costume had a touch of blue and plenty of embroidery. The arrival of the King and Queen of Spain in the church caused a shiver, so majestic were the black costumes embroidered in silver, and the transition from the happy court of the Valois to the sombre one of the Spanish Hapsburgs was marked. Visconti's vision of Spain was Mauresque; the blinding light of the courtyard of the Queen's quarters showed a Princess d'Eboli in lilac surrounded by ladies of the court in white and off-white, shades of ochre and gold; the black figure of the King, surrounded by his huge greyhounds held by his black slave, made the audience tremble. One felt the majesty and sadness of that mighty figure – the true protagonist of the opera, into whom Visconti put some of his own torments and solitude. In the garden there was an infinite line of fountains and a turquoise, starred sky. The *auto-da-fé* scene was so different from the former interpretation: it was a sunlit stage studded with bejewelled courtiers headed by the King and Queen, who looked like reliquaries, contrasting with the Calvinist group of Flemish envoys led by Carlos. The sense of pomp and history was tremendous.

It was a stunning experience, an extraordinary *tour de force*. Filippo Sanjust designed the costumes – Enrico Medioli, knowing that Visconti could not be persuaded to employ anybody unless he decided to do so himself, left some of Sanjust's drawings around Visconti's house. Maurizio Chiari designed the sets and Enrico Medioli was assistant to the director. Boris Christoff was the almighty King, Jon Vickers the desperate Infante, Tito Gobbi his faithful friend Rodrigo, Gré Brouwenstijn played Elisabetta di Valois, and Fedora Barbieri was la Principessa d'Eboli: vocally, too, under Carlo Maria Giulini, they made a superb team.

London, at last, captivated Visconti totally. 'He adored England, which coincided with the peak of his success, with his maturity,' said Medioli. The shopping in Jermyn Street, the search for small restaurants serving delicate oysters, the delights of the uncrowded and special London of the late 1950s – including the theatre and a stimulating social life – Visconti discovered all this. 'London was the place where he had come to buy horses in his youth, he loved the English way of life. And *Don Carlos* turned into a triumph,' Enrico Medioli recalled.

Visconti and Medioli had first come to London in February for a fortnight and stayed at the Ritz. It snowed and snowed. They had gone to see Webster at his house, where they arrived late because of the snow and had found a delighted and tipsy general administrator. 'Luchino and Webster liked each other very much from the start. David Webster was very happy, every detail was discussed and arranged,' said Medioli. When they returned to London for the rehearsals, they went to a small hotel in St James's where there was a hydraulic lift. 'It was dusty and old. Luchino used to say, "This is no hotel, it's a den," but then, when he shaved in the mornings, I would hear him singing "Beloved den!" He was happy. It was a beautiful stage of his life, nice, pleasant.' John Gielgud gave a large dinner party in Visconti's honour at l'Ecu de France; Visconti liked Gielgud's company and particularly his scholarly wit. During the evening Visconti was asked if he would like to direct a comedy starring Vivien Leigh and Claire Bloom, but he refused on the grounds that his English was not good enough.

He was delighted with Covent Garden Opera House and the people who worked there. There was a tiny dressmaker in the costume department who always protested about the quantity of costumes required. She would say that two page boys would suffice. 'Please!' Visconti would bow to her, 'give me two more! Just two more!' and wheedle her into producing two extra costumes by pirouetting around her. It was one of the happiest periods of Visconti's life; not only was he at the pinnacle of his fame, career and success, but he had also achieved a degree of inner peace.

Don Carlos was an overwhelming success: London had never seen an opera staged with such respect for history and for the musical score, so carefully detailed and magnificent to the eye: at the time of writing it is still in the repertoire and, although it has lost many of Visconti's touches, it is still a moving, splendid production. 'He was a musical man, he expressed himself in opera,' Uberta Visconti explained. 'He used to say that he loved the things he did for the cinema best because in the cinema he was more the "author", even if films like *Death in Venice* or *The Leopard* came from stories by Thomas Mann or Lampedusa. But in his choice of opera, there was a choice of identity.'

Visconti would have liked to stay on in England and visit the countryside; he discovered that London suited him – the difference from Rome was striking. And the hunting for antiques! Visconti bought quantities of ornaments and pictures, furniture and materials – it was such an amusing and rich market. However, he had to leave the country because he had promised Menotti to open the new Festival at Spoleto.

Spoleto was a new adventure. Gian Carlo Menotti had lived in America and been very successful as the composer of several operas. He admired two Italian directors, Strehler and Visconti. With courage and generosity (he spent a lot of his own money and an immense amount of his energy), Menotti decided to start a festival in the beautiful Umbrian town of Spoleto, where there were two splendid theatres, but the local people felt little desire to co-operate and there was hardly any accommodation. The aim of the festival, which was to become an annual event, was to link the cultures of America and Europe. Menotti had found a young American conductor: 'To my great surprise, when I asked Luchino to open Spoleto, he accepted at once. And he even admired Thomas Schippers and was delighted to work with him, in spite of the fact that nobody had ever heard of him. Schippers was rather like Luchino in character, a bit of a snake who would never give in on any point, an iron character – and this Luchino liked. Luchino was admirable. When he asked me "Who is the conductor?" well . . . Tony must have been twenty or twenty-one. . . . "Can he conduct?" he asked. And the singers . . . all Americans. . . . "My God!" he said. "Where shall I live?" "In my house," I replied. He accepted everything at once. He didn't do it free, he had a thing about fees, professionalism, but he said "Talk to my agent"; for Spoleto his fees were always low.' They decided to open with Verdi's *Macbeth*, another forgotten opera.

'He loved the first years of Spoleto,' said Enrico Medioli; 'he was modestly paid, but did it because he enjoyed it. For *Macbeth* he used a novelty – transparent painted gauzes, which would create different effects depending on the lighting, and disappear when lit from a particular angle. Nowadays everybody uses them, but when I asked Luchino who had invented the method, he answered, "Zeffirelli says that he was the first." '

Menotti remembered that on the evening of the first night, 'Luchino came to my house to change, and in the washbasin we saw a scorpion. I shrieked and was about to kill it, when Luchino said, "For Christ's sake! It brings luck: tonight will be a triumph, because I was born under the sign of Scorpio." '

Macbeth was indeed a triumph and a revelation: not only was Schippers hailed as a great conductor, but *Macbeth* was recognized as a masterpiece. Visconti had revealed and revalued *Macbeth*, once again clarifying, not justifying.

His new 'court' had followed him to Spoleto. Alain Delon and Romy Schneider were staying at Gian Carlo Menotti's house. Also there was Laudomia Hercolani, nicknamed Domietta, a fragile beauty who had found in Visconti a father and a friend who was enormously stimulating: 'His friendship – he wanted total dedication. There was also a moral sense, a great affection in him. He was very keen on rites, anniversaries, occasions. He was a point of reference which was solid and secure, but his judgment could vary because he was emotional. However, his moral rigour was fundamental and very great.' She was like a daughter to him, she told him everything, and they were seldom apart for long. 'He loved work and eating well; we travelled so often together . . . journeys made always with the idea of a film – around Austria, Sicily, and with him for his premières. In museums he was very attentive: sometimes he would see something he liked very much, and you'd notice him gazing at it and realize that he was following a train of thought; and he would do the same with music. He was an extrovert, a force of nature. And he was with friends all the time, ten, twenty of them, never alone. He was generous and greedy.'

Domietta had worked on the décor of *Il Lavoro* (*Work*); it was typical of Visconti to involve somebody he loved in his projects. She came from the same background as he and she was beautiful. 'When he wanted to, he frightened me; at work he was exacting, because he would not admit that one could be slack. A couple of times he caught me laughing during work and he was furious.' His parents had been friends of her parents. 'When I was a child I remember them coming to dinner in Rome, but Luchino was different from the Viscontis. Knowing the environment from which he came, I knew how he had evolved.' Change and evolution were a preoccupation in which Luchino Visconti was trying to help her. 'He felt nostalgic about his childhood, about his world which had disappeared. He spoke about his mother: he often portrayed her in his films, and he looked like her. I don't see anything decadent in Luchino, who was a man who contributed to making Italy into a modern country.'

Visconti loved the company of women. Bice Brichetto regretted being a 'reserved, shy woman: I didn't amuse him. He had an enormous curiosity. He was interested in everything, painting and literature, and followed the latest books; he always had three or four by his bedside, which he would read at the same time. When he travelled he wanted to see everything.' But with women he was also bashful and he was displeased 'if they talked in a vulgar way. Nobody talked about his relationship with Callas to him; he never mentioned it himself. If he had an *histoire* with someone which was meant to be secret, he would hide in a thousand ways.' His behaviour towards women was gentle. 'He was so very secure – he would push me onto the stage, I was afraid, and he was behind me in the wings, watching,' Adriana Asti recalled. In October 1958 she played Laura James in a rather weak, unsuccessful production of *Look Homeward, Angel* by Ketti Frings from Thomas Wolfe's novel, directed by Visconti in Rome. 'I don't know if this sense of security was something that he had succeeded in achieving. "Go, go on," he would tell me. He was not a guru, but I, on the other hand, hung on his every word.'

Visconti returned to Paris in November 1958 to direct William Gibson's *Two for the Seesaw*, which had been translated and adapted by Louise de Vilmorin, a friend of his who was a famous beauty and a woman of literature. She herself revelled in the art of conversation, of mixing people and of holding open house. In Paris Visconti also directed his first play in another language. 'There was a play I had to do with the young Annie Girardot called *Deux sur la Balançoire*, with two characters. I didn't want to direct it myself,' said Jean Marais, to whom it had been offered. He was asked whom he would like to direct it, and he suggested Visconti. ' "You are a fool!" they told me, "Can you imagine he'd ever do a play in Paris?" "Well," I said, "why don't we ask? If he were to accept, it would be a dream!" ' Visconti accepted at once. Jean Marais marvelled at how well Visconti himself could act: 'His French was fantastic and so was his knowledge of French culture.' During Visconti's brief stay in Paris for this play (the year was crammed with work), Georges Beaume, who was Alain Delon's agent, organized a dinner party at Chez Maxim's for Luchino, Alain Delon, Gian Carlo Menotti and Maria Callas. Callas talked to Beaume about Luchino: 'You have no idea how he treats me. He is a tyrant. I need that. Sometimes I don't understand why he asks me to do something. I look out into the darkness of the theatre, and I say, "Luchino, why do you ask me to do that?" And do you know what the traitor answers, with a smile from one side of his mouth to the other? "Shut up, *conne*! sing – which is the only thing you are able to do!" '

In December 1958 in Rome Visconti staged *Mrs Gibbons' Boys* by Will Glickman and Joseph Stein, once again starring Paolo Stoppa and Rina Morelli. The script was weak and it was not a great success.

During 1959 he worked on only one play (*Figli d'Arte – Sons of Art* – by Diego Fabbri) and an opera for Spoleto, *Il Duca d'Alba*, because he was busy with the preparation and then the filming of *Rocco and His Brothers*, one of his most ambitious films.

The second festival at Spoleto was problematic due to lack of finance and Menotti was tempted to give it all up; 'but I am stimulated by injustice and when a plane flew over Spoleto throwing leaflets directed against us, full of vulgarities, I decided we had to go on.' *The Duke of Alba*, an opera by Donizetti which had been rediscovered by Thomas Schippers, was in a sense a continuation of *Don Carlos* (although, of course, it had been written before).

Alba was the tyrant sent by Philip II to crush the revolution of Spanish Flanders. Eighteen thousand people had been executed, including Count Egmont, beheaded in 1568. (Goethe wrote Count Egmont's tragedy, which Visconti staged later at the Boboli gardens in Florence.)

As there was no money, Visconti said that he would use old scenery stored in Italian theatres. 'Imagine Luchino saying that! We started looking around the Italian opera-houses, and with the luck which Luchino had, we found the original scenery of the *Duca d'Alba* – almost all of it!' Menotti recounted. The costumes, which were missing, were designed by Filippo Sanjust; Enrico Medioli was assistant to the director. Once again the atmosphere of Spoleto was amusing, improvised, electric. Luchino slept in a tiny room in Menotti's house, which he used to compare to Rome's prison, and he enjoyed himself immensely.

Both the play and the opera were but brief interruptions while he worked on his film, *Rocco and His Brothers* (*Rocco e i Suoi Fratelli*). When he started work on the project, Visconti explored a side of Milan he did not know: the grim new Milan in concrete which was growing around the old Austrian Milan of his youth, the new immigrants from the south, their districts, their habits.

Rocco and His Brothers was Visconti's most difficult child – likewise he loved it best: too much went into it, too many ideas and material to make it into a totally successful film, but it is a grand statement. Although there is a link with *La Terra Trema* in the subject matter, *Rocco and His Brothers* is not the documentary which *La Terra Trema* sought to be. *Rocco* was intended to be an historical film while dealing with contemporary events.

History was Visconti's main preoccupation, it was the broad canvas on which he expressed himself, it was the human drama, his great theme; and it gave him room to recount his own saga as well. In *Rocco* he looked at the problem of southern emigration, which was starting then in a massive way, seeing it from Milan, his own city, which, with Turin, had become Italy's industrial capital. Visconti did not share the contempt of the northerners for the wretched southerners who came northwards in order to find work and lead that 'modern' life which was denied them in the south; on the contrary, he took their side. In the north the small, hairy southerner encountered difficulties in the factories and from hostile neighbours, because he spoke an almost totally different language. The emigrants wanted to make money and become like the more polished northerners: the problem of the Italian south was a colonial problem, and Visconti was alerted to it before most of Italy realized that it existed at all.

Rocco is a violent film; it shocked audiences more than any other film by Visconti – and yet it was his first popular commercial success. In *Rocco* he told the story of a southern family which is compelled to go and live in a huge metropolis (censorship did not allow him to specify that the very recognizable metropolis was Milan). The weakest in the family are driven to violence, losing themselves, but the strong man is Rocco (Alain Delon), the character who reacts with love rather than violence. In spite of its violent scenes (like the one in which Nadia, a prostitute, is stabbed dozens of times), *Rocco* is Visconti's most human film because the observation is kind, the message many-layered and the characters convincing.

It took a long time and many literary sources to produce *Rocco*. The title-part – not in fact the leading role, which instead belonged to the 'baddy', Simone – was named after Rocco Scotellaro, a peasant from the deep south who had died young and whose beautiful poetry had just been published. The rest of the title, *and His Brothers*, derived from Thomas Mann's *Joseph und seine Brüder*. Rocco's ignorance of violence, his total goodness, his determination to overcome by understanding, came from Mishkin, the character which Dostoievsky, like Visconti, had counterposed to a violent human being, Rogozin. There is hardly any need to point out that *Rocco and His Brothers* was not *The Idiot* and that the two media, fiction and film, are very different; but there are many more points which Visconti took from Dostoievsky: Nadia, the prostitute, is loved by both Rocco and Simone, in the same way as Nastasia Filipovna is loved by both Mishkin and Rogozin. Nastasia and Nadia are killed in the same way; and in Claudia Cardinale's interpretation of Ginetta, one can see a hint of Aglaja.

But in spite of its moral message, once again Visconti was in trouble with censorship and had to cut some sequences and tone down others. When the script of *Rocco* was almost finished, Visconti read some short stories by the Milanese writer, Testori, and new elements were added. The film was made in black and white. 'At first I thought of filming *Rocco* in colour, but in the end it seemed right that it should be grey: that's the way Milan would look to the lonely peasant from the south,' Visconti said to Penelope Gilliatt in November 1961.[5] Although the film was intended to be primarily historical, it contains a couple of episodes which were utterly political and which were worked on with Antonello Trombadori, the 'liaison officer' between Visconti and the Party, between Visconti and Togliatti. This applied not only to *Rocco*: as long as Togliatti was alive, Visconti would 'submit' all his final scripts to Trombadori as the representative of the Italian Communist Party.

Rocco was filmed between 1959 and 1960 with actors who, at the time, were virtually unknown: Alain Delon, Renato Salvatori, Annie Girardot, Katina Paxinou, Claudia Cardinale, Adriana Asti and Claudia Mori. In September, it was shown at the Venice Film Festival where it provoked the usual scandal – due mostly to the radical nature of Visconti's message: the southerner was Italy's second-class citizen, the south was northern Italy's colony. The film was awarded a special prize by the Festival jury, which avoided giving it the first prize it deserved; Visconti did not collect it.

Rocco was boycotted in every way. Even in Parliament Christian Democrat and neo-Fascist MPs demanded to know why the film was shown at all since it slandered southern emigration. Some local magistrates banned *Rocco* and demanded that certain sequences should be 'darkened' – a new form of censorship.

The upper class of Milan accused Visconti of having betrayed his roots; most of the press mocked the Communist aristocrat who had tackled one of those subjects which are better left untouched and swept under the carpet. This was motivated mainly by the effort of the Christian Democrats to defeat the expression of popular culture, which was championed almost exclusively by Left-wingers and Communists; genuine culture, as Graham Greene says, is always in opposition.

This offensive was not only directed against Visconti. While Catholic directors and writers received grants, a good press, and were protected by associations, the Communists were to be wiped out because, with neo-realism, 'they shamed Italy abroad,' as Andreotti, then Minister for the Arts, said at the time. The Communist Party never did anything to build a counter-offensive, to rally its supporters and protect them, and this was because, in spite of having inherited an organization from the Resistance movement, the Party was losing its militancy. Togliatti thought that culture should be left to find sponsors from the usual private channels, and he spoke of this to Visconti; when the Christian Democrats started their big offensive against Left-wing culture, Togliatti was ill and about to die. Otherwise, he – a man who felt the importance of cultural expression – might have acted.

Visconti needed to establish a close working relationship with his actors, 'sometimes a cruel one,' said Francesco Rosi. 'I understand this well, in the type of work we do: it is impossible for a director making a film which he wants to succeed to avoid establishing a love relationship with his interpreters. I always fall in love with the actors who are to be the interpreters of my film, it could not be otherwise. I love to be with people if I love them; if not, why should I care? – I prefer to be on my own. Unless the person one hates – and that is so similar to love! – is so interesting that one establishes a dynamism which is different: a tension, the taste of provocation, of prevailing, of getting to know the other, of vanquishing the other . . . we are talking about Visconti, not about me – as far as I'm concerned, alas, the game of love I play is a massacre!'

There must have been something similar in Visconti's make-up, in his need to know and love his actors; his intense interest embraced those he could love and he too needed 'massacres'.

He loved his actors and often 'consumed' them, but he loved his actresses as well. The latter would confide in him all the details of their love affairs. With some of his favourite actresses he had an extraordinarily close relationship: he enjoyed going to dances with them, and would tell them what to wear, how to solve their love affairs, how to make up their faces and how to cut their hair.

He kept his distance from writers and intellectuals, who in Rome, as in most other places, formed a tightly-knit group. He saw them, but only occasionally; he preferred the company of those who shared his work, and was annoyed by the pretentiousness of the Left-wing intellectuals and by labels. Within his group he preferred those who, when he played one of his nasty cruel jokes, would step aside and disappear for a while, maintaining their integrity and dignity. Among his lovers, or occasional lovers – because there was an immense number of them – he fell for those who did not yield. The man who resisted became his god, and because of Visconti's constructive, paternal character, it was this type of man that he concentrated on building up as an actor, thrusting him onto the public. Alain Delon never yielded: Visconti had a sublime and unrequited love for him. *Rocco* was a vehicle for the handsome, unknown actor, but Visconti wanted to do more for him and with him. Thus, when a play by Testori called *L'Arialda* (realistic in form, but decadent in content) was banned by the censors, he decided to cancel all his Italian plans because he was genuinely disgusted with magistrates and politicians hunting him, but also because he wanted to make new plans in order to work with Delon. *L'Arialda* had already opened in Rome and when it arrived in Milan in February 1961 it was banned because of 'obscenity'.

In addition, he staged another opera: this time *Poliuto* by Donizetti, at La Scala with Maria Callas. But the magic had gone: he was otherwise sentimentally involved and so was she. In November 1961 he sent her one of his long 'bureaucratic' telegrams apologizing to her because he refused to work for La Scala as a protest against political harassment. She answered at once in a warm and loving letter, but was concerned about her own trouble rather than his. She was involved with Onassis and was longing to obtain a divorce from Battista Meneghini. Visconti would comment 'Poor Battista!' He disapproved of the vulgarity of the 'turtle' – his nickname for Onassis – and of the publicity which surrounded their affair: he hated publicity about this kind of thing, while Onassis loved it.

Poliuto, according to its designer, Nicola Benois, suffered because of Visconti's defection: 'Visconti and I had planned every detail, but he withdrew from the project, leaving the direction to Herbert Graf, who had to prepare a staging at the last minute. Despite these problems, Maria was no trouble – simple, human and sympathetic during rehearsals, always ready with a smile. But she badly needed a strong hand to guide her, to give her courage – the hand of Luchino.'[6]

Visconti then withdrew to his villa at Torre San Lorenzo, about fifty kilometres from Rome (he later sold the villa to one of 'his' actors, Renato Salvatori, who had married Annie Girardot, one of 'his' actresses). He was looking for an adaptation of a play for Alain Delon. Georges Beaume

(Delon's and Romy Schneider's agent) was staying with Visconti, Delon and Romy Schneider: 'He told me he felt like doing something Elizabethan for the stage because there were many things in the plays of that time which still had relevance. We read Webster and John Ford and fell for *'Tis Pity She's a Whore.*' The play featured incest – a theme which haunted Visconti – between brother and sister and, like so many English plays of the period, it was set in an Italian city, Parma. Parma was visited, explored and researched: it was fun for him to be there with Delon, Beaume and Schneider, to eat well and, guided by Enrico Medioli, to play the inquisitive tourist in this Stendhalian city.

Romy Schneider, the star of popular films such as *Empress Sissi*, was the official fiancée of Alain Delon. 'Alain had the role of the man,' Georges Beaume continued, 'but who was to be his sister? I knew, but I didn't want to tell Luchino, because the ideas always had to come from him, and because Romy was my client.' After a while Schneider was chosen.

Both young actors were facing the theatre for the first time, and in *'Tis Pity* Romy Schneider was acting in a language which was not her native tongue. Ford's play had been 'adapted' by Georges Beaume, and Piero Tosi designed the costumes – the finished production was a great success. Visconti demanded endless rehearsals, and his anger, his most insulting words and tempestuous scenes were directed against Romy Schneider, who was young and beautiful, who had the kind of Austrian aristocratic looks which Visconti liked and who reminded him of Pupe.

There was a small incident: Sam Spiegel had asked Delon to act in *Lawrence of Arabia* in the role which later went to Omar Sharif. Beaume suggested to Visconti that *'Tis Pity* should have a limited run, so that Delon could start his film. 'He was furious, didn't want to hear about it, insulted everybody, it was terrible: there was even a fight. Alain missed an important role, but we all adored Luchino all the same.' Visconti wanted Delon to work for him and him alone. 'Luchino transformed Delon as an actor,' said Adriana Asti. 'Luchino was extremely sensitive to beauty, in men and women. I regret not having been more beautiful; I must say with dismay that he became almost blind when confronted with beauty: even imbeciles were judged well if they were beautiful. It was his weakness, he saw his reflection in these beautiful creatures, he felt at ease in their company.'

A handsome young German actor who longed to meet Visconti asked Sanjust to introduce him to the director. When Filippo later met Luchino at his house, he told him that he had asked the actor to come that day. 'You must be mad!' said Luchino, 'we have to work, we have no time to lose! I don't want to see him.' But, when the amazingly handsome young man arrived, Visconti changed totally. 'Do come in! How nice of you to come!' And he asked the actor about himself, his ambition and even what he thought of Visconti's own films. The boy explained that he had not liked most of them, at which Luchino, who would generally erupt with anger over much less, merely said 'How interesting! Really? You didn't like that? Tell me, why?' His respect, even adoration for beauty had made him accept pompous, ill-informed criticism from a stranger, whereas he would have not tolerated the slightest reserve on the part of someone of the greatest intellect.

Visconti returned to see Jacques Lacan, the famous Freudian psychoanalyst married to Sylvie Bataille.

His love life was tormented, but sentimental despair resulted in creativity.

In the summer of 1961, while Visconti worked for the Spoleto Festival on *Salome* by Strauss, the object of his love was locked up in Torre San Lorenzo: locking people in towers for one reason or another seems to have been a habit of Visconti's — yet another insight into the overbearing insecurity of his character. His production of *Salome*, inspired by Gustave Moreau's paintings, was strangely and surprisingly homosexual. The beautiful negro soprano had few veils to shed since she arrived on the stage already naked, and the sensuous dance was actually performed not by her, but by a group of young boys. Salome held St John's head, which dripped blood all over the place, and she rolled about on the floor as if masturbating with the horrendous object. 'Every night three or four people fainted,' Gian Carlo Menotti recalled. It certainly managed to *épater les bourgeois*, but that was all.

In 1962, while he was already working on the script of *The Leopard*, a film which would provide an important role for Alain Delon, Visconti agreed to direct one episode of *Boccaccio '70* (the others were directed by de Sica and Fellini) based on Maupassant's short story *Au Bord du Lit*.

In an interview with Oriana Fallaci, Visconti said that he had directed *Il Lavoro* (*Work*) because he had seen in it a splendid opportunity for Romy Schneider. What he meant was an opportunity to transform her into a cerebral, sophisticated woman, dressed by Chanel, surrounded by superb *objets d'art* and white cats. She played the part of Pupe, a rich German bourgeoise and the daughter of a powerful industrialist who is married to Ottavio, a good-looking, spoilt aristocrat. The story is interesting. Their marriage, which has progressed against a background of bottles of Guerlain scent, bibelots, opalines, statues by Donatello and Sarah Bernhardt (she had been a pupil of Carpeau), reaches an impasse when the scandal breaks that Pupe's husband is involved with call-girls. When negotiating their divorce, Pupe proposes a financial settlement based on her sole job qualification: sex. Ottavio must employ her if he does not want others to do so, and the settlement must be backdated. In the scenes in the apartment of Pupe and Ottavio — who never succeed in being a sympathetic or interesting couple — were paintings lent by Domietta Hercolani and some *objets d'art* from Visconti's house. Every day Carlo Ponti, the producer, would send fresh freesias from his gardens near Rome; and two hundred roses and two hundred gladioli were flown daily from Holland. The luxury of the decadent décor (the cost of the production was enormous) underlines one of Visconti's favourite themes: that a sexual relationship is always contaminated by other factors such as money or possessiveness. Despite all the time and trouble spent on it, this was a rather trivial film, especially after the commitment of *Rocco and His Brothers*.

11
Turning to the Past

Visconti's baroque style of working and living provoked a virulent attack in *Il Mondo* (in those days the best Italian weekly) by Alberto Arbasino, the bright young writer who had been one of Visconti's entourage. The title of the article was 'From Marx to Opalines'. To attack him from within, to mock him as Arbasino had, to present not the face of the hard-working Communist director persecuted by censorship, but that of a decadent man who loved opaline and blond boys, was regarded by Visconti as *lèse-majesté*. Arbasino had desecrated the god of the theatre, wittily, but with a heavy hand and with knowledge. He had also achieved his intellectual independence. Henceforward, Arbasino was on his own, no longer part of the golden group; he was 'cut' by many people, regarded as a leper, and won recognition only after a long time. Visconti was profoundly wounded by this attack, which came from a new and unexpected quarter: not from the Right wing or the bourgeoisie, but from an intellectual who spoke his 'language' and who knew him well. As his fame increased and he became more secure, he began to 'shed' those friends whose company was intellectually demanding. 'At a certain point, I stopped seeing him,' said Hans Werner Henze, 'it had become impossible to talk to him; he was surrounded by *ragazzini*, watching television all the time.'

His 'society' games had become obsessive; a form of relaxation in earlier days, now they had become an escape from any kind of intellectual exchange. He had invented a new game called *la pagella* (the report). An absentee, known to all, would be awarded written marks according to his or her intelligence, beauty, sympathetic qualities, etc. The totals, which were added up and read out, frequently provoked great hilarity.

Television (exceptionally poor in Italy) had also become an addiction, another form of escapism, enabling him to be alone while surrounded by people and chatter. Even in other people's houses, he would switch it on and sit in front of it for the entire evening, killing any discussion or conversation.

When he came to the casting of *The Leopard*, he had in mind either Marlon Brando or Laurence Olivier for the part of the old prince. Brando had been consulted and was interested; he was an intellectual actor, and *The Leopard* had been the literary sensation of the time. But the producers rejected Luchino's first choice and, as so often in the past, Visconti had to forgo his ideal actor. Negotiations with Laurence Olivier began, but it proved impossible to effect insurance of the great actor, who had been seriously ill. As alternatives, 20th Century-Fox offered Spencer Tracy, Anthony Quinn or Burt Lancaster. Visconti chose the latter.

The Leopard was written by one of the many impoverished Sicilian princes, Giuseppe Tomasi di Lampedusa, whose vast culture, like Visconti's, was European rather than Italian and *The Leopard* is about social change in history – one of Visconti's favourite themes in his work so far; it is also the story of an aristocratic class plunging towards the end, towards death – of the individual and of the entire class. The book thus embodies the themes which most appealed to Visconti: the story of his fate and the history of his class – History as the great leveller.

Tomasi had written his novel in cafés (in fact, mainly at the table of a good *gelateria* in Palermo), as far away as possible from his crumbling palace on La Marina. The novel had been rejected by many publishing houses, and Tomasi died without witnessing its enormous success which spread throughout the world.[1]

The novel was finished in 1958, four years before it was filmed. In 1962, Ernesto Ruffini, the Cardinal of Palermo, said that the book was one of the three factors which had contributed to the dishonour of Sicily – the Mafia and Danilo Dolci being the other two. The fact that *The Leopard* was to be made into a film would damage Sicily even further.

The filming of *The Leopard* was a major operation. Visconti entrusted Lampedusa's adopted son, Gioacchino Lanza Tomasi, with finding the ideal locations; his old Sicilian friend from Chanel days, the Duke of Verdura, was to advise on how the Sicilian aristocracy danced the quadrille, which liveries were worn by various households, and so on. A team left Rome to prepare Visconti's own house; he had bought a crumbling but magnificent tower by the sea just outside Palermo. He had it gutted, and new bathrooms with old tiles, drawing-rooms and bedrooms were made ready by Giorgio Pez, Domietta Hercolani and Bice Brichetto, who combed local antique shops for furniture and *objets d'art*. The new house, in which Visconti was to live for a few months, was designed to contain an apartment for Alain Delon. Also his chef from the Abruzzi arrived.

A huge team moved into Palermo to recruit hundreds of people who would become Garibaldi's soldiers, rebellious populace and Bourbon and Piedmontese troops. Aristocrats would play themselves in the long sequence of the ball, for which Visconti was to use a recently-discovered waltz by Verdi.

The Leopard marked the beginning of a downward curve in the inventive output of Visconti's artistic career. In fact, it may already have started with *Work*. From now on, his output became less interesting and his entourage less stimulating, possibly because his *raison d'être* had faded. He made films now because they afforded an opportunity of working with his protégés. It seemed as if he were losing the breadth and experimental drive of such films as *Ossessione*, *La Terra Trema*, *Senso* and *Rocco*, as if he had no more statements to make, and had lost faith in politics or in a better vision of humanity. In his work from this point onwards Visconti developed a theme which had remained subdued in his previous output: that of his own life. The striving towards an understanding of his roots and motivations, though disguised by diverse stories and varied protagonists, emerged as his main preoccupation, verging on artistic egocentricity. Some years later, when I asked him if he were writing his own biography in his films, he denied it vehemently, and gave many reasons for his denial. He was probably doing it subconsciously.

The costumes for *The Leopard* were all-important. Piero Tosi had employed Vera Marzot to help him; she did not know Visconti and did not like what she had heard about him 'because things one read about him were often irritating, he was described as a bully, a capricious aristocrat.' She and Tosi worked together on the designs for months, until one day Tosi told her that Visconti was coming to inspect their drawings and that all the sketches should be prepared in stacks, one for Lancaster, one for Morelli, and so on; she should throw away all unwanted sketches and put everything in order. 'It was as if the Pope were about to arrive; Piero never lost his terror of him. He said to me, "Now you can go." I had no intention of going, I wanted to meet Luchino; I had to work with him, after all.' Tosi kept on saying to her, 'Don't be agitated, don't worry, everything will be all right!' In the event, Visconti's visit, his first encounter with Vera Marzot, was professional; as usual he showed respect for good work. He stopped at her table to discuss the details of her designs. 'In particular I had designed all the costumes for the children, the servants and for some of the army. He was severe with people who were slack, but never unfair; he certainly had a better relationship with women than with men.'

The film, which was to triumph at the Cannes Film Festival, is a story of torpor and fatalism: the old order is forced to accept a new leadership, which is going to behave just the same, if not even worse, than the old one. Sicily has a stagnant economy, while the land-owning aristocrats watch its and their own impending downfall, which will pave the way for the middle-class Mafiosi and for the northern Italians to take over. The noble head of the Salina family, who in the book represents Lampedusa himself (in the film the character portrays Luchino Visconti as impersonated by Burt Lancaster), understands that he belongs to a class doomed to die. Salina's favourite nephew, Tancredi, has become a rebel by joining the Garibaldini, but he slowly adapts to the changing times. He betrays his class by choosing a sexy wife from the new Mafia middle class. He forsakes Garibaldi's army to become a Piedmontese regular officer and he gradually becomes a conservative. Prince Salina's crisis resolves itself in a long, beautiful ball sequence. The prince has grown old; he has tried to adapt and protect his family, but he sees no role for himself in the new order: everything has remained the same, but the leadership has changed for the worse. 'The Prince of Salina knew he belonged to a class doomed to die. Finally he sensed death all around him: it was the only thing that held any meaning for him,' Visconti explained:

> I can understand his nostalgia, but his world *had* to go and that is what I want to show in the film. I am not a southerner and we in the North have a kind of remorse towards the South: a bad conscience. The support we promised has never been given. The movement which released Sicily from the Bourbons came about, like all revolutions, through promises made to the people. And, as always, those promises were never kept. Garibaldi acted in good faith, but the opportunistic landlords were quick to exploit the changing situation for their own advancement, setting up a new bourgeois oppression. Through centuries of servitude, Sicily today still lies in a kind of torpor and the Mafia persists like a gangrenous growth. All this must and will change. For me the theme of *The Leopard* is very similar to that of another film of mine, *Senso*. Only this time the vision is less cruel, the events viewed with more pathos.[2]

Visconti spent four months in Sicily filming in the summer, when the island is yellow and dusty. There he was, shading himself under an umbrella or standing for hours under the fierce sun, with the sirocco and the heat. During the first two weeks, shooting the revolt in Palermo, the crew kept frightful hours. The dressers started work at 4 a.m. and did not finish until 10 p.m., but no one thought of stopping, resting or going on strike. It was difficult finding locations which had retained a nineteenth-century atmosphere: telegraph poles were removed and asphalt was covered with paving stones. The Mafia bosses of villages where Visconti wanted to film were consulted; their permission was necessary, but Luchino was not told about this until later.

Visconti was often in a bad mood, even though most of his friends were in Sicily with him. Georges Beaume was in Palermo, as were Enrico Medioli and Filippo Sanjust, who, with Visconti, were working on the libretto for an opera.[3] But Alain Delon and 'Romina' (Luchino's nickname for Romy Schneider) had turned down the invitation to stay in Visconti's beautiful tower and instead had rented a villa on the other side of Palermo. 'Luchino idolized Delon,' Fulco della Verdura recalled. 'Delon was the only actor to have a dressing-room; poor Burt Lancaster stood around for hours, waiting.' Alberto Fassini seemed to be the recipient of most of Visconti's bad temper. There were terrible scenes which came to blows. 'I know what he wanted to show: the end of a class, the death of something which, however many faults it had, he minded seeing dying,' he said. 'He never stopped working. At night we all dined together, there were tables of twenty-odd people, friends, those who came to see him; while dining he would also be listening to the music for the film . . . and no matter what time he went to bed, he would read for hours and absorb what he read.'

Gioacchino Tomasi recalled that, within a few days, Visconti spent sixty million lire on *objets d'art* for his house in Palermo. 'Like d'Annunzio, surrounding himself with possessions. And like d'Annunzio he carried with him the idea of torment, a court of people to torment. He maintained a rigid division between males and "queens".'

If Visconti fell for something Sicilian such as an eighteenth-century ceramic called Malvica, whole factories of defunct Malvica would rise overnight; his actors would buy huge pieces of 'old' Malvica to give Visconti. Lancaster gave him a whole stove. 'There he was, a man of the Renaissance, followed by his serfs, slaves, tarts, buying and buying. At any given moment various people would not be on speaking terms,' Tomasi recalled. Delon and Visconti were not speaking to each other; the producers and Visconti were not speaking to each other.

Visconti had taken sixteen days to film the first sequences of the film (which eventually appeared behind the credits) and had literally demolished a part of Palermo in order to make it look as it did in the nineteenth century. Lombardo, the producer, suggested that the last part of Garibaldi's triumphal entry into Palermo could be filmed in a studio. Visconti refused. As usual, he had given the producers a professionally exact estimate of how much *The Leopard* would cost; he was always precise in his estimates and would keep within them, despite his reputation to the contrary. But by the time the sixth version of the script had been accepted by Lombardo, the producer was losing money on another film, *Sodom and Gomorrah*, whose initial budget of two million dollars had risen to eight. Lombardo was hardly in a position to embark on *The Leopard*, so American backing was found, on condition that it star an American actor and that it be shot in English. Visconti having refused to comply with this latter condition, a compromise was found: the scenes involving Lancaster were shot in English, the remainder in Italian to be dubbed later for the English version. Eventually 20th Century-Fox made cuts and reprinted the Technirama soft colours, the sombre yellows, the dim candlelit tables, in strong, full colour. Critics said that there were two films, the original and the American version. The American and British public never saw the original film, which was far more beautiful. Visconti later declared: 'For *The Leopard*, an American version was prepared without my supervision. It was, in my view, badly cut and dubbed with ill-chosen, unsuitable voices. Moreover the film, which is in colour, has been processed as if it were a bright piece of Hollywoodiana.'[4] To which the executive vice-president of 20th Century-Fox replied: 'We may be forced to initiate action against Visconti, who seems intent on harming his own picture with statements which seem to damage the film.' In December 1963, Visconti even wrote a letter to *The Times*.

One weakness of *The Leopard* lay in its actors; Lancaster rose above expectations, but Alain Delon never approached the complex character of Tancredi, nor Claudia Cardinale that of Angelica. Yet, at times, Visconti did not serve his actors well either. Horst remarked how unerotic was the sequence of Tancredi and Angelica roaming the vast cellars of the palace – a scene which was charged with sensuality in the book – and without that element it became meaningless. 'It was as if he didn't know what love was,' Horst said, 'and yet he was so passionate!' Fulco della Verdura would have disagreed because he thought that Visconti had only ever loved himself.

Before leaving Sicily for Rome, Visconti was interviewed by Gioacchino Tomasi; they knew each other quite well by then. Tomasi worked for a Communist paper, was the adopted son of the author of *The Leopard* and had the wit and the culture to please Visconti. In the film, he said to Tomasi, he had tried to broaden the writer's vision, which saw events exclusively from the protagonist's angle. It was the revolt of the people which brought the 'leopards' down. 'But I don't think I've added anything to the ideas of Lampedusa; I have only enlarged on some themes which interested him less and are just hinted at in the novel, although hinted at with great clarity.'[5] And to the boy who had served as the model for Tancredi – and Visconti knew it – he said: 'Tancredi was the kind of man who always swims with the tide, betting on a certainty. Like those who marched on Rome or fought in Spain in order to regain the power which had slipped from their hands, behaving then like their predecessors or worse.'[6] Lampedusa's pessimism became his.

Trombadori visited Visconti several times while he was filming *The Leopard*. When a journalist said in an article that in *The Leopard* Visconti had abandoned realism, Trombadori wrote to Visconti, saying that he was remaining truer to the Communist Party than the Communist Party was keeping true to him.

The Leopard was attacked for its decadence – and when the attacks came from the Left, Visconti felt like an orphan. Once again Togliatti came to his rescue by writing a letter addressed to Trombadori on 2 April 1963: *The Leopard* was a masterpiece, he said, better than the book, and Visconti should not allow anybody to cut it.

In Togliatti, Visconti saw a father-figure whose authority he recognized and also a constructive politician whom he – oddly enough – compared to Cavour. 'Visconti, in his films, always had a vision of salvation,' Trombadori observed. 'He wanted there to be hope in his films, a solution. In him there was a strand which was quasi-religious.' There were two or three people whom he totally respected, 'and he even made certain things with them in mind,' said Enrico Medioli. 'One of these was Togliatti, and also Trombadori, who was close to Togliatti.'

When Togliatti died, later in 1963, Visconti lost a father: much to the horror of some relatives, older friends and admirers, he kept vigil at his body, and the photograph of the famous director next to Togliatti's corpse was printed in the whole Italian press, with sarcastic or respectful comments, depending on the political colour of the individual newspaper. Visconti said that Togliatti had been very close to him, had seen all his plays and films, and that he wrote to him commenting on sequences. But they had not in reality been as close as Visconti pretended: they did not say '*tu*' to each other, there were no direct letters and no telephone calls; when Togliatti attended his first nights, it had been because Visconti had asked him through Trombadori, because Togliatti could not be officially seen with Visconti and could not write directly (Communist leaders never do anyway) to a well-known homosexual, however talented he was: the Party was prim as prim can be.

In fact, even this most respected 'father' had kept his distance from his 'son'; he had not rejected him, but he had not wanted him too near either. 'Visconti was very lonely, very attached to his family,' said Domietta Hercolani; 'all his life he was nostalgic for the world he left behind.'

In fact there were two worlds: his friends – a 'family' he had created – and his own family, a living symbol of that world which had gone forever; but the former was becoming a more and more important element in his life. With his relatives he was united particularly in moments of sorrow and convention, funerals and marriages. He was part of the clan and respected the rules – telephoning and remembering everybody's birthday, and staying at Cernobbio with his sister Nane and at Sperlonga with Uberta. He did not, however, often go back to Grazzano-Visconti, where his elder sister, Anna, lived, because the old house was haunted by visions of his mother being outlawed, of Guido's funeral and his father's too. His brother Luigi lived in Via Cerva, in the old Visconti *palazzo* in Milan, while his beloved younger brother Edoardo was at Colle Val d'Elsa, in Tuscany.

Luchino had that particular *chic* typical of the family: a fake shabbiness, clothes which never looked new, desert boots, shirts in small, dark checks. All his care was lavished on the interiors of his homes – the bowls of flowers, the great effects; his houses were like theatre stages, but his stages were like houses, lived in.

Via Salaria and La Colombaia on Ischia, Visconti's favourite houses, were used by his second family, that of his friends. It was open house at Via Salaria and its décor changed as Visconti's taste changed. He bought endlessly; knowing that dealers and artisans charged him exorbitant sums, he retaliated: 'I know that you rob me and I shall pay you in two or three years.' There were always scenes – but they accepted it, since it was true. However, he was almost always in debt.

New Year's Eve was an important occasion when he would give buffet dinners for between sixty and eighty people. The tables were decorated by him with vast bunches of gardenias, and his faithful old friend Gnam Penati would organize sophisticated dishes. At such parties, a Roman princess might be seen talking to a whore; Marlene Dietrich, dressed in white sequins and turban, to a new arrival on the social scene. Ferocious Great Danes and Irish Wolfhounds barked outside the large double-glazed windows reflecting the lovely Roman garden. But Visconti preferred intimate social evenings when he would play games with his close friends, and they would act out a film, book or play title, dressing up with a few overcoats, scarves and improvised hats; but even during these small gatherings only the best champagne and caviar were served by menservants in white gloves.

When going to Ischia he would leave Rome with his friends in a procession of several chauffeur-driven cars. Once in Naples, they would board a ship, and on Ischia various taxis would be waiting on the docks for the arrival of the uncrowned king of the island. Up at La Colombaia, a wonderful Arab tower overlooking the island of Ponza, everything was ready: there were embroidered linen sheets on every bed. He liked the sea in a northern way, he loved it aesthetically, he loved the colours but he rarely swam: he even used to say that the strong light on Ischia prevented him from concentrating. Each room at La Colombaia had an internal telephone: he loved – and hated – both telephone and television, and used them a great deal. In the mornings (he woke around 8 a.m.) he would ring up on the internal telephone system to wake his guests and have a chat, crack a joke or make plans.

During the morning, processions of local antique dealers would come to sell him all sorts of objects. Lunch was at 1.30, and at 5 p.m. he would interrupt everybody's siesta because at 6 p.m. every day a procession of taxis took Visconti and his guests down to a café in Porto d'Ischia. From there he would take a walk with his friends, stopping at every shop to buy presents for everyone. Another ritual was that of buying the tuberoses, the summer's flowers. Inside the house the scent of these white, fleshy flowers was so strong that it gave many of the guests a headache. At night television was obligatory, however bad and irritating: when the woman announcer said goodnight at the end of transmissions for the day, Visconti would shout at her 'You swine!'

On Ischia his ferocious dogs were everywhere, including some vicious Great Danes, one of whom ripped the back of a guest, much to Visconti's amusement. On another occasion, when a producer Visconti disliked came to see him with some friends, a particularly nasty Great Dane jumped out from behind a bush and the producer, terrified, shot it dead. He was even more terrified when he had to face Visconti and tell him what had happened. 'He also had a mad dog which bit everybody,' says Enrico Medioli, 'and another which he had bred by crossing Great Danes and Bull Mastiffs, as he used to do with horses – it was a hideous-looking dog. During lunch Ignazio, his butler, would serve a meal to the dogs.'

In 1963 the Festival of Spoleto was in serious difficulty due to lack of funds. It opened, however, in June with *La Traviata*, directed by Visconti, the second *Traviata* of his career. It was a very different production from the previous one at La Scala: this was a cosy, middle-class *Traviata*, in which the courtesans were not grand and Violetta's house was in questionable taste. Violetta was sung by a beautiful, intelligent soprano called Franca Fabbri, a newcomer, whose voice had some similarities to Callas's. But by the time the opera opened in Spoleto, la Fabbri was ill and her voice had gone – so, too, had *La Traviata*.

'The programme that year was weak,' Menotti explained, 'so I asked Luchino whether he could stay on and help.' Visconti had been one of the Festival's mainstays; indeed, he enjoyed its atmosphere and the people there. He also liked Gian Carlo Menotti and appreciated him as a man of the theatre, a great impresario. At Spoleto, after work, they would meet and spend time together, often not talking, as was his wont with close friends. In order to enliven the meagre programme, Visconti thought of a small play by André Gide, *The Thirteenth Tree*, a 'curiosity' which he asked his faithful Rina Morelli and Romolo Valli to learn at short notice. There was not enough money to buy new sets, but Visconti had seen the ideal 'set' in a sitting-room of a private *palazzo* in Spoleto. He decided to use it as it was, but there was a capable, elderly female custodian who would never have allowed anyone to take anything out of the palace. This presented a welcome challenge to Visconti, and when Menotti's servant informed him that the custodian loved to drink, Visconti knew what his next move would be. On the very afternoon of the performance, Visconti went to see the woman in question with some bottles of good wine: when she was happily asleep, a van came to collect all the pieces from the small drawing-room, just in time to furnish the stage of the Caio Melisso theatre.

Asked which field he preferred to work in, Visconti answered: 'The one I'm not doing at the time. When I'm directing an opera, I dream about a film, when I'm working on a film, I dream about an opera, and when I'm doing a play, I'm dreaming about music. Working in another field is a change, a rest. You must always work with pleasure, the work is bad if you do not do it with pleasure.'[7]

During the same year he worked on yet another staging of *Troilus and Cressida*, this time set against the background of the Franco-Algerian war, but the project fell through. So, too, did another: Visconti was to film the episode of *Joseph and His Brothers* for a film on the Bible. Other episodes were to be made by Orson Welles and Robert Bresson; in the end it was filmed by John Huston.

In May 1964 he produced *Le Nozze di Figaro* (*The Marriage of Figaro*) for the Rome Opera House: it 'was superb, sensual, exciting, moving, it also had great suspense,' said Hans Werner Henze.

There was always music in his houses, even when he was working, but rarely Mozart; it was Verdi, Wagner and a lot of Richard Strauss. He loved *Il Trovatore*, but he always said that he could not grasp its story (admittedly, a

16 The director at work in 1962

17 Rina Morelli as the Princess being comforted in a scene from
The Leopard (1963)

18 Discussing a scene in *The Leopard* with Burt Lancaster, Ottavia Piccolo (*left*) and Anna-Maria Bottini

9 Visconti at his beloved home La Colombaia on Ischia

0 At his palazzo in Via Salaria, Rome

21 A scene from *The Damned* filmed in 1968. Visconti had ambivalent feelings about Nazism

22 Exercising his eye for detail. The dinner table was a symbol of family life which he used repeatedly

23 Helmut Berger's features were typical of the kind which inspired Visconti – here in *The Damned*

24 The funeral scene which was cut from the British version of *The Damned* – industrial might and bourgeois pomp

25 Visconti recreated the image of his mother (played by Silvana Mangano) in *Death in Venice*

26 Directing Dirk Bogarde at the Hôtel des Bains on the Lido in Venice

Romy Schneider as the Empress Elizabeth of Austria in *Ludwig* had the Teutonic aristocratic looks which Visconti admired

With his old friend Enrico Medioli, answering awkward questions after a preview of *Conversation Piece* (1974)

29 On location for his last film, *The Intruder* (1976)

most complicated one). He still could not do so after staging *Il Trovatore* for La Scala's tour to Moscow, into which he hardly put any work: the faithful Fassini did most of it, but Visconti took the credit. Suso Cecchi d'Amico and Antonello Trombadori joined him in Moscow and Leningrad for the first nights of *Il Trovatore*. They were given an Intourist guide called Svetlana towards whom Visconti took an instant dislike and on whom he enjoyed playing tricks, evading her control. In Leningrad he made a point of visiting the canals described by Dostoievsky and Prince Yusupov's house (enquiring in which room Rasputin had been killed). 'He loved Russia,' said Suso d'Amico, 'he liked the atmosphere even if he himself said that the lack of freedom of expression resulted in poor artistic output. But since he was a conservative – he loved the conservation of certain values – he liked Russia's order.' A few years earlier Visconti had refused to film *Anna Karenina* with Sophia Loren because Ponti had asked him to spend eight months in Russia. 'I think that eight months in Russia are too much for anyone,' he said then.

In November another production of *Il Trovatore* opened in London; it was very different from the La Scala-Bolshoi version because this production was almost entirely the work of Filippo Sanjust (but, once again, Visconti took the credit). Rudolf Bing tried to re-unite Callas and Visconti for *Carmen* at the Metropolitan; the project, later cherished, equally unsuccessfully, by Zeffirelli, came to nothing.

Once again *Maria Tarnowska*, the story on which Antonioni had worked, looked as if it were about to be filmed. Georges Beaume stayed on Ischia with Natalie Delon, whom Alain had married, and Visconti discussed the film with him. *Maria Tarnowska* is the true story of an aristocratic woman who killed her lover. The script, based on a famous trial, was seen from three different viewpoints, like *Rashomon*, so to speak. Visconti described it thus: 'It will be an *art nouveau* film. If I were to think about figurative art, I'd point at Redon or the later Renoir rather than Boldini; and over all I think of Debussy's music. Something soft, languid, decadent. Slightly putrefied but with that violence, with that fever which one finds in decomposed matter.'[8]

This project was an early attempt to portray his mother physically. In the same interview he talked about being old and started reminiscing – a new turn for Visconti, who up to now had been so discreet and secretive. He described training his horses at dawn in the empty plain surrounding Milan, back in the 1920s, when there was no concrete: 'An artisan like me has a duty to recount what he can with precision, with a substantial amount of critical analysis.'

Another project which did not materialize was a film on Puccini, *Portrait of an Unknown Man* (*Ritratto di uno sconosciuto*), which he should have filmed with Mastroianni as the composer; it would have been a portrait of his own past, his family and of his Milan.

Instead he filmed *Vaghe stelle dell'orsa*. (In the UK the film was called *Of A Thousand Delights*, in the USA, even worse, *Sandra*.) The title came from one of Giocomo Leopardi's most desperate poems; the story was inspired by the *Oresteia* of Aeschylus and by events in Luchino's own life. The star was Claudia Cardinale, who gave a particularly inept performance. It was filmed in Volterra, a beautiful Etruscan city dramatically divided by a deep ravine. The theme is that of a family curse transmitted from one generation to the next. Being Jewish, the children of 'the mother' (Marie Bell) are 'different'. The protagonist, Sandra, thinks that her father, a Jew, has been betrayed to the Germans by her mother and stepfather: the wicked mother is an overwhelming presence in this story, but is she really wicked, was she really guilty? The closeness of brother and sister is seen by Sandra's husband (an outsider, an American) as incestuous, and he is right. The mother has withdrawn into madness, playing the same Franck prelude, choral and fugue which Donna Carla used to play at Via Cerva: she nurses a real hatred for her daughter. Gilardini, the children's stepfather, is a character close to Visconti's biography as well, and he is a lawyer, like one of Donna Carla's lovers. Sandra thinks that Gilardini is the man who denounced her father, which is why she hates him. For Sandra's brother, Gilardini is the ravisher of his mother, and so he hates him too. The obsession in this film is with the family, with the balance of hatred, resentment and suspicion in a tormented, interlocking circle. 'In *Vaghe stelle dell'orsa* women are the victims of disorderly passions – woman is always an element of upset,' said Visconti explaining what had always been his image of womanhood. Being a conservative, he had a patriarchal vision of the family, of the role of womanhood. Modern woman had forgotten her duties, 'her reason to exist,' he said.[9] In the film both women, mother and daughter, are negative characters.

He was happy at Volterra; as usual friends and helpers had followed him, including Domietta Hercolani, Bice Brichetto, who worked on the film, and Fulco della Verdura, the sharp-witted old Sicilian duke. Luchino Visconti loved this part of Etruria and the Tuscan countryside and, naturally, he bought a house. This was a Renaissance villa designed by Baldassarre Peruzzi, and its main attraction was that it faced his brother Edoardo's house. Visconti embarked upon an enormous amount of converting and decorating. It was the kind of mansion which had its own theatre and chapel. Visconti was trying to recapture the grand old ways of his family – Via Salaria and Ischia were for the other 'family'; he felt the division between the two forces, the bond with those to whom he was related by blood, and with the 'family' he had chosen; at times he felt almost schizoid about it, rejecting one for the other. The old grudge he felt – and never verbalized, perhaps not even to himself – against his parents, his passionate love for his mother, was transferred to his friends, whom he could pick and choose, love and reject, like his mother had done among her crowd of children, lovers and admirers. By expressing his thoughts about his family through his films, he succeeded in detaching himself from it and, gradually, he became more involved in the other 'family', and his lovers became his sons.

Once, when he was looking round the chapel of his new villa with some friends, he declared: 'And here, every evening in May, we'll recite the Rosary.' He loved not only the rite but also the idea of faith. He was strangely traditionalist in his relationship with the Church. 'I've always believed in God, since I was a child, I was educated in a Catholic way.... I believe in a mysterious force, larger than the individual, but the possibility should not be excluded that the individual might be as great as that force.'[10]

The villa was restored, ancient tiles covered the beautiful floors, antique shops were combed and emptied, and Tuscan Renaissance furniture was placed in the large halls and rooms. When the film was finished, the house was ready and, the preoccupation with his family partially exhausted by the outlet of confession in the film, Luchino went back to his other 'family'.

Visconti's interpretation of the play *After the Fall* by Arthur Miller in Paris (starring Annie Girardot and Michel Auclair, and with costumes by Christian Dior) had been a fiasco. Despite this Visconti remained loved and respected in France, where he was considered a *maestro*.

In October 1965 he opened the Teatro Stabile in Rome with *The Cherry Orchard*, and in November he staged a production of *Don Carlos* which was far weaker than the one in London. Costumes and sets were designed by Vera Marzot, but Visconti took the credit: he was under contract to direct and design the opera and, by asking Vera Marzot to design the costumes for it, he was giving her an opportunity to start in a new field. Visconti's weakness for taking the credit for work which was done by others was growing increasingly apparent.

In November he joined the Pacifist demonstrations organized by the National Committee for the Liberation of Vietnam, but his political involvement was fading. What had been a religion when Togliatti was alive, what had been faith in one man, became discipline alone. Indeed his real faith went back to that of his early days when his mother had taken him to Mass.

He had come to terms with his homosexuality, which did not embarrass him – he was never effeminate. Apart from his masochistic approach to love, he became more and more paternal: he wanted to transform the person he loved. His sentimental metabolism was of a nineteenth-century kind, like that of Swann who keeps a tart like Odette, intimately enjoying being 'soiled' by her, being betrayed, covering her with jewels and being lied to by her: ultimately what Visconti could not achieve was a sentimental relationship of equality. He said that the most important thing in the world was love and that its consequence at times was the creation of art.

Visconti was still looking for a film to make. *The Nun from Monza*, a morbid story which was to have starred Sophia Loren, almost came off. He wrote a treatment from Musil's *Törless*, from Camus's *L'Etranger* and a totally new story for a film – *Lee J. Thompson*, with Suso Cecchi d'Amico and Enrico Medioli. He staged *Falstaff* with Dietrich Fischer-Dieskau, Graziella Sciutti and Regina Resnik, conducted by Leonard Bernstein, for the Vienna Opera theatre – it was an opera he loved and felt deeply about now that he was sixty; it was the opera which he should have directed for the opening of la Piccola Scala, with Arturo Toscanini. '... I got it wrong, I got the last act wrong,' he complained privately. The critics agreed.

Another opera he admired, *Der Rosenkavalier*, was strangely mistreated by him. After his great success with *Don Carlos*, Covent Garden had been longing to have him back. Strauss was his own choice (David Webster and Georg Solti had gone to see him in Paris, where Visconti had told them that he wanted to stage this particular opera). Visconti knew Strauss well, understood his world and was attracted by the sexual ambiguities of the opera, by the analysis of old age giving way to youth. However, rather than presenting the opera as it was, as he had always conceived opera, he set the story in an *art nouveau* context, which resulted in a messy production. He was beautifully served, however, by the singers, who included Sena Jurinac, Josephine Veasey, Yvonne Minton and Michael Langdon.

It was April 1966 and London was pleasing, especially when seen from the flat he had rented overlooking Hyde Park; he had brought his cook from Rome and his friends too. There were new faces in his team, including Ferdinando Scarfiotti, his assistant director on *Rosenkavalier* and *Falstaff*. Visconti would start rehearsals of *Rosenkavalier* early in the mornings, and by 2 p.m. he was free for shopping, taking walks and socializing. He loved eating at Wilton's, or he would go to San Lorenzo with Rudolph Nureyev and discuss making a film on Nijinsky. His aim in *Rosenkavalier*, he said, was that of bringing in some fresh air: 'This opera is full of feeling, of love and eroticism. Every production of *Der Rosenkavalier* I have seen has been the same. I want to remove some of the dust.'[11] Some of the dust was indeed removed and Solti was horrified – he looked on Visconti's interpretation as a desecration of the Austro-Hungarian world from which he came. The idea of stressing the *art nouveau* element of the music was overdone, as if the audience had to be told over and over again that Strauss in *Rosenkavalier* was not really talking about the eighteenth century; this interpretation was hammered home with a decidedly Teutonic lack of subtlety; besides, his new team was not on the same intellectual and professional level as his former entourage. But like the Marschallin, the protagonist of *Der Rosenkavalier*, Visconti wanted young people around him because they made him feel young too. In addition to which, they were more beautiful to look at, and the more talented crop of yesterday had reached middle-age.

The critics were cool, although restrained: nobody wanted to damn the producer of *Don Carlos*.

The vogue for films consisting of episodes was waning; one of the last, *The Witches* (*Le Streghe*), was produced by Dino de Laurentis. Visconti directed one episode, *The Witch Burnt Alive* (*La Stregha Bruciata Viva*) – other episodes were directed by Mauro Bolognini, Pier Paolo Pasolini, Francesco Rosi and Vittorio de Sica. In Visconti's episode Silvana Mangano, de Laurentis's wife, was the principal actress; Helmut Berger had a small part in it too. It told the story of a film actress transformed into an idol; the price of this kind of success was her alienation from the family nucleus, from the duties of womanhood. The episode was chopped about and Visconti said that de Laurentis had 'completely ruined it', but while he was making the film, Visconti discovered his ideal actress. Silvana Mangano had changed since her beauty-prize days; she had become a slender, withdrawn woman who was dedicated to her family and an elegant, austere professional who shunned publicity. In her, Visconti saw the ideal mother-figure, aloof but tender, efficient and beautiful. He liked the fact that she had never been divorced and that her family was united and all-important to her (in the same way, he minded and disapproved when his married friends or relatives separated or got a divorce).

Not long after, Visconti began work on a film of *The Outsider*, from Camus's first novel.[12] The novel tells the story of an apathetic *pied-noir*, Meursault, who kills an Arab without motivation and is condemned to die; the conventional community turns against him because of his 'unheroic', passive behaviour. The only biographical detail for Visconti to work on was in the opening of the book, when Meursault rushes to his mother's bedside because she is dying. Visconti's ideal actor for the part of Meursault, another anti-hero, was Alain Delon. Visconti even accepted radical changes imposed by Camus's widow, Francine, who insisted that the script should be as close to the novel as possible, while Visconti had intended to use the book as a point of departure, not as a point of arrival. In the film he had wanted to show that in 'the characters of *The Outsider* I explain the OAS, torture, all of Algeria today'.[13] Even if Visconti no longer believed in the script, there was still Alain Delon. But Delon asked for a huge fee, to which the producers reacted by saying that they did not intend to make the film for Delon alone. Visconti insisted: he had had Delon in mind for the part from the beginning.

Georges Beaume, Delon's agent, has said that there was a misunderstanding about *The Outsider*: 'Alas, I was away. In the definitive contract there was a clause about the publicity which Delon didn't like, so he sent a telegram insulting de Laurentis, who decided that Delon was not to star in *The Outsider*; it was to be Mastroianni.' Besides, said Beaume, Visconti made it a point of principle not to be paid less than any of his stars; evidently Delon had asked for more.

Having lost two of the motivations for making *The Outsider* – one being Delon, the other his own adaptation – there remained a beautiful but impossible novel to translate on to the screen.

Visconti, who was always very specific about the soundtrack, discussed the film with the composer Luigi Nono. Although he was never a man who paid much attention to the *avant-garde*, he had strong intuitions, when not clouded by love or nepotism. Nono was interested in the idea of writing the music for *The Outsider*, but he wanted to work with Visconti on the whole of the soundtrack. He thought that *La Terra Trema* was Visconti's best film because of the continuous presence of the sound of the sea, which thus became the protagonist. Instead of the sound 'happening by chance', Luigi Nono wanted to 'compose' it: for example, the all-important noise of Meursault's prison cell opening for the last time and the footsteps leading Meursault to the guillotine. So it was agreed that Visconti and Nono would work together and consult each other throughout the different stages of the script, so that the music and the sounds would be conceived as a whole while the words were being written. Visconti seemed to be interested and asked Nono to start working on the prison sequence but, after sending him one tape of his music, the composer never heard anything more from Visconti, not a word.

Ultimately Visconti must have been alarmed at the idea of working with Luigi Nono instead of dealing with a subordinate, or with a member of his own group. The music for *The Outsider* was eventually written by Piero Piccioni.

In spite of his horror of travel, Piero Tosi went to Algiers and stayed in a beautiful hotel just outside the city, on the east side, from which one could see the white citadel, the Fort and the harbour. 'We dined together because during the day he was filming. He dined in his room. As usual he didn't like going to restaurants, but it was no snack – they were proper dinners: waiters in white gloves preparing huge tables, beautifully laid because, if he could not buy a house of his own wherever he went, he transformed the hotel into his house.' One night, when Piero Tosi was with him, he talked about his youthful journey to Algeria, but without revealing the motivation for his desperate escape.

Tosi's formerly terror-stricken relationship with Visconti had mellowed over the years and he was more at ease now; Visconti knew how talented Tosi was, but had always enjoyed the awe he provoked in the shy, blue-eyed Tuscan.

'They were half-way through the film, but they hadn't yet found the boy who is killed by Meursault. One day, near the house where Camus lived, in the rain, under a *djellaba*, I saw a face the colour of the earth, long hands. . . .' Tosi lifted the striped hood and 'I saw a face of wondrous beauty and asked the Arab producer to talk to him.' The boy was twenty-two and had just come down from the Kabilia mountains, Tosi took him to the Aletti hotel, in the centre of Algiers, where the pretty living-rooms include a salon for *thé-dansant* and where the *pied-noir* chef, who came from Russia, cooked them a Russian meal.

The boy's screen test showed him to be very photogenic. 'He had beige eyes, beige skin, beige everything. I went to see Luchino and told him that I thought I had found the boy.' Following Visconti's example, Tosi had the boy under lock and key. 'It is him,' Visconti said as soon as he saw him. 'I also want him for *Joseph and His Brethren*.' The boy looked like a Messiah and had the elegance of a prince. Both men were entranced by his beauty, and decided they would play a joke – something which Visconti loved – on Notarianni, the head of the production team. Notarianni was about to return from Rome, where he had gone to arrange finance because, as usual, they were short of cash. Visconti told Tosi to go and collect Notarianni at the airport and tell him that they had found a Moroccan prince who wanted to put money in the film. 'We went to the market and bought fake jewellery, necklaces, turbans in gold and olive green, and dressed the boy up: he looked like an Arab prince from *A Thousand and One Nights*.'

Notarianni arrived and was introduced to the handsome 'prince', who, through an interpreter, could hardly answer Notarianni's questions because he did not in any way understand what he was talking about. Visconti and Tosi were having a wonderful time. 'It was like *la Commedia dell'Arte*.' Late that evening, after the prince withdrew, Visconti and Tosi confessed the truth to Notarianni, but on the following day the boy from Kabilia and his suitcases had disappeared from the hotel.

In spite of the many talented young actors who had been groomed by him, he was still in search of new talent, and it was Helmut Berger who attracted Visconti's attention. They met at Kitzbühel; Helmut had always wanted to lead a different life from his parents', who had an hotel at Mondsee; he had hoped for years to meet Visconti. This confession moved the director, who was now feeling his age, with lines on his forehead turning his profile into a more hawkish one, drawing his mouth downwards. A great deal had to be done, however, in order to turn this frightened boy into an actor, and also into an adult. Berger began to be seen with Visconti everywhere. 'When he was in Paris, he rang me up at the St Regis,' said Salvador Dali. 'He was with Helmut Berger and asked me if I wanted to work on Proust's *La Recherche*. I replied that I would like to continue my collaboration with him.'

Visconti's main preoccupation now was to make a film which would launch Helmut Berger.

In 1967 Berger went with Visconti to London, where he was staging the third *Traviata* of his career. It was to be a black-and-white Aubrey Beardsley *Traviata*.

Visconti was ill with 'flu when he called Vera Marzot: 'Can you come by? I need to see you for a moment.' She found him on his vast bed, behind which there hung a collection of holy images painted on glass. He was dismissive about his illness. 'Sit down,' he said, 'are you free towards March-April 1967?' He had thought of her for *La Traviata*. 'But it is obvious that the blacks and the whites must not be all blacks and whites, as you know, Verina; they must span throughout the possible range of black, which can be off-mauve, off-livid-green, and the same goes for the whites, which can be lacquered, cream, ice. In the middle of these: all greys.' He offered no explanation then nor did Vera Marzot ask for any, but a few days later he told her the motivation for such an interpretation: 'In order to shock the English a bit.'

He succeeded in annoying more than shocking. 'In London they were furious,' Vera Marzot recalled; 'The wardrobe department were indignant, we got little collaboration; they seemed to think that the naughty boy had decided to indulge a whim of his at their expense. Visconti enjoyed the *malaise* which surrounded him at rehearsals.'

In fact, when Covent Garden's administration saw the designs for *La Traviata*, they decided to ask for changes. 'It seemed capricious,' said John Tooley, 'but David Webster thought that we should take it as it was or leave it.' Tooley was conscious of Visconti's dependence on his team, whom he knew and trusted, and who did the 'dirty' work for him. Giulini, who attended the public dress rehearsal, did not like what he saw, though he worshipped Visconti and they had been genuine friends after working together on several magnificent projects.

This was the last occasion on which Visconti worked in London. Critics, on the whole, were negative about the production, but he never cared about criticism whether good or bad. Sometimes he even despised those who were too appreciative when he knew they should not have been.

Two months later, in Florence, he produced *Egmont* by Goethe, with incidental music by Beethoven, at the Boboli gardens. I saw it with Harold Acton and Alberto Arbasino, with whom Visconti was no longer on speaking terms. *Egmont* is a tragedy about the governor of the rebellious Spanish Flanders who was beheaded. Fedele d'Amico, who had translated it, wrote a letter to Visconti a week before the opening of the play, criticizing certain things and pointing out others: for example Romolo Valli's interpretation of the Duke of Alba, the 'baddy' of the story, made that dignified character into a caricature. Visconti himself had interpreted the tragedy as a political one, but the theme was really Count Egmont's *joie de vivre*, d'Amico said. Visconti read this letter out to the company, but it was too late to change anything; anyway, he always needed time in order to be persuaded and then to absorb ideas. The production of *Egmont* demonstrated a lack of intellectual discussion, of real thought, just like the London production of *La Traviata*.

Visconti's team no longer provided a critical contribution; if one thought of *Ossessione*, in which Visconti had employed the best people in Italy, from Ingrao to Moravia, one could see the intellectual gap between then and now, and realize the importance that the team had for him.

After several artistic failures, he was thinking of *The Damned*, a film in which he was going to express some of his most hidden secrets, in which he was going to go back to History as the spring of all events, the great leveller; in which he was going to launch Helmut Berger.

Berger was beginning to be difficult, and Visconti tried to justify this, like an old parent justifying a young son. Outwardly secure, Visconti was still a tormented man, though he did not like to show this to others, as he would have felt it was a sign of weakness. He had doubts, but he did not like to consult others, seek for the comfort of other people's points of view.

His energy was still tremendous, but he was beginning to get old: he was sixty-one. In New York, where he went with Helmut Berger, he was rehearsing the Rome production of *The Marriage of Figaro* for the Metropolitan Opera House; there he displayed a newly-acquired patience. When the Met suddenly announced to him and to Sandro Sequi, who was directing another opera, that they both were to have less time for rehearsals, Sequi became furious, and wondered to what heights of anger the 'Almighty', famous for his tempers, would reach. Instead, Visconti just accepted the Met's decision.

He did not like America at all, was unhappy there, hated American food, and in American restaurants he ordered nothing but scrambled eggs since he thought that it was the only dish that they knew how to prepare. Helmut Berger did not improve matters: he would tell Visconti that he was old and in his dotage. Visconti tolerated it; in his masochistic way he even enjoyed being insulted in public. Once, at a large dinner-table in a New York restaurant, he seemed not to have noticed any of Berger's asides. 'He's deaf!' Berger said to the other diners, 'he has become deaf....' In fact it was true, Visconti had become a little deaf. But this time Visconti rolled his eyes and everybody around the table trembled because he suddenly looked like a lion: 'I hear everything and I see everything because I am intelligent,' he said, and then exploded in a fury.

During the same trip to New York, he paid a visit to Wanda Toscanini, who was married to Vladimir Horowitz, and they talked about the good old days when they used to hide under the table, a visual recollection which Visconti was to use in *The Damned*. For a man who did not like talking about the past, he was beginning to take surprising pleasure in reminiscing.

In October another play by Testori, called *La Monaca di Monza* (*The Nun from Monza*), which Visconti directed, made a brief and scandalous appearance in Rome; it dealt with forbidden love and Visconti had changed the text. Both public and critics condemned it and then official censorship put a sudden end to its performance. But 1968 and 1969 were the years in which the old symbols of authority, the ones recognized, respected and needed by Visconti, were being overthrown. Visconti did not accept, nor did he have any sympathy with the students' movements, with the rejection of all discipline, of order, of the system. He did not like the present either, nor did he try to understand the new symbols. In the young, he minded the attitude of passivity, the lack of education and culture: he came to hate politicians more and more, so that he took refuge in his own past, and the present became the symbol of the end, the death of better days. 'He felt a sense of guilt for being an aristocrat,' said Piero Tosi; 'the livery of a valet, the uniforms in his plays, films, all had to be exact: it was part of a culture which was his own. This world which was disappearing, which was decaying ... you discover that that was his world. His own battalion of menservants at home: at times you could hear them walk like an army. Nowadays there is nobody who bodies forth an insular world like Luchino used to.' But his insular world was coming to an end and he knew it.

12
Interior Twilight

'I'm very German. I like German culture, German music, German philosophy; and the origins of the Visconti family are in Germany,' he said, referring to the fact that the old Viscontis were Longobard, when interviewed about *The Damned*.[1] 'In this picture I want to ask where the responsibility lay for the Nazis in Germany. The most grave responsibility was with the bourgeoisie and the industrialists because, if Hitler had not had their help, he would never have achieved real power. Books say that the Krupps paid Hitler, so I am inventing nothing. And I like in all my films to have a nucleus of humanity, a family. I try to explain, in the development of the family, the parallel of what happened in the whole of Germany and later all over the world.'

However, Hans Werner Henze and Horst, two Germans who knew him well, thought that Visconti did not understand Germany. 'For him Germany was dangerously mysterious,' Henze said, 'and he painted a fascinating story in a melodramatic way, as if Nazism had developed from the upper-middle classes. In fact Nazism was the triumph of mediocrity, of the *petite bourgeoisie*, of their psychological and sexual morality. It was the gentility of the *petite bourgeoisie* which made Nazi Germany, not those handsome and perverted Krupps.'

The Damned was a spectacular and expensive film; it took three months of preparation and eight months to film, and cost nearly two million dollars. As usual, the story contained different elements. 'I always dreamt of making Thomas Mann's *Buddenbrooks*, but I never managed it. Then I had the idea of *Macbeth*, but that was stopped. Then once again I thought of making *Buddenbrooks*, set at the beginning of the Nazi movement, and from this the script emerged. There are one or two similarities with *Macbeth* in the murders, but not more. The focus is on other things.'[2]

The search for locations entailed many journeys to Germany, Austria and Bavaria – some of Ludwig's castles had been considered when Visconti thought of concealing the identity of the Krupps. When the cast and the film crew finally moved on location, it was almost as if the Third Reich were back in power. The Austrian resort of Unterach am Attersee was taken over and flooded with Nazi banners and stormtroopers; a Jew who was driving through the holiday resort had a heart attack. The whole of Düsseldorf's traffic was brought to a halt for a funeral scene. German sausages were sent daily to Austria because of the different colour: Visconti refused to have pink Austrian Würstels on a Bavarian table, which produces pale sausages made of veal, not pork. There were tremendous difficulties with the production.

Originally *The Damned* was called *Götterdämmerung* or *The Twilight of the Gods*, the title of the last opera of Wagner's Ring cycle. *The Twilight of the Gods* was a better title than *The Damned*, and Visconti hated the title that the distributors imposed. He thought that this film was European, as his culture was, and when told that a farmer in Iowa might never have heard of the *Götterdämmerung*, he said that it did not matter. In fact the film made a lot of money in America – perhaps due to the multiple murders, the many sadistic scenes, and the beginning of a wave of nostalgia for the Nazi era. *The Damned* was to be the first of many a film on the subject: Nazism, sadism, homosexuality and uniforms were 'launched' and made respectable under a veneer of complacent criticism.

He would not have liked to think of *The Damned* in this context; it is, in fact, a story of the decline and decomposition of a family whose fortunes are linked to wider historical events. The von Essenbeck family is involved in the rise of Nazism. Baron Joachim (Albrecht Schonhals) is due to retire as head of the family steelworks and his heir is his decadent grandson Martin (Helmut Berger), but he has two other possible successors: Herbert (Umberto Orsini), a liberal, and Konstantin (René Kolldehoff), a fanatical member of the *Sturmabteilung*. Joachim would prefer the anti-Fascist Herbert but, due to the political situation, his choice has to fall on Konstantin and, in order to control him, Friedrich Bruckmann (Dirk Bogarde), an outsider, is made managing director of the gigantic steelworks. But Friedrich is not totally an outsider because he is the lover of Baroness Sophie (Ingrid Thulin), the mother of Martin. In his rise, Friedrich is also helped by a cousin of the von Essenbecks who is in the SS and opposes Konstantin. In the struggle for leadership, Friedrich almost achieves both marriage to Sophie and total control. With the political help of the SS, young Martin is able to force both Friedrich and his mother to commit suicide on the day of their mock marriage. After this Martin, who is only a tool of the regime, will be swept away by the tide – a visual tide of elegant SS men who engulf the 'wedding' party in the house of the von Essenbecks.

The film begins with Baron Joachim's birthday party, which is also his retirement party and which coincides with the burning of the Reichstag. At this party, Martin's little cousin, Günther, becomes young Luchino Visconti when he plays a Bach cello sonata. The younger children, under the direction of the French nanny, who could be Mademoiselle Hélène, recite a poem in Italian; Martin's contribution to this private show in honour of his grandfather is a cabaret song which he sings in drag. He is a depraved boy who injects himself with drugs and loves little girls – he is also in love with his mother, who, to some extent, encourages him in order to gain his consent to her marriage to Friedrich; but his seduction of her turns into rape.

The assassination of Konstantin during the Night of the Long Knives, in which the SS eliminate the SA, is an opportunity for Visconti to recount an historical event; the orgy of the men and the massacre which follows is detailed. Visconti stresses visually the difference between the SA, the brown shirts, instruments of counter-revolutionary violence during the rise of the Nazis, and the efficient, cold militarism of the SS. And there, at the centre, is a family of monsters: 'A family nucleus which is heading for ruin, always negative stories . . . I recount them as if in a requiem. . . .'[3]

Visconti was looking at the waning gods of early industry, Wagnerian gods whose female divinities were tiresome Frickas or aggressive Valkyries.

On location in Austria and Germany there was a certain amount of hostility towards Visconti, who was recreating times best forgotten; this antagonism was heightened by the fact that money from Rome failed to arrive and occasionally there was not even enough cash to pay for the hotel. Once the whole crew were locked in their rooms as a reprisal – this time not by Visconti, but by the hotelier. The organization was appalling: Bogarde sat in Rome for three weeks waiting to be called; Thulin waited to work for five weeks; at times even Visconti did not work, in protest against not being paid. The actors stuck to the film and to Visconti, who bewitched them all; Bogarde, who began by being sceptical about him, came to like and admire the director; they became friends and grew to understand each other.

The Damned often recalls opera, even in the way it is conceived – in the duets and chorus, and in the strong, sweeping, clear-cut passions it recounts. Visconti made no bones about it – most of his films were operas anyway – and sometimes when directing he even quoted *Parsifal*. But the bleakness of Nazism was seen with the duplicity of an eye which was partly fascinated by it (apart from a reference to Dachau, the story concentrates on the family's struggle for control); the beauty of the people and often the décor hid the horror of Nazism. He wanted to interpret the psychology of the Nazi, without any rhetoric; he said Aschenbach, the colonel of the SS, was a cultivated man, like Hess, who loved flowers and played the piano.

In the film, colour was used dramatically, as he had used it in *Senso* and *The Leopard*, and he analysed his way of using colour as a means to re-invent reality.

The von Essenbecks, in their fall, gave way to another class, which represented the reactionary populism of Germany. And the fall of one class which gives way to another – a worse one – was Visconti's theme, the theme of his life. *The Damned* was heavily cut by Visconti, by the censors and then by the distributors.

When *The Damned* was shown in New York for the first time, Helmut

Berger had tears in his eyes, for he saw that Visconti had made him into an actor as well as a star. People queued to see it. Visconti went to the States for the premiere; though he went to collect Visconti and Berger at their hotel, Horst refused to see the film: he thought that his old friend Visconti was incapable of understanding the petty populism of Nazism. The film was hailed as a masterpiece by most critics and it drew an enormous public. It was his first film to make a lot of money.

In January 1969, Visconti directed a new play by Natalia Ginzburg. 'But *L'inserzione*[4], which I staged in Milan, was slight: I couldn't find anything in it which really involved me in the production. On the other hand, I think I made a personal contribution to *La Monaca di Monza* by Testori – so much so that the author protested. I may do things which are more or less successful, but I cannot do them without believing in them,' declared Visconti later.[5] In fact, after directing *La Monaca di Monza*, Visconti's relationship with Testori cooled; it grew even colder after he failed to cast a boyfriend of the playwright's in *The Damned*. Seeing that so many good-looking newcomers were launched by Visconti, friends would insist that he should use their protégés – but Visconti was only interested in the people he loved and felt close to. Occasionally Visconti would actually promise to find a small part for this or that boy and, in the end, enjoyed disappointing the expectations he had aroused. Such episodes always led to hatred of him.

In March he staged *Simon Boccanegra* at the Staatsoper in Vienna. He did not like working with Joseph Krips, who conducted the opera, nor did he get on with some of the glittering cast, and all agreed that the production was bad.

Enrico Medioli was one of the old entourage who almost always worked for Visconti and towards whom Visconti felt tenderness – indeed there was mutual respect. Together they worked on a script for an episode of a film which was to be called *Three Steps from Frenzy* (*Tre passi dal delirio*). The actual episode was to be called *I giocatori di scacchi* (*The Chess Players*), but the film was never made. When working on a script, they would start with endless meetings, during which they would discuss and disagree. 'Then,' said Medioli, 'we would share things, with Suso too, and with Luchino, because he also wrote. Say I wrote two or three scenes; if they were no good, he would say so, with great courtesy, explaining why, and it always seemed right. If they were good, he would be silent for days. He wouldn't call because he enjoyed my vexation.'

Visconti was also working on *Death in Venice*.

Thomas Mann was a writer whom Visconti had loved and absorbed throughout his life, and with whom he identified – the more so as he grew older. Visconti did not himself feel old, merely older in the sense that his desire to work was as strong as ever and he was still tremendously energetic, but his artistic motivation was different and he was beginning to talk about the past, to regret it. He was also, now, to face more private themes, his past of artistic militancy could justify his late return to his privacy, he said, a privacy which for years he had protected. And he who had felt the power that beauty gives was no longer so handsome. He was strong, but he smoked an amazing amount – about eighty or more cigarettes a day. At times he tried to go without smoking for a couple of days in order to train himself to do without tobacco, but he then would go back to chain-smoking and his long fingers were stained yellow from the nicotine.

While preparing *Death in Venice*, he went repeatedly to the Lido with friends and, in silence, he would look at the Hôtel des Bains, at the long white beach and at the melancholy light on the lagoon: in silence he was remembering things past, and this was what *Death in Venice* was going to be, his past and his present intertwined, evoked through Thomas Mann, with scenes of great beauty – maybe the most beautiful of all Visconti's wonderful images. During these silent inspections, he already saw the images he was going to recreate; Aschenbach, the protagonist of the novella, in the film was going to be the composer, Gustav Mahler; and Mahler's music became a languid, morbid element of the story. This film was to be no opera, for once no great passions, no family dramas: just a photograph album.

He took over the Hôtel des Bains for three months. He insisted that Piero Tosi work on the film: he wanted the most accurate and scholarly person he could find to evoke the images.

Thomas Mann recounted his feelings, Visconti photographed them, but then fell into the trap of explaining: there was too much dialogue in *Death in Venice*, which was at its best when visual. And for the spoken 'explanations', Visconti had plunged into *Doctor Faustus*, Thomas Mann's last book, so that the middle-class Aschenbach, who dressed for dinner every night in order to sit in the dining-room surrounded by a well-bred clientele, speaks in the words of the demoniac protagonist of Mann's last book.

Alberto Moravia pinpointed this weakness when he wrote that Mann's Aschenbach was described as 'a middle-class intellectual of the turn of the century, not a Nietzsche or a Strindberg, and that is why the infatuation for a boy of fourteen brings about the collapse of the man's values. In other words, the drama of Aschenbach is social while Visconti's Aschenbach is intellectual. The difference is to be found in the two authors. Mann was the historian of aesthetic decadence; Visconti was a decadent aesthete who could well figure as a character of Mann's.'[6] This change allowed Visconti to recount the story of Luchino Visconti as seen by Luchino Visconti – or many aspects of it – using that fourteenth-century technique in which one painting depicts the various stages of a saint's life. In Visconti's story we see a famous upper-class aesthete (Mahler), in whom Visconti can reflect himself; it would have been impossible for him to make the same transposition into the conventional middle-class unknown writer of Thomas Mann's novella. And yet the upheavals that a homosexual crush could create in a conventional man could not take place in an intellectual, at least not in the same way. But Visconti's adaptation was deliberate, the transposition was intentional. The film was an explicit recollection of Visconti's life revived by Piero Tosi, under strict instructions from his director. A silent Silvana Mangano, who gazes at her children dressed so beautifully and neatly, was just like Donna Carla Visconti: Visconti himself said that seeing Mangano reading on the beach under large hats and parasols, a haughty profile, distant, husbandless, gave him the eerie feeling of watching his mother. The manners of her children were as rigidly disciplined as those of the Visconti brood, who also wore sailor suits. There is a governess who accompanies these aristocratic Polish children, who could have been the one who worked at Via Cerva. And mirroring himself in both Tadzio and Aschenbach, the tormented reaction of the latter to the discovery of his homosexuality became the exaltation of an upper-class intellectual, of himself, not of a bourgeois.

Although, when young, Visconti had inherited a certain Puritanism, a northern element, a form rather than an essence, which had tormented his awareness of being 'different', in his more mature years he had shed these doubts and sufferings. His only regret – that of not having a family – was to some extent allayed by acquiring sons through his lovers, something quite common in homosexuals.

The film of *Death in Venice* contains many contradictions; this makes it, of all his films, the most revealing of Visconti himself, because his nature too was very contradictory. And an important component of his 'confession' was to be found in his juxtaposition of present and past. To the present belongs the story of a middle-aged man who, after arriving in Venice and after exchanging a provocative glance with a boy, dies on the beach in front of an hotel. From the past, on the other hand, we learn that the same man, a successful composer, has a family life and has certain values, a concept of beauty, a philosophy, which, however, does not satisfy him. In one of the flashbacks – which represent the past – the protagonist encounters a prostitute, whose name, Esmeralda, is the same as that of the boat on which he arrives in Venice; for Visconti homosexuality is pure, while womanhood is contamination, prostitution.

When he arrives on the boat, Gustav von Aschenbach is accosted by a drunken old man whose face is made up; a strange gondolier takes him to the Lido; on his arrival the *maître d'hôtel* receives him with much servile bowing. The protagonist hardly speaks, words are peculiarly rare. Finally an English clerk from Cook's tells the composer the truth: the city is swept by plague. Both *maître d'hôtel* and gondolier were servants deceiving the master; in the same way the barber who dyes von Aschenbach's hair and makes him up deceives the passive protagonist: there were no instructions for the barber to do so. And the composer will not look any younger. This is again Visconti surrounded by a servile court which uses him, deceives him and disobeys him.

Aschenbach arrives in Venice alone, he is always alone, surrounded by people who speak languages and dialects which he does not understand, by mutters and whispers – and he dies alone. The theme of solitude among crowds is also a reflection of Visconti's own life.

Visconti's concern with ageing is apparent in several ways in the film. There are several masks of made-up men, not only Aschenbach's but also that of the singer and of the old man in the boat. The ageing face of the protagonist underlines the purity of the face with which he has fallen in love: Tadzio, the image of youth. Youth – Tadzio – is always surrounded by people, by his mother, his governess, his sisters and his young friends, thus the barrier between youth and old age is total: when Aschenbach tries to speak to Tadzio's governess in French, she answers in Polish. Tadzio is also the innocent young Luchino, playing on the beach unaware of his purity and beauty. The one-sided relationship of voyeurism which the protagonist enjoys – just content to watch the youth (old Luchino watching young Luchino) – is broken by the eloquent glance which the boy exchanges with him.

The plague, the sirocco sweep Venice in contrast with the purity of Tadzio's face. The scenes from the past, which do not contribute to the understanding of the film, but do contribute to Visconti's self-analysis, suggest that Aschenbach is a puritan, that his inspiration is spiritual, yet he feels attracted – and frightened – by sensuality. The flashbacks continue to suggest elements of Visconti's life and his doubts and preoccupations. But far from enlightening, they confuse the audience; Visconti had let himself go, remembering things past without telling the full story.

Death in Venice was praised and criticized; it won awards, and Visconti loved it dearly. He came to London, where the film was given its world première attended by the Queen and Princess Anne, who had read Mann's novella especially for the occasion.

Horst liked *Death in Venice* and he wrote to his old friend to tell him so. In fluent French, Visconti answered from Ischia on 9 August 1971; he was delighted. Visconti really cared about the recognition of those he esteemed – not of audiences, of critics; in this (and other things) he was no populist. His regular correspondence was immense and, in addition, he answered letters from unknown admirers and would send money to many who asked for it – though only after checking as far as he could that they were really in need.

Visconti returned to Ischia to recover from *Death in Venice*, for it had been a tiring film to make. One day, while he was in a shop at Porto d'Ischia for the ritual present-buying, he suddenly felt very ill and collapsed on the floor. Though he soon recovered, his doctor warned him that he had suffered a mild heart attack and said he must stop smoking, have a rest and take the medicine prescribed. Visconti, who hated doctors, threw away the medicine and never told his friends about the mild attack.

While at La Colombaia, he worked on a cherished project, a film of Proust's *A la Recherche du Temps Perdu* – or of a part of it. In Proust, as in *Death in Venice*, he was 'fascinated by the theme of the impossibility of love'. Both works, he said in 1970, attracted him because of their elements of decadence, degeneration and finality which had always been at the roots of his films: putrid Venice is besieged by a secret epidemic; Paris society is afflicted by the corrupting vice of futility. The film was to open with the protagonist and his mother staying in Venice, after the death of Albertine, and end after the orgy in Julien's homosexual brothel, with Marcel merging with the frightened Parisians, seeking shelter from the bombardment in 1918. Having such vast material to draw upon, Visconti decided just to hint at the love story of Swann for Odette de Crecy, while the central themes would be Marcel's love for Albertine and Baron Charlus's for Morel, a story of love and jealousy.

The rights for *A la Recherche* belonged to a French producer called Nicole Stephane, whose agent was Georges Beaume. She wanted Réné Clement to direct the film, but Beaume thought that Visconti should. Beaume and Nicole Stephane went to Milan for lunch with him at the Principe di Savoia. Visconti talked of his conception of Proust, but said nothing of the film. 'You are saying all I wanted to hear,' she said, 'I must kiss you!' And she asked him to direct *A la Recherche*.

Visconti was due to start filming in August 1971. He worked on it for eight months. With Mario Garbuglia (who designed the sets) and Suso Cecchi d'Amico, he combed France for six weeks; he had selected his locations at La Ferrière, the *belle-epoque* château which belonged to Guy de Rothschild, Combray, Trouville, Doncières, Cabourg, Paris and Venice; in addition, he had accumulated hundreds of photographs and sketches. He had chosen his cast, some of whom already had a contract. Silvana Mangano was to be Oriane de Guermantes; Alain Delon, Marcel the narrator; Helmut Berger, Morel; maybe Charlotte Rampling, Albertine. For Charlus, once again, Visconti had thought of Marlon Brando, whom he judged an 'extraordinary actor', but once again the producers preferred another actor, maybe Laurence Olivier. Brigitte Bardot had let Visconti know that she would like to take part in the project and he had included her, in the small role of the ageing Odette de Crecy. Piero Tosi dreaded designing the costumes because Proust had been so precise in their description. The dialogue was going to be taken from the original; there were already 363 pages of script. The film would have lasted just under four hours and would have cost five billion lire, in those days far too much. Nicole Stephane did not have this amount and asked Visconti to postpone the date of shooting in order to give her time to find more money.

Instead of waiting, Visconti started working on another film (*Ludwig*), which, in turn, took longer than expected, and Nicole Stephane, thinking that he had given up *A la Recherche*, sued him. She felt betrayed and was so furious that she turned to director Joseph Losey, who commissioned Harold Pinter to write the script of a film which Visconti considered his by inherited right..

Although he was distraught at the idea of not being able to make this much-cherished film, Visconti felt a strange sense of relief, because he had decided that *A la Recherche* was to be his last film. He was very superstitious and was convinced that, after completing it, he would have died. Since *A la Recherche* was going to be the most autobiographical of all his films, after completing it he would have been left with nothing more to say, which for a man like Visconti meant death.

Colour would have been evocative and images would have doubled and tripled as if in a mirror: present and past were going to intertwine more explicitly than they had done in *Death in Venice*. But what kind of Proust would this have been? Certainly Visconti would have projected himself in the narrator (interesting to note that for this key role he had chosen Alain Delon) and in Charlus. Oriane de Guermantes was Visconti's mother, even in the pages of the novel.

When we talked about it, a few months later, I told him that he had been lucky not to have been able to make the film; the transposition of a novel like *A la Recherche* was impossible, it was too elusive to stand the grossness of explanation, of images. He did not agree and told me that he had counter-sued the producers and that he still hoped to make it. The situation was stalemate: Losey could not make the film without Visconti's permission and the French producers were losing money.

Instead Visconti started work on *Ludwig*. Although there were some themes of his own even in this story, *Ludwig* was not part of his autobiography. The idea for it had come to him while he was combing Bavaria in search of locations for *The Damned*. There was an important reason, however, for Visconti to film *Ludwig* as soon as possible: this was a way to consecrate Helmut Berger as an actor, to launch his difficult 'son' by giving him an important role.

I went to see Visconti at Bad Ischl, a sleepy Austrian town, where he had arrived with three Panavision cameras, a vast number of electricians, cameramen, sound-technicians and actors. It was a cold February with no snow. On the hilltop of Bad Ischl stood the hunting-lodge where the last Emperor of Austria, Franz Joseph, and his wife Elisabeth used to spend their holidays.

I watched Visconti as he worked, his sharp profile outlined by the powerful lighting. He was giving detailed directions to Romy Schneider – the Empress Elisabeth – about her lady-in-waiting: 'Come on, Romy, you hate that woman, Countess Ferenczy; also she came from a brothel in Budapest.

She is spying on you because your husband has put her in this post to do just that. She is a subordinate. Come on: contempt. And detachment.'[7]

I wanted to read the script, for I was curious to see how Visconti and Medioli had managed to portray Wagner and his wife Cosima. Visconti lent me his own copy, as there were no spare ones. Ludwig had first heard *Lohengrin* at fifteen; within four years he knew all of Wagner's librettos by heart (although the score for *The Ring* was not written, the librettos were). He decided that his first task as King was to rescue Wagner from his creditors and to stage his operas. 'Very difficult for me,' said Visconti; 'Wagner treats Ludwig very badly, but I cannot show him in a totally mean light.' The mature and cunning composer saw the potential of the young King's infatuation. 'If I am Wotan,' Wagner wrote in a letter, 'then he is my Siegfried.' But although signs of homosexuality became accentuated in Ludwig, his relationship with Wagner remained one of hero-worship. Wagner meanwhile drained the King's finances, interfered in politics and became highly unpopular. 'One must remember that when Wagner came to Ludwig, he was suspected by the Bavarian ministers: he had a revolutionary past, he hated the Germans for not accepting his music. And then he finds a man who says "Do you want to have a theatre? Have all the money you need,"' Visconti explained. 'Actually to have understood that Wagner was Wagner, that is quite something. Was Ludwig mad? No. Before his time, of course, but highly intelligent. Bismarck, who was no fool, respected Ludwig's brains. There is no doubt that his first political gesture, to call Wagner to his court, was an enlightened one.'[8]

When Ludwig II succeeded to the throne, he was only nineteen, extremely handsome, tall and romantic-looking. He was also vain: Ludwig would not appear in public before his hairdresser had curled his otherwise straight black hair. Not that he appeared much: he shunned society, hated crowds and loathed public engagements. Ludwig's chaste love for his cousin Elisabeth, his senior by six years, plays a substantial part in the film. 'She too was a fascinating character, who also suffered a terrible death, murdered like a pig; a woman whose physical fascination is still a legend. Cocteau was very taken with her.' Visconti was intrigued by these characters; he pointed at the actress who played the role of Elizabeth's sister, Maria Sophia, who for a short time was officially engaged to Ludwig. 'She will become Queen of Naples, the last Queen of Naples, a Bourbon. Isn't it odd?' He loved history.

Ludwig's extravagance, his search for solitude and his refusal to marry became increasingly marked. For political reasons Wagner had to leave Munich: once he could no longer build his dreams through Wagner's music, Ludwig started building castles. 'Ludwig had the mind of an architect,' Visconti said, 'and of a constructor. Herrenchiemsee and Linderhof are beautiful, although creating a dream of the eighteenth century in the nineteenth: Neuschwanstein is totally Wagnerian and ugly. As an architect

Ludwig had quite advanced concepts. As he was a man who loved a spectacle, he built into life a pomp that he alone could enjoy. He was something of a Medici, but he had no Michelangelo to work for him. And that was not the Renaissance period, it was a kitsch era: it was a moment when Europe was bourgeois and engaged in thoughts of conquest and supremacy, not of idealism.'[9]

Few links between Visconti and Ludwig existed, but enough for Visconti to mirror some of his own self and be interested: there was the interpretation of Ludwig as a man outside his times, there was the love for Wagner, and, in a more modest way, the preoccupation with building: 'building a pomp which he alone could enjoy.' Visconti too had a mania for 'making' houses, for leaving behind him a trail of villas and towers, a grand trait. And there was the homosexuality, although not with the same guilt which haunted Ludwig; Ludwig's last favourite was a young actor called Kainz.

The last scene in which Richard and Cosima Wagner appear in the film is on Cosima's thirty-third birthday. A small orchestra assembles on the stairs and under Wagner's direction plays the Siegfried Idyll, his birthday gift to his wife. Among those present was the young Friedrich Nietzsche – another god in Visconti's pantheon (though he does not appear in the film). 'So I really see Wagner for the last time in a beautiful setting. I wanted to include his death in Venice. But then I even cut his funeral, when the body comes by train through Munich,' said Visconti. He had to cut the script because of lack of money; producers were once again a problem in *Ludwig*. 'You know, Ludwig had said that Wagner's body belonged to him. I think he actually would have liked to keep the corpse. As it was, he had all the pianos in his castles covered and bound with crepe.' Wagner's coffin was brought to Bayreuth by way of Munich. The station was crowded with mourners carrying torches; Beethoven's Eroica Symphony and Siegfried's Funeral March from *Götterdämmerung* were played: one can well understand that Visconti was sad not to be able to recreate these scenes.

In a circus, which had been faithfully reproduced just outside Bad Ischl, they filmed during the night because of the load on the electricity supply; it was extremely cold. Visconti looked like an aristocrat from *War and Peace* in furs and boots, with a perpetual cigarette in his hand. He had a thermos with coffee and brandy in his pocket which he would gladly share. When he felt Helmut Berger was not responding to his directions, he became the wrath of God. The circus echoed Visconti's voice, and so did the faces of those present. His anger was no laughing matter.

In *Ludwig* he was fascinated by 'the personality of a man who, although believing in absolute monarchy, is unhappy and a victim. What fascinates me is his weak side, the impossibility of living a daily reality. Ludwig is a man one feels sorry for, even when he thinks he is the winner. He loses in his relationships with Wagner, with Elisabeth, with Kainz....' And when I told him that I was tempted to think that he – Visconti – was writing his own autobiography also in *Ludwig*, he said: 'No, absolutely not. I am fascinated by the man as a clinical case; the story of a person who lives at the extreme limits of the exceptional, outside the rule. And so did the other two, Wagner and Elisabeth. I am interested in this story of monsters, people outside the reality of daily life. But as to the affinities with these characters, I don't see any. I don't feel like a weak person, a loser in life. Out of all the betrayals and double-crossings which I've suffered, I have come out in one piece while Ludwig didn't. The feeling I would like this film to arouse is that of pity.'

While I was at Bad Ischl, the general administrator of the Vienna Staatsoper came to talk to him: he agreed to stage *Tristan and Isolde* in 1973, which was to be conducted by Leonard Bernstein, and, later, he was to produce the *Ring* for La Scala: he really longed to do that. But he also told me that he feared he had not enough time left for it; he laughed, but I felt that he was often thinking of time running out, of death.

13
Working to Live

Suso Cecchi d'Amico was with him on the night Visconti had a stroke. It happened in Rome, in the heat of the last days of July, on the terrace of the Eden Hotel. He was sixty-six. That evening he had decided to dine out with two producers whom he wanted to charm, something which he could do well: he hoped to change a project with one and persuade the other to invest in a film. When Suso Cecchi d'Amico arrived at his house to collect him, he was very white. 'On the telephone he had told me that he had spent some days in Tunisia, where he had suffered from the heat and he had felt a particular weariness under the strong light. He had also filmed the last scenes of Ludwig's coronation in terrible heat,' she recalled.

He was exhausted. Filming *Ludwig* had taken longer and been more tiring than he had anticipated. The cold of Ludwig's castles (some of which Visconti had restored, much to the consternation of his producers and to the joy of the Bavarian Tourist Board), the heat of Rome, the endless problems, all took their toll.

Later, 'on the terrace of the hotel, suddenly he seemed to have grown bigger and one of his eyes looked askew. We took him into a spare room,' Suso Cecchi d'Amico continued. 'I called a doctor; he never lost consciousness. One of his legs moved as if it had gone mad, without any control: I've never seen anything of the kind.' He went on apologizing to her while his leg was thrashing about on its own, so much so that Suso Cecchi d'Amico chose to spend most of those long hours outside the room: she didn't want to worry him further. When Enrico Medioli, who had rushed to the hotel, took his shoes off, Visconti could not help noticing his own electric-blue socks and thought to himself what an unpardonable error the colour was.

Visconti later gave a lucid account of the evening. 'I had worked at home that day. They came to collect me, the British-Italian producer Janni, the Italian producer Perugia and Suso Cecchi d'Amico. It was about 8 p.m. We should have talked about my next films. But now that I remember, I had smoked a lot during that day.'[1] By then he smoked over eighty cigarettes a day, sometimes even a hundred and twenty, especially when working in the cutting-room; he smoked 'like a locomotive' without being aware of lighting one and stubbing out another.

They had gone to the top floor of the Eden Hotel, where there was a beautiful terrace with a bar and garden where Visconti had never been before; they drank champagne and he remembered observing that the champagne was not cold enough, when he suddenly felt as if he had been struck by lightning. Suso Cecchi said, 'Luchino, Luchino, what's the matter?' He recollected that as he was taken to a room in the hotel he heard voices saying, 'Let's take him to a nursing-home.'

The nursing-home was hot, his room was tiny, hundreds of people came to see him, he could get no rest and he heard people chatting in the corridor, all the time. He even remembered the face of a Professor Lopez who had been summoned from Madrid and had arrived on the day following his stroke: Lopez wore grey moustaches and a black tie, and leaned over him; he looked like an undertaker. Every day forty to fifty fresh gardenias from his gardens were brought in and arranged in a bowl at the end of his bed. 'There was this stink of flowers, of death,' Fedele d'Amico recalled; 'his face showed dramatic pain, controlled with infinite dignity, the face of a Rembrandt. Throughout his illness he conducted himself superbly.'

He had never been ill before, he was not accustomed to disease, quite the opposite . . . apart from those few seconds on Ischia, that warning which he had dismissed. But this time he knew that something serious had happened: his arm had turned to lead, like somebody else's arm. He spoke only with tremendous difficulty. His visitors would arrive to find him looking lost, but almost at once he would make a joke and force himself to look happy. 'The day following his stroke,' said Domietta Hercolani, 'I found him in his bed sitting up and eating spoonfuls of caviar.' But on another day, when Alberto Fassini and the actress Lilla Brignone went to see him, and he talked about things which he would no longer be able to do – taking a walk in the centre of Rome, shopping, etc. – there were tears in his eyes. Brignone and Fassini, who had known Visconti for so long, had never seen him crying before, though he soon recovered himself. Fassini and Brignone exchanged a desperate glance, but never talked about the episode to each other.

The Roman nursing-home was swarming with journalists, who that August were short of news, all hoping to catch a sensational picture of the director or learn about his death before the others. It was decided therefore to send him to Switzerland as soon as he was able to face the journey. Three weeks after his collapse, he was flown to Zurich for treatment in the Zurich Cantonal Clinic, where Thomas Mann had died, though nobody told him that. He spent two months there.

His sister Uberta, his niece Meralda, Enrico Medioli and Suso Cecchi d'Amico were often at his side. Others came to see him; only when one is ill, he said, could one find out who one's real friends were; he speculated on the horror of being ill and deserted – maybe because, in spite of his denials, he felt deserted: Helmut Berger came to see him only once. Visconti would ask where he was or whether he had written; his friends would lie to him, of the place where Donna Carla's nuns had embroidered damasks and where a priest had discussed theology with the young Luchino. Once again, he felt a great longing for his family, for his sisters and brother; memories would come back, he talked about his grandmother, the lake, his mother (but never about his father); he still felt that it was vulgar to let himself go to the length of confession but he allowed himself to give in to reminiscing.

His brother and sisters rallied around him and he felt the strength of his own family, of his roots. On the other side there were those few with whom he had shared so much: Enrico Medioli stayed near him, at times being tiresome in order to protect him from his excessively energetic self.

At Cernobbio in the late autumnal days, Visconti finished editing *Ludwig*, but he was restless and started thinking about future projects. He had abandoned his cherished plan for the *Ring* at La Scala, on which Mario Chiari had already started work. His doctors told him that Milan's climate was dangerous to his health. He still hoped to film *The Magic Mountain*; Thomas Mann's son was enthusiastic at the idea. But over *Zelda*, a script which he had written the previous year, there were difficulties; Fitzgerald's daughter, fearing that her mother might be misrepresented, wanted to have a final say on the script. She asked for a lot of money, Visconti said, inventing reasons for Berger's absence.

Though Visconti received mountains of mail from friends and unknown well-wishers, he also received vulgar messages of real hatred with obscene drawings and letters saying that he deserved what had happened to him, that he should have died. Enrico Medioli, who read all his correspondence to him, would shelter Visconti from the abuse, quickly making up another text.

Visconti could not bear the idea of *Ludwig* unfinished, unedited, unshowable. The left side of his body was still paralysed and his left eye was slightly less open than the other, but he was lucid. At first he could not even stand up, then little by little he was able to spend some time in a chair answering letters, then walking a little more each day. He had to go through hours of physiotherapy, exercising his paralysed muscles, but he was determined to get better in order to finish *Ludwig*.

He started working on the music for the film, detailing the sequences. A month and a half after his arrival in Zurich he was better, and his doctor, friends and relatives realized that, unless he was allowed to go back to his work, he would give up fighting. At the end of September, he left Zurich for Villa Erba at Cernobbio, by the lake where he had spent so many summers. Before his arrival the villa was equipped with a cutting-room, which contrasted with the old furniture, with the atmosphere and besides, how could one damage further the memory of a woman who had been an alcoholic and had died in a lunatic asylum?

He answered the many letters that came, but his handwriting had become distorted. He also wrote to Romolo Valli, who was by this time the artistic director of the Spoleto Festival, telling him that he had secured Lila de Nobili to design the scenery for *Louise* by Charpentier, the opera he wanted to stage at Spoleto the following year. By asking him to open the festival, Romolo Valli, like so many friends, wanted him to feel needed, to feel that he had plenty of offers, but never really thought that he would be able to stage an opera or work again. They knew that work was ultimately the only thing Visconti cared for and that, in order to go on living, he had to look forward to more.

Time passed slowly at Villa Erba, where he would sit on the lawn and look at the steep, wooded hills which rose behind the house. The creepers on the wall turned yellow and pink. The gardens echoed with the old noises, the plants were the same, and in the house he recognized objects from his childhood. It was sweet, yet sad, to be at Cernobbio. He resented the long sessions of physiotherapy twice a day, four hours of ridiculous gestures to retrain his dormant limbs.

He resolved to get accustomed to his new state of dependence on others, but he would not have lived without his *raison d'être*, his work, his means of expressing ideas and liberating himself from doubts and memories. He had in fact made up his mind to leave Via Salaria forever, he did not want to set foot in it again or even to see it from the outside. His friends and relatives, who were naturally distraught because they had grown to love the house, tried to persuade him to change his mind. Suso Cecchi d'Amico told him that, with a few changes, with a lift built in, the house would be perfectly habitable. But Visconti adamantly refused to return to the house which had been his father's and which had witnessed his agile self, where every object would remind him of better days. He therefore engaged a secretary and rented a little flat near Uberta's, leaving all details of dismembering the vast Via Salaria house to others. The paintings, the *objets d'art*, the bibelots, the opalines, the silver, the Sèvres, the engravings, the bric-à-brac, the linen, were to be moved to his new house.

During 1972 Visconti had bought an *art nouveau* villa near Castelgandolfo (the summer resort of the Pope) on the lake – a lack-lustre lake 'compared to which the Bavarian ones looked like the Mediterranean,' Henze commented. 'The sun shone for a couple of hours on the house, that was all. It was a grim place.' It was a villa which he had rented in the past because he could reach it from Rome if the capital became too hot for comfort and when he was working at Cinecittà. Visconti had begun to hate Rome with its noise, its vulgarity, its traffic, its corruptive Byzantine disorder. He had grown fond of gardening – a straw hat on his head, a rake and a pair of secateurs in his hands – and would spend hours engaged in the care of plants, especially on Ischia. Typically he knew everything about botany and his approach was on a grand scale.

He had bought the villa at Castelgandolfo for a large sum of money and now he was spending an incredible amount on doing it up. He had ordered thirty fully-grown palm trees to line a boulevard leading to the house – each tree costing about one million lire and, naturally, each tree, in the humid shade of the lake, died almost immediately. 'Financially he was a disaster,' his sister Uberta said, 'but he was right, why shouldn't he spend his money? He had no concept of finance and his generosity was frightening.'

When the furnishings from Via Salaria had been assembled at the villa in Castelgandolfo, two lorries arrived one night not long afterwards and took almost everything away. Visconti knew who had organized the theft, but did not want to prosecute; he did not care, for he had an unnerving detachment from possessions, once he had possessed them. And he never actually lived at Castelgandolfo, which went on being decorated with the usual extravagant expenditure; artisans cheated the man who could no longer shout at them. Visconti's lawyer was appalled, for Luchino no longer kept any accounts. 'Visconti was attached to money only when he needed it. Now he couldn't care less,' his lawyer said.

While the garden which stretched to the dark lake was being filled with hundreds of roses and palm trees, Visconti lived in a third-floor apartment in Via Fleming: on the ground floor, next to his doorbell, 'L.V.' had been marked in blue biro. The flat was some way from the centre of the city, near his sister's, and had a large terrace overlooking the capital. It consisted of two rooms: one stacked with books and paintings with a little dining-table and an enormous quantity of flowers; the other, his bedroom, looked like a room in a hospital. From Via Salaria he had brought only two dogs called Teodoro and Conrad, a painting of *Icarus Falling* by Galielo Chini (Puccini's friend who had designed the sets for *Manon Lescaut* and *Turandot*) and two photographs, one of Helmut Berger, the other of Marlene Dietrich with the dedication 'Luca, I always think of you'. While he had been in Zurich and then at Villa Erba, Marlene Dietrich had written many letters to him: 'Let time go by,' she would write, 'that's the best way to defeat it.' Time went by, but he could not defeat it. He hated being dependent on others; he would walk a few steps on the terrace, then he started taking short walks in the street. 'What is happening to me?' he would say to his sister, 'I am a cripple,' but gradually he managed to readjust. 'Enrico wants me to be ill because the doctor says that I am ill. If I were to keep to the diet that these imbeciles have prescribed! . . .'

A Swedish nurse was with him during the day, for he still had to exercise his reluctant muscles two hours in the morning and one-and-a-half in the afternoon. By sheer willpower he developed a quality which he had never before possessed: patient endurance. He started writing a diary of his illness, 'a radiology of my experience',[2] and did not believe what everybody told him, that within one year he would have recovered: he thought it would take far longer. He made some progress, but by January 1973 he was still unable to be present at the first night of *Ludwig*.

He watched television much of the time and would often fall asleep in front of it. His cousins Ida and Ottorino, who dined with him, sometimes snored away, at which Visconti would wake up and cry: 'Look at them! They always sleep!' Then he would realize that he, too, had been asleep and would feel angry with himself: 'I didn't follow a bloody thing!'

By this time most of Visconti's films were being shown on television and he would watch them with a curious detachment, as if they had been made by somebody else. 'That was not so bad after all!' he would say. He wanted to have them all on videotape, in order to watch them on the little screen. He liked other directors as well, but there were only a few whom he really admired professionally: Bergman, Fellini, Rosi and Antonioni.

Gradually he began to regain his confidence: he could open the door on his own and would demonstrate the gesture in a self-mocking way, 'Look how clever I've been!' But he had nothing to do. 'We could see that he was in despair, we had to find something for him to do,' said Suso Cecchi d'Amico. So they picked on a new play, which featured only three actors.

Visconti started rehearsing Pinter's *Old Times* in his apartment. By staging a contemporary play he wanted to demonstrate that, though he was handicapped, he was not out of touch. Ten days before the opening of the play, he began rehearsals in the Theatre Argentina, where his Rolls-Royce was literally driven inside the auditorium; sitting in a box, using the stick on which he leant when walking to point at people, and sometimes to hit them as well, he directed the whole play. He was not well but his face was radiant, because he was back at work.

Visconti had turned down an 'official' translation offered by Pinter's agent and had commissioned his own. He had also turned the theatre upside down: the stage disappeared and a kind of boxing-ring was built in the centre; the stalls were moved to surround this new stage 'in the round'. His interpretation of *Old Times* was, to say the least, ambiguous: lesbian relationship, naked bodies, masturbation. Pinter was furious, and so was his agent, who had the play stopped two days after it opened. Though it is a play about a family – a subject Visconti had analysed in its most sinister aspects from his first production, *Les Parents Terribles*, to his last, *Old Times* – he had substantially changed Pinter's creation in order to suit his own theme.

Pinter had further reasons for feeling annoyed with Visconti: owing to a clause in the contract, nobody could film *A la Recherche* without Visconti's consent; the production team was losing money, while Losey and Pinter were waiting. Georges Beaume went to see Visconti in Rome with a letter in which the production company asked Visconti to sign a clause which would have allowed Losey to go ahead. As soon as Beaume arrived from Paris, he rang Visconti, who at once understood the reason for his visit. Instead of the usual immediate invitation, he said, 'I can't see you tomorrow, we are rehearsing. Come on Tuesday.' He engineered the meeting so that Beaume would see him at work, undiminished by his illness. Visconti's face was wrinkled and grey, and his voice had become less powerful so that he had to use a microphone; so much had he changed that Beaume felt upset, but when Visconti started giving orders he became once again himself, the efficient director he wanted Beaume to see. 'I didn't know when and how to give him the letter, but Luchino understood: he accused everybody of being Verdurins. Before leaving, I handed the letter to somebody else: I knew he would never sign it.'

After the closure of *Old Times*, Visconti gave a press conference from that very box at the Argentina from which he had directed. Somebody flew to London to placate Pinter, but without much success: Pinter came to Rome to see the play for himself (performances had resumed after Visconti had modified the production), and he stuck his protest against the distortion of his text onto the glass door of the theatre. Visconti had invented a new play, said Pinter: *Old Times* was not a story about two lesbians, and all the sexual acts in Visconti's version were against the spirit and intention of his play. Visconti retorted that Pinter was a radio playwright and that his plays needed 'filling out' by a director.

Fortunately Visconti had started working on *Manon Lescaut*, which was to open on 21 June at Spoleto. Schippers had persuaded him to give up Charpentier's *Louise* in favour of Puccini, whom he wanted to conduct. His old team rallied around him; not only Lila de Nobili, who had refused to work for many years (she sent one hundred preliminary sketches for the scenery), but also Piero Tosi, who designed the costumes. They started work three months ahead of the performance – Alberto Fassini, who was his assistant, would go and have breakfast with Visconti and then they would leave together for Spoleto at 11 a.m. in Luchino's chauffeur-driven Rolls-Royce. 'Luchino and I sat in the back, talking and often working on *Manon*. Once we gave a lift to two prostitutes, though he only realized that later. "How nice they are!" he said. They had recognized him and knew who Helmut was; Luchino was very pleased with Helmut's popularity. He loved Helmut. Luchino often identified himself with the Marschallin in *Der Rosenkavalier*.'

His Rolls would stop behind the theatre so that he could enter directly on to the stage, but there was a staircase and it was a tremendous effort for him to climb it: he would lean on his driver and on Alberto Fassini. In front of the stage a little armchair was ready for him. Before rehearsals, he would slowly walk over the route which he would cover later in order to learn his way; he had gone as far as having a high step built in his flat the same height as that up to the stage at Spoleto. He used his stick and was making a tremendous effort.

He knew what kind of *Manon* he wanted to stage – a dark and tragic story –and he asked for a soprano who would be able to emerge naked from a bathtub. The auditions for the role caused quite a stir. After hearing Nancy Shade, Menotti sent Schippers a famous telegram: 'She has a beautiful bottom.'

Nobody thought that *Manon* would ever come off, let alone be a success. Instead it was arguably the most accomplished and thought-out opera Visconti ever staged. Romolo Valli wrote:

> This was the last, inspiring expression of his catalysing talent, of his sensibility, of his intuition. It was an event which seemed to sum up, in an admirable synthesis, every aspect of his personality: his passion for music, his penetrating understanding of drama, his incisive comprehension of the psychological and aesthetic implications of a human situation, the splendour of his visual sense, plus his scrupulous and impeccable taste in reconstructing different settings and customs.[3]

On the first night, I went to see him during the interval before the second act; outside his box, the watchful Alberto Fassini would allow only one person at a time to see him; with him in his box was Wally Toscanini, his old friend. He let me kiss him on the cheek, something which immediately suggested to me that he was no longer the frightening man he once was; although we had known each other for years and said *'tu'* to each other rather than *'lei'*, I would never have dared to kiss him before. He was looking older and paler, his colour had faded, his bushy eyebrows were less severe and his jaw less powerful; there was suddenly something fragile about him. Had he known that such thoughts crossed my mind, he would have been hurt, and yet this sick man had produced the masterpiece I was watching. As the lights dimmed again and the public hastened to regain their seats, Visconti stopped me: 'Stay with us, there is plenty of room.'

At the end of *Manon* there was an ovation for him: the whole theatre turned towards his box and cheered. There was something uncanny about the fact that this man who was old and ill had been able to produce an opera in such detailed perfection, with a new vision, 'thinking of Zola, really'. One could not but admire him. The ovation went on and on; visibly moved, he waved a white handkerchief, just a little, almost shyly. Visconti had succeeded not only in staging the opera but also in making it into something unforgettable: he had put so much of himself into *Manon*.

After the opera we went to dine in a restaurant; Visconti did not seem tired, for he was too proud to show his weakness, but as usual the service was slow and half-way through dinner he decided that it was time to go to bed. We all got up – there must have been twenty of us – and left with him.

The feeling of affection, which before his illness he was unable to demonstrate, found some expression. He recognized the faithful help of Alberto Fassini, so often mistreated, forever bewitched; he had been the vehicle of Visconti's orders to singers and workers. When *Manon* was, contrary to usual practice, staged again at Spoleto the following year, Fassini repeated Visconti's direction down to the smallest detail: 'He only came for the first night and embraced me tightly just to tell me that the staging had been well cared for.' Once, and only once, in the past, Visconti had praised Fassini – for the La Scala production of *Il Trovatore*, which he had prepared for Visconti: 'Not bad, it is almost like Zeffirelli!' Knowing that the mere name of Zeffirelli was anathema, Fassini sulked. 'It is no insult: Zeffirelli is not bad, you know!' That was as far as he could go.

Visconti kept La Colombaia on Ischia, but he transformed it in a grand manner, *à la* Ludwig: a new swimming-pool was built for his exercises and he cut through sixty metres of mountain rock so that a lift with coloured glass panels could carry him up and down from his bedroom to the sea. Showing great vitality, he also supervised planting in the grounds. When he was told that the new owner of Via Salaria had cut down the thick creepers which covered the outside walls of the house and had it painted 'a horrible red', he was angry at the insult to his old home.

Dinners remained a rite when on Ischia, though cooks came and went every two months (the death of his old chef from the Abruzzi had been a tragedy). He would send dishes away: 'Horrible! Disgusting! Sack the cook.' In the past he had always eaten two full meals a day from lobster to dessert; he had an incredibly strong stomach and loathed dieting. He ate much less now, but he had started smoking again. 'What do I care?' he said. 'I've lived long enough. I have enjoyed life, I lived it fully, I never gave up anything. I don't care if I die. But I still have enough power to defeat my illness.'[4]

It was important for him to make a film, but all the ones he had planned were out of the question. He needed a story for which no travel, no moving about Rome was required. Enrico Medioli wrote an adaptation from Mario Praz's *Conversation Piece*, which Suso Cecchi d'Amico, Visconti and Medioli himself then turned into a script. Burt Lancaster, who was asked to play the leading role of the professor, dashed to Rome when Visconti called him. So too did Silvana Mangano and Claudia Cardinale. Helmut Berger was offered the part of a lost son who is more of a victim than a scoundrel.

The next problem was who was going to invest in a film with a sick director and which did not look like being a commercial success? It was difficult to find backing, but finally a Right-wing producer came forward. The fact that Visconti was going to make a film with Right-wing money produced fierce controversy. Visconti himself did not care, money was money: what was the difference between Italian Right-wing money and American money? The truth is that Visconti had to make this film in order to stay alive, and his friends would have gone to any lengths to find a producer. Put in this context, Visconti's gesture is understandable. Moreover, to a non-Italian audience, the sin of being paid by Right-wing money may seem venial and yet, given

Visconti's principles, he should have resisted it. It is not true that the end justifies the means and certainly not in this case, when the end was to enlist a famous Left-wing name to give a veneer of respectability to what had always been Visconti's opposition. Many Italian directors had soiled their hands with Fascist or Christian Democrat money. Visconti, on the contrary, had been the man who had paid from his own pocket to make films like *La Terra Trema*, who had sold family jewels to make *Ossessione*, and who had turned down projects which he had found politically harmful. But, necessarily, his illness changed him.

Conversation Piece tells the story of a sixty-year-old professor who collects paintings, a scholar of the history of art, a collector of conversation pieces. He is divorced and is a lonely man. His father was American, while his Italian mother is the rich owner of the Roman *palazzo* where he lives in an apartment decorated with frescoes and covered with books. The professor is a cultivated man who has chosen solitude in order to cultivate music and art, but he is overpowered by a family which is not his.

Working on the set became exceedingly fatiguing and Visconti no longer enjoyed it. There were no longer any jokes or gossip, 'and he always stood, never wanted to use a wheelchair,' Suso Cecchi d'Amico commented, 'and to see him walk was so sad.' At a certain time in the afternoon he liked a strawberry ice, which the executive producer would go and buy personally; everybody on the set was trying to help. Visconti hated all this, though he was gratified that so many people should show their concern for him.

He suffered, but was ashamed to let anyone see it. Once or twice he exploded in one of his furies when Helmut Berger or one of the others turned up a few minutes late. In his letters to Berger, which were published after his death, Visconti begged him to be careful and work hard, because work gave one dignity and strength; the job of an actor was a serious one. Life, he said, was to be faced with discipline and was to be enjoyed, while it was still possible, while there was youth – and health.

In *Conversation Piece* one of the characters recites a poem by Auden, written shortly before his death:

When you see a fair form
   chase it
      and if possible embrace it
Be it a girl or a boy
Don't be bashful, be brash, be fresh
Life is short, so enjoy
   whatever contact your flesh
      may at the moment crave
There is no sex life in the grave.

Visconti pinned up these lines in his room. In his flat there was no room for anybody else but a nurse and perhaps he already felt he was in the grave.

14
To Burn until Death

Visconti felt trapped by his own cultural roots, but he was too analytically lucid not to perceive the change in himself. Had Visconti not produced *Manon*, one could talk of his artistic decline, but he had been able to create a masterpiece, even with a poor libretto; he had taken the opera seriously, as he always did with whatever he tackled. He had changed however, as he himself recognized – he had become more introspective. In the past he had fought battles by trying to convey a message and stimulate the public as well as to entertain it. Not that he thought of the public as an entity to be pleased, but he certainly considered he had a duty to retain the audience's attention, as is evident in the stern criticism he made of many film directors of the new generation: he judged them boring or without purpose. This judgment, though, was given in the later years of his life and thus was clouded by the fact that he was ill and that, deluded by events, he had taken refuge in the past. What he had often analysed in his films (the Italian inability to change) had become too evident; the proliferation of corruption and disorder hurt him. He used to grumble about political violence, but he was no longer a participant, merely an ageing spectator; he was no longer tempted to portray Italian contemporary life: bombs planted by the Italian Secret Service, chaos, violence, extremism. His last analysis of contemporary events had been *Rocco and His Brothers*.

In the very last years of his life many of the hangers-on disappeared, but most of his valuable assistants and friends came back, and the watchful eye of his sister defended him. Visconti saw it thus:

> I have ten, fifteen people whom I dearly love and who love me, who always showed me that they were frank, truthful. . . . I have been very ill. Two months in hospital . . . hard, believe me, very hard. There were those who sent me a little telegram, nice, friendly. . . . But there were also those who came to Zurich and stayed one day, ten, thirty days. . . . So it may be a cliché, it may be a well-known fact, but I shall tell you that eternal friendship is like this, while others. . . . What a terrible disappointment, you know. . . . How painful. . . . I loved them so, they seemed to love me so . . . and where were they in the end?[1]

This streak of masochism pervaded the last stretch of his life: when he started smoking again after his return from Cernobbio, when he watched his possessions being stolen, saw his former friends do the stealing, there was an element of self-destruction, a revenge against himself.

In his physical suffering he was stoic. During the filming and editing of *Conversation Piece* he was often in pain, stuck in the same position until somebody came to help him, depending on others to be taken upstairs, downstairs, to be washed or to eat:

> But I swear that neither old age nor illness have quenched my desire for life and for challenge. I feel ready for ten other films, not just one. . . . Films, theatre, musical comedies, I want to do them all. With passion. Because one must always burn with passion when facing something. Besides, we are here for that, in order to burn until death, which is the last act of life, completes the deed by transforming us into ashes. I am already at an age when, generally, people retire. But if I were obliged to lie on a bed, waiting for time to come to an end . . . well, there is no doubt that I would die much earlier.[2]

Once again, after finishing *Conversation Piece*, it was necessary for him to start work as soon as possible. To find a producer for *The Magic Mountain* proved impossible; Italy was swamped by hard-core pornographic films which made a lot of money; producers were clearly scared at the mere idea of a film about the fascination of disease directed by a cripple.

Always searching for a literary thread with which to embroider his own canvas, Visconti turned to d'Annunzio and, together with Suso Cecchi d'Amico and Enrico Medioli, started considering *Il Piacere* (*Pleasure*), perhaps d'Annunzio's best-known novel.

The film rights for *Pleasure* were taken, so he opted for *The Intruder* (*L'Innocente*) instead, maybe a more apt story for a film.

Visconti hated d'Annunzio as the precursor of Fascist Nationalism, but he was also attracted by the decadent lifestyle which d'Annunzio had invented for himself (over-decorated grand houses, debts, champagne and haughtiness), by the abundance of his mistresses, by his sexual appetite, which had not been dissimilar to his own. Visconti thought that *The Intruder* had valuable elements for a film: 'In it there is a precise fact: the killing of a child. Also the relationship between Tullio Hermil and his wife Giuliana is very interesting. . . . It is true that Tullio Hermil is a superman, more fantasy than reality, but we have modified him. Today nobody tolerates a man who kills a child. So that, in the film, we show him differently. After killing the baby that Giuliana had by her lover, he kills himself. He punishes himself. Therefore the character is right.'[3]

For *The Intruder* he would have liked to sign Alain Delon and Romy Schneider, according to Georges Beaume, but they were otherwise engaged. Instead the new beauty of the Italian cinema, Laura Antonelli, and Giancarlo Giannini were to star in the film, and Rizzoli was to produce it.

The routine of work, of writing the script, finding the locations and designing the sets, made Visconti forget about his dependence on others. He was also getting better and was beginning to be able to move his right leg. Fidelma, the maid who had been with his sister Uberta since the war, and his manservant Antonio were the only people allowed near him at all times, to wash him and hold him. Visconti had always trusted Fidelma's judgment: he would show her his films before anybody else. He had patiently trained himself to achieve some small movements: he wanted to acquire some independence, a degree of freedom so as not to appear weak or ridiculous in front of his film crew:

> Oh God, I was free before, I used my body as if it were the most natural thing in the world ... and then, all of a sudden.... The blow! The re-thinking! The sudden discovery that I wouldn't be able to do certain things ever again. That freedom gone forever.... Because of this, I hate my illness: because it deprives me of my liberty. Because it humiliates me and goes on humiliating me all the time. Because I have to learn to walk again, to move my hands again, to use them ... and then the need to be looked after, the necessity for somebody to be always there, ready to dress one, to put on one's shoes, to shave one, to comb one's hair.... It is so debasing, it wounds one in such a horrible way.... And so one rebels, of course. But only within oneself, it wouldn't be fair to others, it would be of no use. On some days I can hardly bear myself. And so, in order not to think, not to feel, I apply myself, I make an even greater effort. Not that I am generally very disciplined, no: I still smoke and work more than I should; if before I gave one hundred per cent, now I try to give at least ninety. I have lost some liveliness, that is natural.[4]

He exercised his leg as well as doing other exercises, alone in his bedroom, not using his cane because he was determined to start his next film without having to use a stick: he would send everybody away from his room and practise in silence. But one day he slipped and fractured his right leg. It was 3 April, he was sixty-eight and once again everything collapsed, the work of months, the exercises, the massage, all had been in vain. When it was decided that an operation was necessary, he realized that he had lost the use of his other leg too, and then he really let himself go. He did not speak, he did not eat. Everything was ready for filming – they were losing their actors, the producers were losing money, and Suso Cecchi d'Amico told him that either they must decide to make *The Intruder* or they should cancel. He agreed to use a wheelchair, but he hated his physical weakness being 'on show'. In the evenings he would go on with his exercises to improve his mobility, but he had so many sores, his body was ulcerating.

They filmed at Villa Badiola, near Lucca in Tuscany, among *fin de siècle* shapes and atmosphere: Laura Antonelli looked like Eleonora Duse, the elegance of her clothes, the flowers, the colours; the soft morbid decadence of the story was rendered superbly. Seeing the film one would never guess that Visconti was in severe pain while working on it; there was little of himself in the story, but a lot in the form. In spite of the agonizing pain, he took great care over every detail. 'The veils for Laura Antonelli were never enough,' Piero Tosi recalled. In the book there is a lovely description of these veils: three Proustian pages written before Proust. That is when Tullio sees that his wife is escaping him; she is calm, not desperate, he vaguely senses this. For this scene Visconti wanted Laura Antonelli in a hat which he had seen Duse wear, which was like the sculptures by Medardo Rosso, deforming the face. The hat had to be perfect. Tosi made four tiny ones with many veils which suited her. Luchino chose the smallest, which suited her least but which had a lot of veils. When Antonelli lifted them, looking at herself in the mirror, they had to stay above her mouth ... hours of torture with these veils because they would not stay where he wanted them! After many trials, Piero Tosi put two long invisible pins behind Laura Antonelli's ears and asked the actress to try and rest the veils on these dangerous pins. 'My mother wore veils just like these,' Visconti told Tosi. 'She was swathed in veils, in 1910, when she went to La Scala followed by a valet, and she also travelled in veils.'

Filming was exhausting. When giving details to the scene-shifters, he would shout into his microphone, because his voice had become softer: 'Move the corpse!' pointing at himself and his wheelchair.

'He was a martyr, he suffered very much, one can't even imagine how much,' said his sister, 'but I never heard him complain. In the last year he didn't feel like going on; though if he hadn't broken his leg, maybe he would have done so. And if he hadn't made his film, he would have died earlier. In the nursing-home, he was practically dead, but his doctors realized that if he hadn't made *The Intruder* he would have died. "That film will destroy him," they said, "but it's better if he makes it."' He tried to turn his condition into a joke, to relieve others of any embarrassment: nephews and nieces, brothers and sisters, maids and menservants were involved in pushing Uncle Luchino's wheelchair. He was given a huge tape-recorder and, as he always did when he had a new toy, bought hundreds of tapes and played music all the time.

When the filming was complete, he slowly started editing it with his assistants. His body was ulcerating, he was suffering more and more, life had become intolerable. The last year was terrible; his sister had to use the wheelchair to get him from his bed to his armchair; he had accepted his condition in order to finish his film. 'I've been independent all my life,' he used to say, 'now I have to depend on everybody.' When he came close to finishing the editing he realized that he could not start any other work.

His close friends came to see him at home; he would spend some time on the terrace of the flat, and asked after Castelgandolfo; the house had become a worry, the gardener, the builders, the thefts. He asked after his dogs. 'The last time I saw him,' said Antonioni, 'was at his house, sitting in his wheelchair in his tiny flat or, rather, in a normal flat – something that amazed me because I had always seen Luchino in surroundings which were more appropriate to him. As soon as he saw me, he called me: "Michele, embrace me." In this way our old friendship was revived.'

Some months before he died he called his lawyer and told him that he wanted to be cremated, which in Italy was not easy for one had to join a special association. He wanted to be buried in a special corner of his house at Ischia, but this was not allowed. He told Uberta: 'Look, I want you and Fidelma to go and throw my ashes into the sea.' Uberta would try to avoid the subject. 'You can forget about it,' she told him, 'imagine me taking a boat carrying your ashes in my hands!' He would often talk about death: 'I am curious: I want to see what happens on the other side. I am interested to go and see.' And he would tease his sister, Antonio and Fidelma when they put him to bed in the evening. 'Tie the handkerchief here, in this way, for the dress rehearsal.'

After he had finished editing *The Intruder*, he wanted to die. He started smoking heavily again.

While his film was being dubbed, he tried to pretend that pain did not disturb him. He could no longer travel or walk – and perhaps he could no longer work. 'The last time I saw him,' said Suso Cecchi d'Amico, 'we were in the cutting-room working on *The Intruder*; he was slow, he understood that we were in a bad mood.' He went home and she wrote him a long letter. He rang her up: 'I'll be back in the studios soon.' But on the following day they rang up from his house saying that he was not able to come because he had a bit of temperature. 'I didn't go and see him during the two days he was in bed, then his blood pressure went down and he died, just like that, very suddenly. I really minded Luchino dying, but I suffered seeing him in that state. He was so brave, I never, never heard him complain, at the most "Ahhh", almost with nonchalance.'

'I shall die with my gardenias,' he had said to his niece, Meralda, and his room was indeed filled with roses, tuberoses and gardenias. On the day of his death he had been listening to Brahms's Second Symphony almost all day long and then, he made a gesture and whispered to his sister, 'Now it's enough.' 'Have you had enough music?' she had asked him in Milanese dialect. 'Yes,' he said, and a few hours later, at 5.30 in the afternoon, he died. His body was laid out on his large bed, a handkerchief tied to support his jaw just in the way he had asked his sister and Fidelma to rehearse it and a red blanket over him. Friends and family came to see him at once; even Berlinguer, Togliatti's successor as leader of the Italian Communist Party, called at Via Fleming.

There were difficulties about finding a church for his Requiem Mass, not only because strictly the Mass should have taken place in his parish church near Via Fleming, which was not suitable, but because Luchino Visconti's funeral was to be two days later, on the nineteenth, a Sunday, the day of St Joseph. Not many churches celebrated Requiem Mass on Sundays, but Fedele d'Amico knew somebody at St Ignatius, the Baroque Counter-Reformation church dedicated to Ignatius de Loyola, the heart of the Jesuit school, of the Roman College. Its Baroque frescoes in perspective, the false dome, the richness of the marbles, the stuccoes, the delicate carved angels turned the church into a theatre: on the high altar, in gold, the arrogant words Ignatius said to God, '*Ego vobis Romae proditus ero*' – in Rome I shall be useful to you.

Outside the church is one of Rome's loveliest squares, and it was here that the first 'lay' funeral took place.

In the square, among hundreds of flowers and wreaths, were friends and admirers known and unknown, many of whom had brought red flags. 'It wasn't a Party funeral,' said Antonello Trombadori, 'people had come spontaneously, all those who thought that his presence in life had been important.' Trombadori made a moving speech opposite the grand façade of the church. 'He had never asked me to speak at his funeral, because he didn't like talking about death and didn't like talking about his illness.' In his speech Trombadori said that the memory of Visconti should be entrusted to the written page for those 'who hadn't met him, for those who will come after him, not only a literary, critical, historical portrait, but a human one'.[5]

Some of those who had been outside the church for the lay funeral joined the crowds inside the church of St Ignatius for a solemn Requiem Mass; Fedele d'Amico had chosen the music. When the bier came out into the square, the crowds applauded Luchino Visconti in a way they had never done when he was alive.

His villa at Castelgandolfo was raided by thieves again: even his papers were stolen and then burnt; letters, personal documents, photographs disappeared or were reduced to cinders. His sister could not face the melancholy of visiting it. His house at Ischia was locked up.

Thus ended a long life, fully lived and experienced, the exceptional life of an exceptional man.

To whatever he had applied himself, from horses to war, to the cinema, he worked with vigour, never troubled by doubt, rarely changing his mind, so that his errors were many, but sincere. What he did, he did with virile firmness, never considering what would be said about him.

He could not love women after having loved his mother passionately. His mother had been for him a continuous standard of comparison; in the last years he often talked about her: he had many photographs of her reprinted and framed them and put them in his room. In every film of his there was something to do with his mother: his mother in evening dress; on the beach; his mother playing the piano; and he talked about his beautiful mother swathed in veils kissing him goodnight – an apparition, an angel. He saw her going away in a cloud of veils out of his door.

His involvement with women, however interesting and intelligent they were, never made a dent in his sentimental make-up, they never kept him awake at night; at times they were almost a cover-up, an excuse: his engagement to Pupe, the impossibility of marrying her; Maria Callas, who suffocated him, and Elsa Morante, who stimulated him, but ultimately scared him. There had been Marlene Dietrich and Coco Chanel, but how much more important, in his life and in his work, had been the young men who *had* kept him awake at night, whose insolence had struck his masochistic chord; because this was the only love of which he was capable.

One of the major contradictions in his character was that he never lost his capacity for dominating others and yet at the same time he was a masochist. Strong in his work and in his relationships with his equals, at the same time he took pleasure in being humiliated by his inferiors. His relationship with them was very similar to that of men of a century earlier with their lower-class mistresses – an old-fashioned attitude: his loved one was an object to be kept, to be patronized. There was no mature exchange. And because his passions which were invariably stormy and all-involving were, in his eyes, sinful, he wanted to be punished, debased and humiliated. This streak not only pervaded his art, but because of it he used some actors and actresses who were not good enough. This was also due to his dominating side, his desire to rule over other people who accepted that rule; whoever resisted or did not want to accept went away; some who stayed exploited him financially and otherwise.

He depended on a team at all times, and its composition was vital to him. While he preferred the weaker, his work profited by the stronger. He did not leave an heir, but he left a school. Many of those who had taken their first steps with him worked successfully on their own but, in a sense, having turned against their artistic past: Rosi and Zeffirelli have covered different ground from Visconti's. Others whom he formed, whom he 'launched', were unable to proceed without him. After the war he restructured the whole profession of acting in Italy. Mastroianni, de Lullo, Adriana Asti, Delon, Romolo Valli, Stoppa, Morelli, Alida Valli, Berger – they were 'made' by him, but not all of them had real talent or were able to develop: Visconti had a way of acting all parts for them, like a conductor who sings the various instrumental parts to the orchestra, thus ensuring a good interpretation – for one performance only; moreover by doing this he often undermined people's security, making them feel that he was a better actor than they would ever be. He also, of course, undermined other people's security simply because he enjoyed doing so.

His homosexuality, in a man of his generation, had, at the start, been an important affirmation. It had been a sin, a forbidden fruit, chosen as a rebellion against a certain society. But towards the end of his life that society no longer existed, could no longer provide him with stimulating and interesting obstacles; that society had gone forever and he never ceased to regret it; that which had come in its place – the jackals instead of the leopards

– did not interest him. The family, as he said, was the only remaining nucleus which provided him with the 'necessary' terror and chains.

A friend said of him that 'he was duped by his own lack of humility; in the end he had nobody, he had fallen into the Roman pit, he was terribly bored.' This is not necessarily true. He had chosen, in the end, to avoid intellectual confrontation and to liberate himself from his memories by pouring them out. He was bored by intellectualizations: he severed his links with intellectuals and even in his work became more of a populist, in spite of the decadence and sophistication of some of his later movies.

That he was insecure is apparent in his need to sport the photograph of a well-known actress like Marlene Dietrich, of slightly adding to or changing the truth. Ultimately his family came to be the only repository of his security, but even within it, at times, he was almost shy.

He left many orphans. All those who worked for him and to whom I talked underlined the fact that, after his death, there was nobody – in Italy or elsewhere – who took the pleasure and the trouble, the time and the dedication, to make a film in the way Visconti had.

Enrico Medioli said of his friend and colleague: 'From the start he always knew exactly what he wanted. For example, he wanted to describe the anger and suffering of a peasant from Lucania; or he wanted a lucid and cool vision of hell, exemplified by a Nazi family; or he wanted a representation of the fascination and illusory charms of a privileged class (his own); or the solitude or perhaps, rather, a visionary interpretation of the Spain of *Don Carlos*; or Macbeth seen as a sublime pastiche in the manner of Hayez; of the *Duca d'Alba* as if it was done in the days of Queen Marguerite.... The idea was very clear, so it should naturally be easy to carry it out. But this, in reality, could be extremely difficult.'[6]

Piero Tosi, Vera Marzot and many others had little desire to work for others, for that Visconti's death had left them feeling idle and uninterested. 'He was such an important person that my life changed when I met him,' Vera Marzot said, 'and changed again when he died.' Also because in whatever they did, work or life, he had become a point of reference: 'One would think of what he would have said.'

He was a focal-point for his peers, but he also liked to shape people, to get them ready for a future which eventually would not involve himself. He was conceited and yet he had some humility in so far as he was willing to learn from others and from books providing he could assimilate the ideas and make them his own. His knowledge of human nature was the result of close observation and he used this knowledge, when it suited him, to charm and conquer people, as well as in his films and other work.

Visconti had the capacity to feel very happy and secure; he loved being the star when he 'performed' his famous terrifying scenes, when he felt terror rising in others, when he played Ivan the Terrible; but at heart he was a man of contradictions, often hiding his depression or, more often, suppressing his despair by plunging into work.

One of his great strengths was to believe in what he did and to turn disadvantages into advantages, not only throughout his career as a director – and I use career for lack of a better word – but in his personal and sentimental life. When he could not have Anna Magnani for *Ossessione*, he made himself believe that Clara Calamai was the ideal actress, and it worked. The same happened with Alida Valli, who took Ingrid Bergman's place in *Senso*. The actors or scripts available were no surrogates; for him they became the best. 'He had the nature of a winner even when he lost: a battle lost, he showed that he had won it, in his films, in his love affairs. That is the beautiful side of his character: his strength, and with that he achieved what he did,' said Alberto Fassini. When it became obvious to him that it was not possible to film *Pleasure*, he declared to an interviewer that he had discarded it because *The Intruder* was a better subject. He really believed that the choice had been made by himself, not by events.

In spite of his despair, Visconti possessed a *joie de vivre*, a sense of living his life to the full, of proving himself. He showed great courage in all he did; in his films and in his actions he was brave. Antonioni, who considers himself a pupil of his, summed him up: 'Luchino was feared, respected and envied. Everybody was afraid of him. They were even afraid of helping him make films. That's why he often made his films with his own money. But his name opened many doors.' Visconti also showed courage in the way he bore his illness. 'He was a lucky man who succeeded, with the strength he had, in winning right until the end, from his wheelchair,' Rosi said. 'He had a deep respect for work, and in this he was a real Lombard. He took things seriously. When he talked about horses, he never joked; he took that seriously as well.' Rosi remembered his authoritarianism, which he used to overcome difficulties. While filming *The Damned*, for example, Visconti was worried, he was behind schedule and there were difficulties with the production; a little girl had been repeating her scene and getting it wrong for the umpteenth time. 'Had it been me, I would have tried to calm her down. Instead Luchino went to her, with his thick, angry, bushy eyebrows, and told her, "Look, if you are not good, I'll send you to Biafra!" With his authority, he reassured her.'

He read an amazing amount, though only in the sphere which interested him – his culture was not wide, but deep in those areas, deeper than most. He had inherited that kind of culture which was also a way of life, of behaviour, the horror of appearing weak, of being caught without the cloak of his dignity.

Visconti's Marxist commitment came from his deep sense of history and of his personal situation in the historical process. It was a genuine commitment, not done merely to shock people: he did like to shock, but never with his personal life. He had done everything possible to defeat the class to which he belonged and yet he regretted its defeat. His class had made the mistake of allowing Fascism – the industrial class to which his mother belonged had actually promoted it – in the same way as the Krupps had financed Nazism and for the same reasons. His first form of Marxism had taken the shape of opposition, of rebellion. He was a rebel by choosing the life of a homosexual, by surrounding himself with people from all walks and classes. He was a silent rebel in his later years when, after Togliatti's death, he did not like the new shape of the Italian Communist Party, the signs of opportunism, the new leadership and, indeed, his last works lacked a political message, even those two or three sentences he had liked to 'fit in' in his previous works. But his relationship with the Communist Party and the Communist Party's relationship with him remained an interesting facet of his life: he was a discreet presence, afraid to disturb but ready to help, he underwent the discipline of being in a populist party, wearing the habit of a monk, for self-punishment. But he never used his films for overt propaganda: the Party never asked this of him, nor would he have accepted it: over and over again he preached freedom of expression, the right of ideas to remain uncontaminated by political dictates.

Although he had lost interest in the present, although he did not see any figure of prominence in politics in whom to believe, he was never a pessimist because he never allowed himself to be one.

Those who went to see him while he was filming *The Intruder* and were embarrassed at seeing him confined to a wheelchair were immediately put at their ease by a joke or two: 'You'll see me directing my next film from a stretcher!' They were also amazed to see the change in his face when he started work, shaping a scene or correcting a move; this last lordly exercise of his mastery erased the wrinkles of his suffering. He died working, as he had wished to.

Bibliography

Ajello, Nello, *Intellettuali e PCI 1944/1958* (Ed Laterza, 1978)
Amendola, G., *Lettere a Milano* (Editori Riuniti, 1973)
d'Amico de Carvalho, Caterina, *Album Visconti* (Sonzogno, 1978)
Ardoin, John, and Fitzgerald, Gerry, *Callas* (Holt, Rinehart, 1974).
Baldelli, Pio, *Luchino Visconti* (Mazzotta, 1973)
Cameron, R., *The Golden Riviera* (Weidenfeld, 1978)
Costantini, Costanzo, *L'Ultimo Visconti* (Sugar, 1976)
Faldini, Franca, and Fofi, Goffredo, *L'Avventurosa Storia del Cinema Italiano* (Feltrinelli, 1979)
Ferrara, Giorgio, *L. Visconti* (Seghers, 1978)
Hamilton, Nigel, *The Brothers Mann* (Secker, 1978)
Horst, H., and Hoyningen-Heune, H., *Salute to the Thirties* (Viking Press, 1970)
Lacouture, J., *Léon Blum* (Seuil, 1977)
Lifar, S., *Ma Vie* (Juillard, 1965)
Marais, Jean, *Histoire de ma vie* (Albin Michel, 1975)
Metropolitan Museum of Art, *Diaghilev* (1978)
Monelli, P., *Rome 1943* (Migliaresi, 1947)
Nowell-Smith, Geoffrey, *Luchino Visconti* (Secker, 2nd ed., 1973)
Renoir, J., *Ma Vie et mes films* (Flammarion, 1974)
Sachs, Harvey, *Toscanini* (Weidenfeld, 1978)
Spenser, C., Dyer, P., and Battersby, M., *The World of Serge Diaghilev* (Penguin, 1979)
Stirling, Monica, *A Screen of Time* (Secker, 1979)
Tesio, F., *Il Purosangue* (Hoepli, 1978)
Tosi, Piero, catalogue introduction by Rosi, F., *Visconti's Film Costumes* (Charleston, 1978)
Trombadori, A., d'Amico, Fedele, and Guerrieri, Gerardo, *Visconti, il Teatro* (Reggio Emilia, 1977)
Visconti di Modrone, G. C., *England and Italy* (Royal Academy, 1932)

Scripts of films with introductions, all edited by Cappelli: *Ossessione* (1977), *La Terra Trema* (1977), *Bellissima* (1978), *Senso* (1977), *Rocco e i suoi Fratelli* (1960), *Le Notti Bianche* (1957), *Boccaccio '70* (1962), *Il*

Gattopardo (1963), *Vaghe Stelle dell'Orsa* (1965), *La Caduta degli Dei* (1969), *Morte a Venezia* (1971), *Ludwig* (1973), *Gruppo di Famiglia in un Interno* (1974)

Sources and Source Notes

My heartfelt thanks are due to: the Cineteca Nazionale, Centro Sperimentale, Roma, in particular to Signor Baldi and Dr Cereda; and to Paolo di Valmarana; to the Museo Teatrale alla Scala in Milan and to its director, Maestro Gianpiero Tintori; to il Teatro alla Scala, Milan, and its musical director, Claudio Abbado, Bianca Zedda and Paolo Mezzadri; to the British Museum Library; to Jean-Pierre Angremi of the Ministère du Spectacle; to André Zavriew, Conseilleur Culturel of the French Embassy in Rome; to Harvey Sachs for his valuable help.

My most grateful thanks to all those who gave of their time in talking to me, in answering my queries and in replying to my letters: Claudio Abbado, Manolo Borromeo d'Adda, Anna Maria Aldobrandini, Giorgio Amendola, Fedele d'Amico, Silvia d'Amico, Suso Cecchi d'Amico, Alberto Arbasino, Madina Visconti Arrivabene, Niki Visconti Arrivabene, Adriana Asti, Luigi Barzini Jr, Georges Beaume, Pierre Branberger, Marlon Brando, Bice Brichetto, Clara Calamai, Rory Cameron, Meralda Caracciolo, Caterina d'Amico de Carvalho, Wally Toscanini Castelbarco, Henri Cartier-Bresson, Camilla Cederna, Mario Chiari, Maurizio Chiari, Corrado Corradi, Salvador Dali, M. Erve-Miller, Giulia Devoto Falk, Alberto Fassini, Giorgio Ferrara, Franco Ferri, Ignazio Gardella, Giuseppe Patroni Griffi, Maria Denis Guani, Renato Guttuso, Lord Harewood, Hans Werner Henze, Domietta del Drago Hercolani, Laura Lombardo-Radice Ingrao, Pietro Ingrao, Sylvie Bataille Lacan, Gioacchino Tomasi di Lampedusa, Willy Landels, Luigi Lanzillotta, Franco Mannino, Uberta Visconti Mannino, Jean Marais, Vera Marzot, Laura Mazza, Enrico Medioli, Gian Carlo Menotti, Umberto Morra, Luigi Nono, Giuliano Pajetta, Ubaldo Pandolfi, Pier Luigi Pizzi, Francesco Rosi, Filippo Sanjust, Giuseppe de Santis, Sandro Sequi, Umberto Tirelli, Sir John Tooley, Piero Tosi, Antonello Trombadori, Luisa Valerio, Romolo Valli, Fulco della Verdura, Filippo Visconti, Ida Gastel Visconti. And to those who didn't want me to record their names.

I also thank those authors, journalists, publishers and newspapers who allowed me to quote from their work.

1: BELLE EPOQUE

1 San Carlo Borromeo, 16th century
2 *The Canterbury Tales*, Book VII, 11. 2399–2402
3 *Cristina, Portraits of a Princess*, Beth Archer Bomberg (Hamish Hamilton, 1978)
4 Archives of the Museo del Teatro alla Scala. Printed in Bergamo
5 Daniela Pasti, *Il Mondo*, 14 March 1971
6 Lina Coletti, *L'Europeo*, 21 November 1974
7 *L'Ultimo Visconti*, Costantini
8 Opera by Ponchielli
9 Camilla Cederna, *L'Europeo*, 28 November 1954
10 Lina Coletti, op. cit.
11 Franco Rispoli, *Settimo Giorno*, 28 May 1963
12 Interview with Lietta Tornabuoni, *L'Europeo*, 10 April 1969
13 Ibid.
14 Franco Rispoli, op. cit.

2: ESCAPING THE COCOON

1 Milanese bookshop
2 Lina Coletti, op. cit.
3 Ibid.

3: THE GOLDEN SET

1 *Ma Vie*, Lifar
2 *L'Allure de Chanel*, Morand
3 *Histoire de ma Vie*, Marais

4: FLYING FREE

1 Gaia Servadio, *Observer*, 30 July 1972
2 *The Brothers Mann*, Hamilton
3 Interview with Lietta Tornabuoni, *L'Europeo*, 10 April 1969
4 *L'Allure de Chanel*, Morand
5 *Gente*, 4 April 1976, '*quel giorno Luchino mi disse*' by Peter Dragadze

SOURCES AND SOURCE NOTES

5: NEW FRONTIERS

1 Lina Coletti, *L'Europeo*, 21 November 1974
2 Lina Coletti, op. cit.
3 *L'Action Française*, May 1936
4 *Léon Blum*, Lacouture
5 *Ma Vie et Mes Filmes*, Renoir
6 Ibid.
7 Interview with Jean Renoir, *Tempo*, no. 37, February 1940
8 Renoir, op. cit.
9 Article by Visconti, *Rinascita*, 24 April 1965
10 *Le Dernier Tournant* by Pierre Chenal, with Michel Simon. Garnett's version was acted by Lana Turner and John Garfield. In 1981 *The Postman Always Rings Twice* was remade by Bob Rafelson, starring Jack Nicholson.

6: CHANGING ROLES

1 *L'Avventurosa Storia del Cinema Italiano*, Faldini and Fofi
2 Ibid.
3 G. L. Rondi, *Tempo*, 21 January 1976
4 *L'Eco del Cinema*, 21 January 1959

7: UNDERGROUND

1 Lietta Tornabuoni, *L'Europeo*, 10 April 1969
2 Franco Rispoli, *Settimo Giorno*, 28 May 1963
3 Partially published in *Cinema e Resistenza* edited by Giovanni Vento and Massimo Mida (Luciano Landi, 1959)
4 His future favourite scriptwriter: she also translated for him *Tobacco Road, Life with Father, Look Homeward, Angel, Mrs Gibbons' Boys, Le Treizième Arbre*
5 Koch had fled to Milan and, after the fall of the regime, he had hidden in Florence, where he was arrested on 18 May; his trial took place seventeen days later.
6 Luigi's wife after his marriage to Madina Arrivabene was annulled in Hungary.
7 Giorgio Strehler, *Milano Sera*, 5 December 1945
8 *L'Avventurosa Storia del Cinema Italiano*, Faldini and Fofi

8: AGAINST THE CURRENT

1 *Cahiers du Cinema*, no. 93 (Paris, March 1954)
2 *Luchino Visconti*, Ferrara
3 Lina Coletti, op. cit.
4 Luchino Visconti, *Rinascita*, 7 December 1948
5 Visconti interview with Penelope Gilliatt, *Observer*, 10 September 1961
6 From a conversation with Franco Mannino
7 *Luchino Visconti*, Baldelli
8 *Premier Plan*, no. 17 (Lyons, 1961, A.A. V.V.)
9 *Cahiers du Cinema*, no. 93
10 *L'Avventurosa Storia del Cinema Italiano*, Faldini and Fofi

9: WORKING WITH CALLAS

1 *Callas*, Ardoin and Fitzgerald
2 Ibid.
3 Ibid.
4 Ibid.
5 Ibid.
6 Camilla Cederna, *L'Europeo*, 26 November 1954
7 Ardoin and Fitzgerald, op. cit.
8 Article by L. Visconti, *Il Contemporaneo*, 26 January 1957
9 *Toscanini*, Sachs
10 Ibid.
11 Ibid.
12 *Il Contemporaneo*, op. cit.
13 Camilla Cederna, op. cit.
14 Ardoin and Fitzgerald, op. cit.
15 Ibid.

10: THE OTHER FAMILY

1 *L'Avventurosa Storia del Cinema Italiano*, Faldini and Fofi
2 Ibid.
3 *Il Contemporaneo*, 18 January 1958
4 This is a pity. The opera should be sung in its original French (libretto by

Joseph Mery and Camille du Locle from the tragedy by Friedrich Schiller). In fact the Italian translation often doesn't fit the musical phrase. Visconti and Giulini discussed this possibility but the singers, who already knew the part in Italian, were reluctant to relearn it in the difficult French. Later, Claudio Abbado also wanted to perform the opera in its original, but ran into similar difficulties.

5 *Observer*, op. cit.

6 Ardoin and Fitzgerald, op. cit.

11: TURNING TO THE PAST

1 *The Leopard* was finally printed by Giangiacomo Feltrinelli in a very small first edition

2 Interview with Derek Prouse, *The Sunday Times*, 8 July 1962

3 *Il Diavolo in Giardino*, from the *Affair du collier*, music by Mannino, performed in Palermo in February 1963

4 *Observer*, 27 October 1963

5 Interview with Gioacchino Tomasi di Lampedusa, *L'Ora*, 26 November 1962

6 Ibid.

7 S. Edwards, *Evening Standard*, 18 April 1966

8 Interview with Lietta Tornabuoni, *L'Espresso*, 6 June 1965

9 *Visconti Impossibile*, Sennuccio Benelli (1973)

10 Costanzo Costantini, *Playmen*, no. 5, May 1973

11 *Evening Standard*, op. cit.

12 Camus in 1957 received the Nobel Prize for literature; in 1960 he died in a car crash which was probably suicide.

13 *L'Ora*, 26 November 1962

12: INTERIOR TWILIGHT

1 Interview with Mark Shivas, *Guardian*, 4 April 1970

2 Ibid.

3 Lina Coletti, *L'Europeo*, op. cit.

4 In London it was played at the National Theatre (October 1962) by Joan Plowright, directed by Laurence Olivier

5 Lietta Tornabuoni, *L'Europeo*, 6 June 1965

6 A. Moravia, *L'Espresso*, 14 March 1971

7 G. Servadio, *Observer*, 30 July 1972

8 All quotes from the author's articles in the *Observer*.

9 Article by the author, *Il Mondo* 3 March 1972

13: WORKING TO LIVE

1 *L'Ultimo Visconti*, Costantini

2 Costantini, op. cit.

3 From the catalogue of an exhibition of costumes used in Visconti's works which opened at Charleston, USA, and was later shown at Spoleto and Reggio Emilia.

4 Costantini, op. cit.

14: TO BURN UNTIL DEATH

1 Lina Coletti, *L'Europeo*, 21 November 1974

2 Ibid.

3 Costantini, op. cit.

4 Lina Coletti, *L'Europeo*, op. cit.

5 *Visconti e il Teatro*, Teatro Municipale di Reggio Emilia, 1977

6 Enrico Medioli, Introduction to the catalogue of an exhibition of costumes from Visconti's films (Charleston)

Visconti's Works

The compilation of this list has been made possible thanks to *Album Visconti*, edited by Caterina d'Amico de Carvalho (Sonzogno, 1978); *Visconti* by Geoffrey Nowell-Smith (Secker, second edition, 1973); *Callas* by John Ardoin and Gerry Fitzgerald (Holt, Rinehart, 1974); *Luchino Visconti* by Pio Baldelli (Mazzotta ed.); and *The Catalogue of the Spoleto Festival* (Black Lock House, College of Charleston, 1978).

Theatre

Carità Mondana (Social Charity) by Giannino Antona Traverso, 1936
Director: R. Caló and R. Simoni
Sets and costumes: Luchino Visconti
Cast: Andreina Pagnani, Luigi Cimara, Paolo Stoppa

Sweet Aloes by Jay Mallory (Joyce Carey), 1936
Director: R. Caló and R. Simoni
Sets and costumes: Luchino Visconti
Cast: as above

The Journey by Henry Bernstein, 1938
Sets and costumes: Luchino Visconti
Cast: Andreina Pagnani

Les Parents Terribles (The Dreadful Parents) by Jean Cocteau, 1945
Director: Luchino Visconti
Sets and costumes: Luchino Visconti
Cast: Andreina Pagnani, Lola Braccini, Rina Morelli, Gino Cervi, Antonio Pierfederici

The Fifth Column by Ernest Hemingway, 1945
Director: Luchino Visconti
Sets and costumes: Renato Guttuso
Cast: Carlo Ninchi, Olga Villi, Arnoldo Foá, Carlo Lombardi

La Machine à Ecrire (The Typewriter) by Jean Cocteau, 1945
Director and sets: Luchino Visconti
Cast: Ernesto Calindri, Antonio Battistella, Vittorio Gassman, Laura Adani, Nora Ricci

Antigone by Jean Anouilh, 1945
Director: Luchino Visconti
Sets and costumes: Mario Chiari
Cast: Mario Pisu, Rina Morelli, Olga Villi, Giorgio de Lullo, Paolo Stoppa

Huis Clos (Vicious Circle) by Jean-Paul Sartre, 1945
Director: Luchino Visconti
Sets and costumes: Mario Chiari
Cast: Paolo Stoppa, Rina Morelli, Vivi Gioi, Valentino Bruchi

Adam by Marcel Achard, 1945
Director and sets: Luchino Visconti
Cast: Laura Adani, Vittorio Gassman, Ernesto Calindri

Tobacco Road by John Kirkland from Erskine Caldwell's novel, 1945
Director: Luchino Visconti
Sets and costumes: Cesare Pavani
Cast: Ernesto Calindri, Renata Seripa, Vittorio Gassman, Laura Adani

Le Mariage de Figaro (The Marriage of Figaro) by P. A. Caron de Beaumarchais, 1946
Director: Luchino Visconti
Sets and costumes: Veniero Colasanti
Music: Renzo Rossellini
Cast: Nino Besozzi, Lia Zoppelli, Vittorio de Sica, Vivi Gioi, Vittorio Caprioli, Maria Mercader, Antonio Pierfederici, Alberto Bonucci

Crime and Punishment by Gaston Baty from F. Dostoievsky's novel, 1946
Director: Luchino Visconti
Sets and costumes: Mario Chiari
Cast: Memo Benassi, Massimo Girotti, Franco Zeffirelli, Giorgio de Lullo, Paolo Stoppa, Luisa Fares, Achille Millo, Vanna Polverosi, Arnoldo Foá, Mariella Lotti, Rina Morelli

The Glass Menagerie by Tennessee Williams, 1946
Director: Luchino Visconti
Sets and costumes: Mario Chiari
Cast: Tatiana Pavlova, Rina Morelli, Paolo Stoppa, Giorgio de Lullo

Life with Father by Howard Lindsay and Russell Crouse from the novel by Clarence Day, 1947
Director: Geraldo Guerrieri
Sets and costumes: Maria de Matteis
Supervisor: Luchino Visconti
Cast: Paolo Stoppa, Rina Morelli, Giorgio de Lullo, Franco Interlenghi, Mariella Lotti, etc.

Eurydice (Point of Departure) by Jean Anouilh, 1947
Director: Luchino Visconti
Sets and costumes: Mario Chiari
Cast: Giorgio de Lullo, Antonio Gandusio, Paolo Stoppa, Cesare Fantoni, Achille Millo, Alberto Bonucci, Franco Zeffirelli, Rina Morelli

As You Like It by William Shakespeare, 1948
Director: Luchino Visconti
Sets and costumes: Salvador Dali
Cast: Cesare Fantoni, Gabriele Frezetti, Vittorio Gassman, Ruggero Ruggeri, Luciana Salce, Paolo Stoppa, Luigi Almirante, Franco Interlenghi, Rina Morelli, Vivi Gioi, Marcello Mastroianni, Sergio Fantoni

A Streetcar Named Desire by Tennessee Williams, 1949
Director: Luchino Visconti
Sets and costumes: Franco Zeffirelli
Cast: Carla Bizzarri, Vittorio Gassman, Marcello Mastroianni, Vivi Gioi, Rina Morelli, Franco Interlenghi, Cesare Fantoni

Oreste by Vittorio Alfieri, adapted by Luchino Visconti, 1949
Director: Luchino Visconti
Sets and costumes: Mario Chiari
Cast: Ruggero Ruggeri, Paolo Borboni, Rina Morelli, Vittorio Gassman, Marcello Mastroianni

Troilus and Cressida by William Shakespeare, 1949
Director: Luchino Visconti
Sets: Franco Zeffirelli
Cast: Vittorio Gassman, Giorgio de Lullo, Mario Pisu, Paolo Stoppa, Giovanni Cimara, Franco Interlenghi, Renzo Ricci, Marcello Mastroianni,

Memo Benassi, Giorgio Albertazzi, Rina Morelli, Elsa de Giorgi, Eva Magni

Death of a Salesman by Arthur Miller, 1951
Director: Luchino Visconti
Cast: Paolo Stoppa, Rina Morelli, Giorgio de Lullo, Marcello Mastroianni, Franco Interlenghi, Flora Carabella, Mario Pisu

A Streetcar Named Desire by Tennessee Williams, 1951
Director: Luchino Visconti
Sets and costumes: Franco Zeffirelli
Cast: Flora Carabella, Franco Fabrizi, Marcello Mastroianni, Giorgio de Lullo, Rossella Falk, Rina Morelli

Il Seduttore (The Seducer) by Diego Fabbri, 1951
Director: Luchino Visconti
Sets and costumes: Mario Chiari
Assistant director: Giorgio de Lullo
Cast: Paolo Stoppa, Rina Morelli, Rossella Falk, Carla Bizzarri

La Locandiera (The Innkeeper) by Carlo Goldoni, 1952
Director: Luchino Visconti
Sets and costumes: Luchino Visconti and Piero Tosi
Cast: Marcello Mastroianni, Paolo Stoppa, Gianrico Tedeschi, Rina Morelli, Rossella Falk, Flora Carabella, Giorgio de Lullo, Ruggero Nuvolari

The Three Sisters by Anton Chekov, 1952
Director: Luchino Visconti
Sets: Franco Zeffirelli
Costumes: Marcel Escoffier
Cast: Paolo Stoppa, Rossella Falk, Sarah Ferrati, Rina Morelli, Gianrico Tedeschi, Memo Benassi, Giorgio de Lullo, Marcello Mastroianni, Ruggero Nuvolari

Tobacco is Harmful by Anton Chekov, 1953
Director: Luchino Visconti
Costume: Mario Chiari
Cast: Memo Benassi

Medea by Eurypides, 1953
Director: Luchino Visconti
Sets and costumes: Mario Chiari
Cast: Sarah Ferrati, Memo Benassi, Sergio Fantoni, Giorgio de Lullo

Festival (musical comedy) by Age, Scarpelli and Vergani, 1954
Consultant: Luchino Visconti
Cast: Wanda Osiris, Henri Salvador, Nino Manfedi, Raffaele Pisu

Come le Foglie (Like the Leaves) by Giuseppe Giacosa, 1954
Director: Luchino Visconti
Sets and costumes: Lila de Nobili
Cast: Salvo Randone, Lina Volonghi, Lilla Brignone, Gianni Santuccio

The Crucible by Arthur Miller, 1955
Director and designer: Luchino Visconti
Cast: Tino Buazzelli, Edda Albertini, Paola Boboni, Cesare Fantoni, Adriana Asti, Gianni Santuccio, Lilla Brignone

Uncle Vanya by Anton Chekov, 1955
Director: Luchino Visconti
Sets and costumes: Piero Tosi
Cast: Eleonora Rossi Drago, Rina Morelli, Paolo Stoppa, Marcello Mastroianni

Death of a Salesman by Arthur Miller, 1956
Director: Luchino Visconti
Cast: Paolo Stoppa, Rina Morelli, Marcello Mastroianni, Franco Interlenghi, etc.

La Locandiera (The Innkeeper) by Carlo Goldoni, 1956
Director: Luchino Visconti
Sets and costumes: Luchino Visconti and Piero Tosi
Cast: Marcello Mastroianni, Paolo Stoppa, Romolo Valli, Rina Morelli, Rossella Falk, Giorgio de Lullo, Ruggero Nuvolari

Fröken Julie (Miss Julie) by August Strindberg, 1957
Director: Luchino Visconti
Sets and costumes: Luchino Visconti
Cast: Lilla Brignone, Massimo Girotti, Ave Ninchi

L'Impresario delle Smirne (The Impresario from Smyrna) by Carlo Goldoni, 1957
Director: Luchino Visconti
Sets and costumes: Luchino Visconti
Cast: Paolo Stoppa, Ilaria Occhini, Rina Morelli, Corrado Pani, Giancarlo Sbragia

A View from the Bridge by Arthur Miller, 1958
Director: Luchino Visconti
Sets and costumes: Mario Garbuglia
Cast: Paolo Stoppa, Rina Morelli, Ilaria Occhini, Sergio Fantoni, Corrado Pani

Immagini e Tempi de Eleonora Duse by Gerardo Guerrieri, 1958
Director: Luchino Visconti
Cast: Lilla Brignone, Robert Brown, Giorgio de Lullo, Rossella Falk, Edmonda Aldini, Vittorio Gassman, Emma Gramatica, Rina Morelli, Annibale Ninchi, Luise Rainer, Romolo Valli

Look Homeward, Angel by Ketti Frings from Thomas Wolfe's novel, 1958
Director: Luchino Visconti
Sets and costumes: Mario Garbuglia
Cast: Gianna Giachetti, Lilla Brignone, Corrado Pani, Tino Bianchi

Two for the Seesaw by William Gibson, 1958
Director and designer: Luchino Visconti
Cast: Annie Girardot, Jean Marais

Mrs Gibbons' Boys by Will Glickman and Joseph Stein, 1958
Director: Luchino Visconti
Sets and costumes: Mario Garbuglia
Cast: Bice Valori, Rina Morelli, Paolo Stoppa, Sergio Fantoni

Figli d'Arte by Diego Fabbri, 1959
Director: Luchino Visconti
Sets and costumes: Mario Garbuglia
Cast: Paolo Stoppa, Rina Morelli, Sergio Fantoni

L'Arialda by Giovanni Testori, 1960
Director and designer: Luchino Visconti
Cast: Rina Morelli, Umberto Orsini, Pupella Maggio, Valeria Moriconi

'Tis Pity She's a Whore by John Ford, 1961
Director and sets: Luchino Visconti
Costumes: Piero Tosi
Cast: Romy Schneider, Alain Delon, Valentine Tessier, Sylvia Montfort, Lucien Baroux

Le Treizième Arbre (The Thirteenth Tree) by André Gide, 1963
Director: Luchino Visconti

Cast: Rina Morelli, Giacomo Piperno, Romolo Valli, Vittorio Caprioli

After the Fall by Arthur Miller, 1965
Director: Luchino Visconti
Sets: Mario Garbuglia
Costumes: Christian Dior
Cast: Annie Girardot, Michel Auclair, Clotilde Joano

The Cherry Orchard by Anton Chekov, 1965
Director: Luchino Visconti
Sets and costumes: Luchino Visconti and Ferdinando Scarfiotti
Cast: Rina Morelli, Ottavia Piccolo, Paolo Stoppa, Massimo Girotti

Egmont by J. Wolfgang Goethe, 1967
Director: Luchino Visconti
Sets and costumes: Ferdinando Scarfiotti
Cast: Elsa Albani, Giorgio de Lullo, Romolo Valli, Piero Yaggioni, Nora Ricci, Ottavia Piccolo

La Monaca di Monza (The Nun from Monza) by Giovanni Testori, 1967
Director: Luchino Visconti
Cast: Lilla Brignone, Sergio Fantoni, Valentina Fortunato, Mariangela Melato

L'Inserzione (The Advertisement) by Natalia Ginzburg, 1969
Director: Luchino Visconti
Sets and costumes: Ferdinando Scarfiotti
Cast: Adriana Asti, Franco Interlenghi, Mariangela Melato

Old Times by Harold Pinter, 1973
Director: Luchino Visconti
Assistant: Giorgio Ferrara
Sets and costumes: Mario Garbuglia
Cast: Umberto Orsini, Adriana Asti, Valentina Cortese

Operas and Ballets

La Vestale by Etienne Jouy
Music: Gaspare Spontini

Milan, Teatro alla Scala, 1954
Conductor: Antonino Votto
Director: Luchino Visconti
Sets and costumes: Piero Zuffi
Cast: Franco Corelli (Licinio), Maria Meneghini Callas (Giulia), Enzo Sordello (Cinna), Nicola Rossi Lemeni (il Sommo Sacerdote), Ebe Stignani (la Gran Vestale)

La Sonnambula by Felice Romani
Music: Vincenzo Bellini
Milan, Teatro alla Scala, 1955
Conductor: Leonard Bernstein
Director: Luchino Visconti
Sets and costumes: Piero Tosi
Cast: Giuseppe Modesti (Conte Rodolfo), Gabriella Carturan (Teresa), Maria Meneghini Callas (Amina), Cesare Valletti (Elvino)

La Traviata by Francesco Maria Piave
Music: Giuseppe Verdi
Milan, Teatro alla Scala, 1955
Conductor: Carlo Maria Giulini
Director: Luchino Visconti
Sets and costumes: Lila de Nobili
Cast: Maria Meneghini Callas (Violetta), Silvana Zanolli (Flora), Giuseppe di Stefano (Alfredo), Ettore Bastianini (Giorgio)

Mario e il Mago (Mario and the Magician)
'Choreographic action' by Luchino Visconti from the novella by Thomas Mann
Music: Franco Mannino
Milan, Teatro alla Scala, 1956
Choreography: Leonide Massine
Conductor: Luciano Rosada
Sets and costumes: Lila de Nobili
Cast: Jean Babilée (Mario), Salvo Randone (il mago Cipolla), Luciana Novara (Silvestra)

Anna Bolena by Felice Romani
Music: Gaetano Donizetti
Milan, Teatro alla Scala, 1957
Conductor: Gianandrea Gavazzeni
Director: Luchino Visconti
Sets and costumes: Nicola Benois

Cast: Nicola Rossi Lemeni (Enrico VIII), Maria Meneghini Callas (Anna Bolena), Giulietta Simionato (Giovanna Seymour)

Iphigénie en Tauride by Nicolas-François Guillard
Music: Christoph Willibald Gluck
   Milan, Teatro alla Scala, 1957
Conductor: Nino Sanzogno
Director: Luchino Visconti
Sets and costumes: Nicola Benois
Cast: Maria Meneghini Callas (Ifigenia), Dino Dondi (Oreste), Fiorenza Cossotto (Artemide)

Maratona di Danza (The Dance Marathon)
Libretto: Luchino Visconti
Music: Hans Werner Henze
   West Berlin, Städtische Oper, 1957
Choreography: Dick Sanders
Conductor: Richard Kraus
Director: Luchino Visconti
Sets and costumes: Renzo Vespignani
Cast: Jean Babilée (Jean), Marion Schnelle (Marion), Gundula von Woyna (Celestine)

Don Carlo by Joseph Mery and Camille du Locle from the tragedy by Friedrich Schiller
Music: Giuseppe Verdi
   London, Royal Opera House, Covent Garden, 1958
Conductor: Carlo Maria Giulini
Director: Luchino Visconti
Sets: Luchino Visconti and Maurizio Chiari
Costumes: Luchino Visconti and Filippo Sanjust
Assistant producer: Enrico Medioli
Cast: Boris Christoff (Filippo II), Jon Vickers (Don Carlo), Tito Gobbi (Roderigo Marchese di Posa), Marco Stefanoni (il Grande Inquisitore), Gré Brouwenstijn (Elisabetta di Valois), Fedora Barbieri (la Principessa d'Eboli)

Macbeth by Francesco Maria Piave
Music: Giuseppe Verdi
   Spoleto, Teatro Nuovo, 1958
Conductor: Thomas Schippers
Director: Luchino Visconti
Sets and costumes: Piero Tosi

Assistant director: Enrico Medioli
Cast: Carmine Torre (Duncano), William Chapman (Macbeth), Ferruccio Mazzoli (Banco), Shakeh Vartenissian (Lady Macbeth)

Il Duca d'Alba by Eugene Scribe
Music: Gaetano Donizetti
  Spoleto, Teatro Nuovo, 1959
Conductor: Thomas Schippers
Director: Luchino Visconti
Sets: Carlo Ferrario
Costumes: Luchino Visconti and Filippo Sanjust
Assistant director: Enrico Medioli
Cast: Luigi Quilico (il Duca d'Alba), Wladimiro Ganzarolli (Sandoval), Renato Cioni (Marcello di Bruges), Ivana Tosini (Amelia d'Egmont)

Salome by Oscar Wilde
Music: Richard Strauss
  Spoleto, Teatro Nuovo, 1961
Conductor: Thomas Schippers
Director: Luchino Visconti
Sets and costumes: Luchino Visconti
Cast: George Shirley (Erode), Lili Chookasian (Erodiade), Margaret Tynes (Salome), Robert Anderson (Jokanaan)

Il Diavolo in Giardino (The Devil in the Garden) Historical and pastoral comedy by Luchino Visconti, Filippo Sanjust and Enrico Medioli
Music: Franco Mannino
  Palermo, Teatro Massimo, 1963
Conductor: Franco Mannino
Director: Luchino Visconti
Sets and costumes: Luchino Visconti and Filippo Sanjust
Assistant directors: Enrico Medioli and Marcello Aliprandi
Cast: Jolanda Gardino (Madame de Tourzel), Glauco Scarlibi (Boehmer), Rosario Guanziroli (il Delfino di Francia), Rosanna Peirani (Madame Royale), Clara Petrella (Jeanne de la Motte)

La Traviata by Francesco Maria Piave
Music: Giuseppe Verdi
  Spoleto, Teatro Nuovo, 1963
Conductor: Robert La Marchina
Director and designer: Luchino Visconti
Costumes: Piero Tosi and Bice Brichetto
Cast: Franca Fabbri (Violetta), Daniela Dinato (Flora), Franco Bonisolli (Alfredo), Mario Basiola Jr (Giorgio)

Le Nozze di Figaro (The Marriage of Figaro) by Lorenzo da Ponte
Music: Wolfgang Amadeus Mozart
  Rome, Teatro dell'Opera, 1964
Conductor: Carlo Maria Giulini
Director: Luchino Visconti
Sets and costumes: Luchino Visconti and Filippo Sanjust
Cast: Ugo Trama (il Conte Almaviva), Ilva Ligabue (la Contessa Rosina), Rolando Panerai (Figaro), Mariella Adani (Susanna), Stefania Malagú (Cherubino)

Il Trovatore by Salvatore Cammarano
Music: Giuseppe Verdi
  Moscow, the Bolshoi Theatre, 1964
Conductor: Gianandrea Gavazzeni
Director: Luchino Visconti
Sets and costumes: Nicola Benois
Assistant director: Alberto Fassini
Cast: Piero Cappucilli (il Conte di Luna), Gabriella Tucci (Leonora), Giulietta Simionato (Azucena), Carlo Bergonzi (Manrico)

Il Trovatore by Salvatore Cammarano
Music: Giuseppe Verdi
  London, Royal Opera House, Covent Garden, 1964
Conductor: Carlo Maria Giulini
Director: Luchino Visconti
Sets and costumes: Filippo Sanjust
Cast: Peter Glossop (il Conte di Luna), Gwyneth Jones (Leonora), Giulietta Simionato (Azucena), Bruno Prevedi (Manrico)

Don Carlo by Joseph de Mery and Camille du Locle
Music: Giuseppe Verdi
  Rome, Teatro dell'Opera, 1965
Conductor: Carlo Maria Giulini
Director: Luchino Visconti
Sets and costumes: Luchino Visconti
Cast: Cesare Siepi (Filippo II), Gianfranco Cecchele (Don Carlo), Kostas Paskalis (Don Rodrigo), Martti Talvella (il Grande Inquisitore), Suzanne Sarroca (Elisabetta di Valois)

Falstaff by Arrigo Boito
Music: Giuseppe Verdi
  Vienna, Staatsoper, 1966
Conductor: Leonard Bernstein
Director: Luchino Visconti

Sets and costumes: Luchino Visconti and Ferdinando Scarfiotti
Cast: Dietrich Fischer-Dieskau (Sir John Falstaff), Rolando Panerai (Ford), Juan Oncina (Fenton), Ilva Ligabue (Mrs Alice Ford), Graziella Sciutti (Anne), Regina Resnik (Mistress Quickly)

Der Rosenkavalier by Hugo von Hofmannsthal
Music: Richard Strauss
London, Royal Opera House, Covent Garden, 1966
Conductor: Georg Solti
Director: Luchino Visconti
Sets: Luchino Visconti and Ferdinando Scarfiotti.
Costumes: Vera Marzot
Cast: Sena Jurinac (Marschallin), Josephine Veasey (Octavian), Michael Langdon (Ochs), Joan Carlyle (Sophie)

La Traviata by Francesco Maria Piave
Music: Giuseppe Verdi
London, Royal Opera House, Covent Garden, 1967
Conductor: Carlo Maria Giulini
Director: Luchino Visconti
Sets: Nato Frasca
Costumes: Vera Marzot
Cast: Mirella Freni (Violetta), Anne Howells (Flora), Renato Cioni (Alfredo), Piero Cappucilli (Giorgio)

Simone Boccanegra by Francesco Maria Piave
Music: Giuseppe Verdi
Vienna, Staatsoper, 1969
Conductor: Josef Krips
Director: Luchino Visconti
Sets and costumes: Luchino Visconti and Ferdinando Scarfiotti
Assistant director: Alberto Fassini
Cast: Eberhard Waechter (Simon Boccanegra), Nicolai Ghiaurov (Jacopo), Gundula Janowitz (Amelia), Carlo Cossutta (Gabriele)

Manon Lescaut by Marco Prago, Domenico Oliva, Giulio Ricordi and Luigi Illica
Music: Giacomo Puccini
Spoleto, Teatro Nuovo, 1973
Conductor: Thomas Schippers
Director: Luchino Visconti
Sets: Lila de Nobili and Emilio Carcano
Costumes: Piero Tosi and Gabriella Pescucci
Deputy director: Alberto Fassini

Cast: Nancy Shade (Manon Lescaut), Angelo Romero (Lescaut), Harry Theyard (Renato), Carlo Del Bosco (Geronte)

Films and Documentaries

Partie de Campagne, 1937
Director: Jean Renoir
Assistant directors: Jacques Becker, Henri Cartier-Bresson and Luchino Visconti
Script: Jean Renoir from a short story by Guy de Maupassant
Costumes: Luchino Visconti
Photography: Claude Renoir
Producer: Pierre Braunberger for Les Films du Panthéon (shown for the first time on 8 May 1946)
Cast: Sylvia Bataille, Georges Darnoux, Jacques Borel, Gabriello, Jean Renoir, Marguerite Renoir

La Tosca, 1940
Directors: Jean Renoir and Carl Koch
Assistant director: Luchino Visconti
Script: Luchino Visconti, Jean Renoir and Carl Koch from the play by Victorien Sardou
Music: Giacomo Puccini
Cast: Michel Simon, Rossano Brazzi, Massimo Girotti

Ossessione, 1942
Director: Luchino Visconti
Assistants: Giuseppe de Santis and Antonio Pietrangeli
Script: Luchino Visconti, Mario Alicata, Giuseppe de Santis, Gianni Puccini and Alberto Moravia from the novel *The Postman Always Rings Twice* by James Cain
Editor: Mario Serandrei
Production company and distribution: ICI, Rome
Cast: Clara Calamai, Massimo Girotti, Juan de Landa, Elio Marcuzzo

Giorni di Gloria (Days of Glory), 1945
Directors: Marcello Pagliero, Luchino Visconti
Commentary: Umberto Calosso
Editors: Mario Serandrei and Carlo Alberto Chiesa
Production company: Titanus

La Terra Trema (Episodio del Mare), 1947
Director: Luchino Visconti
Assistant directors: Franco Zeffirelli and Francesco Rosi
Script: Luchino Visconti, freely taken from the novel *I Malavoglia* by Giuseppe Verga
Photography: G. R. Aldo
Editor: Mario Serandrei
Production company: Universalia
Cast: fisherman and people from Acitrezza

Bellissima, 1951
Director: Luchino Visconti
Assistant directors: Franco Zeffirelli and Francesco Rosi
Script: Suso Cecchi d'Amico, Francesco Rosi and Luchino Visconti based on a story by Cesare Zavattini
Sets: Gianni Polidori
Costumes: Piero Tosi
Photography: Piero Portalupi and Paul Ronald
Production company: Bellissima Films
Cast: Anna Magnani, Walter Chiari, Tina Apicella, Gastone Renzelli, Lola Braccini, Alessandro Blasetti, Mario Chiari

Appunti su un fatto di cronaca (Notes on a happening), second episode of a news film, 1951
Director: Luchino Visconti
Commentary: Vasco Pratolini read by Giorgio de Lullo
Producers: Marco Ferreri and Riccardo Ghione

Siamo Donne, 1953
Film in episodes
Fifth episode: Anna Magnani
Director: Luchino Visconti
Script: Suso Cecchi d'Amico and Cesare Zavattini from an idea by Cesare Zavattini
Editor: Mario Serandrei
Production company: Titanus, Film Costellazione
Cast: Anna Magnani

Senso, 1954
Director: Luchino Visconti
Script: Suso Cecchi d'Amico and Luchino Visconti from a short story by Camillo Boito
Costumes: Marcel Escoffier and Piero Tosi

Photography: G. R. Aldo and Robert Krasker
Editor: Mario Serandrei
Production company: Lux Films
Cast: Alida Valli, Farley Granger, Massimo Girotti, Heinz Moog, Rina Morelli, Marcella Mariani, Christian Marquand

Le Notti Bianche (White Nights), 1957
Director: Luchino Visconti
Script: Suso Cecchi d'Amico and Luchino Visconti from the story by F. Dostoievsky
Music: Nino Rota
Sets: Mario Chiari assisted by Mario Garbuglia
Costumes: Piero Tosi
Editor: Mario Serandrei
Production company: CIAS Vides
Cast: Maria Schell, Marcello Mastroianni, Jean Marais, Clara Calamai

Rocco e i suoi Fratelli (Rocco and His Brothers), 1960
Director: Luchino Visconti
Script: Luchino Visconti, Suso Cecchi d'Amico, Pasquale Festa Campanile, Massimo Franciosa and Enrico Medioli from *Il Ponte della Ghisolfa* by Giovanni Testori
Sets: Mario Garbuglia
Costumes: Piero Tosi
Editor: Mario Serandrei
Production company: Titanus, Film Marceau
Cast: Alain Delon, Renato Salvatori, Annie Girardot, Katina Paxinou, Paolo Stoppa, Claudia Cardinale, Corrado Panni, Alessandra Panaro, Claudia Mori, Adriana Asti

Boccaccio '70, 1962
Film in episodes
First: **Le Tentazioni del Dottor Antonio** by Federico Fellini
Second: **Renzo e Luciana** by Mario Monicelli
Fourth: **La Riffa** by Vittorio de Sica
Third: **Il Lavoro**
Director: Luchino Visconti
Script: Suso Cecchi d'Amico and Luchino Visconti
Music: Nino Rota
Editor: Mario Serandrei
Producers: Carlo Ponti and Antonio Cervi
Cast: Romy Schneider, Tomas Milian, Romolo Valli, Paolo Stoppa

Il Gattopardo (The Leopard), 1963
Director: Luchino Visconti
Script: Suso Cecchi d'Amico, Enrico Medioli, Pasquale Festa Campanile, Massimo Franciosa and Luchino Visconti from the novel by Giuseppe Tomasi di Lampedusa
Sets: Mario Garbuglia
Décor: Giorgio Pes and Laudomia Hercolani
Costumes: Piero Tosi
Editor: Mario Serandrei
Production company: Titanus, SHPC/SGC
Cast: Burt Lancaster, Alain Delon, Claudia Cardinale, Paolo Stoppa, Rina Morelli, Serge Reggiani, Romolo Valli, Mario Girotti, Pierre Clementi, Ottavio Piccolo

Vaghe Stelle dell'Orsa (Of a Thousands Delights, or Sandra), 1965
Director: Luchino Visconti
Story and script: Suso Cecchi d'Amico, Enrico Medioli and Luchino Visconti
Art director: Mario Garbuglia
Photography: Giuseppe Rotunno
Editor: Mario Serandrei
Production company: Vides
Cast: Claudia Cardinale, Jean Sorel, Michael Craig, Marie Bell, Renzo Ricci

Le Streghe (The Witches), 1966
Film in episodes
The Witch Burnt Alive (La Strega Bruciata Viva)
Director: Luchino Visconti
Story and script: Giuseppe Patroni Griffi in collaboration with Cesare Zavattini
Sets: Mario Garbuglia and Piero Poletto
Editor: Mario Serandrei
Production company: Dino de Laurentis's Cinematografica
Cast: Silvana Mangano, Annie Girardot, Francisco Rabal, Massimo Girotti, Else Albani, Clara Calamai

Lo Straniero (The Outsider), 1967
Director: Luchino Visconti
Script: Luchino Visconti, Suso Cecchi d'Amico and Georges Conchon from the novel by Albert Camus
Costumes: Piero Tosi
Art director: Mario Garbuglia
Photography: Giuseppe Rotunno
Editor: Ruggero Mastroianni

Producer: Dino de Laurentis
Cast: Marcello Mastroianni, Anna Karina, Georges Wilson

La Caduta degli Dei (The Damned), 1969
Director: Luchino Visconti
Story and script: Nicola Badalucco, Enrico Medioli and Luchino Visconti
Sets: Pasquale Romano
Costumes: Piero Tosi and Vera Marzot
Editor: Ruggero Mastroianni
Production company: Praesidens Films, Zurich, Pegaso Films and Italnoleggio
Cast: Dirk Bogarde, Ingrid Thulin, Helmut Griem, Helmut Berger, Umberto Orsini, Nora Ricci, Charlotte Rampling

Alla Ricerca di Tadzio (Looking for Tadzio), 1970
Director: Luchino Visconti
Production company: RAI-Radiotelevisione Italiana

Morte a Venezia (Death in Venice), 1971
Director: Luchino Visconti
Script: Luchino Visconti and Nicola Badalucco from Thomas Mann's novella
Sets: Ferdinando Scarfiotti
Costumes: Piero Tosi
Editor: Ruggero Mastroianni
Production company: Alfa Cinematografica and Productions Editions Cinématographiques Françaises
Cast: Dirk Bogarde, Silvana Mangano, Bjorn Andresen, Romolo Valli, Nora Ricci, Marisa Berenson

Ludwig, 1973
Director: Luchino Visconti
Story and script: Luchino Visconti and Enrico Medioli with Suso Cecchi d'Amico
Sets: Mario Chiari
Costumes: Piero Tosi
Editor: Ruggero Mastroianni
Production company: Mega Film, Cinetel, Dieter Geissler Filmproduktion and Divina Film, Munich
Cast: Helmut Berger, Trevor Howard, Romy Schneider, Silvana Mangano, Isabella Telezynska, Umberto Orsini, Sonia Petrova, Adriana Asti, Nora Ricci

Gruppo di Famiglia in un Interno (Conversation Piece), 1974
Director: Luchino Visconti

Story: Enrico Medioli
Script: Suso Cecchi d'Amico, Enrico Medioli and Luchino Visconti
Sets: Mario Garbuglia
Costumes: Piero Tosi and Vera Marzot
Photography: Pasqualino de Santis
Editor: Ruggero Mastroianni
Production company: Rusconi Film and Gaumont International
Cast: Burt Lancaster, Silvana Mangano, Helmut Berger, Claudia Marsani, Romolo Valli

L'Innocent (The Intruder), 1976
Director: Luchino Visconti
Script: Suso Cecchi d'Amico, Enrico Medioli and Luchino Visconti from Gabriele d'Annunzio's novel **L'Innocente**
Sets: Mario Garbuglia
Costumes: Piero Tosi
Editot: Ruggero Mastroianni
Producers: Giovanni Bertolucci for Rizzoli Films, Les Films Jacques Letienne, Société Imp. Ex. Ci and Francoriz Productions
Cast: Giancarlo Giannini, Laura Antonelli, Jennifer O'Neil, Didier Haudepin, Rina Morelli, Massimo Girotti

Index

A la Recherche du Temps Perdu, 200–201, 210–11
Abbadia, S. Salvatore, 118
Abbado, Claudio, 148
Abyssinia, 49
Archard, Marcel, 111
Acitrezza, 73–4, 116
Acquasanta Golf Club, 98–9
Acton, Harold, 190
Adam, 111
Adani, Laura, 110, 111
Aeolian Islands, 64
Aeschylus, 184
After the Fall, 185
L'Age d'Or, 54
Agnese di Hohenstaufen, 141
Alassio, 21
Aldo (camera man), 117, 138
Alexander, Field-Marshal, 102
Alfano, Franco, 26
Alfieri, Vittorio, 122
Algiers, 188–9
Alicata, Mario, 67, 70–2, 82–3, 85–6, 102, 104, 108
Amendola, Giorgio, 67, 71, 83, 84–5, 86
Amendola, Giovanni, 67
Amidei, Sergio, 120
Amman, Paul, 46
Anna Bolena, 151
Anna Karenina, 183
Anne, Princess, 199
Anouilh, Jean, 110, 115
Antigone, 110
'Antiparnaso', 125
Antonelli, Laura, 216, 217–18
Antonioni, Michelangelo, 71–2, 104–7, 116, 128, 183, 210, 218–19, 223
Anzio, 89
Aosta, Duchess of, 22

Arbasino, Alberto, 133, 174, 190
Ardeatine, 93–4
Arduini's, 73
L'Arialda, 170
Ariosto, Ludovico, 119
Arrivabene, Niki, *see* Visconti, Niki
Art Nouveau, 25, 43, 128
Art Theatre Company of Milan, 33–4
As You Like It, 120
Asti, Adriana, 142, 150, 156, 166, 168, 171, 221
Auclair, Michel, 185
Auden, W. H., 214
Austria, 21, 46, 124, 193–4, 195
Avanzo, Baroness d', 96
Avanzo, Carlo Libero d', 87
Avanzo, Renzo d', 73, 87, 126

Babilée, Jean, 127, 159
Bad Ischl, 201
Badoglio, General, 84, 85, 86
Baker, Josephine, 31
Balanchine, Georges, 58
Baldwin, Stanley, 60
Balthus, 41
Balzac, Honoré de, 30, 138, 155
The Barber of Seville (Rossini), 158
Barbieri, Fedora, 163
Bardot, Brigitte, 200
Barzini, Luigi, 33
Bataille, Sylvia, 61–63, 161, 172
Bavaria, 193, 201–202
Bavarian Tourist Board, 205
BBC, 80
Beaume, Georges, 166, 170–71, 177, 183, 187, 200, 210–11, 216
Beaumont, Etienne de, 31, 53–4, 55
Beethoven, Ludwig van, 190
Belgiojioso, Princess Cristina, 6

Bell, Marie, 184
La Belle et la Bête, 54
Bellini, Vincenzo, 145, 160
Bellissima, 130–131, 154, 158
Benassi, Memo, 115, 123
Benois, Nicola, 170
Bérard, Christian, 41, 48, 54, 58
Berger, Helmut, 187, 209, 211; Visconti's letters to, 154; and Visconti, 189, 191; in *The Damned*, 194, 195–6; and *A la Recherche*, 200, 201; in *Ludwig*, 201, 203; and Visconti's stroke, 206–207; in *Conversation Piece*, 213, 214; debt to Visconti, 221
Bergman, Ingmar, 210
Bergman, Ingrid, 134, 137, 223
Berlin, 30, 43, 46, 160
Berlin Philharmonic, 58
Berlinguer, Enrico, 219
Bernasconi, 94, 96, 99
Bernhardt, Sarah, 31, 123
Bernstein, Henry, 65
Bernstein, Leonard, 146–7, 186, 204
Bible, 182
Bing, Rudolf, 183
Bismarck, Prince Otto von, 202
Black Shirts, 25, 30, 44
Bloom, Claire, 163
The Blue Angel, 43
Blum, Léon, 59–60
Boboli gardens, Florence, 119, 122, 167, 190
Boccaccio '70, 172
Bogarde, Dirk, 194, 195
Boito, Arrigo, 7, 14, 134
Bolognini, Mauro, 187
Borghese, Elizabeth Mann, 127
Borrelli, Professor, 23
Borromeo family, 4–5, 10, 22, 23
Borromeo, Manolo, 5, 11, 22–3, 65, 103
Bosé, Lucia, 120–1
Bourdet, Edouard, 53
Bousquet, Marie-Louise, 52
Brando, Marlon, 137, 139, 174–5, 200
Braunberger, Pierre, 62–3
Brecht, Bertold, 30, 53, 66, 160
Bresson, Robert, 182
Brianza, 10
Brichetto, Bice, 149, 165–6, 175, 184

Brignone, Lilla, 150, 206
Brivio, Countess Anna, 8
Brouwenstijn, Gré, 163
Bruckner, Anton, 136, 138
Bufalini, 71
Buñuel, Luis, 43, 52

Cagliostro, 141
Cain, James, 63, 70, 75, 78
Calamai, Clara, 44, 73, 74, 77–8, 81, 128, 223
Calasanziani fathers, 31
Caldwell, Erskine, 111
Caligula, 107
Callas, Maria, 125, 129, 183; in *La Traviata*, 27, 147–9; relationship with Visconti, 101, 121, 140–141, 142, 146–7, 151–2, 165, 166, 221; and La Scala, 141; in *La Vestale*, 142–4; in *La Sonnambula*, 145–6, 147; affair with Onassis, 151–2, 170
Camerini, 131
Cameron, Rory, 49, 51
Camus, Albert, 107, 186, 187
Camus, Francine, 187
Cannes Film Festival, 176
Canova, Antonio, 142
Capo, Gian, 33
Carabella, Flora, 123
Caracciolo, Meralda (niece), 31, 206, 219
Cardin, Pierre, 151
Cardinale, Claudia, 168, 179, 184, 213
Carità Mondana, 63
Carmen, 183
Carretta, Governor, 109
Cartier-Bresson, Henri, 61
Caruso, Pietro, 109
Cassino, 88
Castelbarco, Countess Edoarda, 12
Castelbarco, Count Emanuele, 15, 18, 24
Castelgandolfo, 208–209, 218, 220
Castiglioncello, 156–7
Catholic-Communists, 92
Cavour, Camillo, 179
Cederna, Camilla, 143–4
Cernobbio, 15, 27, 29, 36–7, 40, 84, 180, 207–208

Cerrutti, Maria, 94
Cervi, Gino, 106
Cesarini-Sforza, Marco, 85
Chamberlain, Neville, 60, 65
The Chandelier, 107, 108
Chanel, Coco, 40, 41, 47, 58, 64, 150, 172; and Visconti, 42, 49–50, 51, 56, 63, 221; at La Pausa, 49–50; Horst photographs, 52; designs costumes for *Oedipe Roi*, 54; introduces Visconti to Jean Renoir, 59; visits set of *A Day in the Country*, 62 suggests Dali should work on *As You Like It*, 120
Charpentier, Gustave, 208, 211
The Charterhouse of Parma, 29–30
Chaucer, Geoffrey, 5
Chekov, Anton, 132–3, 134, 149
The Cherry Orchard, 185
Chiari, Mario, 80, 115, 134, 144, 207; in occupied Italy, 86, 87–91, 93–4, 100; and *Pensione Oltremare*, 104; designs for *Les Parents Terribles*, 106; on Koch's execution, 110; and *La Terra Trema*, 117
Chiari, Maurizio, 133, 163
Chiari, Walter, 128
Le Chien Andalou, 52
Chini, Galielo, 154, 209
Christian Democrats, 169
Christoff, Boris, 163
Chronicles of Poor Lovers, 120–121, 129
Ciano, Count, 31, 57
Ciano, Edda, 57
Cinecittà, 129, 130, 157, 208
Cinema, 67, 68–9, 71–2, 75, 81, 82
Cineteca Nazionale, 161
Clement, René, 200
The Coach of the Blessed Sacrament, 125, 129
Cocteau, Jean, 31, 40, 41, 42, 48, 50, 54, 58, 106, 110, 202
Colle Val d'Elsa, 180
La Colombaia, 123–4, 127–9, 137, 180, 181, 200, 213
Comédie Française, 48, 54
Committee for Assistance to Those Persecuted by Fascism, 85
Committee of National Liberation, 86

Communist Party (Italian), 67, 68; Visconti and, 59–61, 71, 102–103, 113–14, 151, 223–4; members arrested, 82–4; resistance to German occupation, 85, 92–3; and *Morts sans sépulture*, 113; opposition to, 118; Visconti submits film scripts to, 168; loses militancy, 169; after Togliatti's death, 224
Como, 63, 111
Como, Lake, 8–9, 15
Conversation Piece, 213–14, 216
Le Corbusier, 56
Corelli, Franco, 142, 143
Corradi, Corrado, 28, 34, 43, 64, 66, 103, 124
Così fan Tutte, 150
Covent Garden Opera House, London, 146, 161–4, 186–7, 189–90
Crespi, Fosca, 8, 159
Crime and Punishment, 115
Cristaldi, 157
The Crucible, 149, 150
CVD, 43

Dada, 47
Dali, Gala, 120
Dali, Salvador, 43, 52, 58, 120, 189
d'Amico family, 156–7
d'Amico, Fedele, 134, 138, 151, 159, 190, 206, 219–20
d'Amico, Suso Cecchi, 128, 129, 133–4, 154, 186; translates *The Fifth Column*, 108; first collaboration with Visconti, 125; Visconti chooses Cardin dress for, 150–151; and *White Nights*, 157; visits Russia, 183; works on *A la Recherche*, 200; and Visconti's stroke, 205–206, 208, 210, 214; prepares script for *Conversation Piece*, 213; and *The Intruder*, 216, 217, 219
The Damned, 23, 47–8, 154, 191, 193–6, 201, 223
Dance Marathon, 159, 160
d'Angelo, Salvo, 129
D'Annunzio, Gabriele, 5, 14, 25, 82, 178, 216
David, Jacques Louis, 142
A Day in the Country, 61–3, 69

Days of Glory, 109–10
Death in Venice, 164, 196–9, 200, 201
Death of a Salesman, 126
Debora e Jaele, 141
Debussy, Claude, 7
De Cespedes, Alba, 126
de Giorgi, Elsa, 123
de Laurentis, Dino, 187
Dell'Anna, Livio, 43, 74–5
Delon, Alain, 165, 166, 183, 216; in *Rocco*, 161, 168, 170; and *'Tis Pity She's a Whore*, 171; in *The Leopard*, 172, 175, 177–9; and *The Outsider*, 187–8; and *A la Recherche*, 200, 201; debt to Visconti, 221
Delon, Natalie, 183
Delos, 64
de Lullo, Giorgio, 107, 108, 110, 114, 115, 221
Demidoff, Countess, 31
Denis, Maria, 44, 73–4, 76, 83, 87, 90, 93–101, 115
de Nobili, Lila, 150, 208, 211
de Sabata, Victor, 143
de Santis, Giuseppe, 67–72, 75–6, 77–8, 92, 102, 108
de Sica, Vittorio, 44, 112, 172, 187
Deux sur La Balançoire, 166
Diaghilev, Sergei, 9, 31, 33, 40–41, 127
Diaghilev Prize, 150
Dietrich, Marlene, 180–181, 209, 221, 222
Dior, Christian, 185
di Stefano, Giuseppe, 148, 152
Doctor Zhivago, 154
Dolci, Danilo, 175
Don Carlos, 141, 161–4, 166, 185, 186 222
Donizetti, Gaetano, 131, 151, 166, 170
Doria, Prince, 85
Dostoievsky, Feodor, 157, 168, 183
Il Duca d'Alba, 166–7, 222
Dufy, Raoul, 58
Dumas, Alexandre, 70
Duncan, Isadora, 31
Duse, Eleonora, 123, 217, 218
Düsseldorf, 194

Eden Theatre, Milan, 34

Edmunton-Low, Captain Richard, 88–9
Edward, Prince of Wales, 48
Egmont, 190
Eisenstein, Sergei, 60, 100
L'Elisir d'Amore, 131, 158
Elizabeth II, Queen of England, 199
Erba family, 8
Erba, Anna, 13, 14, 15
Erba, Lina, 8, 15, 24, 25
Erba, Luigi, 8
Escoffier, Marcel, 133, 138, 144
Euripides, 134
Eurydice (Anouilh), 115
Existentialism, 110
Experimental Film Centre, Rome, 66, 68
Expressionism, 30, 47

Fabbri, Diego, 126, 166
Fabbri, Franca, 182
Fairbanks, Douglas, 64–5
Fallaci, Oriana, 172
Falstaff (Verdi), 26, 144–5, 186
The Fan, 150
Fascism, 28–9, 32, 46, 57, 224; rise of, 24–6; Don Giuseppe's opposition to, 44; Visconti's rejection of, 60, 102; opposition to in Rome, 70–2; and decadence, 82
Fassini, Alberto, 129, 141, 148, 177–8, 183, 206, 211–13, 223
Fellini, Federico, 172, 210
Fenice Theatre, Venice, 138
Feodor, Grand Duke, 55
Ferida, Luisa, 44
Ferrara, 75, 77, 81
Ferrara, Giorgio, 114
Ferreri, Marco, 129
Ferri, Franco, 95, 97, 100–101, 104
Festival, 150
Festival of Nations, Paris, 150–1
Feuillère, Edwige, 160, 161
Fidelma (maid), 217, 219
The Fifth Column, 108
Figli d'Arte, 166
The Firebird, 48–9
First World War, 20, 21–4
Fischer-Dieskau, Dietrich, 186
Flaubert, Gustave, 58

INDEX

La Fleur du Pois, 53-4
Florence, 115, 121, 190
Ford, John, 171
Forlanini, Colonel, 35
Fort, Paul, 21
Forte dei Marmi, 27
Fortuny, 31
Fournier, Alain, 69-70
France, 21, 44
Franciolini, 134
Franck, César, 15, 184
Franco, General, 60, 120
Frank, Jean-Michel, 58
French Communist party, 59-61
Frings, Ketti, 166
Fröken Julie, 159
Fürstenberg, Prince Hugo, 50, 51, 53
Fürstenberg, Princess Leontine, 50, 51
Fürtwangler, Wilhelm, 58

Gabin, Jean, 139
GAP, 90, 92-5, 99, 118
Garbuglia, Mario, 200
Gardella, Ignazio, 28, 29, 34
Garibaldi Brigade, 84
Gassman, Vittorio, 110, 111, 121, 122
Gatti-Casazza, Giulio, 7
Genoa, 118
Genovese, Vito, 31
Gente, 50
Gerace, Princess of, 32
Germany, 30, 44-5; Visconti visits, 45, 46-8; war declared, 66; occupation of Italy, 84-91, 92-100; *see also* Nazism
Gestapo, 93, 160
Ghiringhelli, Antonio, 141, 144, 145
Giacometti, Alfredo, 40, 55, 58
Giacosa, 14
Giannini, Giancarlo, 216
Gibson, William, 166
Gide, André, 52, 53, 56, 60, 182
Gielgud, John, 163
Gilliatt, Penelope, 168
Ginzburg, Natalia, 196
Gioi, Vivi, 73
Girardot, Annie, 166, 168, 170, 185
Giraudoux, Jean, 56, 58
Girotti, Massimo, 74-5, 78, 81, 87, 107, 114-15, 120, 123, 128, 135, 158-9
La Gita in Campagna, 141
Giulietta e Romeo, 139
Giulini, Carlo Maria, 144, 162, 163, 190
GiViEmme, 11
The Glass Menagerie, 115
Glickman, Will, 166
Gluck, Christoph Willibald, 151
Gnecchi, Vittorio, 28
Gobbi, Tito, 125, 163
Goethe, Johann Wolfgang von, 46, 167, 190
Goldoni, Carlo, 18, 34, 131-2, 150, 159
Graf, Herbert, 170
Granger, Farley, 135, 137
The Grapes of Wrath, 108
Grazzano-Visconti, 10-11, 15, 27, 29, 33, 37, 42, 44, 75-6, 80, 180
Greece, 64
Green, Henry, 72
Greene, Graham, 169
Griffi, Peppino Patroni, 110, 115, 123, 154
Grosz, George, 30
Guarino, Alfredo, 106
Il Guerrin Meschino, 21
Guglia, Maria, 98-9
Guptman, Toto, 65
Guttuso, Renato, 73-5, 81, 84, 85, 93

Hammamet, 56-7
Helen, Queen of Italy, 22, 58
Hemingway, Ernest, 70, 108
Henze, Hans Werner, 159-60, 174, 182, 193, 208
Hercolani, Laudomia (Domietta), 165, 172, 175, 180, 184, 206
Hitler, Adolf, 45, 47, 65, 66, 193
Hollywood, 64-5
Horowitz, Vladimir, 191
Horst, 193; affair with Visconti, 51-2, 55, 56-8, 64, 65; hatred of Nazism, 60; continuing friendship with Visconti, 124, 151; on *The Leopard*, 179; refuses to see *The Damned*, 196; likes *Death in Venice*, 199
Huis Clos, 110
Hungarian Revolution, 151
Huston, John, 182

L'Illustrazione Italiana, 18
L'impresario delle Smirne, 159, 161
L'Incoronazione di Poppea, 141
Ingrao, Pietro, 67–72, 82–3, 102, 191
Ingres, J. A. D., 142
L'inserzione, 196
Interlenghi, Franco, 121, 123
The Intruder, 216–18, 219, 223, 224
Iphigenia in Tauris (Gluck), 151
Ischia, 123–4, 127–9, 137, 181, 199–200, 209, 213, 219
Italian Army, 31–3
The Italian Worker, 86

Jeli the Shepherd, 70, 72
Jews, 60
Joseph and His Brothers, 182, 189
The Journey, 65
Jurinac, Sena, 186

Kappler, 93
Karajan, Herbert von, 150
Kazan, Elia, 121, 126
Kienholz, 159
Kitzbühel, 50, 189
Kleist, Heinrich von, 160
Koch, Carl, 66–7, 68, 69
Koch, Pietro, 87, 89–90, 92, 94, 96–100, 109–110
Kolldehoff, René, 194
Korda, Alexander, 58–9
Kortner, Fritz, 160
Krips, Joseph, 196
Krupp family, 193, 224

Lacan, Jacques, 161, 172
Lampedusa, Giuseppe Tomasi di, 164, 175, 176, 179
Lancaster, Burt, 175–9, 213
Langdon, Michael, 186
Il Lavoro (Work), 165, 172–3, 175
Lawrence of Arabia, 171
Lee J. Thompson, 186
Leghorn, 157, 158
Leigh, Vivien, 163
Lelong, Lucien, 41
Lelong, Nathalie, 41–2, 53
Leningrad, 183
Lenya, Lotte, 53
Leoncavallo, Ruggiero, 14

The Leopard, 27, 164, 172, 174–9, 195
Leopardi. Giacomo, 184
Leven, Hugo, 128
Lévy, Raoul, 120
Libya, 38, 42, 79
Liceo Berchet, 23 28
Liebig, 15
Lifar, Serge, 31, 40, 41, 42, 49
Life with Father, 115
Liszt, Franz, 6
Litta, Countess Eugenia, 6
Lizzani, Carlo, 121
La Locandiera, 131–2, 150–1
Lombardo, 178
Lombardo–Radice, Laura, 83, 85, 92, 102
Lombardo-Radice, Lucio, 71, 83
London, 43, 58–9, 161–4, 183, 186–7, 189–90, 199
A Long Day's Journey Into Night, 160
Longanesi, 81
Longo, Luigi, 84
Look Homeward, Angel, 166
Lopez, Professor, 206
Loren, Sophia, 183, 186
Il Lorenzaccio, 119, 122
Losey, Joseph, 201, 210–211
Lotti, Mariella, 44, 115
Louise, 208, 211
The Lover of the Gramigna, 72–3, 75
Ludwig, 201–4, 205, 207, 210
Ludwig II, King of Bavaria, 193, 202–4, 205
Lulu (Bertolazzi), 149
Lux Films, 108, 134, 137

Macbeth (Verdi), 164–5, 193, 222
Macerati (chauffer), 38
La Machine à Ecrire, 110
McNarney, General, 102
Maffei, Countess, 6
Mafia, 118, 175, 177
Maggio Musicale, Florence, 122–3, 134
The Magic Mountain, 207, 216
Magnani, Anna, 73, 76, 77, 83, 131, 134, 223
Mahler, Gustav, 46, 126, 127, 129, 197
I Malavoglia, 72, 73–4, 83, 114, 115, 116–17

INDEX

Malibran, Maria Felice, 6
Mallory, Jay, 64
Malraux, André, 60
La Mandragole, 122
Mangano, Silvanna, 187, 198, 200, 213
Mann, Katia, 127
Mann, Thomas, 46-7, 56, 72, 126-7, 150, 155, 164, 168, 193, 196-9, 206, 207
Mannino, Franco, 126, 127-8
Manon Lescaut, 9, 211-13, 215
Marais, Jean, 41, 43, 50, 54, 73, 80-81, 83, 102, 157-8, 166
Il Marchese del Grillo, 130
Marcia Nunziale, 134
Margherita, Queen of Italy, 22
Margot, 56
Maria Tarnowska, 105-106, 183
Mario e il Mago, 127, 141, 150
The Marriage of Figaro (Beaumarchais), 112
Marseilles, 57
Marx, Karl, 24, 102
Marxism, 25, 30, 59, 102, 223-4
Marzot, Vera, 176, 185, 190, 222
Mascagni, Pietro, 14
Maselli, Francesco, 144
Massine, Leonide, 127
Mastroianni, Marcello, 112, 121, 123, 156-8, 183, 187, 221
Il Matrimonio Segreto, 145
Maupassant, Guy de, 61, 104, 172
Medea, 134
Medioli, Enrico, 146, 167, 171, 177, 186: friendship with Visconti, 133, 196: and *Don Carlos*, 163: on *Macbeth*, 164: on Visconti, 179, 181, 222; writes script for *Ludwig*, 202; and Visconti's stroke, 205-207; prepares script for *Conversation Piece*, 213
Melville, Herman, 70
Meneghini, Battista, 146, 152, 170
Menotti, Gian Carlo, 147, 164-5, 166-7, 172, 182
Merimée, Prosper, 125
Messina earthquake, 13
Metropolitan Opera, New York, 183, 191
Milan, 4-10, 11-13, 26, 42, 43, 63, 84, 102, 103, 167-9
Miller, Arthur, 126, 149, 161, 185
Ministry of Arts, 75
Ministry of Defence, 136
Ministry of Industry, 86
Ministry for Popular Culture, 70, 72-3
Minne, George, 128
Minton, Yvonne, 186
Mirabello, Teresa, 23
Miranda, Isa, 106, 134
Mistinguett, 158-9
Mrs Gibbons' Boys, 166
Mocci, Paolo, 86, 87, 90, 93-4
Modigliani, Amedeo, 57
La Monaca di Monza, 191-2, 196
Il Mondo, 174
Monte Carlo, 12
Morandi, 132
Morante, Elsa, 129, 221
Moravia, Alberto, 81, 87, 129, 191, 197
Moreau, Gustave, 172
Morelli, Rina, 110, 114, 121, 123, 128, 166, 176, 182, 221
Moreno, Marguerite, 120
Mori, Claudia, 168
Morra, Umberto, 85
Morts sans sépulture, 113
Moscow, 183
Mozart, Wolfgang Amadeus,, 132, 150, 152, 182
Munich, 43, 47
Musil, Robert, 46, 186
Musset, Alfred de, 107
Mussolini, Benito, 13, 25-6, 30-2, 43-4, 49, 65-7, 81, 84, 103, 127
Mussolini, Vittorio, 67, 81

National Committee for the Liberation of Vietnam, 185
Nazism, 45, 46-8, 60, 102-103, 127, 193-6, 224
Neue Sachlichkeit, 47
New York, 64, 65, 191
Nietzsche, Friedrich, 203
Nijinsky, 40, 41, 186
Noailles, Marie-Laure de, 31, 40, 41, 52, 57
Noailles, Vicomte de, 54
Nono, Luigi, 188

Notarianni, 189
Notes sur un fait divers, 129
November, 58–9
Le Nozze di Figaro (Mozart), 182, 191
The Nun from Monza, 186
Nureyev, Rudolph, 186

Ochetto, Roberto, 109
Oedipe Roi, 54
Old Times, 210, 211
Olivier, Laurence, 119, 174–5, 200
Onassis, Aristotle, 152, 170
O'Neill, Eugene, 160
Oreste (Alfieri), 122
Orlando Furioso, 119
Orléans, Duke of, 10
Orsini, Umberto, 194
Osservatore Romano, 138–9
Ossessione, 73, 75–6, 77–82, 83, 101, 105, 106, 109, 161, 176, 191, 214, 223
Ostia, 142
Otello (Verdi), 121, 141
The Outsider, 187–9
OVRA, 71, 86

Pagnani, Andreina, 34, 63, 65, 106, 107–8
Pajetta, Giuliano, 125
Palazzo Pitti, Florence, 119
Palermo, 175, 177–8
Pandolfi, Ubaldo, 35–7
Les Parents Terribles, 54, 106–7, 108, 210
Paris, 15, 31, 40–2, 43, 48, 53, 58, 150–151, 161, 166, 200
Paris Opéra, 8
Parma, 171
Parsifal, 195
Partisans for Peace, 125
Pascal, Gabriel, 58–9
Pasolini, Pier Paolo, 161, 187
Paul Alexandrovitch, Grand Duke, 41–2
La Pausa, 49–50
Pavlova, Tatiana, 115, 123
Pavolini, 72–3
Paxinou, Katina, 168
Penati, Gnam, 36, 128, 180
Pensione Jaccarino, 87, 89–90, 93, 95–6, 97–8, 101, 104, 109, 113
Pensione Oltremare, 104

Peregallo, 141
Perugia, 205
Peruzzi, Baldassarre, 184
Petipo, 125
Pez, Giorgio, 175
Philipe, Gérard, 120
Piacenza, 10–11
Picasso, Pablo, 41
Piccioni, Piero, 188
La Piccola Scala, Milan, 144–5
Pickford, Mary, 64–5
Piedmont, 32
Pierfederici, 107
Pietrangeli, Antonio, 108, 120, 125
Pinerolo, 31–3
Pinter, Harold, 201, 210–211
Pintor, Fortunato, 97
Il Pirata, 160
Piscistrello, 88
Pius XII, Pope, 92
Pizzetti, Ildebrando, 141
Pizzi, Pier Luigi, 111
Pleasure, 216, 223
Polignac, Princess de, 42, 52
Poliuto, 170
Ponti, Carlo, 172, 183
Popular Front (France), 59–60, 61
Porto Marghera, 118
Portrait of an Unknown Man, 183
The Postman Always Rings Twice, 63, 75, 78
Poulenc, Francis, 49
Pozzi, 33
Prague, 125
Pratolini, Vasco, 104, 120–1, 129
Praz, Mario, 213
Prévert, Jacques, 63
The Prince of Hombourg, 160
Proust, Marcel, 30, 44, 70, 155, 161, 189, 200–201, 218
Psychological Warfare Board, 108–109
Puccini brothers, 73, 80, 102
Puccini, Dario, 67, 75–6
Puccini, Giacomo, 8–9, 14, 21, 26, 67, 154, 183
Puccini, Gianni, 67, 68, 70, 71, 72, 84, 92–4, 104
Puccini, Massimo, 67
Puccini, Tonio, 26

Quinn, Anthony, 175
Quirino Theatre, 112

Radiguet, Raymond, 41, 50
Rampling, Charlotte, 200
Rapallo, 25
Rasputin, 183
Ravel, Maurice, 41
Redon, Odilon, 154
Reggimento Savoia Cavalleria, 32
Regina Coeli, 83, 85, 93, 98, 109
Regnoli, Piero, 139
Reiniger, Lotte, 67
Renoir, Jean, 59, 60–63, 66–9, 75, 79, 81
Renoir, Marguerite, 61, 62
Resnik, Regina, 186
Ricci, Renzo, 123
Ricci, Rinaldi, 93, 104, 144
Riccio, Attilio, 75
Ricordi, Giuditta, 8
Ricordi, Giulio, 8, 9, 14, 16
Riefenstahl, Leni, 47
Rigoletto, 141
Rilke, Rainer Maria, 5
Rimini, 20
Rinascita, 120
Der Ring des Nibelungen, 194, 204, 207
The Rise and Fall of the City of Mahagonny, 53
Rizzoli, 216
Rocco and His Brothers, 161, 166, 167–9, 170, 173, 176, 215
Rome, 30, 191–2, 208; Visconti goes to live in, 68–73; German occupation, 86–7, 90, 92–100; Liberation, 100, 103; in *Bellissima*, 131
Rome Open City, 130
Rome Opera House, 121, 125, 182
Rosai, Ottone, 132
Der Rosenkavalier, 16, 186–7, 211
Rosi, Francesco, 110, 115, 116–17, 119, 144, 169, 187, 210, 221, 223
Rossellini, Renzo, 112
Rossellini, Roberto, 130, 134, 137, 141
Rossini, Gioacchino, 125
Rosso, Medardo, 218
Rothschild, Guy de, 200
Ruffini, Ernesto, Cardinal of Palermo, 175

Ruggeri, Ruggero, 123
Russian Ballet, 9, 40–41

Sahara, 38–9
Salerno, 86
Salome (Strauss), 172
Salsomaggiore, 81
Salvatori, Renato, 168, 170
Salzburg Festival, 150
San Carlo Opera House, Naples, 141
San Gregorio prison, 97, 99
Sandra, 154
Sanjust, Filippo, 133, 146, 163, 167, 171, 177, 183
Santa Marinella, 133
Sanzogno, Nino, 145
Sardou, Victorien, 67
Sartre, Jean-Paul, 110, 113
Satie, Erik, 41
Savoy, House of, 22, 44
La Scala, Milan, 5–10, 19, 25, 140, 141–9, 151, 170, 183, 204
Scarfiotti, Ferdinando, 186
Schiaparelli, Madame, 54–5
Schiller, J. C. F. von, 162
Schippers, Thomas, 164–5, 166, 211–212
Schlumberger, 60
Schneider, Romy, 165, 171, 172, 177, 201–202, 216
Schonhals, Albrecht, 194
Sciutti, Graziella, 186
Scoccimarro, 85
Second World War, 66–110
Il Seduttore, 126
Senso, 67, 130, 134–9, 141, 155, 158, 176, 177, 195, 223
Sequi, Sandro, 191
La Sera, 23
Serandrei, Mario, 78, 109
Serato, Massimo, 73
Sert, Misia, 40, 41, 42
Sforza, Francesco, 6
Shade, Nancy, 212
Shakespeare, William, 19, 120, 122, 133
Sharif, Omar, 171
Siamo Donne, 134
Siciliani, 121–2
Sicily, 13, 64, 73–4, 116–118, 175–9
Simon, Michel, 69

Simon Boccanegra, 196
Simoni, Renato, 18, 63
Sodom and Gomorrah, 178
Solti, Georg, 186
Somalia, 57
La Sonnambula, 145–6, 147
Sordello, Enzo, 143
Soviet Communist Party, 158
Soviet Union, 80, 183
Soviet Writers' Union, 151
Spain, 44
Spanish Civil War, 82, 85, 113
Sperlonga, 154, 180
Spiegel, Sam, 171
Spoleto Festival, 164–5, 166–7, 172, 181–2, 208, 211–213
Spontini, Gaspare, 141
SS, 86–7, 90, 93–4, 97
Stalin Joseph, 118
Starace, 44
Stein, Joseph, 166
Steinbeck, John, 70, 108
Stendhal, 30, 133, 138, 155
Stephane, Nicole, 200–1
Sternberg, 25, 43
Stignani, Ebe, 142
Stoppa, Paolo, 110, 114, 123, 128, 166, 221
Strauss, Richard, 172, 182, 186
Stravinsky, Igor, 40–1, 48, 54
A Streetcar Named Desire, 121, 126
Strehler, Giorgio, 107, 111, 145, 149, 164
Strindberg, August, 159
Suor Letizia, 131
Sweet Aloes, 64
Switzerland, 206–207

Tassili mountains, 38–9
Tchelitchew, Pavel, 58
Teatro Eliseo, Rome, 106–107, 121
Teatro Stabile, Rome, 185
Tebaldi, Renata, 141
Tecchia, Piero, 42
La Terra Trema, 83, 114, 116–119, 125, 161, 167, 176, 188, 214
Testori, 168, 170, 191–2, 196
Theatre Argentina, Rome, 210, 211
The Thirteenth Tree, 182

The Three Sisters, 132–3
Three Steps from Frenzy, 196
Thulin, Ingrid, 194, 195
Tibet, 160
Tiepolo, Giovanni Battista, 151
The Times, 178
Tirelli, 132
'Tis Pity She's a Whore, 171
Tobacco Road, 111
Tofano, Sergio, 123
Togliatti, Palmiro, 113–114, 118, 120, 168, 169, 179–80, 185, 224
Tomasi, Gioacchino Lanza, 175, 178, 179
Tooley, Sir John, 162, 190
Torre San Lorenzo, 170, 172
La Tosca, 66–9
Toscanini, Arturo, 5, 7–9, 19, 21, 23–4, 26, 28, 30, 43, 103, 107, 140, 143–5
Toscanini, Wally, 10, 12, 18, 24, 144, 145, 212
Toscanini, Wanda, 23, 28, 30, 144–5, 191
Tosi, Piero, 122–3, 144; works on *Bellissima*, 130; designs for *La Locandiera*, 132; and *Senso*, 137–8; on Callas, 145–6; and *'Tis Pity She's a Whore*, 171; costumes for *The Leopard*, 176; and *The Outsider*, 188–9; on Visconti, 192; and *Death in Venice*, 197, 198; and *A la Recherche*, 200; and *Manon Lescaut*, 211; and *The Intruder*, 218; after Visconti's death, 222
Totó, 125
Touareg, 38–9
Tracy, Spencer, 175
Traversi, Giannino Antona, 63
La Traviata, 27, 145, 147–9, 181–2, 189–90
Trenno, 43
Tripoli, 38, 65, 123
Tristan und Isolde, 158, 204
The Triumph of the Will, 47
Troilus and Cressida, 122–3, 182
Trombadori, Antonello, 60, 92, 112–113, 114, 118, 153–4, 168, 179, 180, 183, 220
Il Trovatore, 8, 134, 158, 182–3, 213

Tunisia, 21, 56–7, 205
Turandot, 26
Il Turco in Italia, 125, 140
20th Century-Fox, 175, 178
Two for the Seesaw, 166

Umberto II, Prince, later King of Italy, 22, 32, 36, 42, 43, 114
Uncle Vanya, 149
L'Unità, 82, 93, 114
United States of America, 64–5, 191
Unterach am Attersee, 193–4
L'Uomo di Pietra, 21

Vaghe Stelle dell'Orsa, 15, 184
Valli, Alida, 44, 134, 135, 137, 138, 221, 223
Valli, Romolo, 182, 190, 208, 212, 221
Vatican, 139
Veasey, Josephine, 186
Venditti, Roberto, 93
Venice, 40, 41, 42, 49, 196–9, 200
Venice Film Festival, 119, 131, 138–9, 168
Venice Theatre Festival, 126
Verdi, Giuseppe, 8, 129, 133, 138, 141, 147, 155, 162, 175, 182
Verdura, Fulco, Duke of, 9, 16, 175, 177, 179, 184
Verga, Giovanni, 69, 70, 72–4, 83, 114–117
Vespignani, Renzo, 159
La Vestale, 142–4
Vickers, Jon, 163
La Vie est à nous, 59, 61
Vienna Staatsoper, 186, 196, 204
Vietnam war, 185
A View from the Bridge, 161
Villa, Luisa, 28
Vilmorin, Louise de, 54, 58, 166
Visconti family, 4–12, 21, 29, 193
Visconti, Anna, 16, 23, 29, 66, 76, 180
Visconti, Carla (mother), 23–4, 30–1, 33, 63; background, 8–12; and Visconti's childhood, 13–20; marriage ends, 21–2, 25, 27; in retirement in Cernobbio, 27, 29, 36, 37; relationship with Visconti, 74, 147, 154, 165; in Visconti's films, 183, 198, 220; death, 65–66, 74
Visconti, Carlo, 6
Visconti, Edoardo, 16, 19, 25, 29, 31, 33, 36, 66, 103, 120, 180, 184
Visconti, Filippo, 16, 27
Visconti, Gian Galeazzo, 10
Visconti, Giuseppe (father), 23, 24, 36, 63; background, 8, 9–12; and Visconti's childhood, 13–20; marriage ends, 21–22, 25, 27; and Queen Helen, 22, 58; Visconti runs away from, 29–30; love of the theatre, 33–34; relations with Visconti, 37; superstitious, 37; dislike of Fascism, 44; death, 75–76, 180
Visconti, Guido, Duke of Modrone (grandfather), 6–8, 9
Visconti, Guido (brother), 16, 23, 29, 31, 38, 51, 65, 76, 79–80, 123, 180
Visconti, Guidone, 7, 9
Visconti, Ida (cousin), 210
Visconti, Ida Pace (Nane), 19, 21, 27, 29, 63, 66, 180
Visconti, Luchino: family background, 4–18; love of music, 6, 23–4, 129; childhood, 12–20; superstitious, 13; education, 14, 19–20, 23, 31; autobiographical influences in his films, 17–18, 176, 184–5, 197–9; early interest in theatre, 18–19, 28; character, 22–23, 153–7, 221–4; first interest in the cinema, 26, 44; relations with his mother, 27, 31, 74, 154, 165, 220; religious beliefs, 29, 37, 40, 155–6, 185; runs away from home, 29–30, 31; joins Army, 31–33; attitude to women, 31, 32, 149, 165–6, 184, 198, 220–221; homosexuality, 32, 40, 41, 43, 74, 153–4, 170, 185, 198, 221; political awareness begins, 32; trains and breeds horses, 35–36, 42–43; relations with his father, 37; car accident, 37–38; in the Sahara, 38–40; in Paris, 40–42, 48. 58; friendship with Chanel, 42, 49–50, 51, 56, 63; textile designs, 43; visits Germany, 45, 46–48; and Facism, 47–48, 57; contemplates marriage, 50–51, 53; affair with Horst, 51–52, 55, 56–58, 64, 65; first

film, 52–53; works for Gabriel Pascal, 58–59; works for Jean Renoir, 59, 61–63; and Communism, 59–61, 71, 102–103, 113–14, 151, 223–4; and his mother's death, 65–66; and the Roman communists, 68–73, 82–84, 85; and his father's death, 75–76; and German occupation of Italy, 86–91, 92–102; arrested, 95–99; rejects Maria Denis, 101; relationship with Callas, 101, 121, 140–141, 142, 146–7, 151–2, 165, 166, 221; writes novel, 108; theatre company, 114–15; as a director, 119, 123; relationship with Zeffirelli, 121; love of opera, 121; as a host, 124, 127–9, 180–181; persecuted by officialdom, 125; works with Callas, 142–4; 'society' games, 155, 174; relations with his actors, 169–70; takes credit for others' work, 183, 185; and Helmut Berger, 189, 191; heart attack, 199–200; suffers a stroke, 205–14, 215–19; death, 219; funeral Mass, 219–20; *see also* individual films, operas and plays
Visconti, Luigi, 16, 19, 20, 23, 29, 31, 35, 36, 65–66, 180
Visconti, Madina, 36, 37, 40, 42, 50, 53–54, 55, 61, 65
Visconti, Marcello, 21
Visconti, Matteo degli, 5, 6
Visconti, Niki, 36, 40, 42, 50–54, 61, 66
Visconti, Otterino (cousin), 210
Visconti, Uberta, 37, 44, 66, 73, 129, 180, 206; childhood, 19, 27, 29; on Visconti, 33, 47, 59, 65, 164, 209; in Second World War, 87–88, 90; and Visconti's arrest by the Germans, 96, 98, 99; second marriage, 126; and Visconti's last illness, 218, 219
Visconti, Uberto, Duke of Modrone, 7, 9
Visconti, Valentina, 10
Vittorio Emanuele III, King of Italy, 25, 84, 86

La Voix Humaine, 48, 54
Volpi, 49
Volterra, 184–5
Votto, Antonino, 143
Vuitton, Louis, 48, 129

Wagner, Cosima, 202, 203
Wagner, Richard, 7–8, 46, 129, 155, 182, 194, 202–204
Weber, Carl Maria von, 7
Webster, Sir David, 146, 161, 163, 186, 190
Webster, John, 171
Weill, Kurt, 30, 40, 53, 66
Weimar, Republic, 45, 47
Welles, Orson, 182
West Berlin Festival, 159
Wharton, Edith, 72
White Nights, 157–8
Williams, Tennessee, 121, 137
Windisch-Graetz, Irma (Pupe), 50–51, 53, 171, 221
The Wise Wife, 34
The Witch Burnt Alive, 187
The Witches, 187
Wolfe, Thomas, 166
World Peace Prize, 125

Yusupov, Prince, 183

Zavattini, Cesare, 104, 130–31
Zaza, 125
Zeiffirelli, Franco, 125, 142, 144, 164, 183, 213, 221; first meets Visconti, 115; works on *La Terra Trema*, 117, 119; friendship with Dali, 120; relationship with Visconti, 121, 128; designs for *A Streetcar Named Desire*, 121; designs for *Troilus and Cressida*, 122; designs for *The Three Sisters*, 132; row with Visconti 149
Zelda, 207
Zuffi, Piero, 142
Zurich, 215
Zurich Cantonal Clinic, 206